Cecil County Public Library
301 Newark Ave.
Elkton, MD 21921

O9-BRZ-033

A CASE FOR SOLOMON

BOBBY DUNBAR AND THE KIDNAPPING
THAT HAUNTED A NATION

Tal McThenia

and

Margaret Dunbar Cutright

FREE PRESS

New York   London   Toronto   Sydney   New Delhi

Free Press
A Division of Simon & Schuster, Inc.
1230 Avenue of the Americas
New York, NY 10020

Copyright © 2012 by Tal McThenia and Margaret Dunbar Cutright

All rights reserved, including the right to reproduce this book or portions thereof in any form whatsoever. For information, address Free Press Subsidiary Rights Department, 1230 Avenue of the Americas, New York, NY 10020.

First Free Press hardcover edition August 2012

FREE PRESS and colophon are trademarks of Simon & Schuster, Inc.

For information about special discounts for bulk purchases, please contact Simon & Schuster Special Sales at 1-866-506-1949 or business@simonandschuster.com.

The Simon & Schuster Speakers Bureau can bring authors to your live event. For more information or to book an event, contact the Simon & Schuster Speakers Bureau at 1-866-248-3049 or visit our website at www.simonspeakers.com.

Maps Copyright © 2012 by Jeffrey L. Ward

Book design by Ellen R. Sasahara

Manufactured in the United States of America

1   3   5   7   9   10   8   6   4   2

Library of Congress Cataloging-in-Publication Data

McThenia, Tal, and Cutright, Margaret Dunbar.
A case for Solomon : Bobby Dunbar and the kidnapping that haunted a nation / Tal McThenia and Margaret Dunbar Cutright. —1st Free Press hardcover ed.
        p.   cm.
1. Dunbar, Bobby, d. 1966. 2. Dunbar, Bobby, d. 1966—Kidnapping, 1912. 3. Kidnapping—Southern States—Case studies. 4. Missing children—Southern States—Case studies. 5. Mistaken identity—Southern States—Case studies. 6. Dunbar, Bobby, d. 1966—Family. 7. Cutright, Margaret Dunbar—Family. 8. Opelousas (La.)—Biography. I. Cutright, Margaret Dunbar. II. This American life (Radio program) III. Title.
HV6603.D86M35 2012
364.15'4092—dc23   2011051965

ISBN 978-1-4391-5859-3
ISBN 978-1-4391-9325-9 (ebook)

All photographs in the text and inserts are courtesy of the Dunbar Family Private Collection unless otherwise noted.

For Bobby and Marjorie

Then came there two women, that were harlots, unto the king, and stood before him.

And the one woman said, O my lord, I and this woman dwell in one house; and I was delivered of a child with her in the house. And it came to pass the third day after that I was delivered, that this woman was delivered also: and we were together; there was no stranger with us in the house, save we two in the house. And this woman's child died in the night; because she overlaid it. And she arose at midnight, and took my son from beside me, while thine handmaid slept, and laid it in her bosom, and laid her dead child in my bosom. And when I rose in the morning to give my child suck, behold, it was dead: but when I had considered it in the morning, behold, it was not my son, which I did bear.

And the other woman said, Nay; but the living is my son, and the dead is thy son.

And this said, No; but the dead is thy son, and, the living is my son.

Thus they spake before the king.

Then said the king, The one saith, This is my son that liveth, and thy son is the dead and the other saith, Nay; but thy son is the dead, and my son is the living.

And the king said, Bring me a sword. And they brought a sword before the king.

And the king said, Divide the living child in two, and give half to the one, and half to the other.

Then spake the woman whose the living child was unto the king, for her bowels yearned upon her son, and she said, O my lord, give her the living child, and in no wise slay it.

But the other said, Let it be neither mine nor thine, but divide it.

Then the king answered and said, Give her the living child, and in no wise slay it.

She is the mother thereof.

—1 Kings iii, 16-27

Thy wish was father, Harry, to that thought

—William Shakespeare, *Henry IV, Part II*, Act IV, Scene 5

Contents

Character List

The Boys

Bobby Dunbar
Bruce Anderson

The Parents

C. Percy Dunbar
Lessie Dunbar
Julia Anderson

The Accused

William C. Walters

Siblings

Alonzo Dunbar, Bobby's brother
Bernice Anderson, Bruce's sister

Dunbar Family

Ola and S. Harold Fox, cousins
Katie Dunbar, Percy's sister
Archie Dunbar, Percy's brother
Preston King, Percy's uncle

Walters Family

James Pleasant and Ailsie, parents
D. B. "Bunt" Walters, brother
Frank Walters, brother

The Lawyers

For the Defendant:

Hollis C. Rawls
Thomas S. Dale
Edward B. Dubuisson

For the State:

R. Lee Garland
John W. Lewis
Edward P. Veazie

Officials

Sheriff Marion L. Swords, Sheriff of St. Landry Parish, Louisiana
John M. Parker
Earl Brewer, Governor of Mississippi
Judge Benjamin H. Pavy, St. Landry Parish, Louisiana

Reporters

For the *Item*:

Ethel Hutson
Mignon Hall
Sam Blair

For the *Daily States*:

A. J. McMullen
F. S. Tisdale

For the *Times-Picayune*:

Herman Seiferth
Stanley Ray

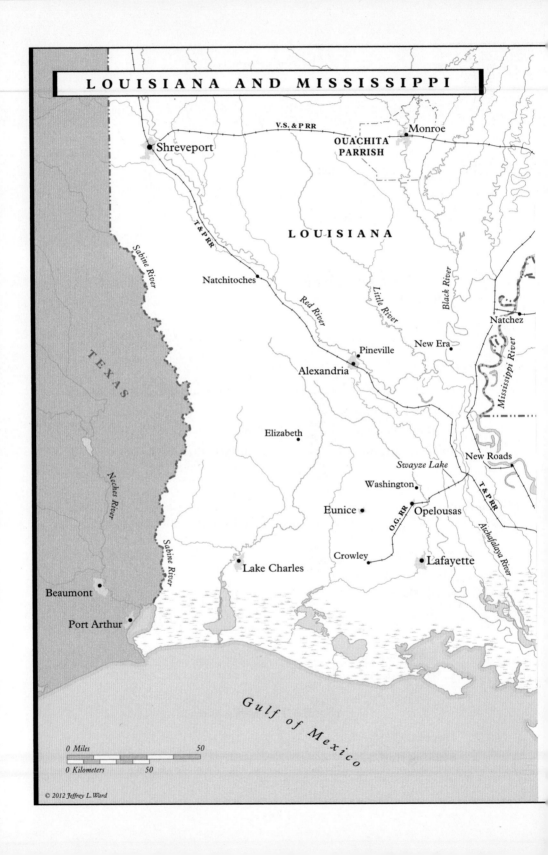

LOUISIANA AND MISSISSIPPI

V.S. & P RR

Shreveport

Monroe

OUACHITA PARRISH

LOUISIANA

T & P RR

Natchitoches

Sabine River

Red River

Little River

Black River

Natchez

New Era

Pineville

Alexandria

Mississippi River

TEXAS

Elizabeth

Swayze Lake

New Roads

Washington

T & P RR

Eunice

Opelousas

Neches River

O.G. RR

Crowley

Lafayette

Atchafalaya River

Sabine River

Lake Charles

Beaumont

Port Arthur

Gulf of Mexico

0 Miles   50

0 Kilometers   50

© 2012 Jeffrey L. Ward

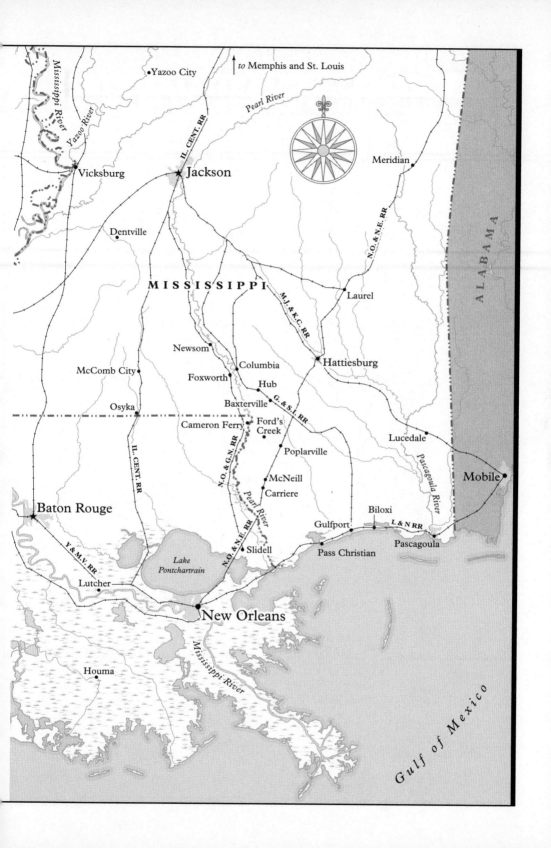

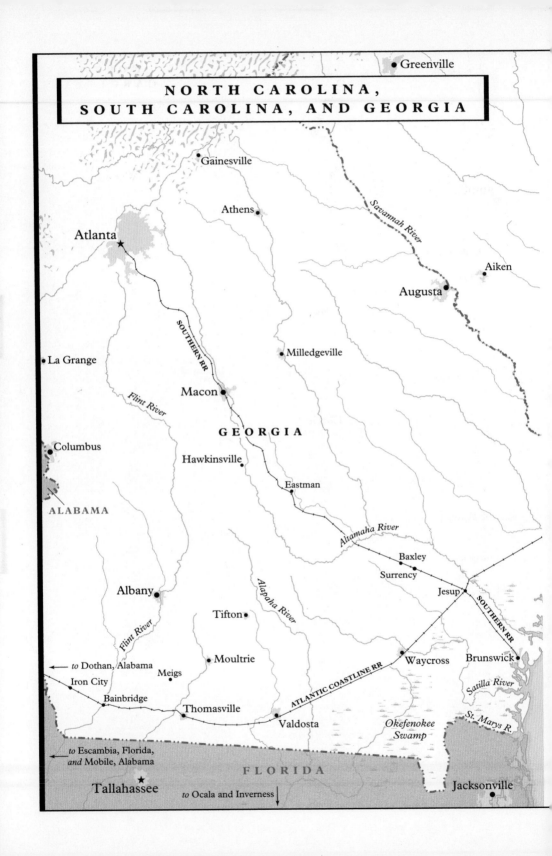

NORTH CAROLINA, SOUTH CAROLINA, AND GEORGIA

Greenville

Gainesville

Athens

Atlanta

Aiken

Augusta

SOUTHERN RR

La Grange

Milledgeville

Flint River

Macon

GEORGIA

Columbus

Hawkinsville

Eastman

ALABAMA

Altamaha River

Baxley

Surrency

Albany

Jesup

SOUTHERN RR

Tifton

Alapaha River

Flint River

Moultrie

Waycross

Brunswick

to Dothan, Alabama

Meigs

ATLANTIC COASTLINE RR

Satilla River

Iron City

Bainbridge

Thomasville

Valdosta

Okefenokee
Swamp

St. Marys R.

to Escambia, Florida,
and Mobile, Alabama

FLORIDA

Tallahassee

to Ocala and Inverness

Jacksonville

W. K. Patrick, New Orleans *Times-Democrat*, June 10, 1913

Foreword

Mark Dunbar, age twelve: Can you talk about your husband?

Marjorie Dunbar, Mark's grandmother: Well, I got married in 1935. And when I first started dating him, I found he had been kidnapped when he was a little boy . . . Everybody was always interested in that. He was kidnapped and taken, and he was kept for nine months. He was a little over four years old, and his mother and father didn't get him back until he'd been gone nine months.

Mark: Did they beat him a lot?

Marjorie: Yes, an old peddler was there that picked him up. And he would make him go out and beg for food and money. And when he would try to tell his name, he would whip him. He had scars on his back when they brought him back.
  And he'd been dressed as a girl and . . . they had dyed his hair. And you could hardly recognize him as being the Bobby Dunbar that had been kidnapped.

Marjorie Dunbar was my grandmother, and the story she repeated to my cousin Mark for his eighth-grade social studies project was the one I grew up with too. Back in 1912, when our grandfather, Robert Clarence Dunbar, was a little boy, he had wandered off from a camping trip in Louisiana and been kidnapped. Many months later, he was miraculously found in Mississippi and returned home.

Grandma first told me the story during a visit when I was in fifth grade, six years after Grandpa had died. No matter that it had a happy ending and had happened long ago, the story frightened me. She showed me a collection of newspaper articles about the kidnapping, but the thing most seared into my memory was an illustration of the kidnapper himself: a man named William Walters. For many nights after that, I still saw his thick handlebar mustache and piercing eyes when I tried to go to sleep.

There was another part of the story that I found more bewildering than terrifying, embodied in the title of one of the articles: "A Case for a Solomon." When my grandfather was returned to his parents, Percy and Lessie Dunbar, another mother named Julia Anderson had come down from North Carolina to claim him as *her* son, not Bobby Dunbar. After much controversy and a court trial, she was proven wrong. I couldn't help wondering: Where was this other mother's son? Did she ever find him? I tried to make sense of it all in a short essay for school entitled "The Lost Boy." Apparently I failed: the teacher told me it was too confusing.

As I grew older and heard the story again and again, the mystery and questions at the edges of it wore down, and it achieved the soft simplicity of a childhood fable, complete with a moral at the end: don't wander too far from home and don't talk to strangers. As a mother, I even used the story as a lesson for my own children as well.

In 1999, not long after losing Grandma, my brother Robert Clarence Dunbar III was killed when the small plane he was piloting crashed in New Mexico. Afterward, I spent time with my parents, grieving and helping them through the shattering loss of their firstborn son. One day, as we were looking through old family photos and remembering Robbie, my dad handed me a thick, heavy black binder. It was a copy of the family scrapbook devoted to my grandfather's kidnapping, passed down from my grandfather's mother, Lessie Dunbar, to my grandmother, and when she died, passed on to her children.

The binder was stuffed with newspaper clippings, handwritten letters, and telegrams, taped in with little if any discernible order. I stopped suddenly on an editorial cartoon, dated 1913 and entitled "Fifty Years from Now." It depicted a boy, whose shirt collar read "Bobbie III," on the floor reading a newspaper story about the kidnapping mystery and asking his grandfather, labeled "Boy Taken from the Tinker," the following question: "Grandpa, do you ever think we'll know for certain what our right name is?" Next to that caption, a long time ago, someone had scribbled a confident retort: "Why sure! It's Bobbie Dunbar." The cartoon was a mirror to the moment I was living as I stared at it. The little boy, Bobbie III, was my brother.

The scrapbook was like a jigsaw puzzle without the picture on the box, and over the next few months, I lost myself in trying to piece it together. At first it was easier to explore a mystery in my grandfather's past than to make sense of the aching questions about life and death in my own present. But soon the scrapbook—and the story it told—was no longer a safe source of escape. The controversy over my grandfather's identity, hurried through in my grandmother's retelling, in fact had been front and center in the kidnapping case for two full years after he was recovered.

And the very first time I looked beyond the scrapbook, my family legend was turned squarely on its head. One quick online search of "Bobby Dunbar" led me to the genealogical website of Tammy Westmoreland, who had posted this note about her great-grandmother, the "other mother," Julia Anderson:

"Julia had a son from her first marriage named Bruce that was kidnapped from NC when he was six years old and taken to LA. She tried to get him back, but the people who kidnapped him won him in court and changed his name to Bobby Dunbar."

In this version, the kidnapper was not William Walters at all, but rather my own ancestors, Percy and Lessie Dunbar. As much as I had absorbed the controversy playing out in the pages of ninety-year-old newspapers, it had not occurred to me that my grandfather's identity—*my own family's identity*—was still being challenged in the age of the Internet. Bobbie III's question was now fully my own.

Within months, I was piecing together a broader historical record in libraries, archives, and courthouses across several states. I explored the story's landscapes as I read about them, peering into the swampy murk of Swayze Lake from the wooden railroad trestle where little Bobby Dunbar had disappeared; wandering across the Mississippi farm where the lost boy had made friends with a fox terrier named Rambler; marveling at the lovely white mansion where Lessie Dunbar had given my grandfather a bath when he first was recovered; and roaming the halls of New Orleans's Hotel Monteleone, where the future governor of Louisiana had examined the boy's foot to determine that he was Bobby Dunbar—a decision, it dawned on me then and there, that had made my life possible.

With great apprehension, I ventured to Poplarville, Mississippi, to meet the descendants of Julia Anderson in person: not just Tammy Westmoreland and her aunts and uncles but also two of Julia's own children from a later marriage, Hollis Rawls and Jewel Tarver. Right away, I could tell that for Julia's children, two generations closer to the story than I was, the case was far more than a genealogical mystery. It was a festering injustice, reflected vividly in the childhood story that Jewel's daughter Linda had grown up hearing:

I knew that . . . Mother's brother Bruce had come down from North Carolina with Mr. Walters; they came on a wagon. And . . . [t]his little boy had taken missing over in Louisiana . . . [T]here was a hearing, the people in Louisiana proved that he was their child, [but] he really wasn't. They just got him. *They just took him.*

For all their indignation over the past, Julia's family was only kind and open with me. I shared my research with them, and they shared their stories. One in particular was strange and unnerving: Hollis told me that some fifty years ago, my grandfather—then a grown man—had come to Poplarville to see him. It would be years before I fully believed the story and understood its significance.

In Georgia, I met the family of William Walters, my grandfather's alleged kidnapper. Jean Cooper and Barbara Moore, Walters's great-nieces, recalled that long after his conviction, William Walters adamantly maintained his innocence, though his motivation in taking Bruce Anderson in the first place remained a dark mystery even to his immediate family. Jean and Barbara's grandfather could not fathom why his brother would have carried a small boy halfway across the country. Nearly a century later, neither could I.

As far from home as I would travel, the most significant chapter of my search occurred in Lumberton, North Carolina, just a few hours from where I'd grown up. I sat at the hospital bedside of ninety-year-old Bernice Graves Hardee, Julia Anderson's oldest living child, who had lived with her brother Bruce for the first year of her life in North Carolina, before the kidnapping controversy. Holding Bernice's fragile hand, staring into her watery blue-gray eyes, and hearing her memories of her mother, I felt as if I were with Julia herself—the woman who might or might not be my great-grandmother. When my father, Bobby Dunbar Jr., came into the hospital room, Bernice glowed with life. Just months before she died, God had answered her lifelong prayer: her brother had returned. Neither my dad nor I dared to challenge her belief that we were kin. "It is the truth, what I know, isn't it?" she asked before I left. All I could do was smile and nod weakly.

As much as I accepted that the descendants of Julia Anderson and William Walters had their own truths, I still believed that my truth was the *right* one. My grandfather was Bobby Dunbar, the lost boy who was found. But eventually, the historical record put up too many challenges to that belief for me to ignore. Everything I thought I knew seemed to be crumbling out of my grasp. And far more than a question of roots was at stake.

My brother Robbie's memorial service, for all of the anguish I felt, had been one of the most profound moments of coming together that I had ever experienced with my extended Dunbar family. As we gathered around the smoky barbecue pit, a Dunbar ritual that originated with Grandpa and Grandma, I felt my family's unquestioning love and embrace. Researching this story, I hoped, naïvely, that my work might somehow help to recapture that connection and bring us all closer in a new way. Instead it threatened to do precisely the opposite. I had hurled open the family closet and was yanking out its skeletons. I was betraying, and dividing, my own family.

It has taken years to come to some kind of peace with that tension, and for healing within my family to occur. An essential part of that process has been sharing this story with my coauthor, Tal McThenia, an objective "outsider," and entrusting him to craft and write this book. During our four years of collaboration, we have demanded of each other a clear-eyed loyalty to the story's difficult truths. And we have kept each other's hearts open to the devastation and hope at the bottom of its mystery. Like Tal, I take great pride in the fact that our work exposes and corrects a series of century-old injustices and falsehoods. But ultimately, the most important part of this story comes after the public agony of my grandfather's early years. It is the life he chose to live in private that makes this family story most necessary to share.

—**Margaret Dunbar Cutright**

In synopsis, this story invariably prompts a barrage of incredulous questions. How can two mothers claim the same boy as their own? How could there be any uncertainty, from either mother, in knowing the child she bore? The answers to these questions are complex, incremental, and cumulative, and in the end, the issue of recognition is probably the least relevant and certainly the least compelling.

This is a story of loss: one mother's agonizing surrender to it, and another mother's terrified, scorched-earth fight against it. It is a story of the ferocious, selfless, and seemingly irrational maternal instinct to protect a child.

But what of the boy himself? He must have known who he was.

The answer, in this story, for this boy, is not so clear-cut.

If a child's memory, like anyone's, is imperfect from the moment of its inception, an infinitely evolving alchemy of lived experience, imagination and speculation, cues and suggestions, then how do they know what is "true"? If a child's sense of self depends on owning memory, on attaching to concrete and stable forces around him—home and family—and on the simple act of having a name and knowing it, what happens when all of that is challenged, when all of that is constantly in flux?

It is the boy who is the puzzle, and the quiet hero of this story.

—Tal McThenia

Authors' Note

THIS IS A WORK OF NONFICTION. Anything in these pages that appears in quotation marks, including spoken dialogue, is taken from authors' interviews, written letters, legal records, newspaper reports, archival collections, books, and articles. Where critical discrepancies exist in the historical record, we note them in the text. In newspaper reports, Robert Clarence Dunbar is often referred to as "Bobbie" or "Robbie," both of which are preserved in quotations. Otherwise, we refer to him as Bobby, the name and spelling that he himself preferred.

Chapter 1

A. R. Waud, Cypress swamp on the Opelousas Railroad, Louisiana,
Harper's Weekly, December 8, 1866

August 23, 1912

LESSIE DUNBAR TUCKED her son's little toes into one sandal, then another, and fastened the straps. She harbored no illusion that they'd stay on for long. She lifted his hand and coaxed his baby ring into her palm. If *this* came off, it would never be found, not out here.

All the while, she felt him studying her eyes. Deep blue like his own, this morning Lessie's were swollen and bloodshot. It was hay fever season, after all, and on top of that, they'd spent last night in a silt-encrusted cabin. But being only four, Bobby might wonder if she was crying or hurt.

Lessie had no time to explain or reassure. As soon as she released his hand, he was off, down toward the lake with his father and all the other boys and men. Maybe he hadn't been worried about her at all.

She darted into the cabin to put the ring someplace safe and then returned to cooking. The fish fry had been called for noon, and at last count, she had at least a dozen mouths to feed.

Today, a Friday in late August, was the perfect time to fish. The record-breaking spring floodwaters, which had burst over the banks of the Atchafalaya River and into its surrounding bayou basin, were receding. And the ensuing explosion of giant red river crawfish, infamous for stealing bait, had subsided as well. "Craw-fish Are Vamoosing; Fishing Is Getting Good," read a headline in the local paper in late July. From all the narrow bayou-lakes in the area, delighted reports of fat catches of perch and trout were making their way back to Opelousas, where the townspeople were wilting in the heat, weary of the summer dust settling over their sidewalks, and itching for escape.

The Dunbars took refuge at this place on Swayze Lake, as they had in years past. Owned by Lessie's uncle, it was a largely wooded parcel with two primitive cabins wedged between a dirt wagon trail and the bayou's ever-shifting shoreline. There were eleven in the party in all: along with Lessie, her husband, Percy, and their sons, Bobby and Alonzo, came Percy's cousin Wallace, his wife and two sons, Lessie's younger sister, Rowena Whitley, a family friend named Paul Mizzi, and a servant girl. With a crowd this size, and others expected to stop by soon, they had arrived a day early to ensure an ample catch. And since the camp had been underwater for months, there was also the chore of returning it to habitability. The women spent hours scrubbing mud from the walls and windows, as the men hacked out a clearing through the overgrown canebrake down to the lake.

Nothing could be done about the shoreline, however, where the rapidly receding floodwaters had left a five-foot-wide bank of soft, deep mud. Fishing from here was a mucky, clumsy business, Percy and the other men learned quickly, and direct access to the water was utterly precarious.

In the late morning, a young black boy entered the camp, bearing a message for Percy. Mr. David Thornton, who lived a mile to the north, was finalizing a land deal and needed the deed transfer notarized back at his farm. Percy, a notary, had either accepted the job earlier, or this was an on-the-spot request. In any case, fishing would have to wait.

As his father headed up to the road with the boy, Bobby tried to tag along. But Percy turned him back. He couldn't watch Bobby and do his job at the same time, and, besides, he'd return before noon. Bobby grew distraught, screaming and clawing at his father as Percy moved to mount his horse.

In the struggle, the rubber band strap on Bobby's straw hat snapped. His father stopped and leaned down to face his son. He didn't have the patience to repair the strap, so he simply pressed the hat down harder onto the boy's head. Then he turned away, climbed onto the horse, and swung his cork leg (a prosthetic he'd had since childhood) over and into its stirrup. As Percy set out down the road, he instructed the boy to take Bobby back to camp.

About that time, more guests arrived: John Oge, a planter and well-known state politician; Dr. Lawrence Daly; and Daly's twelve-year-old son, who were happy to join in the fishing. Ambling down to the lake, rotund Oge challenged rotund Wallace Dunbar to a contest for the biggest catch.

For Lessie, the presence of Oge and Daly injected an air of formality into the gathering, and a reminder of the time, hastening her efforts in the kitchen. Every incoming fish needed to be cleaned, fried, and then drained over a bed of Spanish moss. She had Rowena to help in this process, and the nurse girl kept two-year-old Alonzo out of the way. But swollen-eyed Bobby would have to fend for himself.

The other three boys were several years older, and though he could tag along while they made their fun, he would never be part of it. So when Bobby saw Paul Mizzi heading down to the lake to shoot garfish, he begged his mother to let him follow. Thirty-year-old Paul had a unique friendship with Bobby. He often took the boy riding at his horse and cattle farm, on a big buckskin horse. And Paul was the only one who could call stout, little Bobby by his odious nickname "Heavy" and make it sound like a term of endearment. Plus, of course, few things were more thrilling than the firing of a gun.

As soon as Lessie agreed, Alonzo inevitably wanted to follow, as did one of Wallace's sons. Before turning back to her work, she warned the boys away from the shore. It wasn't just the mud; the lake plunged quickly to a depth of fifteen feet.

Searching the water with Paul and the other boys, Bobby saw the flash: just beneath the surface, the razor teeth of a garfish, panicking a school of sac-a-lait. Paul kept the boys back, raised his pistol, and started to fire. The shots ripped into the water's surface and decimated an island of hyacinth, their echoes booming against the walls of cypress that lined the lake. A dead garfish floated to the surface, its head the shape of an alligator.

Overlapping with the excitement of gunfire was the madcap commotion of the fishing contest. With the boys cheering them on, Oge and Wallace baited hooks and cast lines at a furious pace. With the gars out of the way, the catching sped up substantially.

Then someone from the cabin called for help setting up for lunch, which ratcheted up the bustle. Later, no single person could quite remember all that followed. Lessie recalled finishing up the mayonnaise in the kitchen. Wallace recollected being instructed to move the dining table and benches away from the cabins into the clearing for a better view of the lake. John Oge knew only that he was lingering down by the shore, drinking ice water and waiting for the meal to be called. Paul Mizzi remembered hoisting Alonzo onto his shoulders and bouncing him back up to camp, nearly trampling Bobby on the way.

As the newspapers would later report, "Bobby's last words were characteristic." When Paul warned, "Get out of the way, Heavy, or I'll run over you," Bobby scuttled away and shouted back, "You can't do it! You ain't no bigger than me!"

EMERGING FROM THE cabin with the first plate of fish, Lessie scanned the crowd of men and boys swarming around the table. It wasn't long into setting out the meal before she put her finger on what was wrong.

She asked where Bobby was. Her question landed on Paul, who still carried Alonzo atop his shoulders, but she knew before he could open his mouth that Paul had no idea. With a quick glance at the other men, she knew that neither did they.

She called Bobby's name. Her eyes darted from one end of the clearing to the other. She called again, louder. And when Paul finally echoed her cry, Lessie's panic burst open. She turned from the table and dashed toward the lake. They all watched her, mute, impotent. Her shoes sunk into the mud, and she stopped, her eyes racing across the water, the weedy shoreline, and the gnarled roots of the bank.

Lessie rushed from one end of the camp to the other, calling for Bobby, and the others joined in. Bewildered, the boys watched the adults spin out of control all around them. Little Alonzo gaped in horror as his mother collapsed to the dirt.

Wallace, Oge, and Daly struck out on the wagon trail behind the camp, to the north. It was possible that Bobby had taken off, once again, after his father. The three men trotted up the road, calling the boy's name and getting no response, scanning the dense woods and spotting no one. They ran into Percy, riding back from the Thornton place, and broke the news.

Percy raced back to camp, where flies covered the uneaten fish on the table, and his wife's tiny frame lay crumpled on the ground. He knelt beside her and held her, as Paul and the others filled him in on the details.

Within moments, Percy was up again, scouring the area just as the others had before him. He remembered Bobby's straw hat with its broken strap and told them all to keep an eye out. It couldn't have stayed on long.

There were footprints in the mud everywhere, but closest to the water's edge where the earth was soft, none the size of Bobby's. The tangle of brush that bordered the camp seemed impenetrable, but Percy dropped to his knees nonetheless and scrambled into it. As the rest of the party continued the search in every other direction, Percy tore through the roots and weeds and canebrake on his hands and knees, dragging his cork leg behind him, searching for Bobby, his hat, or his footprints. He crawled north and south, his voice hoarse from calling, and, too close to the water's edge, he sunk elbow deep and deeper into the mud.

Lawrence Daly and John Oge burst back into camp. After searching northward on the trail, they had just now turned south, where they came upon bare infant footprints in the dirt. They weren't sure if the prints were Bobby's, and they didn't know if he had been barefoot or not. Lessie grabbed Bobby's sandals from the ground, and she and Percy followed the men back to the road.

She knew in an instant that the tracks were Bobby's. They matched the size of his sandals, and none of the other children had gone unshod. On this question, one newspaper would later report her sworn oath that she was "willing to lay down her life."

The four followed the prints south along the wagon trail, all the way to its dead end at a T with the railroad tracks, just a few yards west of a wooden trestle over the lake. The footprints crossed the railroad tracks and dropped down an embankment into a sandpit on the other side. Damp sand had clung to the child's feet, and they detected signs of a scramble or a fall on the way back up the embankment. Then on the railroad tracks, the prints appeared again clearly. Percy led the group after them, but it wasn't long before he stopped dead, staring down. The footprints, he would later recall, had "suddenly disappeared."

They looked everywhere for the boy's path to pick up again: up and down the tracks and in the grass alongside, then, defeated, back to the spot where Percy had stopped. The final footprints pointed west, toward Opelousas, away from the railroad bridge. Where had the boy gone?

Speculating that perhaps the prints were not Bobby's after all, Daly and Oge hurried to retrieve several children from the black settlement to the north. With Percy and Lessie watching, they coaxed the children's feet into position, side by side with the footprints in the dirt. All of the children's feet were larger than the prints.

The westbound excursion train returning to Opelousas lumbered over the bridge, and someone flagged it down. Its passengers, relaxed and happy from a day at lakes nearby, gaped down at the odd scene: a frantic, mud-spattered search party clustered around barefoot black children. When the passengers heard the news, their summer bliss fell away, and many rushed off the train to aid in the search. The engineer promised to call for more help when the train made it back to town.

Indeed, two hours later, railway superintendent Harry Flanders had dispatched a special train carrying one hundred men, all hunters and fishers who knew the terrain well. From the east, a car carrying a rail gang home from a day's work at nearby Second Lake stopped and joined in the search. As late afternoon turned to evening, the hunt broadened for a mile through the woods and tangled shoreline of the lake. They all knew what to look for: tiny footprints, a straw hat, a scrap of blue rompers, a shivering four-year-old boy. They found none of it.

A crossbred dog owned by someone up the road was brought in to follow the scent of the footprints. It zigzagged into the woods, was detoured by a coon and a jackrabbit, then finally darted out onto a log extending from the shore into the water. There, on the log, sat a ham bone, remnants of lunch left by one of the searchers.

By dark, Lessie's sister Rowena had been sent back home to Opelousas with Alonzo and the servant girl. Although it had begun to rain and there was nothing for Lessie to do here but worry, she could not leave. With Percy occupied, helping to supervise the crowds of searchers, she huddled in one of the cabins, paralyzed.

Last night, as she had put Bobby to bed, the swamp beyond these thin plank walls was loud with life: pig frogs grunting, nighthawks shrieking, the gurgle-laughs of a barred owl. Tonight it was a more ominous din, and not just the rain, either. The woods outside were alive with barking dogs, roaring flames, and men screaming her son's name.

A CENTURY BEFORE, the idea of a family camping trip into the Atchafalaya River basin would have been unthinkable. Most Louisianans saw the place as an impenetrable swamp, and rightfully so. There were few inroads into the region, no roadways that crossed it, and most of its waterways were dangerous and barely navigable. In 1816 geographer and cartographer William Darby published the popular study *A Geographical*

Description of the State of Louisiana, which afforded curious readers across America a glimpse into the basin's dark interior. "To have an idea of the dead silence, the awful lonesomeness, and dreary aspect of this region," Darby wrote, "it is necessary to visit the spot." It was hardly an invitation.

For the next century, levees were built across the basin to buffer its towns from flooding by the Mississippi, which fed into it from the northeast. Massive clogs of stumps and trees were removed from waterways to create deeper channels for travel and commerce. Low-lying swampland was drained to accommodate an increasing pressure for plantation agriculture. By the outbreak of the Civil War, the Atchafalaya, as untouched and primordial as much of it still appeared, was a thoroughly designed and managed environment.

But the war ended Louisiana's plantation system, and along with it came the destruction and deterioration of the levees. Even more significant was a series of catastrophic floods during which the Mississippi breached the levees and, with the channels clear of timber, inundated the Atchafalaya full force. In 1866, a year after the war's end, reportorial illustrator A. R. Waud ventured into the region to capture the bayou for readers of *Harper's Weekly.* Waud's drawing is a child's worst nightmare. Thick cypress limbs hang heavy across the entire scene, and in their dark shadows lurk grinning black alligators.

The rebuilding of the levees continued through the turn of the century. In the areas where farming had been abandoned, lumberjacks moved in to harvest the cypress. In northern parts, agriculture made a slow comeback with drainage and the planting of rice fields. And across the region, a fishing economy blossomed. Locals staked personal claims to specific streams and channels, setting up camps along the shoreline or traveling in houseboats to fish where the waters were unclaimed. Steamer service through the larger channels was on the rise. Seasonal roads were cut through the woods. And railroads were built to connect New Orleans with the bayou's growing new towns.

In 1905 the Opelousas, Gulf and Northeastern Railway, more commonly known as the O.G., opened its tracks to Melville and linked Opelousas with "the Lakes" along the way. This chain of deep, clear bayous, partially connected and surrounded by woods, had long been a haven for the adventurous sportsman. Percy Dunbar had hunted and fished here since he was a boy. With the railroad came a new degree of civilization to the lakes, which were now accessible to whole families for single-day picnic excursions as well as for weekend campouts.

Swayze Lake was closest in, an easy hour-and-a-half ride. Besides Lessie's uncle's camp, there were a few other fishing shacks scattered around Swayze, none closer than a mile, and a black community to the north. Down the lake from the Dunbars' camp, the O.G. crossed the water via wooden trestle and continued eastward to Half Moon Lake and then Second Lake after that.

Second Lake was private, open only to members of the Opelousas Rod and Gun Club. In 1912 that included political leaders and patriarchs of St. Landry Parish's Civil War–era aristocracies: Edward B. Dubuisson, R. Lee Garland, Sheriff Marion Swords, and Percy's business partner, Henry E. Estorge. While Percy's name wouldn't appear as a member until 1917, he knew and was known by all of these men in 1912, approaching that inner circle, if not inside it already. Unlike Swayze, Second Lake was a resort with amenities, boasting a new clubhouse and kitchen, a wide lawn, and manicured grounds, which the *St. Landry Clarion* credited to "the energy and good taste of '[S]ebe' and 'Aunt Mary,' the keepers there." That year, the club rolled out shooting tournaments as its latest feature. And for one season at least, the lake itself was cleared of the pernicious lavender-blossomed Japanese water hyacinth, which had been fouling the waterways of the Atchafalaya for the past thirty years.

Just north of Second Lake was Half Moon Lake, developed into a resort by O.G. superintendent Flanders to coincide with his inauguration of daily round-trip rail service. Half Moon promised most of the amenities of Second but was open to the general public. A kitchen was being built, swings and other visitor conveniences were to be erected, and grounds were being tidied for what the *Clarion* called "a real 'parky' appearance."

So when the Dunbars ventured out to the lakes in 1912, there was nothing at all pioneering about their journey. On a Thursday in late August, the O.G.'s passenger carriages would be overloaded with families, fishing poles, and bulky gear for camping and cooking. They had every reason to believe that their excursion would be safe.

WELL INTO THE night, the walls of the cabin shook with a series of thunderous explosions. If Lessie had allowed herself to venture outside, she would have faced what looked like a battlefield. Muddy men wandered wild-eyed through the smoke-filled camp. In the dark beyond, lanterns flashed through the trees, and across the lake was a line of massive fires. The surface of the water itself was roiling with the blasts of dynamite. To the south, by the train trestle, a thick cable was stretched from shore to shore, dangling massive hooks to drag the depths.

They were looking for a body.

At last, the explosions brought to the surface something pale and white. A call went up, and a light was brought to bear: it was the bloated belly of a deer drowned in the spring flood.

The dragging and dynamiting continued through the night, in vain. With the break of dawn, men dove into the lake to search the little coves that the hooks had been unable to reach—the places where a body may have been caught up in weeds. John Oge was one of the divers; he plunged into the murk all morning, ripping through the tenuous hyacinth, scouring the dark tangle of roots underwater along the banks.

If Bobby had not drowned, searchers speculated, any number of wild animals could have killed him. Just a few miles from here, a massive black bear killed two calves in 1908. A poisonous snake might have struck, a giant loggerhead turtle might have snapped off a limb, or if Bobby had slipped into the water, a mature garfish could have devoured him. As the search wore on, some even wondered if the boy had met a slower and crueler demise, his blood poisoned from mosquito bites. But the likeliest predator of all was an alligator, well known for lurking beneath the water's surface by the shoreline and waiting for a turtle, bird, or small mammal to make its oblivious approach. In just seconds, a gator could shoot up, snap its jaws around its prey, and recoil underwater, leaving only a splash and a fast-fading ripple. After waiting for the prey to drown, the creature would rise to the surface to swallow it whole.

Four years prior, just weeks before Bobby was born, southwest Louisiana had been horrified by an eerily similar case of a missing boy. About one hundred miles west of Swayze Lake, three-year-old Harry Frye accompanied his parents and their friends on a Saturday-afternoon fishing trip on the Calcasieu River. While the adults took spots up and down the banks, Harry first lingered with his mother at camp, then headed upstream to join a group of men. An hour later, he was noticed missing, and a frantic days-long search ensued. Dragging of the river turned up pieces of the boy's clothing, bloody and shredded. If one believed the national wire, a tooth-punctured teddy bear was recovered as well. Almost everyone concluded that it was death by alligator, and when a fourteen-foot suspect slithered onto the banks nearby, the men raced home for guns. Though the gator eluded the angry hunt, "the search was abandoned, as the evidence seems conclusive as to [Harry's] fate."

But whatever Bobby Dunbar's fate, there was no scrap of clothing to offer resolution.

By Saturday afternoon, Lessie grew physically ill. When an afternoon special arrived with more searchers, Percy boarded the train with his wife for its return to Opelousas. They fled the swamp, but its black mud clung to their clothes and skin.

When they climbed the front steps of their Victorian cottage on Union Street, they could hear family and friends gathered inside. But the Dunbars had moved here only days before, so the place did not seem at all like home. Possibly, this would afford Lessie and Percy a small comfort when they opened the front door. This was not yet Bobby's house either, and they might not feel him in every corner.

LESSIE DUNBAR WAS born Lela Celeste Whitley in February 1886, a decade into her parents' doomed experiment with life in Texas. Newly-weds John and Delia Whitley had settled on a promising parcel along the state's remote southeastern coast, but the nearest town was Morales, a bloody hotbed of post–Civil War anarchy bypassed by the incoming railroad and left to die. Four years and three siblings after Lessie's birth, the Whitleys fled back east to resettle among Delia's kin in St. Landry Parish.

Thomas Quirk, Delia's father, was one of the more prosperous Anglo planters in Grand Prairie, a community fifteen miles north of Opelousas whose greatest wealth and most fertile land were in the hands of French-speaking Acadians. Thomas may not have been able to offer financial support, but as John got the new farm on its feet, Delia had plenty of siblings who could help with feeding and caring for the children.

Lessie's health may well have played a role in the Whitleys' return. She was born with a horseshoe kidney, an anatomical anomaly wherein her two kidneys were fused together into the shape of a U. This was not a grave concern in and of itself, but Lessie suffered from a common ancillary condition: obstruction of the urinary tract, which would gradually lead one kidney to atrophy and, late in her life, the temporary failure of the other. From childhood onward, she likely suffered chronic abdominal and flank pain, vomiting, and recurring infections. At least in St. Landry, unlike in Texas, the family had professional medical care within a reasonable distance.

They also had access to quality Catholic education. In 1902 Lessie and two of her sisters were enrolled in the Mt. Carmel Academy at Washington, Louisiana, run by an order of nuns who taught in remote French-speaking settlements up and down the state's southwestern bayous. In the academy's tuition books, while the Quirk cousins and most other boarders paid $10 to $14 per year, the Whitley girls' records are different: in Mother Melanie Leblanc's delicate script is written "gratis," "in honor of St. Joseph," "give vegetables when they can and help with work."

For her brief schooling at Mt. Carmel, Lessie would remain grateful to Mother Melanie and the order for her entire life. It was a rigorous bilingual curriculum, going far beyond the basics to include Louisiana history, French literature, philosophy, and astronomy. Of the "household arts," Lessie excelled at embroidery, crochet, and sewing, specializing in clothes for dolls and people alike. Hers was a God-given talent, and Mother Melanie and the other sisters nourished it. In a 1902 school photo, Lessie stands in the rear row among the tallest girls, a commanding presence, shouldering ahead of her fellow students. Her wide face is grimly determined, betraying no trace of childhood, and her pale eyes seem to be looking beyond.

As Lessie's final year at Mt. Carmel was nearing a close, her future husband's career was beginning just two blocks down the street. At first Percy Dunbar didn't have an office for his real estate business, so he tucked himself into the shop of an old shoemaker. In these early years, he snapped up tax sale bargains and turned them for a profit, negotiated timber rights for relatives and neighbors, and sold small rural tracts and lots in town, slowly but surely building a reputation. It helped that he was also Washington's town constable, whose duties, in addition to keeping the peace, included seizure and sale of debtors' property.

Though descended from Robert Dunbar, a successful Scottish American planter in Natchez, Mississippi, Percy had not grown up with easy privilege. Before the Civil War, his grandfather Samuel had a modest plantation with fourteen slaves in East Feliciana Parish; after the war, Samuel relocated to St. Landry, and his land and wealth were divided among his sons—Percy's father Robert being one of five. Percy's maternal grandfather was Felix A. King, president of the Opelousas Board of Police during and after the Civil War, but he was an accountant by trade, with nothing like a fortune. Robert and Madeline raised Percy and his siblings on a small family farm between Opelousas and Washington, and while Percy was certainly schooled during boyhood, there are no records of a college education.

What is known about Percy's youth indicates that, like Lessie's, it was a physical struggle. As a boy, he lost his foot and lower leg in a firearms accident. Though he spoke of the incident later, he never specified the person who pulled the trigger, which suggests it was either he himself or someone too beloved for him to name. The local papers of his youth were dotted with accounts of boys' mishaps with guns, and even a foot peppered with birdshot, if not treated promptly, often led to infection farther up the ankle and amputation.

By the time he reached adulthood, Percy had adapted to his cork leg so fully that strangers couldn't even tell he had it. As one family member recalled, he turned his leg into something of a parlor trick: out in public, he would put on a big show of whittling a stick, drawing a crowd close; then, without warning, he would jam the knife through his pants and into the cork, scattering the startled gawkers. A good thing, then, that his young bride was so skilled with needle and thread.

A year before marriage, Percy executed a series of shrewd career maneuvers: he relocated to the larger town of Opelousas, partnered with H. E. Estorge, and added insurance sales to the duo's roster of services. Estorge, fifteen years Percy's senior, was deemed by the *Clarion* one of St. Landry's "noblest Creole sons," a fixture of parish leadership and state politics. In late 1906, the new partners' first ad was designed to attract attention: in a newspaper column flanked by letters to the editor and classifieds, the notice for Estorge & Dunbar was printed vertically in giant lettering. St. Landry was in the midst of a real estate boom, and Dunbar and Estorge cashed in, selling suburban lots around the perimeter of Opelousas, parceling off plantations, and bringing whole new towns to life along just-laid railroads.

Percy may have met Lessie (just turning twenty and fourteen years his junior) via their overlap in Washington, or even in the social circles of Opelousas, which Lessie's sister Mary had entered via marriage into the prestigious Dupre family. As a candidate for wife, Lessie was ideal: a young, attractive, well-liked, nun-schooled Catholic, and a skilled homemaker from a family with a name.

For the Whitleys, the proposal was welcome. By now it was clear that John was too old and infirm to thrive as a planter. Lessie's two older sisters still lived at home, unmarried and supplementing the family income with seamstress work; by 1910, the Whitleys had taken in two schoolteachers as boarders as well. From a financial perspective, marriage to Percy Dunbar was Lessie's best hope for a brighter future.

In the cool early-morning hours of a weekday in June 1907, they were wed at the home of a Dupre relative in Washington. The wedding made the front page of one of the St. Landry weeklies and even appeared in the *New Orleans Item*. In one Opelousas paper, Lessie was called "a popular and accomplished daughter of our sister town," and in another, Percy was described as "the genial and indefatigable real estate and insurance hustler." After a honeymoon in New Orleans, the newlyweds settled into married life in Opelousas, in a rented home centrally located on Court Street and big enough for Percy's younger brother Archie to move in too.

The indefatigable hustler threw himself into public life. In 1910 Percy was elected as board member and secretary of the recently reorganized Progressive League. He became secretary of the local Democratic Party, overseeing party primaries, and in the summer of 1912, he was appointed to the city's board of supervisors. A year into the Dunbars' marriage, Bobby was born, then Alonzo two years later, but given Lessie's health issues, her pregnancies were far from worry free.

IN HIS FIRST few years, Robert Clarence Dunbar was fearless, even in the face of painful consequences. When he was eighteen months old, he bolted away from his nurse into the backyard and put his left foot directly into a pile of red-hot ashes. It was a severe burn, enough to disfigure his big toe and impair its growth. Later, a crash with Lessie's sewing machine left a deep cut above Bobby's right eye. Worried that her son would lose his sight, she took him to the doctor, but fortunately, the wound just left a scar.

Bobby often played with the neighbor's daughter, Margaret Durio, but as he aged, his stomping grounds broadened well beyond the yard next door. Nearly every afternoon, he was known to dash down to the courthouse square to scare the goldfish in the fountain. Inevitably, he would fall in and soak himself, requiring Deputy Chachere to fish him out and carry him home. Bobby had also taken to racing out the gate and down the street to meet his father on his way home from the office. But when a rowdy saloon opened up along this route, Lessie grew so worried that the sight of public drunkenness would taint his childhood that in the summer of 1912, the Dunbars moved. Their new home was a modest Victorian on Union Street, a safer distance from the dangers of downtown. Apparently it was easier to relocate the entire family than to keep Bobby Dunbar inside the yard.

In mid-August 1912, Bobby accompanied his mother on a visit to her third cousin Douce Mornhingveg, wife of an Opelousas jeweler. Lessie and Douce had not spent time together since girlhood, but their reunion was marred by what Douce would later describe as Bobby's "badness." He was "simply outrageous," she would cluck.

Just a week later, that same quality—call it badness or irrepressible wanderlust—finally resulted in the sort of trouble from which Deputy Chachere could offer no rescue. As Lessie collapsed into her bed on August 24, "prostrate with grief," there were hundreds of men scouring the woods and lakes in search of her son, but there would be no dripping-wet homecoming.

Chapter 2

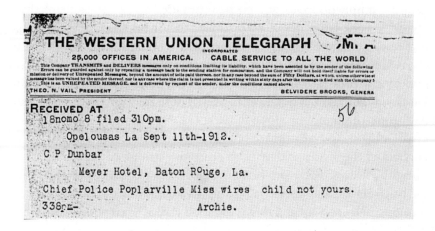

THE WESTERN UNION TELEGRAPH ^Mi ^
INCORPORATED
25,000 OFFICES IN AMERICA.   CABLE SERVICE TO ALL THE WORLD

This Company TRANSMITS and DELIVERS messages only on conditions limiting its liability, which have been assented to by the sender of the following
message. Errors can be guarded against only by repeating a message back to the sending station for comparison, and the Company will not hold itself liable for errors or
delays in transmission or delivery of Unrepeated Messages, beyond the amount of tolls paid thereon, nor in any case beyond the sum of Fifty Dollars, at which, unless otherwise st
message has been valued by the sender thereof, nor is in any case where the claim is not presented in writing within sixty days after the message is filed with the Company f
This is an UNREPEATED MESSAGE, and is delivered by request of the sender, under the conditions named above.

THEO. N. VAIL, PRESIDENT   BELVIDERE BROOKS, GENERA

RECEIVED AT
18nomo 8 filed 31Opm.   5^6

    Opelousas La Sept 11th-1912.·

 C P Dunbar

         Meyer Hotel, Baton R°uge, La.

 Chief Police Poplarville Miss wires   child not yours.
 338p̲ᴇ̲-   Archie.

Telegram, Archie Dunbar to C. P. Dunbar, September 11, 1912

SEARCHERS FLOODED IN from every surrounding town—from Palmetto to the northwest by horseback, wagon, or foot; from Melville to the northeast; and from Port Barre, Opelousas, and Crowley to the southwest—all by special runs of the O.G. By late Saturday afternoon, there were nearly five hundred men. The hunt had widened far beyond its parameters the night before: up to eight miles in any direction from Swayze Lake. As evening came, fires lit up the canebrake again.

The return of darkness brought a surge of desperation, perhaps for no one more than the last man to have seen Bobby alive: Paul Mizzi, who, along with Wallace Dunbar and John Oge, would remain at Swayze Lake for days and weeks to come. But it wasn't just the nightmare of the boy suffering another night in the wild that animated the search. As they tramped through the woods, or clustered at camp to rest, or climbed aboard the train back home, another possibility arose in the men's minds and in their conversations. Their hunt had been thorough and exhaustive, on land and in water, and yet it had produced no trace of a boy or a body. Perhaps, then, the wilderness was not to blame at all.

Perhaps Bobby had been taken.

Someone could have easily ferried the boy away by skiff, it was speculated, out the north end of the lake and into the wider bayou basin. Or
someone could have made off with him down the trail or down the tracks.
Over the past two days, searchers had stumbled across "stragglers" along
the tracks, and as the idea of a kidnapping took hold, the men looked back
on these encounters in a more sinister light.

As the men debated the kidnapping hypothesis, they also took an
opposing theory to its logical extreme. "They even cut open big 'gators,"
Percy would tell the *New Orleans States*. Before they cut them open, they
had to shoot them, best done in darkness, with lanterns aimed at their
eyes. Dragging the creatures to boat or shore before they could sink, hunters hacked the spines with axes to cease the lashing of their tails. Then
came the knives. For years now, owing to the popularity of their hide
for belts, shoes, and purses, alligators had been drastically overhunted,
resulting in a crisis up and down the food chain. Even with a cut up the
belly, these hides would not be left to rot, and the notion of profiting from
such a tragedy was—to some men—unseemly. No surprise, then, that this
aspect of the search would not be eagerly revisited.

Two days into the hunt, when the carcasses and the dredged and dyna-
mited waters refused to yield a body, searchers tried another scheme to
glean a clue as to Bobby's fate. A straw hat, much like the one that the
boy had worn—the hat they'd all been told to look for—was hurled onto
the surface of the water. Mr. Dunbar had said that the boy's hat strap was
broken, so if he had in fact sunk to the bottom, his hat would have floated
to the surface and been spotted. The hat thrower and his companions continued on with their work, but every time they returned to the lake, they
found the hat still there. Its brim filled with water and it listed and curled,
but it didn't sink. Not for minutes, not for hours.

IN OPELOUSAS, THE tragedy cut summer short, and the town was
shrouded in sorrow. Day after day, returning trains from Swayze Lake dis-
gorged an army of filthy, long-faced husbands and fathers. So when they
arrived with the hat story and the talk of a possible abduction, it made
sense that Opelousans latched on. This bristle of speculation was their
only defense against the cruel finality of a young death. And on August
26, hearing reports that Opelousas authorities had contacted police in
New Orleans to search for the boy there, the town allowed itself to feel
positively hopeful.

With more official consideration of a possible kidnapping came a wave of questions and speculation. If the boy had indeed been taken, what was the motive? The Dunbars, while of comfortable means, were not wealthy. Perhaps a kidnapper had mistaken Percy's family with the better-off Dunbars of Opelousas, his cousins. Perhaps the man had intended to snatch the son of Dr. Lawrence Daly, who everyone knew was prosperous. But nearly a week into the search, no one had demanded a ransom.

When New Orleans reporters sought comment from local authorities on the kidnapping lead, they were met with silence. Nor did they get a word from the Dunbars, who remained sequestered in their house on Union Street, surrounded by concerned relatives and inundated with phone calls, cards, letters, and telegrams of sympathy.

Many of these communications prayed for an imminent return of their lost boy. But a few letters, like the one from Percy's aunt Pam in Alexandria, Louisiana, urged the couple to prepare for the worst:

> Now dear ones, should your last effort . . . fail to accomplish that one great boon, the recovery of your darling, the next thought must be your duty to your God—*submission* to his will—your second thought to *comfort each other* in your affliction. Also remember you have another dear little one to live for. God tempers the wind to the shorn Lamb, and thus it will be for you.

When the Dunbars finally broke their silence on August 29, it looked like they might be inching toward such a surrender. Via the *St. Landry Clarion,* they released a letter of gratitude to their fellow Opelousans and the "vast army of human beings" across the region, many of them strangers, who had helped with the search, written words of sympathy, or offered financial support. "We are well aware that all has been done which human effort can accomplish," the letter admitted, "and it is a comfort to know that our country is filled with one of the kindest-hearted people on earth."

But despite the letter's past tense and hints of finality, neither Percy nor Lessie could truly accept that nothing more could be done. This many days in, the theory of kidnapping was their only hope that Bobby was alive. How could they give that up?

And in that, the refusal to abandon hope, the whole town was on their side:

$1,000.00 Reward!

One Thousand Dollars has been subscribed by citizens of Opelousas and deposited with the Planters National Bank of Opelousas, La., to be paid to any person or persons who will deliver to his parents alive little Robert Clarence Dunbar. No questions asked.

Age 4 years and 4 months; full size for age; stout but not fat; large, round blue eyes; light hair and very fair skin, with rosy cheeks.

Left foot had been burned when a baby and shows scar on big toe, which is somewhat smaller than big toe on right foot. Wore blue rompers and straw hat; without shoes. Full name Robert Clarence Dunbar.

In 1912, $1,000 was an enormous sum: the equivalent of $22,000 a century later. The reward contributors included banks and businesses across the parish, from doctors to merchants, from Shute's Drug Store to St. Landry Lumber Company. Mayor E. L. Loeb, Judge Benjamin Pavy, and attorney Edward B. Dubuisson, three of the most well-respected men in Opelousas, pledged $25 each. It was a community effort, just like the search itself. The quest for Bobby Dunbar united Opelousans around a common purpose, and, for a moment, eclipsed the town's long-standing civic tensions.

A BOOMING CITY before the Civil War, Opelousas was nestled on the hills of fertile prairie land where the town's elite had made their fortunes on ranches and plantations. When Baton Rouge came under Federal occupation in 1862, Opelousas briefly became the capital of Confederate Louisiana. In late 1863, Union troops finally advanced on Opelousas, and the town fathers greeted them with surrender. Battles in and around the city had shattered its economy and way of life. Three years after the war's end, the white citizenry of St. Landry—panicked by the threat of the black vote and violent insurrection—launched a parish-wide massacre, killing an estimated two hundred to three hundred African Americans in just two weeks. The event horrified the nation and clouded the town's future with shame, long into its post-Reconstruction embrace of a more "civilized" law-and-order white supremacy.

Nonetheless, Opelousas and St. Landry Parish continued to be major players in state politics, sending their sons into office election after election. The town retained its well-educated professional class, with long-standing familial, social, and political ties to New Orleans, 140 miles to the southeast. With the turn of the century came the railroad and a surge in population, from three thousand to five thousand in just six years. In 1906 the *New Orleans Item* beamed over the town's progress: Opelousas, "to use an expression given recently, has awakened like Rip Van Winkle from a sleep of say twenty years." In 1911 an immense irrigation canal and waterworks was completed, allowing for an expansion of St. Landry's increasingly industrialized agriculture. By 1912, there was a modern sewage system in town, talk of a new streetcar line, political momentum to pave the streets, and a proposed ordinance to keep livestock from roaming free within city limits. Opelousas boasted an opera house, a moving picture show, a magnificent new Catholic church, and a bustling downtown business district.

But there were impediments to the town's resurrection. Time and time again, outside industries made overtures to headquartering within the municipality, only to be tangled in and ultimately repulsed by the internal power struggles of the town's major landowners. While the opera house limped along, the town's legal and illegal saloons were booming, and the 1900 census listed twenty self-proclaimed prostitutes. Though street duels and lynchings had diminished, they were not unheard of in the century's first decade. "There are seldom pistol shots awakening the inhabitants of the city, as in days gone by," the local paper would anxiously boast in 1913. "Something has spread a civilizing hand over those of our people who retain some vestige of the savage."

No barely civilized savage was better known than Marion L. Swords, the portly and dapper four-term fifty-five-year-old sheriff, routinely described as "grizzled." As parish registrar, he had once thrown himself in jail rather than register black voters. During the recent saloon wars, Sheriff Swords punished prohibitionists rather than illegal barkeepers, and when the *New Orleans Item* launched an editorial blitz against his lawlessness, he pistol-whipped the paper's local correspondent, earning statewide derision and dashing his hopes for higher office. By the time he received the first credible lead in the Dunbar kidnapping, Swords was well into his twilight.

IT WAS A phone call, on the afternoon of August 30, 1912, from sixty miles to the east of Opelousas, near Baton Rouge. A few days prior, a woman had been spotted exiting an eastbound train in Port Allen with a small boy in her care. From there she dragged the boy into a skiff and crossed the Mississippi River toward Baton Rouge. The boy's appearance seemed to match the description of Bobby published in the New Orleans *Times-Democrat*: blue rompers, straw hat, barefoot, fair skin. But when a suspicious eyewitness tried to flag down the boat, "the woman at the oars refus[ed] to pay the slightest attention." Sheriff Swords rushed the clue to Percy Dunbar, and together they boarded the night train for Baton Rouge.

When the sighting hit the news, it was the description of the suspect that made the biggest splash: "Italian Woman Disembarks from Frisco Train with Child Not of Her Race," gasped the *St. Landry Clarion*. Later it was reported that she was elegantly dressed in all white and perhaps even wearing a veil. At the time, Italians were just the latest Europeans to suffer suspicion, bias, and violence from the country's earlier immigrants, but Louisiana had a more localized history of anti-Italian fever as well. The turn of the century saw scores of Italians lynched, a form of mob justice traditionally reserved for blacks. Most notoriously, when, in 1891, a jury acquitted a group of Sicilians in the shooting death of the New Orleans police superintendent, thousands of citizens, spurred on by inflammatory editorials in the *States,* stormed the parish prison and shot and hanged eleven Sicilian prisoners—not limited to those who'd been acquitted. One of the mob organizers was the future governor of Louisiana, John M. Parker, who would forever remain unapologetic.

But the reports of an Italian woman with a young boy most brought to mind the horrific case of Walter Lamana. Five years earlier, eight-year-old Walter, son of a wealthy Italian undertaker in New Orleans, was lured with the promise of candy into the hands of kidnappers. The culprits were the infamous "Black Hand," the secret Sicilian gang that had been terrorizing Italian neighborhoods in cities across America since the turn of the century. The gang demanded a $6,000 ransom and moved its young hostage from one hiding place to another to evade authorities. Finally, the trail got too hot. In a swamp hut near St. Rose Walter began to cry for his parents and was choked to keep him quiet, strangled so hard that his neck broke. The body was wrapped in a blanket and dumped in the canebrake. When the police found it, the boy's head had been disconnected from the body altogether.

Nine gang members, including one woman, were captured and

brought to trial, at which point the state militia was called to stave off mob violence. The gang leader was executed, and most of the others were imprisoned for life. But the public wanted them all dead, and outrage was so extreme that in 1910 the state legislature hastily amended the law to make kidnapping (of a boy under fourteen or a girl under twelve) punishable by death, regardless of the fate of the victim.

But in 1912, state-sanctioned execution still was not as quick or hands-on as many southerners would have liked. An August 31 letter to the Dunbars from vacationing Opelousas neighbors put it in stark terms: "I only wish I had been the man who saw the boat pass and had my rifle—the dago would have been extinct and Robert with you . . . at home. A person that causes a father and mother such suffering and anxiety for their son should be executed . . . *fast*."

In Baton Rouge, police drove Percy and Swords out to meet with the eyewitness, and details of the story shifted. The woman and child had taken the ferry, not a skiff. It was actually the witness's wife and her nurse who had spotted the pair, noticed the child's resistance, and speculated that he was being kidnapped.

Retracing the woman and child's steps into Baton Rouge, the team learned that the pair had been seen getting off a streetcar, waiting at the railroad station, then boarding the Yazoo and Mississippi Valley train. Whether they had gone north toward Memphis or south toward New Orleans was unknown.

The trail had gone cold, but Percy could not allow his adrenaline to ebb. He turned to Baton Rouge sheriff Thomas A. Womack, who agreed to scour local orphanages and asylums, in case the kidnapper had abandoned the child. Meanwhile, Sheriff Swords contacted New Orleans police, in the event that the suspect and the boy had traveled south.

But what if they had gone to Memphis? Or farther north, to Saint Louis? A new possibility emerged: many of the seasonal workers at a lumber camp near Swayze Lake were migrants from Saint Louis. Perhaps they had kidnapped the boy and brought him, via this stopover in Baton Rouge, back up to Missouri. But the workers near Swayze were not Italians; they were light-skinned African Americans—"Octoroons." And with that, as the *Times-Democrat* trumpeted, "Suspicion Turns Toward Negroes."

By skiff, Percy and Swords traveled through the lumber camps of the Atchafalaya, built on rafts of floating logs. But among the white lumberjacks and the black laborers, they found neither kidnappers, accomplices, nor witnesses. Searching the woods, Percy's uncle Preston King and a team of men demanded entry to a shack occupied by a family of "half-breed Negroes." Their refusal inflamed suspicion that they were hiding a child, but by the time the searchers returned with arms and more manpower, the family—likely fearing for their lives—had fled.

At Swayze Lake, the fires roared nightly. By now state militia had been called in, with men fanning out in "pickets" for miles. And on August 30, just one week in, the search became national: "Parents Offer $10,000 for Their Missing Boy" was the eye-catching but erroneous headline in the *Omaha World-Herald*, which—along with newspapers coast-to-coast—ran a wire story riddled with sensationalism. Suddenly the cottage on Union Street was inundated with eager sightings of little boys across the country.

As Percy raced off to New Orleans to track a fresh lead on the veiled woman, his Biloxi cousins wrote to urge the Dunbars to hire a private detective. This matter would be best handled by professionals, they insisted, anxious that Percy was flailing himself ragged, too far from home and his suffering wife. But to Percy, waiting idly for someone else to search out his child was unfathomable. His four-day hunt in New Orleans was exhaustive—"I went into every dive, every boardinghouse on the river, and hotel, in my search for the boy," he would later recall—but it turned up nothing. Making a weary-eyed but dramatic appearance at the New Orleans police station, he distributed seven hundred copies of a photo of Bobby and spoke at length with reporters. If nothing else, the genial and indefatigable hustler had won law enforcement and the press over to his cause.

In a September 8 letter, Percy updated Lessie and Alonzo on his plans to follow the river north to Lutcher: after crisscrossing the Mississippi back up to Baton Rouge, "home tonight or tomorrow if nothing new turns up." Percy missed his family: "I hope my little Mama & Buddie are well and am so anxious to get back to them." But he concluded the letter with something of a smile: "Everybody is so nice to me & I am now in Lue Prescotts Drug Store, and he found out I was at the hotel. He came & made me go home with him." Strangers and acquaintances reminded Percy that he was not alone. The vast, anonymous public was searching for his son as well.

In his absence from home, a letter arrived from Poplarville, Mississippi, 170 miles east. It was, like much of the Dunbars' mail these days, from a stranger:

My dear Mrs Dunbar

My heart has gone out to you ever since I saw in the Lake Charles paper the loss of your darling boy: Listen there is an old man here with a little [boy] with light hair blue eyes, and he clames that an old lady came to his hous with him and gave him the little boy. poor little fellow he crys all the time to go home. this old man is trying to tune pianos he has told so many yarns about the boy. They say he is such a smart little fellow. Oh! If I can only be the means of helping you to find your darling child, I'll try and get him to my house this week to tune my piano. I've sent for him to come, for he is now in the county a few miles. I'll do all in my power to help you. Oh! If you could only come you and your husband Just come and come right to my house and stay until you see him. No one will know what you ar hear for. come and feel welcome in my home I'll help you all I can. I just feel like this little boy is yours. He told some of them that the little boy was three and a half years old. Your friend, Mrs. Mattie M. Smith

Though the letter was written to Lessie, it is unlikely that she read it then. If she had, its urgency might have leapt out at her; Mattie Smith's aching hope that this crying boy with the yarn-spinning piano tuner was her son might have reignited her own. And she might have gotten up from bed and insisted, via phone or telegram, that Percy travel over to Poplarville to follow up.

But as Percy would later acknowledge, he was shielding Lessie from many of these incoming clues. In his absence, Percy's brother Archie was in charge of mail, and when he got this letter, he contacted Percy, who instructed him to alert Poplarville authorities. If they deemed the lead worthy, Percy would go there himself. Archie did what he was told. He called the Poplarville police chief, and referred him to the description printed in the newspaper, the photograph, and the reward poster. And then he moved on to the next letter or telegram in the pile. While the Dunbars would later realize that this was a turning point, at the time, Poplarville was just one more town where one more person had seen a little boy.

Two days later, still in pursuit of the veiled woman, Percy received this short telegram from Archie: "Chief Police Poplarville Miss wires child not yours."

IN MID-SEPTEMBER CAME a letter from J. M. Barksdale, a hotel proprietor in Century, Florida, just east of the Alabama border. Here, Barksdale reported, witnesses observed that a crippled tramp was using a child to beg for food along the railroad tracks, and the child resembled exactly the photo and description of Bobby. The sight of the two was heartbreaking and ominous: the boy's "little bare feet struggled, despite the cruel slag which cut them, to keep pace with the man"; his "face was tear-stained . . . as though he were suppressing an outburst of grief"; and the man seemed to be cowing him into silence. Under questioning, the tramp said they were heading to his sister's house in Pensacola, forty miles south, and off they went, down the tracks.

Percy's response was swift and urgent: "Yours of the fifteenth received and enclosed find a photograph and description of my baby. The picture is very good of him, although taken about a year ago. He can easily be identified by the burned toe. If you know anyone between your town and Pensacola, send them one of these cards and ask them to keep a lookout."

But the duo was not found in Pensacola. Instead, days later, they—or a pair like them—were seen due west just over the border at Atmore, Alabama, boarding a train bound for Mobile. A rail worker reported he'd seen them—or a pair like them—climbing aboard another train, still headed west. In Pascagoula, Mississippi, an alarmed reporter spotted a crippled man and a boy selling pencils door-to-door, the boy "shrinking back" from the man in fear. A day later and farther west in Gulfport, Mississippi, a deputy questioned a man and a boy resting on a bench at the depot, but did not detain them. He reported that the boy looked older than Bobby, although he did have an injured left big toe.

When the pair ducked out of sight again, the entire Gulf Coast went on high alert. Little thought was given to why the duo was headed back toward Louisiana, or to the age discrepancy. And while the toe was crucial, what most seized the public's heart was the old cripple's rough manner, the boy's fear, and the compelled begging. "[H]e is forcing the child of tender years to lead the life of a tramp," cried the *Mobile Register*. And there was no greater shame than that.

As long as the word *tramp* had been part of the nation's vocabulary, there had been a "tramp problem." During the deep depression of 1873, the term became popular as a way to characterize the throngs of newly unemployed, homeless transients. With the growth of rail travel, this population became more mobile and more recognizable. So-called tramp laws emerged to keep these men out of the boxcars and barns, off streets and porches, criminalizing every element of their behavior, from seeking employment to seeking food. Naturally, some members of this swelling population were eager to make distinctions: *tramps* didn't work and didn't want to; *hoboes* were on the road in earnest search of work; and *bums* were just drunks who begged and sometimes worked for drink. But in the eyes of settled and employed citizens, such distinctions didn't matter: these men all looked the same. Alongside regular reports of tramps robbing, assaulting, raping, and killing, "the tramp evil" and "the tramp menace" were staples of newspaper editorials, reflecting and exacerbating widespread attitudes of fear, suspicion, pity, and disgust.

Two days after the last coastal sighting, the crippled man and the boy were spotted again, lunching at Brunies Restaurant in Gretna, just over the river from New Orleans. When they headed for the tracks and slipped into a boxcar, police rounded them up.

Yes, the duo had come from Mobile, the man admitted during interrogation, but their movements were innocent. He was forty-five-year-old Tom Warren, in terrible health and grossly crippled, and hobbling his way to Texas, where his brother had offered to take in him and his son John. The boy, in fact, was eight, four years older than Bobby Dunbar. When unnamed Dunbar relatives, most likely Percy's New Orleans kin, arrived to see for themselves, they confirmed that it was not the boy. "[H]e did not tally in any way," the Biloxi *Daily Herald* reported. "There was no scar on the big toe of his left foot. This is especially pointed out in the Dunbar description."

After three full days in jail, the Warrens were sent on their way, their passage funded by contrite court officials and made safer by an official letter from the sheriff, stating their innocence in case of future stops. Yet even after Tom Warren's exoneration, his profile remained etched into the imagination of the entire region.

In late September, an ancient "fakir" and a ten-year-old boy rode the train to Swayze Lake, where the search was finally winding down. Here, the mystic announced, he would lay the child down in an old shanty and place him in a trance. In this state, the boy would speak aloud the location of Bobby Dunbar. But if the boy ever actually spoke, the fakir kept the revelation well guarded from the public.

A string of more plausible leads also ended in disappointment for the Dunbars: a wayward boy in Ohio who matched Bobby's description, only older; a much-anticipated photo from Oklahoma of two waifs, neither resembling their boy.

In early October, when another Baton Rouge lead went cold, it broke Sheriff Womack's heart to report the news to the Dunbars. So on that very day, he made a brash announcement: "I'll give five thousand dollars reward for the return to me of the little Dunbar child, and no questions asked." On top of the thousand dollars already offered, it made nation-wide news.

Womack certainly had the means to put up such a sum. The son of a prosperous planter, he ran a sugar plantation of his own for years, before becoming sheriff that June. He may have known Percy Dunbar through business or political circles already, which would explain his generosity. Or it may have simply been the sympathy of a stranger: during his campaign for sheriff, Womack pledged to allocate $100 a month to orphanages, and he himself was both a father and grandfather.

But the reward announcement had an unintended result: the Dunbar family's mail was reclogged not just with advice from voodoo practition-ers to employ charms and chants but also with menacing notes and threats. "I know where your boy is," read one, "but I'll see that he's kept here forever." Alarmed and overwhelmed, unable to discern real from fake, Percy finally heeded his Biloxi cousins' advice.

The William Burns Detective Agency was a household name nation-wide. A year before, it had successfully cracked the deadly bombing of the Los Angeles Times Building during a labor dispute. Burns himself had been the subject of over a dozen breathless stories in *McClure's* magazine, and the *New York Times* called him "perhaps the only detective of genius whom the country has produced." In New Orleans and across the South, the agency's regional supervisor, Dan S. Lehon, was just as famous as Burns himself. He cut his teeth in detective work as a Pinkerton man, fol-lowed by fifteen years as a special agent for the Illinois Central Railroad, tracking down bank robbers and uncovering graft. In his few years for Burns, he had led the investigation of a labor-related bombing in New Orleans, and was fresh off another major graft exposure, this one in the city government.

Though revered as crime-fighting heroes in the popular imagination, Lehon and the agency had plenty of critics. They operated not so much on the fringes of the law as beyond it entirely, some charged. Their intel-ligence gathering was just strong-arming—and often union busting—by a different name. In the Los Angeles bombing case, Burns's tactics had included at the very least unlawful extradition. During Lehon's stint with the Illinois Central, he was thrown in jail for leading a sledgehammer-wielding mob against a competing railroad crew.

The Burns strategy for investigating a kidnapping was no less aggressive. When the Dunbars signed on with Lehon, they knew that they weren't getting a mild-mannered sleuth. Meanwhile, the incentive for the detective, who presumably had his pick of cases, was a matter of much speculation. Asked by the *States* if the reward had influenced his decision, Lehon bristled. "Of course we do not work for rewards," meaning that the $6,000 would go to whomever provided the decisive tip, and that the Dunbars were paying the agency regardless of results. Rather, he explained, "I took a personal interest in this case because it appealed to me." Lehon was a father himself, his youngest a five-year-old daughter.

In his hands, the search immediately became more professional. The first step was to print a revised circular, one with the new reward and a photo of Bobby on Burns Agency letterhead and without the alarmist Wild West quality of the original. The new circular amended the physical description—"light hair" was replaced with "Hair light, but turning dark"; the description of the toe burn was streamlined—and it outlined the exhaustive Swayze Lake search. Most significant, it highlighted the late-August sighting of "a dark-complexioned woman, supposedly a mulatress," in Baton Rouge.

Less than two weeks later, police as far away as Philadelphia were conducting a house-to-house sweep of the city's black neighborhoods. In Tennessee, a white boy was spotted in the care of a black woman, who struggled to convince her accusers that she was watching the boy while his parents performed in a traveling fair. In Atlanta, a reverend spied a woman dressed as a man with a "modish Alpine hat" and "swinging a rattan cane" escorting a young lad who looked like Bobby Dunbar across a viaduct; by that evening, officers on foot and by motorcycle were turning the city upside down. The Burns Agency had blanketed police stations with some five thousand circulars, and its men were combing cities and towns up and down the Eastern Seaboard and across the South. No surprise, then, that public suspicion was flung in every possible direction.

Nonetheless, Percy Dunbar was now at least cautiously optimistic. "I believe that with the help of the newspapers of the country," he told the *Item* on November 17, "that sooner or later Robert will be returned."

In a chilling coincidence, halfway across the country and on that very day, another father's dwindling hopes for the safe return of his son gave way to horror. In Lackawanna, New York, the body of seven-year-old Joey Joseph, missing for a full year, was found entombed in excrement at the bottom of an outhouse behind a saloon. Authorities had been led to the spot by a confessional postcard from the killer himself, who had spent the past year taunting the boy's father with letters and postcards that detailed how he had taken, tortured, molested, and then finally strangled the boy. The killer also confessed anonymously to the 1902 murder of a newsboy in New York City, and to twelve other attacks and attempted murders on boys as well. On November 17 the shocking story made headlines across the nation, and in the *Item*, it appeared just a page away from the interview with Percy Dunbar. Two days later, authorities closed in on the killer, J. Frank Hickey, whose obsession with recounting his deeds in writing finally did him in and inspired his moniker in tabloid history: the Postcard Killer.

As New York authorities sought to piece together Hickey's movements and track down other victims, investigators across the country wired in details of all their own unsolved cases of murdered and missing boys, on the slim chance that there might be a connection. Naturally, New Orleans police inquired about Robert Dunbar, whose disappearance was still an utter mystery. The *Item*'s report on the inquiry—"the fruitlessness of their search for the Dunbar boy necessitates the grasping of any clue that has the remotest possibility of throwing light on the case"—was far more responsible than its headline: "Fear Degenerate Slew Dunbar Boy."

For Percy and Lessie, Joey's demise embodied their worst and most unspeakable fears about what had happened to Bobby. There had been no ransom demand, after all. Percy had a sheaf of taunting letters not unlike Hickey's. Their son could be long dead, his little body violated, cast off down some hole to rot, and never to be found.

It eventually emerged that Joey's father had kept Hickey's graphic post-cards a secret, not just from authorities, whom he feared might give up their search, but also from his wife. He knew that they would shatter her, and he needed her naïve hope to survive. In this regard, Percy was no different. It is unknown whether Lessie ever learned of the Postcard Killer—whose grisly confessions, hasty trial, and outrageously lenient sentencing were splashed across the New Orleans dailies for a full month—but, undoubtedly, Percy did everything he could to shield her from this news.

The search was destroying Lessie. Though the Burns Agency was now in charge, the tide of leads arriving by mail to the Dunbar home had not diminished, and it was still Percy's job to sort them before passing them on to the professionals. Even if he managed to keep the letters from her, Lessie often saw the photographs. Few of the boys looked anything like Bobby, yet how could each and every one not tear at her heart?

It finally became too much for Lessie; at some point as the search dragged on, she left home for a month. In an April 1913 interview with the *Daily Picayune,* she would mention this time, only fleetingly—not in reference to the circumstances of her departure but rather what happened upon her return: "[M]y 18-month-old baby [Alonzo] forgot me in the month that I was away from it, after Robbie was lost . . . When I went back and snatched up the little thing to kiss it, it screamed, and for a long time would do so every time I went near to it." Coming home to Bobby's enduring absence, her only comfort was the son she still had. But she could not hold him, either.

Chapter 3

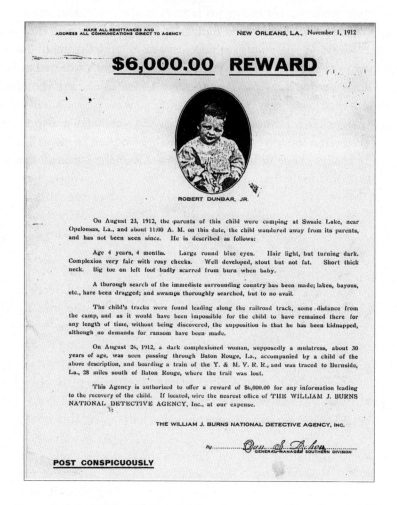

Reward poster, William J. Burns Detective Agency, November 1, 1912

THE EARLY DECEMBER pall upon the Dunbar home was broken by news from Mobile. Burns detective R. C. Cowen and Mobile detective Charles Berge, who had partnered up to sift through Gulf Coast sightings, had apprehended a suspect and were close to locating the boy he had been seen with. Percy was on the next train south.

In late September, the spotting of a lame man and a boy had led Mobile police to apprehend two suspects who were traveling together: Edgar Hooks, a one-legged man who made his way on crutches, and another man, a paralytic. They said they were both peddlers of pencils and shoe-strings. Since their alibis were credible and they had no boy, they were released, and Hooks headed northeast up the Alabama River. But over the next six weeks, a report surfaced that a group of tramps was occupying a house "deep in the canebrake," in the precise vicinity where Hooks had traveled—with a small boy in their custody.

Soon thereafter, Hooks reappeared, outside of Mobile at the dairy farm of Heyman Gabriel—this time with a boy, both of them hungry. Gabriel's superintendent fed them and drove them as far into Mobile as the streetcar, but after they left, Gabriel grew suspicious enough to alert Mobile police. The boy, he felt certain, was Bobby Dunbar. After days of stalking and near misses, Detectives Berge and Cowen finally closed in on Hooks at the Mobile post office—without the boy—seized his mail, and took him in for questioning.

When Percy arrived in Mobile, he registered in a local hotel under an assumed name to avoid scrutiny and joined Cowen and Berge for the interrogation. Hooks maintained his innocence, but the investigators were doubtful. Having read his mail, they now had addresses and a photograph: a family portrait of Hooks, his wife, and a young boy that he insisted was his son. Their first stop was the farm of Heyman Gabriel, who studied first the family photo and then the photo of Bobby on the Burns circular, just under the heading "$6,000 Reward." Without hesitation, Gabriel pointed to the images of Hooks and Bobby: this was the pair he had seen.

Suddenly everything changed. This was the first definitively confirmed sighting of Bobby yet, and Percy's hopes surged. His son was nearby, just up the Alabama River. As the men hurried away, Percy was effusive in his thanks to Mr. Gabriel, who would take pride in his accomplishment for the rest of his life.

Farther northeast, a tipster revealed the precise location of the hide-out of Hooks and his confederates: a shack, miles deep into the nearby marshland. Commandeering a gasoline skiff, Percy and Cowen wove through eight miles of braided, winding channels, unmapped and barely passable, for two full days and nights. At every opening in the overgrowth, they looked for a shanty but found no signs of civilization at all. As Percy would later recall, "We tried to find the house but failed utterly."

Cecil County Public Library
301 Newark Ave.
Elkton, MD 21921

Before defeat could set in, frantic new leads arrived from Lucedale, Mississippi, a timber town just forty miles northwest. On December 12, children walking home from school spotted two tramps, accompanied by a small boy. They raced to tell their parents, who alerted authorities. Elsewhere in town, a lady answered her door to find one of the tramps seeking a meal, and when she refused, he snarled a death threat. She went straight to the mayor, and within hours, a pack of concerned citizens and authorities converged on the old planer shed where the tramps had been seen camping out. No one was inside, but they did spot "a bed of freshly gathered straw and what appeared to be the impression of a child in the straw." Just down the road, an old woman offered an even more ominous detail: she'd heard a child crying from the shed, and one tramp had come to her door for matches. She watched him return to the shed, and shortly thereafter, the crying stopped.

Before the citizens got too heated, however, they needed to confirm that the description of the boy matched Bobby Dunbar. So authorities went right to the best source, phoning the Dunbar residence in Opelousas. In Percy's absence, Lessie took the call. She knew there had been a sighting in Alabama, but this was the first she'd heard of Bobby in Lucedale, and it was a shock. As best she could, on the spot to yelling strangers, she remembered her son: Bobby was four years old and five months, she said (though now it would be eight months); he had "light hair, turning darker, and blue eyes."

As Lessie hung up, left to relive her loss and terror alone, an excited "posse" shot out through Lucedale in search of the tramps and the boy. By nightfall, one man had been arrested: Joseph Marshall, in his late fifties, with mustache and graying hair, "crippled in both feet, and one leg . . . considerably shorter than the other." The next morning, the second tramp was rounded up: Robert Marshall, who identified himself as Joseph's brother, although they looked nothing alike.

Beckoned from Mobile to Lucedale, Percy and Cowen grilled the men for hours. Afterward, they announced a few explosive nuggets to the public: the Marshall brothers had implicated Edgar Hooks as the man who actually snatched Bobby Dunbar. The Lucedale tramps and the Mobile tramps, then, were in it together. In fact, it was Cowen's contention that seven men, if not more, were involved.

Later in the day, interrogators locked up a stool pigeon in a cell alongside Joseph Marshall. The snitch, pretending to be a kidnapper himself, extracted a coldhearted confession: the Marshall brothers had taken

Bobby Dunbar into Mississippi, avoiding the trains, Joseph faking a fake leg to garner free meals. Finally, though, the child became a liability. As the *Pic* worded it, they "had to do away with it on account of money running short and they were about to be overtaken."

Dovetailing with the stifling of cries inside the shed, it was Walter Lamana all over again. "Kidnappers Killed a Boy?" asked the *Kansas City Star*. More responsible papers noted the ambiguity of the phrase "do away with," and officials insisted that the search for Bobby Dunbar, alive, was still on.

"I am convinced, from the statements received from Detective Cowen, that [Hooks] is the one who stole the Dunbar boy," Dan Lehon announced to the press on December 13. Given that there had been no ransom demand, he concluded that the boy had been stolen as a tool for begging, "to arouse the compassion of pedestrians." And apparently the description of both Hooks and the Marshalls roughly corresponded to the "stragglers" that Swayze Lake searchers had spotted back in August.

St. Landry deputy Charles Chachere roused Hooks in the Mobile jail at one in the morning, carried him across two state lines, and deposited him in the New Orleans prison to await the train to Opelousas, where these witnesses could identify him in person. But when reporters spoke at last with the accused in person, his story was far from sinister. A former railroad switchman, Hooks had lost his leg to the job, then lost the job, and was now peddling pencils to support his wife and child. "I have never done a real mean thing in my life," he told the press. "I love my wife and baby boy, and the thought of kidnapping a child would have been the last act I would be guilty of." Most compellingly, Hooks declared he was eager to go to Opelousas to face the Swayze Lake witnesses and clear his name.

Though Hooks was carried on to St. Landry, investigators quietly shrunk away from their bolder accusations against him, and their focus shifted solely to the Marshalls. On Saturday the fourteenth, Percy and Cowen shuffled the pair out of the Lucedale jail and onto the train, taking a secretive, roundabout route to Baton Rouge; they "shanghaied" them, as Percy would later put it, to avoid either lynch mobs or inconvenient legalities, or both, at stops along the way.

When the suspects reached Baton Rouge, jailers relieved them of pocketknives and $22 sewn into their clothes, and then placed them in separate cells. The investigators' plan had been to bring the Marshalls to Opelousas for identification, in addition to Hooks. Instead, the most important Swayze Lake witness traveled to Baton Rouge to see the Marshalls in advance: Preston King, Percy's uncle.

As to the details of King's Swayze Lake sighting, news coverage varied wildly. Most papers reported that he'd spotted two tramps on the tracks near the camp the day or the night *before* Bobby went missing. But another paper suggested that the sighting happened afterward, during the search. For the moment, the crucial issue was more basic: were these the two that King had seen?

When King, Percy, and Cowen entered the Baton Rouge jail, all of its current occupants, including the two new arrivals from Lucedale, were lined up in front of the witness. For a silent eternity, King scrutinized every face.

Finally, he delivered his report, and hearts sank: "None of those are the fellows, as I remember."

He was asked to look again, and failed. The Marshalls alone were brought before him. These were the suspects, he was told. Were these the men he saw?

King glanced at his nephew, who had been so certain these must be the guilty pair; so frantically hopeful that this identification would lead them to his son. It was agony to have to tell the truth.

"I'm not sure. No, I can't say they are the tramps."

With King's failure, one paper observed, "the first link in the chain of evidence . . . snapped to pieces." Noting that the Marshalls had disavowed the testimony by the Lucedale stool pigeon, another paper sniped, "This alleged confession, if it was ever made, was afterwards repudiated."

Yet the pair were taken on to Opelousas anyway and housed alongside Hooks in the St. Landry jail. Here, at least two other witnesses reportedly fingered Joseph Marshall as a tramp they had seen on the tracks at Swayze Lake. But not Robert Marshall. So while investigators now had one viable culprit, they felt sure there were more. With all three suspects held in Opelousas, Burns detectives waged an aggressive campaign to ferret out more kidnappers, to prove the initial theory of a lame hobo and a child-snatching gang. Percy Dunbar and a ginned-up populous were all too willing to cooperate.

Another one-legged hobo, a man named Yates, was spotted on a wagon near Mobile; police staked out his route, but when they tried to apprehend him, he wielded his revolver with drunken belligerence and was summarily subdued. When questioned about the Dunbar kidnapping—in what can be seen only as the investigation eating itself—Yates implicated an unnamed Mississippi "negress" for the crime, although once sobered up in jail, he denied this completely. Percy was called back to Mobile to question him, now with Sheriff Swords, but they, too, were less than convinced that he was worthy of extradition.

On December 18 in Osyka, Mississippi, a man named Hammonds, heading home with his son on the train, was detained so many times that he decided to stop traveling until the storm of wild-eyed suspicion had blown over. From the Alabama canebrake came more gossip for Detective Berge to chase: an able-bodied man ferrying food to a one-legged man and a no-legged man in hiding. Officials in Carriere, Mississippi, telegrammed to Opelousas that "suspicious man here named Walters cripple has little boy . . . might be Dunbar child," but when no scar was seen on the boy's toe, the pair were released. Finally, yet another one-legged tramp was tossed into the Mobile jail where Yates still languished, prompting him to gripe astutely, "What, are you going to arrest all the one-legged men in the country?"

In the late winter and early spring of 1913, St. Landry Parish lost at least four of its children. While bird hunting in Sunset, nine-year-old One-zime Meche was shot in the head by his twelve-year-old uncle. John Earl Chachere, almost two, and Etta Pearl Kerr, seventeen, both died at home with their parents at their bedsides. On the mend from an illness, young Errol Stagg, son of one of Percy's city government colleagues, took a sudden turn for the worse. "Pretty as a girl," Errol was five, almost the age that Bobby would be by now. When he was laid in his coffin, Errol's younger sister Rosa cried insistently that he was just sleeping: "I will wake him up and tell him we'll go out to play."

A grown woman, Lessie Dunbar certainly was not so delicate or naïve as little Rosa. If Bobby had died like Errol Stagg, she would not have wailed foolishly for him to rise from his coffin. She would have been strong enough to survive and move on, regardless of whether she could have another child or not. Young death was tragic, but it was common, a fact of life.

But the Dunbars did not have death's certainty of mourning, and unlike Joey Joseph's parents, they did not have their son's body. In fact, in its absence, they had just the opposite: Bobby could be alive; he could be anywhere. The possibility of kidnapping had initially given Percy and Lessie hope, but now it seemed like a prison. And by early 1913, the Dunbar kidnapping was a cottage industry; a force utterly beyond their control. With every step they might make toward accepting Bobby's death, the newspapers, the detectives—the entire world—tugged them back into hoping he was alive.

> I will admit I have been retained in the Dunbar case . . . In fact, I have been at work on it for two weeks and am now in a position to make a public statement which will for all time settle the fate of this child. I have had hundreds of questions asked me on this matter but have declined to give any answer up to this time. So much interest has been aroused on this subject that I will make a full explanation before my audience on the stage of the Bijou Theater Wednesday night.

Thus spoke "America's Greatest Medium," Julian Barnsall, who had long dazzled audiences across the South with his dramatic journeys into the realm of the spirits. Onstage he appeared comatose, but his spirit voice successfully answered question after question hurled at him from the crowd: numbers, names, places where treasured things had long been lost. Who exactly had "retained" Barnsall in the Dunbar case is unknown, but during his recent Mississippi tour, the questioning on the matter had become so ferocious, and the spirits' refusal to answer so unnerving, that the medium suffered a minor breakdown and postponed the remainder of his Biloxi engagement.

On January 15, after two weeks of "work," the spirits were talkative. According to the *Daily Herald,* Barnsall plunged into his patented Occult Dead Trance and "gave some real facts" on the matter. Which facts precisely were not reported, but the thrust of the message from beyond was this: The Dunbar boy was alive. And he would be found.

IN THE NEW Year, Percy did his best to restart the professional life he had had before Bobby had gone missing. He focused anew on business and tried to keep just as busy outside of work. He volunteered on the entertainment committee for the State Firemen's Convention. The Elks, of which he was a founding member, were in high social gear, with housewarming parties for their new clubhouse, a turkey shoot and banquet, and an Easter circus. In March Percy served out the second session of his term on the grand jury. That spring, he launched a campaign for a soon-to-be-vacant city alderman seat, and his run in the Democratic primary against the equally popular Dr. Jack Perrault offered St. Landry a bit of political excitement in an otherwise dull season. As the primary votes were counted, the opponents "drank coffee together, swapped jokes, played 'crack-a-loo' together, and one would have thought Jack was Percy's campaign manager and Percy was Jack's campaign manager," reported the *Clarion*. Percy came out victorious, fifty-six to twenty-nine, and a month later, he was sworn into office.

From a distance, these might have looked like the signs of a man returning to routine. But Percy's motives for hurling himself so fully into public life were borne of something far more complex and dark.

In March, with no further cause to hold the Marshalls or Hooks, Opelousas authorities at last discharged all three. Soon thereafter, without any formal announcement, the $6,000 reward for Bobby's recovery was withdrawn from the New Orleans bank that had held it, and the funds were returned to their donors: $1,000 to Opelousas citizens, and $5,000 to Sheriff Womack of Baton Rouge.

It was over.

And then, less than a week later, it wasn't.

Percy was unsurprised to see another communiqué from southern Mississippi. Over the past months, he had been in sporadic touch with authorities there, who had reported seeing an old man working in the area and traveling by wagon with a small boy. He was either a tinker, a piano tuner, or a peddler. But that child was said to have red hair, and there had already been at least one false sighting of a piano tuner from Poplarville back in September.

This latest report was different. It was not an ordinary letter but a telegram, arriving sometime around April 6 from a Mrs. C. C. Conerly in the hamlet of Hub. And unlike Mattie Smith, the letter writer of Poplarville, Mrs. Conerly was not alone in her suspicions. Practically the whole town seemed to think that this tinker was a kidnapper and that the boy in his care was Bobby Dunbar. Concerned citizens had attempted to check the youngster's toe for a scar, but his foot was too covered in grime to see clearly. The tinker's name, it was reported, was Walters.

Days later, an equally urgent and much more alarming picture arrived via a letter addressed from the "Ladies of Hub": Mrs. Conerly, along with her neighbor Mrs. Anderson and others. When questioned, Walters had been evasive in explaining the boy's parentage. His own child, his sister's, another woman's entirely—apparently he'd given residents and authorities all of these answers. And when the ladies witnessed Walters brutally whipping the child, an ad hoc "citizens' committee" had confronted the tinker, and deputies had questioned and temporarily detained him. Mrs. Anderson's husband, a local doctor, had even examined the boy. For all of these reasons—the evasion, the abuse, the examination—the outraged ladies of Hub were now utterly convinced that the child was the kidnapped Bobby. They offered a detailed description of the boy, and implored the Dunbars to send more details of their son's appearance, and other photographs if possible. The reward poster photo and description that they had were not enough.

Percy shared the news with Lessie, and it was she who wrote back to the ladies of Hub. She said that their description roughly tallied with Bobby, offered more details of Bobby's appearance, and provided two photos. If the ladies could send photos of the child there, Lessie suggested, perhaps that would make things clear. It was a dangerous path, to let her feel hope again, and they both knew it.

It is not known exactly how many exchanges passed between Lessie and the ladies of Hub, nor what features and markings they discussed, compared, or offered back and forth. But by the end of it, the ladies' firsthand observations of this child in Hub and Lessie's memory of her son's body seemed to be largely harmonious.

Meanwhile, Percy and Hub's deputy sheriff, Charles Day, spoke at least once over the telephone and exchanged several telephone messages. The deputy himself had interrogated Walters, examined the boy, and now—at the urging of the ladies and the "citizens' committee," which had gotten Lessie's letter and photos—was again holding Walters in custody, awaiting word from the Dunbars. Or better yet, a visit in person.

Sometime in these volleys between Percy and Day, the likelihood emerged that Walters indeed was the same old piano tuner who had been detained and released in Poplarville last September. Hub authorities contacted the sheriff there for clarification but received no immediate word. Concluding that he'd been down this dead end before, Percy told Hub authorities that he suspected they held the wrong child.

Two days later, the photos came. They were tiny snapshots of a blond-haired boy wearing a white dress and standing barefoot in the dirt. Out of the stacks of heart-wrenching photographs of anonymous children that the Dunbars had received from all over the country, none had given them a moment's pause. But these two were different.

Percy telegrammed to Hub to keep Walters in custody.

By that time, though, the piano tuner had already been released. No one knew where he was headed, but Day assured Percy that he could be found. He *would* be found.

On Friday, April 18, a telegram arrived from Hub beckoning Mr. Dunbar immediately: the apprehension of Walters and the recovery of the child were imminent. The very next day, Mrs. Conerly herself phoned Percy and repeated the command to come.

Percy hung up and told Lessie everything. The Dunbars' guests, Percy's first cousin Ola Fox and her husband, Harold, from New Orleans, were there to hear as well. The Foxes were childless, but in other ways their lives ran parallel to the Dunbars'. They'd married the same year, Percy was nearly Harold's age, and Lessie nearly Ola's. When their families joined, Ola and Lessie took to each other like flesh-and-blood sisters, and a friendship between the husbands came just as naturally. During Percy's search last fall, whether he was staying in New Orleans or just changing trains, he had been welcome at the Foxes' on a moment's notice. And now, as the drama in Hub was swelling to some kind of climax, it was Ola and Harold, out of all the other family, who were at the Dunbars' side again.

The Foxes agreed to stay with Lessie while Percy traveled to Mississippi. She could not be left alone. Over the past few months, Ola's beloved cousin-in-law had undergone a startling transformation. Her wrists were impossibly thin, and her eyes, deep set to begin with, were like caves. She was skeletal. And now, after despair had ravaged her for months, Lessie's hopes were once again high and fragile.

Chapter 4

"FOR GOD'S SAKE, BABY, SPEAK TO ME!"
CHILD DOESN'T RECOGNIZE HIS MOTHER

Imaginary picture of the scene at Columbia, Miss., Monday night, when Mrs. Dunbar tried in vain to get the little boy, kidnaped eight months ago, to speak to her. It was the first effort at identification, and it failed.

Wood Cowan, *New Orleans Item*, April 22, 1913

April 20, 1913

PERCY TRAVELED ALL night without sleeping. On the train from Opelousas, on the hard benches of New Orleans's Terminal Station while waiting for his connection, on the New Orleans and Northeastern Railroad up into Mississippi, and now on the spur line of the Gulf and Ship Island Railroad to Hub, his mind remained fixed on the child in the photographs, the child that these citizens of Mississippi insisted was his son. For all of last fall, this had been his life: staring out train windows, scouring schedules, waiting at remote depots in the dead of night, his body throbbing with anxious adrenaline or sagging with exhaustion, always imagining that at the end of his journey, his boy would be there. Percy had thought that this was over. And now suddenly he was in it again. There was cause to hope, but far more cause to dread.

As the morning sun rose on plains of barren clear-cuts and scrubby second-growth pine, the train squealed to a halt. Hub, the fourth stop, was a growing lumber hamlet eight miles south of the line's terminus at Columbia, the Marion County seat. It was here, in the homes of Hub's better-off citizenry, that the child-snatching tramp had done odd jobs, and that the boy had been spotted and worried over.

Those worriers, who had gone to great lengths to persuade Percy to come, were most certainly awaiting his arrival: Mrs. S. H. Anderson, wife of the company doctor for two local lumber operations; sawmill manager Mr. T. J. Rankin; merchant C. C. Conerly; and their wives. Deputy Sheriff W. W. Lott was there, too.

But the boy was not, which meant that Walters had not been recaptured yet. Sometime yesterday, Saturday, the old man and the child had been spotted in Foxworth, Mississippi, just across the Pearl River from Columbia. In Foxworth, Deputy Ott Pool had tried to reach Hub's deputy, Charles Day, by phone, since it was Day who had communicated with Mr. Dunbar and sent out the order to arrest. Failing in that, Pool contacted Marion County sheriff Stanley J. Hathorn and asked for permission to arrest. But Hathorn, who knew of Walters's earlier detainment and release, instructed Pool to leave the man alone. Instead, Pool at last got hold of Day himself, who just this morning set out to apprehend the suspect once and for all. Apparently the tinker had been zigzagging the roads northward, which some speculated to be a tactic of evasion. From Hub, Dr. Anderson and a group of concerned neighbors, men and women alike, had set out by automobile to chase the chase. Should Walters be found—and they felt certain that he would—extra muscle might come in handy, and a woman's touch would be required for the boy.

The ladies of Hub added a detail that Percy would not forget: witnesses had seen Walters whip the child yesterday *three times*. And they were sure to repeat to Percy what they had said in their letters and phone calls. "Walters told four different ways here by which he got the child, and we knew that something was wrong," Mrs. Rankin would tell the *Item* in a few weeks, "and we knew, too, that the child ought to have been put into some one's hands that would give him better treatment than he was receiving from Walters."

* * *

TWELVE MILES NORTHWEST of Columbia, Deputy Sheriff Day maneuvered an automobile along a muddy stretch of road alongside the Great Northern Railroad line, following the rutted tracks of a wagon. Bouncing along beside Day were Ott Pool and Jeff D. Wallace, a fifty-two-year-old one-armed farmer and deputy from nearby Foxworth.

Wallace's thoughts were focused on the $6,000 reward. If he, Pool, and Day made the arrest, and it was indeed the right boy, then that money would be theirs to divide. But Day had a more personal investment. Of the three, he alone had spoken with Mr. Dunbar on the phone, and he had heard the near-extinguished hope rising in the father's voice. When questioning Walters, Day had a chance to watch and talk with the little lad in his care. The boy had been skittish at first, but Day quickly established a rapport. He had five children himself, and only recently his young son had died.

The car rounded a corner, and a cluster of buildings appeared ahead. Newsom, Mississippi, was a tiny settlement, a family-run timber operation tucked into a sliver of flat land at the base of a steep ridge on one side, and the railroad tracks and the Pearl River on the other. At its center was the old homestead, long in the Newsom family, now occupied by recently widowed Biddy, who oversaw the operation. There were workers' cabins and outbuildings dotted throughout the property, and then the sawmill itself, up against the ridge and powered by a rushing creek.

Day recognized Walters's big bay horse and his covered wagon right away. They were untended, so the men headed up to the mill.

Nearly thirty years later, the boy would recall this moment vividly. "He remembers being in a sawmill sitting on a pile of sawdust with Walters," the *Shreveport Journal* would report, "when a large group of men came for him."

WORD FINALLY REACHED Percy in Hub by telephone: Pool, Day, and Wallace had detained the tinker at Newsom and recovered the boy safely. Up until this moment, Percy must have found it easy to believe that, yet again, he would meet with failure. But for the first time, there wasn't just a suspect in custody. There was a boy.

Then came more complications. After the arrest, the boy had been taken to Deputy Sheriff Wallace's home in Foxworth, six miles south of Newsom, across the river from Columbia. Meanwhile, Pool stayed in Newsom guarding Walters. For one of many possible reasons—lack of an available vehicle, flooding of the fastest roads—Percy and Lott were forced to head north by railroad handcar. If authorities set out by car with the boy from Foxworth, they could rendezvous in Columbia.

Facing each other on the handcar, Percy and Lott put all their strength into the pumping. With his cork leg, Percy strained to keep balance and wearied fast. Temperatures reached into the eighties that day, and he would recall that the trip took the better part of the afternoon.

When the tracks neared a road, they crossed paths with Dr. Anderson, in his car with "seven or eight others." The auto stopped, and Percy saw right away that, again, there was no child. The rendezvous with the other auto had not yet occurred. Abandoning the handcar, Percy and Lott piled in. Their hands were filthy with grease, and they were drenched in sweat. Anderson could feel Percy's rising tension, and he took the rutted roads as fast as the car would allow.

At five in the afternoon, on the outskirts of Columbia, they met up with the other auto, stopped at an intersection. Percy and Lott leapt out first. They approached the car from opposite sides, both peering into the front seat at the boy, wedged halfway into Day's lap and preoccupied with the dashboard controls.

Every witness described the child the same way, and a photo of the boy, perched on the car's running board just moments before Percy's arrival, bears this out: he was filthy. His hair was matted, his greenish-black frock torn and mud caked, and his bare ankles and feet scaly with dried dirt.

But Percy was looking only at the child's face. It was rough with sunburn and road dust, and the eyes were drawn and squinted. Percy knew all this from the other photos and the back-and-forth with the ladies, so he was ready to see beyond these superficialities. He was looking for some essence in this child's face that was familiar.

It welled up inside him, and before he could think it, he said it:

"Bobby."

The boy looked up at the voice, for the first time, right into Percy's eyes.

Percy was stunned. He had recognized the name. He had answered his father.

But as everyone would recall, the boy's eyes did not stay bright with recognition. Instead they dropped back down and returned to an examination of the car's interior.

Percy, though, had felt the glimmer, and he knew. "That's my boy," he said, and he reached over Day to take the child in his open arms.

The boy looked up again, and, according to all eyewitness testimony, instead offered up his bare, dirty left foot.

Percy flinched and stared mute at the foot.

The explanation probably came from Day: so many folks had looked at this boy's toe, he had come to expect that was all anybody wanted.

Undeterred, Percy reached into the car again. Oblivious to the child's grime and his own greasy hands and sweat, he pulled out the boy and held him close to his chest.

Instantly, the child howled in objection. He thrashed and fought Percy, who was horrified and held the boy tighter to calm him. But this only made it worse. The youngster reached back toward the car for Day. On instinct, Day lifted his arms out to him.

Percy handed the boy over and shrank backward. In the arms of Day, his companion of the past few hours, the child quickly settled down. It stung Percy terribly. The onlookers, who had expected instant recognition and a joyous reunion, were in shock and despair for this lost father. They watched him, standing in the dirt road alone, gaping at the boy.

The last time Percy had seen his son, eight months ago, he'd been crying like this. Only then, on the path by Swayze Lake, Bobby had been clinging to his father, not wrestling away. Wanting him, not fearing him.

The child might have lost his memory, someone posited. He might have been coached, brainwashed, warned not to speak or divulge who he was. For the past few weeks, the tinker had kept him hidden in the wagon, away from the public eye. Clearly, the boy had learned to fear.

This was hard for Percy to hear, but he understood it. In the back of his mind, he had probably turned over these possibilities before. So he continued to watch the boy carefully. If he couldn't know the boy through interaction, he would know him by observation.

But over and over, Percy hit the same snag. The boy's eyes: he looked just like Bobby, Percy said aloud, except for the eyes. This boy's eyes were blue, like Bobby's, but they were drawn and tight. Bobby's were round and open.

Dr. Anderson suggested that, on the wagon on the open road, exposed all day to the sun, wind, and elements, the boy must have been conditioned to squint. This made some sense to Percy, too, and he allowed his hope to trickle back in.

By now the boy had calmed down and was growing restless and talkative. He worked the steering wheel and babbled. His voice sounded like Bobby's, Percy observed. And Bobby was chatty, just like this child.

Then one word from the garbled chatter stood out: "audbeel." This, Percy would recall, was exactly how Bobby pronounced "automobile."

Percy smiled and explained this to the others, and the boy enjoyed hearing his word repeated.

At last, Percy regained enough confidence in his initial recognition that he decided to take the examination further, to the details. He needed to look over the child for the marks, moles, and scars that Lessie had drilled into his head.

He hoisted the boy up, back into his arms, and as Dr. Anderson would recall, carried him behind a nearby house for privacy. The exact nature of this phase of the examination is unknown. In the most immediate reports of Percy's retelling, three particular features are consistently named as those he examined: a brown mole just above his left wrist, a cowlick on his forehead, and the burn scar on the left foot. All, he said, corresponded with those of his son Bobby. The final mark, the scar, was not as prominent as he had expected; the next day, Percy said to a reporter: "The scar is somewhat rubbed off on account of the rough treatment and exposure to the elements." "Other marks" are mentioned, but not named. In great detail, Percy also described his examination of the child's hands: though they were most certainly Bobby's hands, the fingers, "once chubby and dimpled" now seemed distended, "as though he had been forced to hold on to a stick, or been dragged along in some way." Finally, it is quite likely that Percy undressed the boy; he would later testify that his shoulders were raw and chafed, and that his back and legs were covered in welts. What the ladies had said was true: the boy had been whipped.

Sometime later, Percy emerged from behind the building, holding the boy in his arms and, according to both Day and Dr. Anderson, weeping. This was either his son, Percy would later remember saying, "or a twin likeness." Among others, Lott would reiterate that point: "Mr. Dunbar said it was the very image of his kid."

Ott Pool was still up at Newsom, detaining Walters at the mill and awaiting further instructions. The boy had not been unconditionally identified, so there was still a question over whether the tinker should, or could, be arrested. Percy wanted to see the old man himself. He had been hands-on about every aspect of the case since the beginning, and more than any of these men, he knew which questions to ask and which pieces of information might be significant.

So it was agreed: Anderson, Day, and Percy would travel back up to Newsom to question the tinker. As for the child, for the time being,

Wallace would take him to his home, where his wife could bathe, clothe, and feed him supper. Percy gave the one-armed deputy $2 to cover those costs. Depending on when and how the interrogation concluded, they would come back for the boy.

ARRIVING AT NEWSOM with Day and Anderson, Percy peered at the old man limping toward them, watched over by Deputy Pool.

"He was a rough-looking citizen," Percy told a reporter the next day, and "looked like a tramp or an outlaw." There was an eight-month history to Percy's suspicion, and his easy blending of stealthy criminal with hapless itinerant. With Hooks and the Marshalls, and all the other crippled tramps, there had been no sure way to gauge a man's guilt or innocence by appearance alone, and William Cantwell Walters was no different.

In fact, at first glance, he certainly looked like a broken vagrant, plain and simple, and not only because of his age or his limp. Two days later, a rather fashion-conscious New Orleans reporter would describe Walters's appearance in detail, which is the nearest existing approximation of what he looked like on April 20:

"He wears a dark blue serge plaid coat, several sizes too small for a man of his build, a pair of yellowish corduroy pants turned up several inches from the bottom, and an old black string tie. He has a derby, which is apparently a boy's size, and of a style five seasons back, and is softened into a perpetual crusher from exposure to wind and weather. A pair of heavy dust-whitened shoes and some grey yarn socks complete his outer apparel."

What bespoke "outlaw" in Walters's appearance was not his wardrobe but his countenance, the features that struck Percy when the man came close. His face was grizzled and gaunt; his mustache, black and unruly. And underneath steeply sloped brows, his eyes, though bagged and drawn tight, were piercing. Photographs and descriptions do not indicate their color, but their quality was undeniable. A week from now, they would be described by someone who knew him well: "Walters sure had vigorous eyes, there ain't no getting around that."

And then there was his demeanor. While there is no record of the precise exchange that took place at Newsom, Percy would recall with certainty that Walters was belligerent. "I tried to talk with the man," he said, but he was "surly and stubborn." According to Percy, he was also evasive: "he could not tell what he had been doing, or where he had come from, with any degree of satisfaction." The only statement that the old man did make, quite insistently, was that he had not stolen the child. But he wouldn't say how he had gotten the boy or who his parents were. Beyond his mistrust of Walters, Percy felt a protective paternal rage: the old man had whipped and cowed the boy into silence.

It was decided to bring Walters to Columbia for further questioning. If he tried to object to another detainment, and he must have, he would have brought up his earlier run-ins, not just with Day, who had questioned him, but also with Dr. Anderson, who had had occasion to examine the boy a few weeks past. The fact that both Day and Anderson had already determined that Walters could not be held as a kidnapper, and that the boy could not be identified as Bobby Dunbar, was his best leverage against Mr. Dunbar, who was rapidly reaching the exact opposite conclusion. But for both Day and Anderson, the father's recognition of the boy, while qualified, carried much more weight.

At the Columbia jail, questioning persisted late into the night. Though the suspect remained ill tempered, he eventually shed some of his reticence. He became "sort of a 'smart aleck' talker," Percy observed, "that never knows when to stop." What exactly he would not stop about, again, is not known. Walters certainly elaborated on his declaration of innocence: the boy's name was Bruce, not Bobby; he'd had custody of him for over a year, and there were plenty of people, elsewhere in Mississippi, who could corroborate that. And finally, as Percy recalled, "It was not until we had locked him up in the jail," well past midnight, "that we were able to get any admissions from him" on the matter of parentage. The child, one report would quote Walters, "was given to me by a widow in North Carolina about a year ago."

But the disclosure came at the price of any remaining civility. Percy described the bitter standoff: "He said he would fight to get it back if he spent his last dollar. I told him he would have to spend his last dollar, and it might cost him his neck as well."

For all his bravado, Percy was rattled. Some part of him had expected to break Walters, to expose a fatal crack in his story. And when that did not happen, doubt crept back in. He wondered what he would tell his wife.

Near midnight, he found himself starving. The Main Lunch Room, an old-fashioned dive just down the street in the Dr. Pope Building, was likely the only place open this late on a Sunday night. And although Mississippi was four years dry, Marion County was teeming with moonshiners, bootleggers, and blind tigers, so if Percy needed a drink, it wouldn't have been hard to find. As he waited for and then ate his dinner, the question festered: what was he going to tell Lessie? Sometime between midnight and two in the morning, whether induced by liquor, lack of sleep, or the companionship of a roomful of sympathetic strangers, Percy opened up. In two months, proprietor Jack Storm, after listing several other patrons present, would swear to what Percy said:

> [A]t this time and place and in the presence of these people, Mr. C. P. Dunbar said: "If I do not find that child, I do not know what will become of my wife. She has been as one demented for the last eight months and seems to grow worse all the while; she can not eat nor sleep, and it is impossible for me to stay at home with her in this condition. I have become reconciled to the loss of the child, but I don't believe my wife ever will, and I do not know what I will do if I do not find the child."

At two thirty Percy contacted Lessie—by telegram, according to some sources; by telephone, according to others. He was optimistic that the boy was Bobby, he told her, but needed her to see him in person to confirm. He would bring the child to New Orleans by morning train and meet her there. If she took the first train out of Opelousas, he would catch the four thirty out of Columbia and arrive before her. The plan was set, but it did not remain private.

April 21, 1913

AFTER LESS THAN two hours of lying in bed awake, Percy stood in the doorway of the Baylis Hotel, peering down the dead-of-night street for some sign of Anderson and Day. He'd sent them to collect the boy from Deputy Wallace. Instead the phone rang, and the sleepy clerk ushered him over to take the call: it was Day, sheepishly reporting that Wallace refused to give the child up until he'd received the $6,000 reward.

Percy was livid. What claim did Wallace, who'd had nothing to do with sighting the child to begin with or alerting the Dunbars; who'd only been one of several men on hand for Walters's re-arrest, which was all but inevitable—what claim did he have to the reward, much less to the reward in its entirety? He'd gotten $2 for bathing, dressing, and lodging the child, and now he wanted $6,000? In his defense, Wallace would soon claim that he wanted only his fair-and-square one-third of the reward, and that he made the compromise offer to escort the child to New Orleans so that

Mrs. Dunbar might identify it there. That offer, he would declare, was rejected or ignored, but Day and Anderson wouldn't remember it having been made at all.

Percy itched to confront the man, but the four-thirty train to New Orleans was leaving in a few minutes, and he had told Lessie that he would meet her. A last-minute change of plan would be one more source of worry, which he doubted she could bear. So with Day's promise to keep "several reliable men" (including himself) guarding both the child and Wallace until he could return, Percy headed for the train, childless. He would have to bring Lessie back up from New Orleans to see the boy.

ON MONDAY MORNING, households throughout Columbia, Mississippi, were atwitter with Dunbar rumors, and thirty-seven-year-old Thomas Seaborn Dale's was likely no different. For his two children, fifteen-year-old Clarissa and twelve-year-old Roy, it must have been impossible to believe that the famous missing boy had been found here, in their very own Marion County. The thought of a kidnapper in their midst caused their mother, Iris, much alarm, as it did all mothers in town. Dale would have more news to report once he was down at work; as an established Columbia attorney, he was on a first-name basis with every official in town. His trip downtown by bicycle would take no more than a few minutes.

If he wasn't just going to work, which was a stone's throw from home, Dale's twenty-eight-year-old partner Hollis Clifton Rawls would have preferred a much flashier mode of transport: his new automobile. The dapper young bachelor was no aristocrat, however. After his mother died, his father—who navigated log rafts down the Pearl River—sent him off to military school, and he had worked at the post office to pay for law school. Well liked in his hometown, Rawls had been Columbia's mayor from 1910 until 1912, losing reelection the year before by the slimmest of margins. Now, just four years out of law school, Rawls had a thriving practice with Dale, although it was hardly reflected in their cramped office above the Pearl River Bank.

They almost certainly knew who William Walters was. The citizens' committee that had formed against the tinker was major local news two weeks ago, and, of course, by this morning, the entire town had heard of his capture. Now here he was in person before the two attorneys, telling them his story and seeking their representation.

Walters didn't get too far before they surmised that, in fact, he had not been arrested at all. Just like before, he had only been detained, held without charges until Mrs. Dunbar arrived to identify the boy, and the proper charge of kidnapping could be drawn up.

Dale and Rawls weighed the situation. They did not know if this old man was innocent or guilty. But they certainly knew how violently unpopular a celebrity child-snatcher would be with some of the less law-abiding citizens of Marion County. If the child was determined to be Bobby Dunbar, Walters might not stand a chance against a lynch mob. They did their best to impress upon the tinker the gravity of his predicament. Finally, Dale got to the point. "Old man," he said, "speaking as friends and not as attorneys, if that boy is Bobbie Dunbar, the road's ahead of you. You have six hours before they get here."

Walters replied calmly that he had nothing to fear. He was an innocent man.

At some level, both Dale and Rawls must have dreaded the idea of taking on his case. The Dunbar kidnapper would be reviled across the South, and if they represented him, their own lives might be in danger, too. Without committing, they tried to draw more information from the old man. He was ready for them, with a memorized list of people in and around the area of Poplarville, in nearby Pearl River County, where he had spent much of the summer and fall of 1912 with this boy he called Bruce. These were upstanding people who would vouch for his story, Walters insisted. One of the first names he mentioned, the lawyers knew well: Bilbo. Jeptha and Matilda Bilbo, aunt and uncle of none other than Theodore G. Bilbo, the fiery and flamboyant lieutenant governor of Mississippi.

Beyond that high-powered connection, both lawyers felt that there was something in the way this old man told his story that seemed straight. He was odd, and he certainly didn't seem incapable of criminal behavior. But he did not strike Dale or Rawls as a likely kidnapper.

At last, they told him that they were inclined to take his case, but on one major condition: if these Pearl River County witnesses couldn't back up his story, then Walters was on his own. They would not represent him if they were not assured of his innocence. And there was the matter of a fee. Walters had $50 in the bank, his horse Charlie, and his rig, a camera, and some interest in land back in North Carolina. It wasn't much. Dale and Rawls had to have known that if this case went very far at all, money would soon become a critical concern. But they took it anyway.

It was not yet noon when local authorities concluded that waiting to charge Walters until the Dunbars returned perhaps was not the most prudent plan. He had been freed to wander off before; if it happened again, they would be pilloried. Less than three hours after the tinker's release, Sheriff Day retrieved him, charged him formally with abduction, and returned him to the Columbia jail.

Whether during his interview with the lawyers, upon his arrest, or perhaps even earlier, late at night in jail with Mr. Dunbar, Walters made a written statement. Largely, it was a chronology of his purported travels during 1912: from the spring, when he and the boy came south from North Carolina, through Georgia, into Florida, west to Alabama, and, finally, to Mississippi. In the summer, Walters had been a patient at New Orleans's Charity Hospital. But the most dramatic revelations came before all that:

> My name is William Walters. I was born in Robeson County, North Carolina and have three grown sons, Horace, William, and Raymond. Horace is in the Philippines. I suppose the others are in Charlotte, N.C. I don't know where my wife is.
>
> I got the child at the residence of J. P. Walters, Barnesville, N.C., between November and Christmas, 1911. Julia Anderson claimed to be the mother of the child. I don't know the father. The child was about three years old when I got him. I took him away from her about the middle of February.

ACROSS THE PEARL River, the boy woke in another strange bed.

There were children all around him. From a former marriage, Deputy Jeff Wallace had at least five still young enough to live at home. His new wife, Saphronia, a young widow, had four children to bring to the household, and in 1913 she was pregnant with another. There were plenty of clothes for the boy to wear, but with this many mouths to feed, the $2 from Mr. Dunbar was sorely needed.

After breakfast, some of the other children may have been hurried off to school, but the boy was left to his own devices on the Wallace farm, a routine with which he was familiar. In the past, though, it had just been the women, or a few curious neighbors who gathered around to ask questions. But now, all morning, a steady stream of strangers approached the Wallace farm to see him. He kept quiet, but that didn't stop them. Old one-armed Wallace stepped in, but he didn't try to block the questions, so much as moderate them.

Deputy Day was the only one who didn't badger the boy about his name. He had settled on calling him "Little Partner," which the boy liked, and which necessitated that Day be christened "Big Partner." Over the course of this day of limbo, "Big" scrounged up all sorts of presents to keep "Little" busy, an orange, sometimes a nickel to flip or bury. After he handed over the jackknife, however, no other gift existed. The boy spent all afternoon gouging at the Wallace fence rails, and he sliced into both thumbs.

As the day wore on, the crowds swelled and grew more insistent. Most everyone would call one name or another to see if he answered. Sometimes they would try to catch him alone, before Wallace or Day could intervene, and test him with questions. And they would gossip giddily over his answers for days and weeks to come.

IN THE EARLY hours of Monday morning, word of Percy's communication with Lessie (which had happened before the Wallace snag) reached the press. By Monday afternoon, at least one New Orleans paper was in possession of a telegram from an unidentified Opelousas source stating that Percy Dunbar was en route to New Orleans with the child to meet his wife. The *Item* was first to run with the misinformation, scooping its competition by almost a full day with a hurried front-page report: "Kidnapped Boy Found; Dunbar Here with Child."

By the time the Frisco was due in from Opelousas on Monday afternoon, New Orleans's Terminal Station was teeming with reporters and photographers eager to capture the reunion of mother and child. But everyone was looking for a man with a little boy. Percy, of course, was waiting alone. Since arriving from Mississippi that morning, he had checked in at the Cosmopolitan Hotel to rest before returning to meet Lessie's train. When it at last lumbered in, he pushed against the tide of arriving passengers and finally met Ola and Harold, with Lessie between them.

Her brimmed hat sprouted a jaunty feather, and beneath a smart brown frock, the tall collar of her blouse was buttoned and brooched. But the clothes hung off her. Lessie's eyes, sunken and circled, flickered with dread when they saw that Percy was alone.

He stepped in, embraced and kissed her, then did his best to explain the situation as coolly as possible. But his tentative optimism apparently shone through. Two days later, she would recall, "I knew that he had good news, as he had never been so affectionate before in public." Percy led her to a quiet bench beneath the grand vaulted ceilings, and, with Ola and Harold huddled around them, he told her about the boy.

Nearby, a *Times-Democrat* correspondent lurked, growing surer and surer that these were the Dunbars. When he finally made his approach, Percy refused to talk. But the reporter persisted, brandishing his paper's copy of the telegram from Opelousas to call Percy's bluff. At this, Percy relented, softened, and introduced Lessie. He did not want to say too much until he was positive, he explained, and she elaborated, adding that they'd had their hopes lifted and crushed so many times.

Once Percy got started, however, he could not stop. He told everything of his encounters with the boy and with Walters in Columbia. He reiterated how certain he was that the child was Bobby. And he announced an explosive new accusation against the tinker: "I think that this is the same clue we have been following up for months; probably the same that we had near Mobile sometime last December." It was Walters they had been trailing all along, Percy now speculated. His search had not been in vain.

Meanwhile, Lessie fretted more over the boy. She could not understand why he would not respond to his own father immediately. And although Percy had explained the suspicion that the child had been "scared into not recognizing me," Lessie was not convinced. "It's too good to be true," the reporter heard her say, as Ola held her. "I can't believe it until I've had the baby in my arms."

When competing newspapers spotted the group, Percy hurried Lessie back to the hotel. By the time they returned for the four fifteen up to Mississippi, photographers lay in wait and snapped their pictures as they rushed into the station. And when it came time to board, journalists followed. The papers were coming along for the ride.

According to the *Item*'s coverage of the journey, Lessie sat at Percy's side and let him do the talking. He was chronicling his eight-month search in far more detail than he had at the train station, teasing out every lead and twist for an expanding crowd. For most of the trip, Lessie remained composed, breaking in to sound a note of worry or caution, or to ask how far they had to go, or to thank the kind ladies from the parlor car for their comfort when she surrendered to exhausted anguish.

Well into Mississippi, another passenger, a Marion County resident returning home from New Orleans, joined the conversation. He knew that local sentiment was raging against the prisoner, and he warned the Dunbars of the danger of a lynching. Lessie was horrified.

But if there was any doubt over the man's claim, it was put to rest as soon as the train arrived in Columbia at 8:58 p.m. At the station, a throng awaited in the night, almost all men bearing arms. They surrounded the Dunbars as they hurried into an automobile driven by Sheriff Hathorn, and they followed by horseback, buggy, or on foot the five miles out to West Columbia. As the car neared the Wallace place, the crowds along the road thickened. When the convoy finally stopped, according to the papers, nearly a thousand people were gathered on Jeff Wallace's property, surrounding the pine-plank farmer's cabin where the little boy was being kept.

In Mississippi and across the South, the lynching of African Americans was a wild-eyed carnival, a public spectacle of gore intended largely to instill fear in other African Americans. By contrast, the lynching of whites—a far less frequent occurrence—was a sober affair, precise and clinical, almost grim. White lynching victims were most often outsiders, vagrants, and itinerants who in some way were thought to have violated the fabric of a community. They were strung up for sensational crimes and unthinkable moral outrages, which is precisely what Mississippi and Louisiana felt kidnapping to be. Whereas frustration with the criminal justice system's delays, loopholes, and technicalities was often an apology for southern mob violence more than an actual rationale, it was undeniable that the sentencing of little Walter Lamana's kidnappers to anything less than death was still felt as a raw injustice throughout the region. A half decade later, to execute the infamous Dunbar kidnapper would be seen as a badge of honor.

In fact, the gathering here could well have been planned. In the early 1890s, Marion County was under siege by the whitecaps, a stealth band of vigilantes that prowled the countryside, burning African American farmers out of their homes and punishing whites who opposed their authority. Columbia's town leaders stood up to break whitecap rule, but they certainly did not eliminate the menace altogether. It would be rumored that whitecaps were behind not just this night's amassing at the Wallace farm but the "citizens' committee" that had confronted Walters in early April.

Organized or not, in order to execute, this mob needed its confirmation of the kidnapper's guilt. They'd been waiting all day for Lessie to deliver it. At the cabin door, she, Percy, and Hathorn were met by the one-armed deputy, Jeff Wallace. The *Item* reported that for two hours, Wallace refused the couple entry until he was promised his reward, but that story appears in no other paper's account. If there was any delay at all, it was likely for Wallace's announcement that the boy was fast asleep, wearied from a day of play and questioning.

When Percy and Lessie stepped inside behind Hathorn, it took a moment to adjust to the dim light. When they did, all they saw, wherever they turned, were the faces of curious men gaping out at them from the shadows. The cabin was already packed with onlookers, who had staked claim to all but one of its tiny rooms. Their faces, according to the *Item*, were "morbid, curious, but stern." Hathorn ordered more oil lamps to be lit, and cleared a path for Percy and Lessie through the hallway toward the front room. As the grumbling crowd parted, the floorboards sagged and shook.

When the door to the front room was opened, the onlookers gushed in alongside Percy, Lessie, and Hathorn, as unstoppable as a spring flood. The men muscled their way to the bedside, where Mrs. Wallace hovered over the sleeping child, and they allowed only the narrowest spot for the Dunbars themselves. Reporters fought for their own viewing space, as close as possible. Outside, more men jostled for an angle through the windows, pressing so close to the glass that their faces could be seen clearly inside, glowing in the smoky light.

Jeff Wallace shoved to the head of the bed. He owned the place, after all, so he deserved a spot front and center. And here he could see the mother's recognition with his own eyes, in case of any further attempt to deny him his due reward. With his one arm, he raised a lamp over the child.

Lessie knelt at the bedside, lowered her head, and prayed silently. She had stared into the face of the boy in the photographs for the past several days, comparing it side by side, feature by feature, with the photos she had of Bobby and with her own memory. She had been uncertain. Now, in person, she would know.

When she looked up, her eyes went to the boy's face. His eyes were closed, and the light was dim, but she could see his face. For a moment, she was mesmerized by his sleeping. He seemed so peaceful.

Then she remembered the men around her and their expectations. Two days later, she would declare that her recognition was sweeping and instantaneous, but by all immediate accounts, her outward reaction was far more complicated. "I do not know," the New Orleans *Daily Picayune* quoted her. "I am not quite sure."

At first Lessie did not want to wake the child. So Percy sat on the bed's edge, and together they adjusted the boy's body and limbs to examine his various "markings." The *Item* reported the next day that the identification was positive. The *Pic* was more specific, repeating all of the markings that Percy had identified and stating that Lessie checked and confirmed these as well. Lessie herself would recall looking for a remembered mole behind the child's ear, finding it and kissing it. But according to later statements, when Lessie ran her fingers across the left big toe of the child, her face filled with disappointment, "plain to everyone present." The skin where the scar from the ash burn had been was apparently now smooth.

Finally, Lessie decided she needed to see the boy's eyes, and Mrs. Wallace was enlisted to wake the child. He was in a hard, deep sleep and could not be easily roused; some papers described him as comatose or drugged. Lessie took hold of the boy herself and gently tried to stir him.

When his eyes opened, the boy first saw the shadowed face of a woman, then an entire roomful of men. They were all staring at him, as people had all day, only now with a primal intensity. He closed his eyes quickly, but hands tugged at him, and the woman's whispered voice begged him to wake up. When he opened his eyes again, the nightmare was still there, only worse. Ghouls' faces peered in through the window. A giant one-armed man loomed over him with a lamp. He cried out, choked in the reeking oil smoke, and tried to twist his body away, closing his eyes once and for all. The confusion that had welled up in him for the past two days now exploded into a throbbing panic.

The boy screamed and thrashed against Lessie. The rejection stung her, made worse by the presence of onlookers. She did her best to calm him, to try to bring him closer. But he kept fighting her, his eyes still closed. She broke into tears.

The *Item*'s quotation of Lessie's cries was likely embellished: "For God's sake, baby, speak to me! Let mama see your little eyes. O baby, don't you know your mama and daddy[?]" But the sentiment was certainly accurate. As Lessie would acknowledge the next day, she did not recognize the boy's eyes: they "did not seem large enough, and I couldn't recognize the light in them." What's more, his voice did not sound like what she remembered Bobby's to be.

Finally, Percy asked that Sheriff Hathorn clear the room; the crowd was upsetting both Lessie and the boy. The ousted onlookers shuffled through the door but lingered just outside, where they could easily hear through—and likely see between—the thin pine planks of the wall. According to at least one later version of events, once the room was cleared, and with

Hathorn the only witness present, Lessie and Percy stripped the boy and examined his naked body. One paper the next day reported that candy and lemonade were brought in for Lessie to offer the child, but "he remained half asleep." Another paper reported that the ordeal—the attempt to wake and identify—went on for a full half hour. But his eyes stayed closed, and she could not find their light.

By all contemporaneous accounts, Lessie's doubt was visible, and it was spoken. The lynch mob outside waiting for her verdict, together with Percy's warning, was a crushing pressure. But one factor did not preclude the other. The need for caution and the ache of doubt ran together, and finally coalesced into a single result.

Lessie released the boy back to the bed. She turned to face Percy. It is not known what words, if any, were exchanged. They then spoke with Hathorn.

With the couple standing behind him, the sheriff emerged from the room and faced the pressing crowd. As Percy would later report, the question was asked aloud: Is this your child? Lessie leaned into Percy, and he fanned her with a newspaper. The *Item* observed: "It needed but a cry from Mrs. Dunbar, 'It is my child,' to have W. C. Walters . . . in whose possession the boy was found, taken from the Columbia jail for a worse fate."

But instead Hathorn announced that the Dunbars were not certain and needed to see the boy in daylight. They would return in the morning. The throng was crestfallen, denied not just the joyful spectacle of a mother-child reunion but also the grounds on which to enact swift justice.

As Lessie wept, Percy put his arm around her and escorted her out of the cabin into the night air. The "crowds dwindled away in the night, impatient for the morrow," and according to one paper, the boy's sobs rang out from inside the emptied cabin.

Percy helped Lessie into Hathorn's auto; back in Columbia, a generous banker named Ed Lampton had offered them a place to sleep. Critics would damn them for their departure that night, but the Dunbars had little choice. There was no place for them to sleep here, and Wallace still wouldn't let the child out of his sight. Lessie would later recall that leaving the boy motherless for another night was agony.

"Keep quiet and bear up," Anderson would remember Percy saying. "Let's go."

The ride through Columbia to the Lampton home, a few miles south, was a blur. The home itself was a mansion, but the most striking contrast to the Wallace cabin was this place's serenity. With their children asleep, Ed Lampton and his wife greeted the Dunbars, asked a few questions, then ushered them to their room. When the door closed, for the first time since they'd boarded the train in New Orleans, Percy and Lessie were alone with each other.

Chapter 5

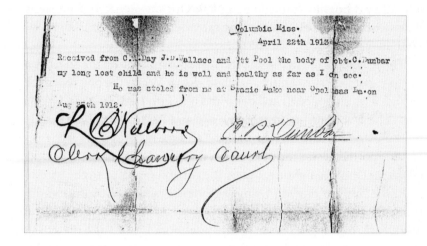

Receipt signed by C. P. Dunbar, April 22, 1913
(Courtesy of Marion County Museum and Archives)

April 22, 1913

MRS. DUNBAR NOT Positive Lad Is Her Missing Boy," blared Tuesday morning's headline in the *Daily Picayune,* with a subheading, "Sure of Body Marks; Eyes Alone Puzzle." The *Times-Democrat*'s headline had a slightly different slant: "Does Not Identify Boy" and "Little One, Half Asleep, Does Not Respond to Endearments." That afternoon, the *Item* stated it plainly: "Child Doesn't Recognize His Mother."

The New Orleans morning dailies would not reach Columbia for hours, a small mercy for the Lamptons' houseguests. Lessie had slept fitfully, if at all, and when she rose, she was anxious to see the child again right away. In his touring sedan, Ed Lampton drove Lessie and Percy, along with Mrs. Lampton, back out to the Wallace farm.

By nine o'clock, the crowds were already gathering again. Their numbers had diminished since last night, with more women now that it was light, but their scrutiny was no less intense. Lessie stayed in the car.

The boy was playing in the yard and road, with Wallace still guarding him, and Day still guarding Wallace. The *States* and the *Item* offered vary-ing—but not necessarily mutually exclusive—details of what happened next. In the *Item*'s version, Percy leapt out of the car and ran toward the boy. When the child looked up, again there was no sign of recognition. Percy tried to usher him toward the car where Lessie waited, but he would not budge.

The *Item* reported that someone placed an orange on the step between the boy and the car to entice the child closer. When the boy made for the orange, Day swooped in and delivered him into Lessie's arms. He fought her, as he had done before, though she and Percy were able to study his markings again—the toe, the moles—and see his eyes in the light. As the *States* reported, it was the eyes, again, that gave Lessie pause. The boy was taken, kicking and fighting, out of the car and returned to the yard.

Lessie felt the crowd's rising impatience with her confusion. It was broad daylight; how could she not know? At the same time, the child was clearly overawed, frozen by the attention. Lessie suggested to Percy and Mr. Lampton that she needed to be alone with the boy; perhaps they could take him back to the Lampton home, away from all these people.

But the child would not return to the vehicle. The *Item* described the standoff:

> While the scene was being enacted, the boy was the center of attraction for two or three hundred people. The auto, with the father and mother, was on one side, and the people on the other. The boy stood there eating his orange, and digging his toes in the muddy ground as though bashful, and looking from one to another with wonderment.

At last, Lessie stepped out of the car and joined Percy in begging. Day, Mr. Lampton, and others tried to goad the child, too. The final, successful inducement was the promise of lemonade, if one believed the *Item,* and the promise to let the boy blow the car's horn, if one believed the *States.* Once lured, the youngster was successfully delivered into the arms of Mr. Lampton in the front seat.

But before they could leave, there was the matter of Wallace. By now the news had been broken to the deputy that the reward had been with-drawn. But Wallace also knew that Deputy Day had contacted Baton Rouge sheriff Womack, who had suggested that the reward could be reinstated. So there would be payment, Wallace believed. And, as he had held all along, he was entitled to a third of it. That point, however, was still up for debate. After much negotiation, Ed Lampton finally brokered a solution: if the child was identified as Bobby, Lampton would agree to personally guarantee the reward—to whichever party or parties rightfully deserved it.

Wallace wanted it all in writing. So Lampton hastily scratched out a note, which Wallace insisted would need to be made more official, should the identification prove successful. But for now, the receipt was enough to mollify him, and at last, a full two hours after it had arrived, the automobile tore away from the gaping crowds.

On Keys Hill, just south of Columbia, the Lampton car turned up a long driveway to the stately white Greek Revival mansion. Just two years old, the home was a testament to Ed Lampton's long, successful career as a dry goods merchant and the president and executive of a network of regional banks. Six thick wooden columns with plaster Corinthian caps lined the front porch, and four chimneys dotted the roof—there were twelve fireplaces in all. Inside were eighteen large rooms, four baths, and two stairways, gleaming red oak floors, high ceilings adorned with massive Waterford chandeliers. To Percy and Lessie, whose rented cottage in Opelousas was a quarter this size, the Lampton home was certainly grand. To the boy, who had slept two nights in a farmer's shack and before that a wagon, it was a palace.

Mrs. Lampton was there, along with a crowd of other ladies, including those from Hub, flocking to comfort and reassure an overwrought Mrs. Dunbar. They retold the stories from their letters, of Walters's cruelty, his suspicious behavior, and the citizens' rising outrage. When the child was brought among them for lunch, the ladies spoke to him with maternal expertise, probed his mind gently, and guided him to interact with the quietly weeping woman at their center. While there is no record of what exactly was said, their clear purpose was to have it proven, to make both Lessie and the boy know that they were mother and son.

For the boy, once again at the center of a crowd's attention, this must have been difficult. It didn't matter that these ladies were warm and motherly or that he was being well fed. He could tell that they wanted something from him, were tugging at him for something, and this was a pressure he had felt and flinched at before. Lessie surely saw this.

But before she could politely intervene, the two youngest Lampton children—twelve-year-old daughter Victoria and seventeen-year-old

Will—pulled the boy outside, where Percy and Mr. Lampton were emerging from the stable with the children's pony. Apparently Percy had it in his mind to use the animal as some sort of test of the child's identity. Lessie and the ladies stepped outside to witness.

Percy lifted the boy to sit atop the pony but allowed him to stay there for only a moment before yanking him off. Predictably, the wronged boy exploded into a rage, and when Percy rebuked him, he began to cry. Percy turned to the crowd. This, he declared, was exactly Bobby's temper and exactly Bobby's wail. He recognized them instantly.

Lessie did not challenge her husband publicly; indeed, she would dutifully repeat his claim later. But it certainly stung her to see the boy led purposefully to tears. And it was preposterous: as much as she shared the desperation that led Percy to this "proof," it was just a show for the crowd. But what good was it for the boy? If he had been terrified into hiding who he was, the weight of that terror would not vanish in an instant, and certainly not through some coarse trick. It would only add to his confusion and mistrust, and make him hide more.

The boy needed not to fear. If Lessie's Bobby was alive inside the body of this tearful, trembling child, he would have to be let out gently. And it would not happen by questioning or begging; they had failed at these before. Lessie needed to open the door for Bobby to walk through, on his own and when he was ready.

Through the mansion's double-hung windows, the ladies in the parlor watched as Lessie offered her hand to the child. When he finally took it, they broke off from the crowd together.

LESSIE TOOK THE boy as far as she could into the massive lawn. She was tender with him, and as they wandered among the live oaks, he quickly forgot his crying. In soothing murmurs, Lessie spoke of their life back in Louisiana. She talked of their home and their family. She recalled his toys, his treasured possessions, his habits and hiding places, things he had known before he had left home. She was reminding him, relaxing his mind open to memory.

He asked if he could see his brother, Alonzo. He had heard his name in the past two days, Lessie knew, but the fact that he remembered it and spoke it aloud—this felt significant. Alonzo was back at home, she replied, waiting for him.

They returned to the big house together, at ease with each other. Lessie told the other adults that she wanted to give the boy a bath—he was itchy with grass, and his feet were caked in mud. She carried the child upstairs.

As she drew the bath, the brick fireplace—there was one in each bathroom—was a source of marvel. She undressed him easily and helped him into the water. When she saw the welts, she ached, and was sure to clean these areas delicately. She ran the rag through his toes and scrubbed away the mud. Mrs. Wallace had performed a passable cleaning of his hair, but it was still darker than Lessie remembered. The filth of the road still clung to its roots. She cupped some water in her hands and dripped it softly over his head. When she scrubbed with soap, the water came down dark at first, then clean.

He kept still, enjoying her touch. It was a pleasure they shared, a pleasure that connected them. His breath was raspy, she suspected from a cold, but it was even and relaxed, interrupted only by the gentle dripping and splashing.

After he was dry and his rough skin softened with talcum, she dressed him in the bedroom. Mrs. Lampton had offered her grandson's clothes, and Lessie picked out a smart little white suit, along with a pair of sandals.

The boy watched as she slipped the sandals over his feet, and then he spoke: "Mamma, they're just like the ones I had before I left home!"

Lessie glanced at the shoes. He was right, of course: these were the very same style of sandal that Bobby had worn and sloughed off to sink his toes into the mud last August 23.

But it wasn't only the sandals. He had just called her "Mamma." At last, he knew who she was. He knew who *he* was. She began to weep. She pulled him close, and his arms wrapped tight around her neck.

It was pure, this moment between them. Nothing that would come after—downstairs, back in the world, with the others—nothing would be this pure. It defied scrutiny or analysis. They knew each other, and that was all. To open the door and face a world that didn't fathom this truth, to Lessie, that seemed impossible.

And yet, she did it. Downstairs, as he ran off with the Lampton children to play with the pony, Lessie made the announcement quietly, first to Percy, who urged her to share it with the others. With each retelling, she grew stronger in its conclusion. The bath, the memory of Alonzo, the sandals, the word *Mamma*. Bobby had returned. Eventually most of the other women were crying along with her. The ordeal of these past few days, the nightmare of the past eight months, was over. As the *Times-Democrat* reported the next day, "After the child had been dressed, and was taken out of doors to play and ride a pony, the mother almost collapsed, and restoratives had to be applied."

As she lay quietly recovering, the boy tore in from outside, enraged, dragging Will Lampton by the arm. Will dutifully showed the boy to the drawer where he could find some twine. In front of all of the adults, the child barked at Will to cross his hands. Will obeyed, and the boy wrapped the twine tight around his wrists. As Percy would recall, he growled, "Now I'll take you into the woods and whip some of the meanness out of you!" then marched his prisoner back outside. It was a disconcerting coda.

THE CROWDS AND the press were gathering at the base of the driveway, restless for news. At last, it came, and as the *Times-Democrat* reported, "within an hour, the Lampton yard on the hill . . . was filled with wagons, buggies, carriages, autos, and saddle horses." People had come from across the county to share in the Dunbars' catharsis, to see the boy and hear the story for themselves. In addition to its usual embellishments, the New Orleans press continued to sculpt the events into a simple fable of rags and riches. "At the Lampton house," the *Times-Democrat* intoned, "the child was once again in gentle surroundings, and began to feel like his former self." Never mind petty distinctions between the fortunes of Lampton and Dunbar. For the newspapers, this was Bobby's manor, the one to which he had been born. And there, among the gleeful and adoring crowds, he at last "answered freely" to his rightful name.

As details of the day's events rippled through the crowds, a current of anger rose beneath the jubilation. It was the same anger felt by the morbid-faced mob at Jeff Wallace's cabin the night before, but now more specific, fueled by reports that the child was covered in welts from Walters's whippings, and a shocking new rumor that the alleged kidnapper might try to block the Dunbars from taking the child back home. In response came a rain of threats against Walters, which eventually made their way to Sheriff Hathorn in Columbia.

Hathorn took action. He called in extra guards for the jail where Walters was held, and even attempted a more drastic safeguard, one long employed by sheriffs facing threat of a lynch mob: he tried to secret the prisoner out of town, on a special train to Jackson. The arrangements fell through, however, leaving Hathorn to do all he could to quell public rage instead.

Weaving his way through the celebration at the Lamptons was Jeff Wallace, but he was not there to congratulate. There was the matter of the official receipt. Earlier, Wallace and Pool had pressed their case for the reward with a Columbia attorney who, though skeptical, had helped to draw up a document. They had roped in Day as well, who admitted assisting with the document's wording but stated clearly that he was not interested in pursuing any reward, especially if it came out of the Dunbars' pocket. Nevertheless, as these were the three who had captured Walters and recovered the boy, they all needed to be present when the document was signed.

So it was that Mr. Lampton drove Percy, Lessie, and the child back into Columbia. Downtown boasted a growing number of banks and hotels, proof that Columbia would not disappear with the forests like other single-industry lumber hamlets around it. But Columbia's real pride and joy, the embodiment of its recent embrace of law and justice, was the brand-new $65,000 Marion County courthouse at the center of town.

Here, the Dunbars were met by Wallace, Pool, and Day, and the receipt was presented for signature, first by Percy and then by Chancery Clerk Welborn. The document would remain in Ott Pool's family for nearly a century, a mysterious artifact of their ancestor's brief role in this momentous case, long after his talk of a reward had been forgotten:

> Received from C. A. Day, J. D. Wallace and Ott Pool the body of Robt. C. Dunbar my long lost child and he is well and healthy as far as I can see. He was stoled from me at Swazie Lake near Opelousas La. on Aug. 23th 1912.

Outside, the celebration, along with its undercurrent of lynch fever, had followed the Dunbars to Columbia. They made it as far as the Lampton auto but found themselves boxed in by as many as thirty cars, on either side of Main Street, from one end of town to the other. Every car was jam-packed, and more people streamed in by buggy or foot. The Columbia Brass Band marched in, too, its exuberant horns adding to the commotion. By three or four o'clock, one estimate put the crowds at three thousand people, which would have meant that virtually every citizen in town, along with hundreds of country folk, had shown up.

The crowds were so thick around Ed Lampton's car that he had to warn them to make their approaches more gradually. Men shook hands with Percy, women kissed and cried with Lessie; every now and then, Ed Lampton held aloft, above his head, the little boy they had all come to see.

Deputy Day climbed into the car, took the child in his arms, and when the crowd had silenced, made a brief speech. "All I did was my duty," he insisted. Then, in a pointed jab at Wallace, who was certainly in the crowd: "I don't want any reward and would not take it." The audience approved enthusiastically. Henry Mounger, a much-esteemed attorney and former state senator, shot to his feet, not just to further shame the reward seekers or to quell the rumors of an attempt by Walters to block the Dunbars' departure, but also to address the more violent-minded contingent in the crowd. The citizens of Columbia and Marion County were law abiding, he reminded them, and they would not do anything to "shame the county and town." Rev. W. E. Farr, the local Baptist pastor, announced that the finding of the Dunbar child was a "modern miracle." Percy's long search had been guided by the hand of God, who had shown His mercy in returning Bobby to his parents. Finally, Percy himself stood, his eyes watery, the child in his arms, to thank Hub, Columbia, and Mississippi for their aid in his search.

"I never saw such a gathering," Chancery Clerk Welborn recalled the next day. "First they cheered; next they cried. Then they cheered some more, and then they fell into each other's arms and cried like children. I doubt if any such rejoicing has ever taken place in any community, at any rate not over a child, who less than twenty-four hours before was a total stranger." And, by the end of all the speeches, Welborn said, "It took all the lynching thought out of them to see the little child in his father's arms."

From where Welborn stood in the crowd, this may have been true. But as the celebration dissipated, several hundred men and women made their way behind the courthouse to the attached brick jail where Walters was being held—their motive unstated but certainly not friendly. From his second-floor cell, the prisoner heard the crowd and, according to the *Item,* "asked that, inasmuch as everyone else had made a statement, his side of the case should be heard." Dale and Rawls were apparently not present to stop him, and so the jailer led the old man down into a first-floor cell where he could address the citizens from behind an iron-barred window.

The crowd peered in at the shadowy figure. They were suspicious, but quieted when he spoke. In a commanding voice, Walters launched into what seemed to be a practiced recitation of details—his background, how he came to be in possession of the child—similar, if not identical to his written statement from the day before. But he didn't get far into his Mississippi travels before someone muscled to the front of the crowd and began badgering him with questions. Thrown off, the old man stammered to answer before another question was fired. "Give me a chance," he pled, though the exchange apparently devolved from there.

Walters had no better luck with his next audience: a visitor to his cell that evening. When Reverend Farr appeared at the door, Walters assumed that he was there to provide spiritual counsel. But Farr, who had just brought the crowd to tears with his exuberant sermon, turned fiery and sharp as soon as he entered: "Between you, me, and God, did you kidnap that boy?" Farr reportedly demanded. Taken aback, Walters issued a prompt denial. As he told his story, the reverend grilled him with questions that, by Farr's estimation, he could not answer adequately. "[T]he man's argument that he was innocent did not appear very strong," Farr informed the *Item*, without offering any details. "I am afraid a jury would convict him within five minutes if he told the same story to the court that he told me."

The *Item*'s own reporter was the next visitor, and now that the crowd and the reverend had worn the old man down, the newsman was able to zero in efficiently on some burning points of contention. The old man admitted that, yes, he had whipped the child, but that he did so to enforce discipline, and never enough to raise a welt. He cared for the boy, he said; just last week, he had bought him a pink umbrella.

When asked about the youngster's parentage, the prisoner looked "cornered" and retreated out into the hall for a drink of water. But eventually he admitted, "I know the boy is my brother's . . . There was a girl living at our home in Barnesville, North Carolina, and she bore a child. A salesman was accused, but my brother admitted that he was to blame. I could not see the girl and my brother disgraced, so I took the little one away."

The jailhouse interrogations wouldn't be public knowledge until the next day, but Walters's indignant stance was already widely known that afternoon. He had stated publicly, more than once, that the Dunbars had taken a boy that was not theirs. Nevertheless, Percy and Lessie were making public plans to leave Columbia with Bobby the next morning on the four-thirty train to New Orleans. At this news, it was reported that Walters had asked his lawyers to file a writ of habeas corpus to stop the child from being removed from the state.

But Dale and Rawls, unconvinced of Walters's innocence, refused to take such a confrontational stance; public sentiment was strongly with the Dunbars, and action taken against the couple to stop them from claiming the child would most certainly reignite public rage against Walters. The best course of action—the fairest and safest course of action—Dale and Rawls concluded, was to bring the witnesses from Poplarville to identify the child and corroborate Walters's alibi. Indeed, these witnesses were expected by car sometime later that evening.

But early evening brought bad news: the roads between Poplarville and Columbia were so flooded that the party of witnesses had been forced to turn around. They would have to take an alternate route and would not arrive until the morning. At this, Dale and Rawls were understandably anxious; if it was true that the Dunbars were planning to leave at four thirty, the arriving witnesses would miss them by several hours. And if the Dunbars crossed state lines, out of Mississippi and into Louisiana with the child, their case would be infinitely more complicated. The lawyers now considered more seriously the option of a writ, but by now the courthouse was closed for the day. By one account, the judge was out of town, anyway. Even if they could track down a judge after hours, the gesture was bound to inflame.

So instead Dale and Rawls agreed to pursue a more polite strategy. Likely, Dale was needed for damage and crowd control over at the jail, so Rawls alone headed out to the Lampton estate to see Mr. Dunbar directly. Though Rawls was gentlemanly, the essence of what he had to say was plainly confrontational: "I immediately told Mr. Dunbar that a mistake had been made and that I would send for half a dozen farmers who could swear to the identity of the boy." Rawls explained the delay with the roads, and may have even directly addressed the rumor he had heard of the Dunbars' early-morning train plans. Percy listened politely as the young lawyer spoke. Of course, he remained firm in his stance that the boy was indeed his son, but according to Rawls's later recollection, Percy's response was quite reasonable: he "promised not to take the child away until we were able to produce these witnesses." Percy would give these attorneys their chance, but he knew they would be proven wrong.

Rawls thanked Percy for his good-faith promise, bid the Dunbars and the Lamptons a polite farewell, then returned to Columbia to confer with his partner. Dale, the more seasoned attorney, knew better than to take much stock in Percy's promise. As the evening wore on, he and Rawls mulled over the other voices that were likely now filling the father's head: those of his wife, the Lamptons, the unshakable ladies from Hub—all certain that the identification was positive and they should feel free to take their boy home. On top of that, the Dunbars were well aware of the possibility of action to prevent them from taking the child, and the fragile Mrs. Dunbar would quickly buckle under such stress. Waiting for these witnesses, the Dunbars must have felt, would not only ensnare them in a protracted legal battle but would also paralyze them in this state of raw emotion. Relief and resolution would come only once they were safely home.

At nine o'clock in the evening, Sheriff Hathorn answered a phone call from none other than Mississippi governor Earl Brewer, in Jackson. The governor had heard reports of the crowd outside the Columbia jail and was worried about a lynching.

While there were plenty of elected officials who shrugged their shoulders at mob violence, forty-five-year-old Earl Brewer was not among them. Since becoming governor in January 1912, he had publicly decried the brutality and irrationality of lynchings and worked to prevent them. As his daughter Claudia would report many years later in her biography of Brewer, the roots of his antipathy for mob violence were very personal. In the early 1880s, when he was an impressionable teenager in the Mississippi Delta, Earl had been invited by a group of older men for a "Saturday night Negro persecution." When his mother spotted him making a mask for the affair, she interceded in horror, pointing out the shame in what he was about to do and bringing his uncle over on the night of the attack to reinforce her point. The intervention had a searing and lifelong impact on Earl Brewer's sense of morality.

The governor listened attentively to Hathorn's update: Mrs. Dunbar had identified the child as Bobby, and Walters was being guarded behind bars. "A great crowd had assembled," the sheriff reported to the governor, "but it was orderly." Brewer thanked the sheriff and hung up. His wife, Minnie, would be happy to hear the news. Claudia, their youngest child, was only seven at the time, and Minnie had been as worried and perplexed by the Dunbar case as every other mother in the two states. Governor Brewer went to bed that night hopeful that the matter would continue to resolve itself in an orderly, civilized fashion.

April 23, 1913

AT THREE THIRTY in the morning, Rawls rushed his new car over to collect Dale, then made their way to the train station, where their suspicions were borne out. In the dark, surrounded by a small crowd, were Percy, Lessie, and the boy, just now emerging from Mr. Lampton's automobile, suitcases packed and ready. They were taking the four-thirty train to New Orleans after all. They weren't going to wait for any witnesses.

Dale and Rawls watched, powerless, as the entire group boarded the waiting train and took over a carriage. Joyful locals heaped farewell presents on the boy, who was wide awake and chatty, playing merrily with both parents, "Big Partner" Day, and young Will Lampton. It was an emotional good-bye, and it would be tricky to interrupt, but that was just what the lawyers needed to do. They had only ten minutes before the train departed.

When Percy spotted Dale and Rawls pushing up the jam-packed aisle, his face darkened. This confrontation would be far less polite than the conversation the evening before. The lawyers implored Percy to honor his word and stay in Columbia for just a few more hours; the Poplarville witnesses were on their way, and any delay in the Dunbars' return home would be minimal. But Percy stood firm. He and his wife were certain that they had their child. Therefore, there was no reason for them to wait; the witnesses were wrong.

It was well before court hours, so Dale and Rawls had no way of securing an emergency writ to stop the Dunbars from removing the child from the state. They had only their powers of persuasion, which were not getting them anywhere. And sentiment in the crowd was most certainly against them. Finally, Percy put an end to the conversation altogether. As Rawls would recall, Dunbar retorted dramatically, "To hell with that—it's my boy, and I'll ride a rotten rail to hell before I give him up."

The warning whistle blew, and the Columbia well-wishers reluctantly left the train. A bleary-eyed reporter from the *Item* stayed on board to report their trip to New Orleans. After begging his folks, Will Lampton was allowed to make the trip, too, to keep his new little friend company. Deputy Charles Day would travel with the Dunbars as well, on account of his personal bond with the boy. However, the presence of two other Columbians suggested a more complicated motivation: chatting with a reporter was Chancery Clerk Welborn, and lurking nearby was Wallace, the one-armed deputy from Foxworth. Apparently the reward imbroglio persisted.

Dale and Rawls were carried down to the platform in the exodus. Rawls in particular was livid. Though Dale had anticipated this stance from the Dunbars, to be confronted with it so blatantly was a whole different matter. Percy had denied them a chance to make their case fairly. He had unilaterally declared that the boy was his, and would listen to no one who said otherwise. It was a breach of trust, and neither lawyer would soon forget it.

The wide-eyed little boy waved out at them from the carriage window lurching ahead into the dark morning.

Chapter 6

W. K. Patrick, New Orleans *Times-Democrat*, April 26, 1913

GEORGE BENZ WAS the only journalist aboard the train. He'd been with the Dunbars on their ride up to Columbia and had kept close ever since. Out of all the reporters from all of the papers, he'd been the only one privy to the family's plans for an early-morning departure. The *Item* could now claim its exclusive.

As word spread that the Dunbars were on board, passengers flocked to the parlor car. The boy, Benz reported, "offered his little sunburned hand to every one of them, but would not talk." Some well-wishers were friends who had come up from New Orleans to meet the train early, but most were strangers who, having followed the story in the papers, now felt that the Dunbars were fair game for discussing intimate details.

Lessie engaged them all, eagerly repeating and pointing to an ever-growing list of traits that had convinced her that this restless boy in her arms was her long-lost Bobby. "Look at that little mole on the lobe of his ear here . . . See this blemish below the knee on his little limb. I have one similar . . . Now, here is another wart . . . And one just where the hair is cut on the back of his neck. Is he my child? Surely he is, and no one will ever get him away from me."

Of course, Lessie was responding to skepticism, reiterated throughout the trip, and so exasperation crept into her voice. But the strangers' questions were chafing more deeply, resurrecting the uncertainty that she herself had felt so nakedly less than twenty-four hours before. With each telling, Lessie grew more resolute, banishing doubt into the realm of the preposterous.

When dawn broke, Lessie was still talking, but the child's attention turned out the window. He stood up on his tiptoes for a better look, then promptly sat back down in pain and yanked off his right sandal and sock. His big toe—not the left big toe, which was the subject of so much discussion—sported a cruel red welt. He touched it and howled. Taking him into her arms, Lessie kissed the sore, applied some ointment, and explained to onlookers that Bobby had grown unaccustomed to footwear and "must have run a thorn in there."

When one tricky onlooker asked the boy, "Where is your mamma?" he pointed up at Lessie. But the follow-up—"And your papa?"—gave him more difficulty. After grave consideration, the boy pointed to Percy. "I guess that is sufficient," one stranger said with a shrug.

In the dining car, the boy devoured his breakfast. He even snuck back to the table to gobble up some leftover eggs with a soupspoon, and when Lessie spotted him, she ordered more food.

While someone in the crowd sought to replicate Percy's "temper" trick by taking away a gift from the boy, Percy himself now opted for a gentler proof. As the boy leaned over a seat, Percy emitted what Benz described as a "peculiar sound with his lips," then pulled away. In response, the boy swung back across the seat and mimicked the sound. "He did that when he was two years old," Percy explained.

This went on for the entire four-and-a-half-hour trip. To an incessant line of strangers, the parents pointed out tic after trick that Bobby had demonstrated before he went missing. "He does so many of them," Lessie maintained, "that I could not be mistaken."

Terminal Station was again mobbed. Photographers and reporters from all of the dailies were lying in wait, the *Item*'s competition eager to regain ground. As word of the Dunbars' arrival rippled beyond the press, the "long-necked mass" swelled into the hundreds, flooding through the waiting areas and down onto the platforms. And when the No. 3 hissed to a stop, a mad dash through the steam ensued. Some misguided gawkers zeroed in on another woman stepping out with a young child in her arms and swept up the startled pair in celebration.

Meanwhile, a *States* photographer turned his camera to capture the real stars, still aboard the train. Framed by the hard edges of the carriage window and popping out from pitch-black shadow, the faces of Will, Lessie, and the boy are slightly blurred, gauzy behind the glass, terrified phantoms looking out at the massing crowd.

When the family finally made it off the train, a cluster of New Orleans relatives surrounded them. The women embraced Lessie, who began to cry. As attention turned to the boy, held tight in the crook of Percy's arm, the *States* reported, "Robert was very cool about it all. In one hand he clutched a little bouquet of red roses—holding them straight and stiff before him. He submitted to the hugs and kisses, making no return, and saying nothing." Aside from expressions of joy, the papers mentioned no other reaction, from anyone in the extended Dunbar family, to the boy himself. If they, like Percy and Lessie, didn't quite recognize him at first, they hid it well behind laughter and shouting.

As the crowd thickened, George Benz ushered the party toward the Basin Street exit to catch a taxi. He had gotten the Dunbars' approval for an exclusive, and his plan was to hustle them down to the paper's offices for photographs. As the *Item*'s coverage would crow, no matter what questions were barked at the couple from competing reporters, they refused to answer. This inflamed the other newsmen and only made the frenzy worse.

Percy handed the boy to Will Lampton and tried to part the crowd, with Will following close behind, then Lessie and the others. They inched up the platform and into the station. Citizens jostled and pushed, hungry for a glimpse of the boy. Balancing on his good leg, Percy shouldered into the crowd. Behind him, they surged toward Will, nearly pushing him off his feet. They touched and kissed the boy, and struggled to claw him from Will's arms. Finally, police arrived and were able to more effectively beat back a path to the street. At last, they were inside the taxi.

At the *Item*'s Camp Street offices, interviewing the Dunbars seemed an afterthought. The real prize was the set of portraits of Lessie and the boy, which would grace the paper's front page the next day, a side-by-side triptych that told a curious and melancholy little story. To the left, in the photo most like a formal portrait, a haggard Lessie holds a morose boy on her lap, staring ahead. In the middle, she pulls him tight trying to kiss him, but he turns his head away and closes his eyes. In the final image, they are facing each other, arms clasped in a pose intended to suggest a loving reunion. In fact, the boy is looking at Lessie, wary and startled.

The impression the photos left was not an accident. Nor were the *Item*'s headlines above: "Boy Called Kidnapped Son Comes with Dunbars"; "Alleged Abducter [*sic*] Starts Strong Legal Fight." The *Item* may have gained the Dunbars' trust and their exclusive, but the paper's task was not to narrate a happy family reunion. Journalistic objectivity wasn't the bottom line, either. Along with its competitors, the *Item* was waging a war over circulation, and the conflict would be won not just by sensationalizing the daily news but also by creating intrigue: withholding resolution each day and building greater anticipation for tomorrow's edition.

At the end of the previous century, New Orleans newsmen battled competitors and political adversaries in streets and saloons, with fists and pistols. When a former private detective snatched up the flailing *Item* and brought his tricks and thuggery to the field of journalism, the paper's circulation soared, and two more staid morning dailies, the *Times-Democrat* and the *Picayune,* straggled far behind. By now, the *Item*'s only real rival was the afternoon *States,* run by Democratic power broker Robert Ewing largely as an extension of his political career. The paper war was now solely one of words, and the Dunbar case would soon prove perfect fodder for a flare-up.

Cars packed with newsmen tailed the Dunbars from the *Item* office downtown all the way uptown to 7031 Freret Street, just blocks from leafy Audubon Park. This was home not just to Ola and Harold Fox but also to Ola's brother, Fred Dunbar, and his wife; Ola and Fred's widowed mother (Percy's aunt), Jenny Dunbar; and Ben Sherrouse, Jenny's brother. It was a large white frame house, with a four-columned porch and single front dormer—modest by comparison to the mansions along St. Charles Avenue, or behind the gates of nearby Audubon Place. Among the family waiting in front was Bobby's cousin, little Lucille DeVerges, eagerly picking flowers to welcome him. But as the reporters crushed in, the family hurried inside.

When the door closed to the crowd, the *States* representative reported an emotional scene in the front hall by peering and eavesdropping through the window. As Percy lowered the child to the floor, Lessie knelt to embrace him. But the boy remained stiff and indifferent, preoccupied with the belt of his linen suit. Rejected, Lessie buried her face in Percy's chest, and he comforted her. In an easy "tell" of fakery, the *States* reported that the Dunbars' spoken words—Lessie's pleas to the child to kiss her like he used to; Percy's advice to be patient—were uttered "in a low tone." Too low for any other reporter to hear.

But aside from embellished dialogue, there was a truth to the *States* report. As the Dunbars themselves would admit, the child had been withdrawn and showed only intermittent recognition, despite Lessie's breakthrough with him the day before. This was a deep, intimate cruelty, and it collided persistently in Lessie with a full day of frenzied public rejoicing. As soon as she finally had privacy, this collision—made worse by days without sleep—came to a head. "Overcome with joy," one paper simplified, Lessie "cried for more than an hour . . . almost screaming, and then she suffered a near collapse, and a physician was called." The doctor urged that she "be kept from excitement," and Lessie retreated to a bedroom and crumpled into a bed.

Meanwhile, the boy took up with Lucille. Though she and Bobby had played only once before, years ago, the connection between the two was instantaneous. Shut out from any drama unfolding inside the house, newsmen and photographers found much of interest in the two youngsters' play in the front and back yards. When the boy, freshly bathed and clothed in a new linen outfit, rolled down the filthy sidewalk, Lucille rebuked him, prompting him to hide his face against the wall and cry. In sunnier moments, he shared with her half a gift box of candy before giving any to the adults, and she hugged him repeatedly. According to one paper, Lucille fancied herself his guardian.

The boy apparently saw Lucille as his confidante, his only of that day. "Alone on the lawn," reported one story, "he talks to her in low tones. He tells his secrets to her, but what they are, no one can say, for if the boy imagines that any one else is about or listening, pop go his lips, they are closed, and he says no more." When asked to share what the boy had said, Lucille was less than helpful, unsure of the questions being posed. The same reporter offered a chilling rationale for the boy's enduring reticence:

> His parents are confident that he has been beaten mercilessly and taught never to speak of the events of his life. Walters, they think, feared that his tongue would give him away. The boy now keeps his tongue well, however, and if he gives any information about any-

thing in the past, it will only be to Lucille, or after he forms a better acquaintance with his mother or father.

In Columbia, Jeptha and Matilda Bilbo emerged from the mud-speckled auto, dazed from the brutal ride up from Pearl River County. Though just in their late fifties, both looked much older—bespectacled, gaunt, and worn from farming life. She kept her dark hair pulled back tight into a long braid; his gray mustache was bushy and unkempt. Dale and Rawls met them and dispensed with the bad news right away: the child they had come here to identify was gone. Opting for the next best course of action, the attorneys assembled as much of a crowd as they could, including the reporters still lingering in Columbia, so that the Bilbos could be heard.

They knew William Walters well. He had boarded with them, off and on, at their home at Ford's Creek, and they recalled his arrival date precisely: "Walters came to our house . . . the Friday before the third Sunday of last July," Jeptha told reporters. "He had a small boy with him." He called the boy Bruce. The inescapable inference was that the boy was in Walters's custody before Bobby Dunbar went missing on August 23, 1912.

But there were nuances in the Bilbos' chronology. During that first visit in July, they said, Walters and Bruce had stayed for two weeks. The pair later left for a few weeks, then Walters returned to leave the boy in the Bilbos' care while he went to Charity Hospital in New Orleans. Four weeks later, he came back and collected the boy.

While the Bilbos' dates would quickly become the subject of intense debate, on this day, most questioning focused on the more tangible matter of the child's identity. When the old couple first arrived, inexplicably there was no photograph of the boy for them to view, so their first public identification was by memory and far from convincing. By midafternoon, that had changed: Dale and Rawls had at least the photo snapped on Sunday, of the boy standing at the car, and possibly one other image of the child taken in Columbia. For comparison was the original photo of Bobby Dunbar published on reward posters and in the news. Though practically buried in all the New Orleans coverage, the Bilbos' testimony was unambiguous: this boy in the photos, the one now in the custody of the Dunbars, was the child the Bilbos knew as Bruce as early as July 1912. It was not the same boy as the one on the reward poster.

Mrs. Bilbo related how Bruce had grown so attached to her during his stays that he called her "Grandma." Asked about his much-scrutinized toes, Mrs. Bilbo, who had bathed Bruce often, remembered a wound on one toe, it was not specified which, from an indeterminate "swelling." The boy had nearly died from it while in their care.

Word of the Bilbos' testimony swept through Columbia, along with a rumor that Matilda would travel to New Orleans the very next day to see the child in person. She and Jeptha had convinced the town that, at a minimum, their claims deserved further consideration. Citizens who had flocked to congratulate the Dunbars now wondered if the happy couple might, in fact, be mistaken. And residents who just yesterday would have carried out or sanctioned a lynching now wondered if Walters might, in fact, be innocent.

But Dale and Rawls knew that they had to do far more than win over a local audience, and the "native son" appeal of Jeptha's nephew Lieutenant Governor Theodore Bilbo, couldn't erase his checkered political reputation. Two years earlier, as a state senator, Bilbo had been charged with soliciting bribes in exchange for votes, and though a later investigation cleared him, plenty of capital insiders felt that he was guilty. Among them was Mississippi governor Brewer, although he didn't say so publicly. By now it was an open secret that Brewer loathed Bilbo for his strong-arm politics, and Bilbo, among other things, wanted Brewer's job. Given this tension, since it was Brewer that would soon be faced with signing the order for Walters's extradition, the attorneys feared that the name Bilbo could just as easily poison the governor against their client as it could help.

BY LATE WEDNESDAY, the Dunbars had decided to remain in New Orleans another day. With the Atchafalaya River pounding the levees near Krotz Springs, the Frisco line between Baton Rouge and Opelousas was under imminent threat of flooding out, making travel by the southern route their only way home. Lessie was still too frayed from Columbia, and the parents were equally concerned about the health of the boy— in particular, his adenoids. In Columbia, Dr. Anderson had advised that swollen glands in the back of his throat might be the cause of not just his raspy "mouth breathing" but also of the apparent change in his facial features.

A physician was called in for a more official diagnosis: Edward Harper, a well-known practitioner of homeopathy. Details of his examination of the boy are not known, though afterward, he suggested that adenoid-removal surgery, while advisable, was not urgent. The doctor cautioned the Dunbars that it might be two full weeks before the child completely recovered his memory, and he furnished them with strategies for helping the lad to recall his old life and home. Undoubtedly, it was agreed, the boy's imminent reunion with his brother, Alonzo, would go a long way toward that end.

But a test of the boy's memory came much sooner, later that evening. The weary child had retreated upstairs when a special visitor arrived, insisting upon his presence: someone he had known from home, before he was taken. This brought anxiety as much as excitement. It meant that he would be expected to remember; that he would be watched.

He paused at the top of the steps, with only his thin, tan legs visible through the banisters to whoever waited below. And then, the instant his face appeared, three voices bellowed all at once: "That's Robbie Dunbar!" It was Dudley Guilbeau, an Opelousas lawyer, and two other friends of Percy's. According to one report, the boy showed no sure sign of recognition, but according to another report, he called one of his old friends by name: "Guilbeau."

By evening, the boy was at the end of his rope. He'd been prodded at, whispered over, and tested by reporters, lawyers, and a doctor. Out of every streetcar that passed, a new mob of strangers spilled out and clambered into the Freret Street house, eager to ogle him, kiss him, touch him, ply him with candy and gifts, and barrage him with the same litany of questions and tricks. Finally, the boy resorted to fighting them off, yelling, crying, and trying to escape. As one reporter observed, "He gouged his eyes with his fingers" and cowered behind his mother's dress until finally, she put him to bed.

AT SEVEN O'CLOCK on Wednesday evening, an envelope addressed to "Mr C. P. Dunbar, Oppolusas La" was postmarked in Columbia. Whether it ever reached its intended destination is unknown. Nearly a hundred years later, it was found in the files of Walters's attorney Hollis Rawls, along with the handwritten letter inside, from the defendant himself:

> I see that you got Bruce. But you have heaped up trouble for yourselves. I had no chance to Prove up, But I know by now you have Decided you are wrong. it is vary likely I will Loose my Life on account of that, and if I do, the Great God will hold you accountable. that Boys mother is Julia Anderson, and He has A Little sister Name Burnece. you ask him, and He will tell you his Momma Name is Julia and His Little sister Burnece. Some people Has Her at Chadburn NC. you write to LF Brown at that Place, and he likely knows. If not you can find out

and it look if you are able to take Bruce you ought to take the other one. I took Poor Little Bruce almost. A Lonely Little tot. He never had Learned any Manners. I Have Given so many statements and no one would Help me, and you took my Little Boy. Now if you will take him And go to Cerro Gordo NC and Evergreen For CK Brown, He will carry you to His mother and prove to you that he is Bruce Anderson and you need not Feel like you will Be Badly treated like I Have Been. now Mr Dunbar, If you had not treated me Like you did, I could Have Proved to you that Bruce was not Robert. Remember what Bad Befalls me From this you will Be Responsible to God. that Boy is A Bastard No doubt and don't contain one Drop of your blood. When you see your mistake it will may Be too late to Do me any Good. But you will Regret it as Long as you Live. I did not teach him to Beg or Bum. But in as much as you Have him, take good care of Him. you will no doubt Have your Hands Full. I never Learned the stait of it until just A Few Minutes Ago. I would Have if I had Got any trace of you[r] poor Little Robert, I should Have Done all For You I could. But now I am where I Can Do nothing. So you Have A Lost Robert and me A Lost Bruce. May God Bless my Darling Boy. Writ me if I Don't get Linched. Hope you are Getting Along with Him. I think you will be sad A Long time. But Hope not too bad.

April 24, 1913

"COME TO DADDY." First thing Thursday morning, Percy opened his arms to the boy and appealed for affection the way he always had with Bobby. But the boy "became terrified" and hid behind Lessie's legs. "From this," the *States* reported, "it is assumed that the boy had cried for this 'daddy' when he was first taken and that every step possible had been taken to make him fear and hate that word."

Later that morning more tensions erupted at bath time. For the entire washing, and drying and powdering after, the boy fought Lessie. It was a "battle royal," according to the *Item*'s reporter on the sidelines, and by the end, a dusting of talcum prematurely whitened her hair. It was at least her third scrubbing of the boy in so many days, and he'd stopped enjoying it. He had been so filthy when they found him, Lessie reasoned. "As his skin becomes cleaner and some of the sunburn disappears from his hands and feet," the reporter noted, "identification marks become more pronounced."

Lessie was after more than dirt. With rag, soap, and powder, she was eradicating sunburn, coarseness, all traces of a life on a tinker's wagon. With each bathing, feature by feature, her son was reemerging.

After the skin came the clothes. As Lessie lifted the boy out of the taxi on the corner of Canal and Chartres Streets, he gaped at the lavish window dressing in the storefront of Godchaux's department store, then tilted his head to take in all six floors above. The emporium was famous throughout the South, and today he was its guest of honor. The store founder's son, Albert Godchaux, stood at the door to greet him, flanked by his advertising manager and a small army of smiling salesladies. Along with Lessie and the boy were Ola Fox, Percy's aunt Jenny, and the press. Godchaux escorted them all across a vast polished walnut floor, past the gleaming glass "Silent Salesmen" displaying neckties and handkerchiefs, and into the magnificent mother's wonderland that was the children's department. Here, surrounded by well-stocked wall shelves, heaping wide display tables, and a growing crowd of onlookers, Mr. Godchaux offered young Bobby whichever suit he wanted, on the house.

" 'Robbie' Knows Just What Kind of Suit He Likes," smirked the *States'* headline, using quotation marks for the child's name to reinforce doubt over his identity. First, Mr. Godchaux produced "a beautiful sailor suit with red and blue trimmings, with stars and anchors, a great big blue string tie and an attractively decorated collar," which the *States* identified as "the same kind worn by the sons of the rich." But the boy, with an air described as haughty, refused it. A saleslady brought out an Irish linen suit, which he liked but refused to try on. He had been undressed in public already too many times and did not want to go through that again. "Not here," the *States* reported his cries, "I won't put it on here. Wait till we get home."

When Lessie tried to coax him, he buried himself away from her, into Jenny Dunbar's arms. Throughout the ordeal, he repeated this rejection, to Lessie and Ola. He would listen only to his great-aunt Jenny, whom he called "Grandma." But when the old woman, leveraging her status as confidante, led him to the dressing room to try on another suit that he seemed to favor, he panicked violently. It took Lessie, Ola, Grandma, and at least one other person to get him inside. As they struggled to dress him, he could be heard shrieking.

WHEN GOVERNOR BREWER arrived at his office, the two deputies from Opelousas were already waiting. On Tuesday afternoon, with the celebration in Columbia roaring, Percy Dunbar had telephoned the good news to his business partner, Henry Estorge, in Opelousas, and the process for extraditing the alleged kidnapper was put into motion. Estorge headed to Baton Rouge for Governor Luther Hall's signature, accompanied by Percy's uncle Preston King, who had recognized a photo of Walters as *another* tramp he had seen at Swayze Lake in August, and who presumably came along now to identify the prisoner in person. But before they went to Columbia, the deputies needed the signature of Mississippi's chief executive.

"I'm up in the air about it," Brewer announced to gathered reporters. At home all morning, he had been on the phone with officials from Columbia and Poplarville, who reported, in his words, that "the people of that place have undergone a complete reversal of opinion during the past two days." Up to fifty Pearl River witnesses, so far, could be counted on to corroborate that Walters had the boy in July, before Bobby Dunbar went missing. Columbia sheriff Hathorn had told the governor that he had received a telegram from Walters's brother-in-law in Chadbourn, North Carolina, confirming Walters's claim that a Julia Anderson had given him her son. And though it was a delicate thing to raise to the two Louisianans, Brewer was sincerely concerned that the angry citizens of St. Landry might lynch Walters if he were delivered there now.

The deputies assured Brewer that there was no such danger; that Louisiana would give the prisoner a fair trial. As evidence of the Dunbars' certainty, they repeated the stories of the sandals and the boy asking after Alonzo, and the Dunbars' identification of markings, chiefly what was reported as a "deep scar" from a childhood burn on his left foot.

Markings aside, "It does seem most remarkable that there should be any doubt about a mother and father knowing their baby," Brewer observed tactfully. In rearguing this point, King told the governor that his own children were playmates of Bobby's, and they had recognized him instantly; he would be happy to have them testify.

To break the impasse, Brewer had his secretary place a call to Lieutenant Governor Bilbo in Poplarville—not a conversation he relished. Apparently Bilbo had been doing some informal investigation, since Poplarville was his hometown and his kin were involved. The town, he told Brewer, was highly agitated over the affair. He had heard that the town postmaster had seen the boy in July and could help to clear matters up. But he had also heard darker rumors: speculation that Walters was part of a kidnapping gang. Hanging up, Brewer faced Estorge and King wearily: "You see, gentlemen, what I am up against. I want to do the right thing, but I want to be sure I am right."

To prove that point, he made another call, to the Burns Detective Agency in New Orleans. The governor had hired detective Dan Lehon before and trusted him, and since Lehon had worked with the Dunbars during their search, the governor hoped that the two deputies would appreciate his involvement now. Brewer asked Lehon to "go see Mr. and Mrs. Dunbar and the child; make a thorough investigation." Lehon agreed. And with that, Brewer announced to the deputies that he would withhold requisition for now. "Owing to all the circumstances, gentlemen, I am going to give Walters a fair show for his white alley . . . If, after we have fully investigated this most mysterious and remarkable affair, any doubt exists, I will favor Mrs. Dunbar. I hope the woman has found her child."

BY MID-MORNING THURSDAY, the Dunbars were back from Godchaux's, and 7031 Freret Street was filled with reporters again. *Times-Democrat* reporter Lee Hawes was visiting with the boy and Aunt Jenny, trying to engage him with questions and conversation, when further "proof" emerged:

> Little Robbie Dunbar gave another confirmation of his identity Thursday morning . . . This was when he denied that his little brother's name was "Alozo," as was claimed by the people of Columbia he had meant in referring to a child at West Columbia.

A reader patient or masochistic enough to unpack that second sentence might, after a long while, come up with the following translation: while in Columbia, the boy had called or referred to another child there as "Alozo." Perhaps the unnamed child was thought to look like Alonzo Dunbar; perhaps the boy was being asked to make a comparison. In any case, the Columbia critics' central, damning point seemed to have been that the boy had mispronounced his alleged brother's name. His brother's name was "Alonzo," not "Alozo."

Of that, the boy was by now well aware. The report continued: "He was asked his brother's name and said distinctly, 'My bubba's name is not Lozo, it's Lonzo.' Not only did he say this, but he repeated it to Aunt Jenny, child fashion, several times."

He may have been repeating because others had repeated to him. He may have been repeating because others had repeatedly asked him. It is also possible that he was repeating to remember.

For the past two days, the Dunbars had been gently questioning the boy, reporting and discussing clues like these with each other and the ever-present journalists: phrases, observations, and fragments of memories that told them this was their Bobby.

Of particular importance to Lessie, who had been crying, the boy observed, "Mamma has a cut eye." This was proof, she insisted, that he remembered that she had been "suffering from swollen and inflamed eyes" the day he disappeared. It had been their last moment of intimacy together as she put on his sandals and took off his ring.

Of course, the Dunbars were interested not just in what he remembered of his old life, before he went missing, but of the intervening eight months. "Both his mother and I have tried repeatedly to get him to say who took him and where he went," Percy told one paper. "Every time we asked him a question, he ran away or hung his little head in fear, and cried a little." At one point, Percy and Jenny tried to coax the boy into telling if he had been taken by a man or a woman, but even when his beloved aunt spoke to him using "terms of endearment," he stayed mum.

When the boy did give them glimpses into those eight blank months, they were fleeting enough to make Lessie and Percy want more; vague impressions and oblique snapshots that instead of giving comfort, made them shudder and cry. They were terrified, not just by the life but also by how much of it they didn't know.

He told his parents that he had lived sometimes in a tent, sometimes in a house, and sometimes in a wagon. It was the wagon and its horse that he spoke of most. It was in the wagon, he told his aunt, that he had been very sick once. When asked where he had traveled in it, he said only "all over." When asked if he had been with other people besides Walters, he said only "yes." He remembered that he used to help out with building a "big fire."

At the Lamptons, he had managed the pony with a skill that he had not exhibited before he went missing. In the Foxes' house, he opened cans of sardines "with as much alacrity as a hungry traveling man." He ate only thick slices of cheese and eggs; the eggs he had always liked; the cheese and sardines were new.

As for Walters himself, the boy did not seem to miss him or even notice that he was gone, according to the *Item*, and "only remembers when questioned about 'the man who was your papa once.' " He recalled Walters ordering him not to talk to strangers. He remembered the old man's whippings.

But the abuse wasn't the darkest thing in the child's mind. When probed about his mother's identity, Percy recalled, "he told me that the reason he didn't know his mamma was because the old man had told him that his papa had killed his mamma and thrown her into a creek." Earlier, the boy had offered a variation of that story to Sheriff Day in Hub, which Percy now repeated: his papa had "stuck [his mamma] in a stump hole." On Friday the *States* repeated the story, with a twist: " 'I had a daddy once,' Robert told his father Wednesday, 'but he cut my mother's throat and threw her in the river.' " Whether the shift from absent mother to both parents absent—and the gory detail—were variations from the boy's mind, from Percy's retelling, or from the sensationalistic *States* is impossible to know.

As for the boy's own identity, the *Item* reported: "He will answer to the name of 'Bruce' as readily as to Robert . . . If asked his name, he will say Robert sometimes, and then Bruce. He has no recollection of a family name."

No matter how hard it was to bear, the Dunbars remained optimistic. "It will be a matter of but a few weeks until he becomes used to us again," Percy predicted, "and then we hope he will tell us something of his experiences."

Today, like yesterday, the probing of the child's mind intermingled with a probing of his body. At a minimum, there were two thorough public inspections in the Freret Street home: one on Wednesday, with at least a representative from the *Times-Democrat* present (most likely Lee Hawes); and another on Thursday, with reporters from both morning dailies and other interested parties. The document that grew out of the examinations tells the story on its own: a telegram, sent late Thursday from the offices of the *Times-Democrat*:

To His Excellency Hon. Earl Brewer, Governor of Mississippi: In a spirit of fairness and a desire to uphold the majesty of the law in the punishment of crime, I respectfully petition your Excellency to honor the requisition of Governor Hall for the extradition of the prisoner, William C. Walters, at Columbia Jail. I desire to assure your Excellency

that both myself and my wife are thoroughly
satisfied with the identity of the child, and to say
that if he were not our boy neither of us would want
to keep him.

We desire to say further that in the presence
of the Times-Democrat; Mrs. Dunbar, Mrs. S. H.
Fox . . . and Mr. S. H. Fox, at the Fox residence,
7031 Freret Street, New Orleans, a full physical
inspection of the child was made this morning to
substantiate our claims as to his birthmarks, etc.
We found the following to tally identically with
the claims of his parents: Curly cowlick on the
forehead, scar on the forehead, mole on the lobe
of the left ear, mole on the back of the neck, mole
on side of neck under right ear (identical with
that on mother), two moles on right cheek, dimples
in corner of eyes, strong resemblance of eyes to
father, separated regular upper teeth, lower teeth
like little brother, back and body covered with
pinhead moles, dark spot in hair (identical with
birthmark of father), deformity of penis, scar on
forehead, cicatrice [sic] of burn on left big toe,
malformation of two little toes on left foot, the
first phalanx of each turning inward slightly,
cuticle of toes not clinging to nails, showing
evidences of burn, familiarity of laugh and sob,
recognition of and affection for mother, responds
to pet name "Mr. Rabbit," playfully bites at father
in "bear game," calls aunt (Mrs. W. B. Dunbar)
"grandma" on account of facial resemblance to
grandma in Opelousas, uses excellent English, free
from grammatical errors common to hill country folk
of North Carolina, where Walters claims to have been
given him, and responds to his Christian name of
"Robbie." Respectfully, C. P. Dunbar

The published versions of the telegram differ by newspaper in only one
key respect: the description of the deformed penis. One paper replaced
"an organ" for the word *penis*, other papers omitted the trait altogether,
and one wrote, "a slight deformity, which none but a male child could

have." Even the most meager understanding of this trait would take a year to emerge, but another was clarified that same night.

One reporter diplomatically broached with Percy a lingering question about the much-debated scar on the boy's foot. Earlier in the day, the child had wanted to remove his socks to show the reporter what he called his "star." But Aunt Jenny told him not to. Then, when the foot was displayed in the afternoon examination, it was plain that the scar had faded dramatically—almost completely.

"That scar . . . was made capital out of by Walters," Percy explained. "He had taught the child to put out his bare foot, as to show there was no scar there, but the little fellow's feet were kept so dirty that it would have been impossible for anybody to tell." And then he went on to explain, in clinical detail, how exactly it had faded: "When he was burned, [w]e used Unguentine, which has a tendency to make scars disappear, and in eighteen months the scar, which had extended to the instep, had disappeared, and it only extended to the base of the toe. Now, if that was possible for it to disappear that much in that time, it was possible for it to disappear from the toe altogether."

With the burn scar so faded, there was another defining characteristic of the boy's left foot that the Dunbars eagerly pointed out: "the malformation of the little toes of the same foot so that the toes turned slightly inward." Both morning dailies observed that the couple highlighted this trait as the feature that made them so certain that the little footprints they saw at Swayze Lake were Bobby's. "Those two little peculiarly shaped toes had dug out a little space in the earth that was unmistakable," Percy told the *Pic*, and in the *Times-Democrat* article, it was Lessie who explained the recognition. In one report, the trait was attributed to heredity, something shared by Lessie; another account suggested that these little toes—with "cuticle separate from the nails"—were visibly affected by the same burn that had scarred the big toe.

Among those participating in one of Thursday's examinations was detective Dan Lehon, present at the behest of Governor Earl Brewer. On Wednesday, when asked, Lehon had expressed "not a doubt" that Walters was the very same elusive suspect that Burns detectives and Mr. Dunbar had tracked through the Alabama swamps last fall. But now his opinion on the case was more enigmatic: "I have had a message from Governor Brewer, and there is going to be a hard fight put up over the little fellow." Lehon left the Freret Street home Thursday evening, and shortly thereafter, he left New Orleans and headed for Jackson, Mississippi. Reporters noted that his departure was sudden, but the Burns office denied that Lehon's business was related to the Dunbar affair.

By Thursday evening, much of the press had thinned out of the house, and the Dunbars were quietly packing and preparing for the next day's train. Since this all began, Lessie explained to one lingering reporter, she had amassed a collection of clippings: letters, telegrams, and newspaper articles from all over the country, all related to the disappearance of, search for, and recovery of her son. "I intend to keep every scrap of paper that has anything about him on it," she said. "I will save them for him, so that when he gets to be a man, he will see the interest and the trouble that everyone has taken in him. I want him to be a good man."

AT NINE THIRTY that night came the governor's telegrammed reply: his refusal of extradition was now official. "I sincerely hope with all my heart that it is your child, and your long and awful suspense is ended," Brewer wrote, "but from the very strong assertions from reliable people to the contrary, I fear you are mistaken in the identity."

The Dunbars tried to remain cool in their public response. But it was easy to guess who these "reliable people" were. The speculation would be confirmed in the *States* the next day: "The head of the Burns New Orleans agency telephoned Governor Brewer late last night that they felt sure the wrong child had been identified as the lost son of the Dunbars."

Lehon, their own investigator, did not believe them.

Chapter 7

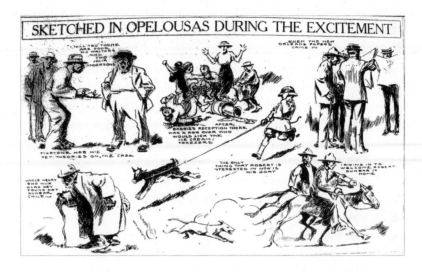

F. S. Tisdale, New Orleans *Daily States,* May 4, 1913

April 25, 1913

SOMETIME AFTER MIDNIGHT, a car jostled down the rutted sandy roads of Evergreen, North Carolina. Inside were a sheriff from Lumberton, twenty miles north, and P. W. Johnson, the thirty-two-year-old editor and proprietor of South Carolina's *Marion Star.*

For the past two days, the New Orleans dailies had barraged the offices of virtually every paper in the Carolinas with calls and telegrams, all after the same story. Hired stringers like Johnson had been sent out in force, scouring the farms and lumber towns of Robeson and Columbus Counties, interviewing citizens and authorities, cobbling together details, and delivering brief dispatches. But until now, their prized quarry had remained elusive. The papers had not been able to find Julia Anderson.

Lawyers and local police had been digging around, too. As of late Thursday, what had been found tended to corroborate Walters's version of events. He had left this area about fifteen years ago and returned in recent years; he had two elderly parents living near Barnesville. Johnson himself had interviewed a Barnesville mail carrier named Walter Murray, who knew both Walters and Julia Anderson, and confirmed that the mother had given her child to the tinker willingly. Murray recalled that he had seen a photo of the child that Walters sent back from Mississippi, and it was clearly the same blond, blue-eyed boy with whom he had left North Carolina.

What was known or suspected about the Anderson woman was murkier. She had been called "loose," with at least one child out of wedlock. There were reports that she had faced charges of adultery with one of Walters's brothers, and even rumors that she had been in jail.

From Mississippi, Dale and Rawls had tried and failed to reach Julia Anderson by telegram. Barnesville, where she was thought to be, was remote: "a town of less than a hundred," "with no telephones and very poor telegraphic facilities," according to the *States*. For the lawyers, the urgency was in seeing justice for their client.

For the newspapers, it was a race for an exclusive.

That evening, Julia Anderson's location was at last identified: the farm of Charlie Lawson, where she was now employed. And Johnson and the sheriff had been on the road out from Lumberton ever since. The journalist might have been tagging along with the sheriff, or, just as likely, he may have orchestrated the whole trip. After all, a scoop for the *New Orleans Daily States*, with his own byline, was at stake.

In the wee hours of the morning, the bouncing headlights at last hit the Lawson farmhouse. A light went on inside.

ON FRIDAY MORNING, with rainfall unrelenting, the Atchafalaya finally broke through the levee near Krotz Springs, as predicted, rendering the Frisco crossing impassible and inundating portions of Iberville and Point Coupee Parishes. The Mississippi was worse. A crevasse had opened up in the levee upriver from Vicksburg, widening to 2,700 feet and getting only wider. Seven counties were flooded, sending thousands of residents clambering to their roofs and clinging to trees. On Thursday night, some six hundred unfortunate citizens spent the night atop a levee, shivering in the rain. Up and down the river, livestock was herded to higher ground, rescue skiffs, motorboats, barges, and steamers were sent out, and armies of workers struggled around the clock to sandbag against more cave-ins. Nonetheless, major ruptures would occur in the next few days, wiping away homes, devastating vast swaths of farmland,

and rendering upward of thirty thousand Mississippians and Louisianans homeless.

Far downriver, there was anxiety over a cave-in near Lutcher, but New Orleans was in no imminent danger, nor were most of the towns along the Southern Pacific rail line. For Louisianans here, flooding was a remote enough worry to celebrate the homecoming of the Dunbar child with abandon.

As the train inched out of New Orleans's Union Station, yardmen chased after it and jostled to shake hands with the smiling boy leaning out the window. Inside the carriage, the aisle was packed with admirers bearing gifts. A kiss from an unkempt woman; Cracker Jacks from a fruit vendor. At the river, when the train was loaded onto a barge to make the crossing, the awestruck boy raced out to see the water, and an engineer offered him the cab seat, where he twisted a valve to release a thrilling burst of steam. On a train parked parallel, a grinning fireman ignited a gob of greasy waste in his palm, and the boy cringed in horror.

At the Schriever stop, a small crowd rushed the train, but by Morgan City, the number surpassed one thousand, almost all women. The mothers of Berwick, dressed in white gowns, flocked aboard and filled the child's lap with bouquets. A little girl brought a note from her grandmother, who had been reading to her all the Dunbar news. A snaggletoothed woman squinted from the boy to Percy, then predicted, "Well, he's going to make a better-looking man than his father." As the Southern Pacific inched through the countryside, pausing at virtually every plantation, people waved from front porches and from cars at the crossroads, and for most of the ride, according to the *States'* F. S. Tisdale, "Robert hung with about 50 per cent of his person out the window or with one foot over the sill." When no one was looking, he snuck a yank to the bell cord and stopped the train dead.

Twenty miles south of Opelousas, the train paused to switch lines at Lafayette, and here the biggest celebration yet was under way. No matter the spitting cold rain, upward of three thousand swarmed the depot: local Elks marching in formation, sprawling packs of schoolchildren let out early. But when they reached the Dunbars' carriage, the main attraction was asleep in his mother's arms. Percy stepped forward to greet the crowd instead, but one towering, bald Elk, the mob spokesman, insisted that the child be brought out of the car for display. Lessie tried to intervene politely, but Percy gave in and woke the boy, who howled when placed in the Elk's arms. Seeing the man's white hat emerge, the crowd roared, and the boy wailed even louder. The Elk lifted the child up in his fat palm, steadying him with the other hand, high above his head. Umbrellas and hats were thrown, while the boy sobbed against the rain.

The Opelousas train pulled in from the north, and delivered an entourage keyed up with expectation: Lessie's sisters, Rowena, Lola, and Douce Whitley; Percy's sister Katie and their father, Robert Sr.; Opelousas mayor E. L. Loeb; and Paul Mizzi, who had been the last to see Bobby at Swayze Lake. A giddy smile was plastered across Paul's face. Before the boy was even carried out, he had scrutinized the windows of the New Orleans train, and in the rear carriage, he would later recount, he saw that it was Bobby right away. Nearby, in Archie Dunbar's arms, sat Alonzo.

Percy and Lessie, having retrieved the boy from the big Elk, made their way toward the gallery of a nearby hotel. Converging from the opposite direction was their Opelousas kin. Word spread that the brothers were poised to meet, and there was, relatively speaking, a hush.

In one account, both boys ended up in Lessie's arms. In another, Percy held them both up before the crowd. One newspaper rosily reported that Bobby recognized his brother right away and kissed him, but the consensus among the other dailies was more realistic. The boy was overwhelmed and crying. Alonzo reached out to hug him, and he pushed the younger boy away, more than once. He gave no sign of recognizing either Alonzo or the other newly arrived family members. None of this was a surprise. The boy had been at the center of a crowd of gaping strangers for hours; faces were by now just an awful blur.

Nevertheless, as the train poked on to Opelousas with the luggage racks of its rear carriage stuffed with flowers, a current of anxiety coursed in. The family would soon be greeted not just by family members but also by a wide community that had known young Bobby before he went missing. To an *Item* reporter, the Dunbars announced that as soon as they arrived at home, they would have the boy examined by two family physicians: Dr. F. C. Shute, who'd delivered the boy, and Dr. R. M. Littell, who'd treated him during his early years. "If they declare the boy is Robert," the reporter predicted, it "will dispel much of the doubt now existing in certain quarters."

"Certain quarters" included the train itself. A fat man waddled down the aisle and asked Lessie if the boy was actually hers. Lessie reportedly snapped back, "Of course he's mine. Don't you suppose I know my own baby after having him with me these last few days?" Tisdale of the *States* asked Percy about a report, just about to run that afternoon, from the paper's stringer in North Carolina: word from the Anderson woman herself, apparently corroborating Walters's story that it had been her son, Bruce, in his custody. According to Tisdale, "Dunbar . . . brought his big fist down on top of the red plush [parlor car] chair in front of him: 'I've got the boy—to hell with the rest of it!' "

Percy's exasperation was understandable: doubt seemed to emanate from *every* quarter. "On the streetcars," began the *States'* Friday commentary, "the thing you hear most often while persons are discussing this case is: 'I have a boy five years old. And he would know me after eight months or a whole year. I cannot understand why he didn't recognize his mother at once.' "

Two days earlier, the *Item* turned to the experts, not just on this question of the boy's recognition, but the parents', too, and the possible motives of the kidnapper. "I know of no precedents," Dr. John Fletcher, professor of psychology at Newcomb College, began, "by which one may arrive at any understanding of the mental processes of the various principals in this case under consideration." In other words, he was just guessing. But while much of the story's analysis smacked of a grandiose pseudoscience typical of yellow journalism, it did accurately reflect the commonsense "questions of the mind" that troubled readers of the Dunbar drama.

It was hard to believe, Fletcher felt, that the kidnapper would have acted for reasons other than ransom, even if he were looking to replace a lost child of his own. As another unnamed expert suggested, Walters's lack of an occupation put him in the category of "psychopathic personalities, by the French savants denominated 'unstable,' of whom almost anything short of crime may be expected." Crazy, but not criminal.

As for the parents, Fletcher found their hesitation understandable after so long an absence, and a sign of sanity: reason had won out over hysteria. On the other hand, the anonymous expert found it "readily conceivable that the year of intense mental strain and the intensity of their desire may have led them into a state of mind where they would not be too critical and could deceive themselves into the acceptance of almost any child."

The unnamed authority found it hard to understand how a child this age could have so totally forgotten parents and his previous life, no matter the trauma he had endured. Tulane University's Dr. David Spence Hill was more circumspect: the capacity for memory is variable according to individuals and circumstances, he noted, and with children, "as in dealing with an animal, we have the disadvantage of not being able to get any introspective testimony."

For its dubious Dunbar fluff, the *Times-Democrat* offered readers a parallel tale from history: the Tichborne case, which "stirred all of England from 1866 to 1875." Wherein a bony, black-haired, French-speaking aristocrat went missing at sea and was replaced by a fat, wavy-haired Australian butcher who didn't speak a word of French. The missing man's mother, so desperate for her son to be alive, ignored these inconsistencies and accepted the impostor as her own, furnishing him with a thousand-pound yearly allowance. Others were not so easily fleeced, and eventually the impostor was exposed and convicted of perjury.

In the field of forensic science, John Norris of the New Orleans Police Department was solicited by the *States* for his analysis as a national expert in the Bertillon method, otherwise known as anthropometry. Bertillon involved the measurements of physical features—head length, length of forearm from elbow to tip of middle finger—to determine individual identity. Its eponymous inventor, French police officer Alphonse Bertillon, was also responsible for the modern-day mug shot, but in 1903 his system of anthropometrics suffered a discrediting blow: two similarly named but different Kansas convicts, Will and William West, were confused because they had the exact same Bertillon measurements; in the end, only the science of fingerprinting could tell them apart. Nonetheless, Bertillon remained in the tool kit of many a police detective.

Since neither Bobby Dunbar nor Bruce Anderson was at his disposal to measure in the flesh, Norris relied on methods employed by untrained laypeople across the South: he put the published reward poster photo of two-year-old Bobby Dunbar under a magnifying glass alongside the recent photos of the boy in question. Norris found three significant differences. First, the ears, which stick out "shell-like" in the Dunbar child's case and which are "drawn" flat in the child in question. Next, the mouth: curving up on the former, curving down on the latter. And lastly, the eyebrows: arched on the Dunbar child, "straight across" on the child taken from Walters. Thus, Norris concluded that they were two different boys, although he did so skittishly: his opinion "must not be construed as any intention on my part to settle a matter which I feel lies with others to do."

Down on Canal Street, the No-Name Theater offered the paying public an alternative to the magnifying glass: the newsreel. "Moving pictures showing the return of the Dunbars with little 'Robbie'," the theater advertised, "are very clear, and there is some resemblance noted between the father and the boy and offer an excellent opportunity to judge them."

It was the children of St. Landry Parish who could best judge, Governor Brewer opined on Friday morning as he prepared to depart for Memphis and Greenville, Mississippi, on flood- and levee-related work. "The old playmates of the baby, if it is really the Dunbar child, will know the little fellow, and he will know them," Brewer told the *States*. "Their actions when they meet will, to my mind, largely be a determining factor in the identification, and we will wait and see how they greet each other."

"Wait and see" was, by his own later confession, the governor's unofficial motto. And given the flooding and the dozens of other more pressing political matters, of course his words had a distracted distance. But he seemed not to have considered that by pointing so publicly to these St. Landry children as judges, he might have an impact on their verdict.

THE RAIN WAS pounding in Opelousas, but people here cared even less than they had in Lafayette. At two o'clock, stores were closed and schools were dismissed, and the town converged on the station. Percy's fellow Elks were there in force, as were officials and ordinary citizens on foot and horseback, in wagons and cars. When the train approached, a "wildcat" fire alarm howled, and mill whistles all over town joined in. It was rumored that their operators hung bricks to the whistle cords so that the noise could continue while they themselves hurried to join the party. Firecrackers were hurled in every direction, punctuating the whistles with maddening pops. Even at top volume, the brass band could not be heard.

All it took was one glimpse of the child at the carriage door, and the crowd of thousands was overcome. As Paul Mizzi carried out his little lost friend, townspeople squinted through the rain and shrieked their lungs out: "That's him!"

Parked nearby was a hook and ladder fire wagon decked out in soggy red, white, and blue bunting, its team of damp horses as ready as they'd ever be to lead a rainy parade. But when Paul tried to lift the boy into the seat of honor, he resisted and began to cry. The crowd, some reported, was terrifying him. It was suggested that he wanted his father to ride with him. Only the *Item* had observed that an old lady so frantic to touch him had instead stabbed the child in the eye with her umbrella.

He didn't stop crying, but he did finally stay put on Percy's lap. With the band in the lead blasting out "Hail, the Conquering Hero Comes" and dozens of cars and carriages following, the parade began. It was about a mile to the Dunbar home on Union Street, with buildings along the route adorned with flags and bunting. Following the fire truck in an automobile, surrounded by friends and family, Lessie wept freely, bowing appreciatively and greeting the friends and neighbors who lined the streets.

"That's the kid!" "That's Bobby!" was the throng's refrain.

When Alonzo was brought up front to the fire truck, the boys at last had their brotherly embrace. But for most of the parade, its king was demonstrably unhappy.

When they reached the Dunbar's cottage—its front gallery draped in red, white, and blue, and "pretty native" flowers everywhere—the parade took over the street and yard. The boy of honor was carried up onto the porch and into the front hall. In the *Item's* photo of the room, bunting abounded, and so did American flags. Two hung vertically on the rear wall; at least one jutted out on a staff; and from the ceiling, two more hung crossed, at a crisp diagonal, forming a processional archway to the room's centerpiece: a miniature "throne," which was, in fact, Bobby's old high chair, draped with white cloth and adorned with garlands of roses, and two flags angling out on either side.

And forming the back of the throne was a giant framed oval infant portrait of Bobby Dunbar, posed in a white gown, holding a toy.

They carried him to the chair and reminded him that it was his. The picture, they pointed out, was him. But when they tried to seat the boy, he balked. As Tisdale observed for the *States*:

> [T]he chair had been so changed by the decoration that he would not have anything to do with it. He refused violently to sit in it . . . As they kept insisting, Robert's famous temper began to rise.
>
> "Say something to your friends, Robbie," one of the family coaxed.
>
> Robert looked on at the smiling and cheering crowd and did as he was told.
>
> "You get out of my house, now." He stormed [away] and swept them all with an angry glance. "I want to go to sleep."

According to one report, he ran into the back of the house. According to another, he cried, but not for long. One far-flung report related that he leapt onto his old red rocking chair and rocked maniacally to block out the hubbub. The behavior might have been fabricated, but it certainly captured the boy's mood.

Then the playmates arrived: eight-year-old Irma May Roos and her little brother Nathan, who had lived next door to the Dunbars in their old house on Court Street. At first the boy was frightened when Irma spoke to him. She then dared him: "Robbie, I'll bet you can't tell who I am." But the boy did just that. The *Times-Democrat* reported that he said her whole name; according to the *States*, he said just "Irma." He then, "almost immediately," called Nathan by name and asked how he was. Later that day, Percy would boast of this encounter, noting that Bobby and Nathan had been "bosom pals."

He wasn't alone in his boasting. "Recognizes Playmates," trumpeted the *Times-Democrat*, the most unequivocal of the next day's headlines, followed by "Dunbar Boy Gives Convincing Proof of Identity."

FRIDAY AFTERNOON AND evening, the New Orleans dailies made their way to Opelousas, and reported one jaw-dropping revelation after another about the case of Bobby Dunbar. Many of them concerned his alleged kidnapper.

Two days earlier, the first known published photo of William Walters had appeared in the Wednesday morning *Times-Democrat* and was reprinted in the afternoon *States*. In this portrait, cropped out from any background, Walters stood in dark clothes and a dark hat, with his hands together, as if wringing them. The image was so poor that the man's most prominent facial feature was his mustache; his eyes appeared as two dark smears. If a reader were to seek out the *Times-Democrat* to finally get a glimpse of the Dunbar kidnapper, he might as well have just closed his eyes and imagined "tramp" and saved himself the nickel. William Walters could have been anyone.

So for the past two days, from across Louisiana, Mississippi, and parts beyond, telephone calls, telegrams, and letters flooded in to newspapers, police stations, and anyone who might listen: this man Walters had been seen everywhere. A New Orleans woman was convinced that Walters was the same man who had held her young son captive in a shanty boat in 1911, only then his mustache was longer. North of Hattiesburg, Mississippi, citizens mistook the imprisoned Columbian for *a different* W. C. Walters who had served time in the federal penitentiary for shooting a black homesteader, prompting this headline from the *Times-Democrat*: "Has William

Walters a Double?" Among the loudest cries of recognition were those from Rapides Parish, seventy miles north. A Pineville blacksmith named McClendon remembered Walters working for him two years back, and trading a watch for a horse. A traveling umbrella maker named Koenig recognized Walters as a traveling stove mender whom he had seen camping in his covered wagon in a vacant lot in Alexandria during January. "His wagon bore a sign, 'The Traveling Stove Mender,' " Koenig told the *States*, "or it may have been 'fixer' instead of 'mender.' I don't remember which."

All of these sightings were chewed over voraciously, nowhere more so than in Opelousas. With practically every visitor or phone call to the cottage on Union Street, the talk turned to Walters and how he had committed the crime. Preston King and a railroad crew had tentatively identified him as the man they had seen near Swayze Lake, and Percy's long-held theory of a kidnapping gang continued to regain traction.

Lessie took a kinder view of the tinker and his motives. She told a reporter that she felt sorry for the man. He had probably taken Bobby as a companion and to gain sympathy for food and lodging. "The ladies at Hub wrote me that he had a real affection for the boy," she told the *Times-Democrat*, "and the boy seemed to return it. He was seen to hug and kiss the old man and call him his 'ugly papa.' "

The talk went on like this as long as the visitors streamed in, well into the night and after the boys were asleep. Friends and family did more than comfort Percy and Lessie; they invigorated them and brought them back to themselves. Lessie even was able to look back at the chaos of the last few days and laugh. Percy joked that now that "he had his own 'gang' about him . . . he had nothing to fear."

Except it wasn't just news of Walters that filled the Friday dailies; it was news of the "other mother." On the *States*' front page was P. W. Johnson's bylined report from North Carolina. His physical description of Julia Anderson was a terse afterthought: "stout" and "well preserved." Instead the report focused on finding and verifying facts about Walters and the identity of the woman's son. Her answers were "steady and without hesitancy," "and the impression left upon her hearers was that she was trying to do the right thing." Johnson did, however, offer this additional indictment: "She is a woman of loose character and has been in the county jail . . . on a charge of adultery."

Early the next morning, the other Carolina stringers' reports made their way into the *Item* and the *Times-Democrat*, with an official statement from the woman herself:

Affidavit of Julia Anderson

William C. Walters left Barnesville, N.C., with my son, Charles Bruce, in February 1912, saying that he only wanted to take the child with him for a few days on a visit to the home of his sister, Mrs. Henry Bell, at Bayboro, S.C., I have not seen the child from that day to this. I did not give him the child. I merely consented for him to take my son for a few days. Walters had been at the home of his father, J. P. Walters, near Barnesville, since November 1911, and while he was there, he and the child were together a great deal and seemed very fond of each other. The boy would go anywhere with Walters.

My son, who left with Walters, is named Charles Bruce. He was born December 18, 1907, at Fork, S.C., at the home of my sister, Mrs. Gilford Bass, who now lives in the country about four miles from Fork . . . D. B. Walters is not the father of that child. He was born before I ever saw D. B. Walters, but D. B. Walters is the father of a girl which was born March 18, 1911. Jim Cowan, a shoe drummer, is the father of the boy. I knew Cowan at Cerro Gordo, N.C., while I was working at the hotel of the lumber company at that place. I have seen Cowan only once since the child was born. He then gave me $5 for the child. I have not seen Cowan since and do not know where he is. I never knew where he lived.

I would know my son if I were to see him, and I am sure he would know me. I am willing to go anywhere to identify him on condition that my expenses be paid and that I be allowed to take the child away from Walters. I do not want him to have the child.

The boy has no marks upon him by which he could be identified. Up to three years old, the boy had a small red speck in the corner of his right eye. At three years of age that speck disappeared, except that it could be noticed in the fruit time. I have no picture of the child, but have a lock of his hair.

My son had dark blue eyes, fair skin, very light hair, and was a strong, healthy child . . .

I had no physician when Bruce was born; only a colored midwife, who is now dead.

On top of the affidavit, the other stringers dug up information reinforcing Johnson's early moral assessment. As for the girl fathered by William Walters's brother, Julia Anderson said she had been given up for adoption.

Apparently there had been another illegitimate child after that, which the Anderson woman had been accused of killing.

Withholding character judgment for the moment, editors of the *Item* and the *Times-Democrat* delivered their verdicts based on "hard facts," via headlines and commentary grafted into the stringers' reports. "Proves Anderson Child Is Not One Held by Dunbars," headlined the *Item*. "Is Not Bruce Anderson," the *Times-Democrat* declared, followed immediately by this, in large type and boxed above the story itself:

> The boy the Dunbars claim as their son bears decided marks as a means of identification.
> The boy taken from Carolina by Walters has *No* marks of identification, according to the affidavit of his mother.
> Therefore, the boy taken from Walters is not Julia Anderson's son, as he claims.

On Friday night and Saturday morning, Dr. Shute, the Dunbar family physician, performed two examinations. He first looked at the boy's foot. The scar, which he had treated three years ago, had undoubtedly faded. The *Item* summarized Shute's explanation: "the child has grown and . . . he had not been accustomed to wearing shoes and stockings lately. So the combination of the two would aid to eradicate the sign to some extent." Shute moved on to the boy's genitalia. According to the story, "Another physical deformity of one of the boy's organs was noted by the physician, and he declared that there could be no doubt about him being Robert Dunbar." Though there were other marks to consider, these two "main peculiarities that he knew the Dunbar boy possessed" were sufficient for Dr. Shute to render judgment.

Percy and Lessie welcomed the identification. Yet as hard as they tried to dismiss this "other mother," the fact that she might actually appear in person was a looming personal threat. "If Julia Anderson is coming to Opelousas to look at this boy, she is welcome," Percy told the *Pic*. "But it doesn't make any difference about Julia Anderson—this boy is mine and I'm going to keep him. I'd just like to see anybody take him away from us."

IN THE SUNSHINE of Saturday morning, as rejoicing and curious country people migrated in from the outer reaches of St. Landry Parish, and Evangeline and Acadia beyond, the boy's recognitions continued to cascade forth. He called out "Jack" to an old man named Jack who used to work for his grandfather. He made an in-joke with Aunt Douce about sewing wooden legs. And he threw a fit when Alonzo was placed in his old high chair, now undecorated and thus recognizable. It was his, he said; his grandmother had given it to him.

"Robert Dunbar recognizes former playmates without 'coaching,'" read a subheading of the Saturday *Item*. A day earlier, the paper had foreshadowed that announcement with this: "A number of little playmates of the boy will be taken to the Dunbar home sometime Saturday in an effort to have the child recall some of them. This is done, not so much in the nature of a test, as to strengthen their already seemingly indisputable proof."

The boy was holding the bridle of his uncle Harold's pony when five-year-old Margaret Durio made her timid approach through the front yard and past the crowd. Their houses had been side by side, Margaret's and Bobby's, before the Dunbars moved; they had been playmates, but they hadn't seen each other in two years. The *States* offered a moment-by-moment retelling of the reunion:

> The two children looked at each other, but neither spoke at once. The familiar puzzled look came into Robert's eyes as he swung the horse's bridle in one hand.
> "Do you know who it is, Margaret?" one of the crowd asked.
> "It's Robert," was the instant answer.
> Robert was still studying her face.
> "You don't know that little girl, do you, Robert?" the uncle asked.
> The puzzled look was gone. "I do, I do, I do," he repeated over and over.
> "You have never been to her house."
> "I have. My grandma took me there; she did, too."
> "When?"
> "A long time ago, a long time ago, a long time ago."

Though he did not speak her name, according to the *States* and all the other papers, the recognition was deemed positive.

At four o'clock, the boy was woken from a nap and driven with his brother down to the courthouse square. The first to greet them were the spiffily dressed young students of the Immaculate Conception Convent, who rushed the car with flowers. Ahead, under a canopy of giant live oaks, was a grandstand, a ragtime band, eighty-five big cakes, forty-four gallons of ice cream, and three thousand people.

Bobby and Alonzo were placed together on a decorated chair, and carried toward the crowd. Inevitably, the boys began to squabble, and "Grandma" intervened, sitting atop the chair with Bobby instead. The crowds exploded when they saw him, and he cried briefly. The throne was perched atop the grandstand, and they all settled in for what would become three full hours of men making speeches.

They were not jubilant speeches to welcome Bobby home, at least not the ones reported in the papers. They were speeches about William Walters and Governor Brewer, extradition, civic honor, mob justice, and capital punishment. Almost all speakers decried lynching and favored the fair course of justice, but at the same time, they had little doubt that Walters was guilty, and if so, they wished for the severest legal punishment: execution. Cried Gilbert L. Dupre, a much-admired former state legislator and judge, and one of Percy's fellow Elks, "I would like to see [Walters] given a fair and speedy trial and hanged to one of these trees as a warning to other child thieves, if he is found guilty. But it is better that ninety-nine guilty men escape than that one innocent man should die. If Governor Brewer fears mob violence, his fears are unfounded." This was less a welcome home party than a righteous town hall meeting.

Perched on his throne, the boy grew bored. He took intermittent interest in the blurring sticks of the ragtime drummer and a kiss from little Rosa Stagg, who so recently had howled for her dead brother Errol to wake up in his coffin. But when Mr. J. P. Boagni handed the boy a shiny new three-wheeled velocipede as a present, he was out of the chair and onto the sidewalks. All the other speech-weary children followed.

The ice cream certainly exacerbated the youngsters' restless excitement. Though the ladies at the refreshment table tried to ration the forty-four gallons, plenty of children snuck back into line for seconds. Once thoroughly sugared, they fixated on the boy and his new toy. Nearly a century later, Aline Perrault vividly remembers chasing the little Dunbar boy around the square, all afternoon. "Everywhere he went, little children followed him . . . [l]ike the Pied Piper. Everybody wanted to be near him."

And in case anyone else needed reminding about the celebration's purpose, the ladies of the social committee had crafted little red paper flags bearing the boy's name. As he zipped through the crowds on his tricycle, a trail of sticky-faced children behind him, he saw his name flashing by on every bosom and lapel. "Robert." "Robert." "Robert."

*   *   *

ON SUNDAY, THE blind ecstasy of St. Landry Parish had peaked. Those unsated curiosity seekers who packed into Catholic Mass were chagrined to learn that the famous boy and his family had stayed home to rest. Especially persistent fans peeked into their backyard, where the reunited Dunbar brothers finally bonded over digging a mud hole and tormenting two new foxhound puppies. The boy's rough handling of one pup's tail—hanging a tin can from it, using it as a handle for hoisting—earned him his very first spanking by Mr. Dunbar since his recovery.

All, however, was not returning to normal. Amid the tide of friends, neighbors, and journalists, one stranger's presence in the Dunbar home was decidedly unwelcome: a flashily attired hulk named Murphy, who had been shadowing the Dunbars since New Orleans, and who claimed to be a Burns detective working for Governor Brewer. For a time, the Dunbars begrudgingly allowed Murphy to linger, to inspect the rooms of their home, and to watch the boys play. But when he followed the family in for dinner to observe the boy's table manners (refined, as one might expect of Bobby Dunbar, or lacking, as one might expect of Bruce Anderson), Percy put his foot down, offering Murphy a chair in the hall or on the porch instead.

But he wasn't the only pesky detective, and by nightfall, the family had become thoroughly unnerved. When three strangers were spotted lurking outside the Dunbar house, local allies were roused from their beds to chase them away. Whether Murphy was among the lurkers is unknown; he made his exit first thing Tuesday morning.

Regardless of whether or not he reported back to Brewer, the governor received another nugget of local insight into the boy's disputed identity via an anonymous letter postmarked from Opelousas and leaked to the *Jackson Daily News.* Its contents were so scandalous that only one New Orleans daily, the *States,* dared reprint it. After congratulating Brewer on his resistance to requisition, the writer offered this:

> Not one-half of the population of Opelousas believe the child to be the missing boy, particularly the women who knew him best, his mother's best friends, those who lived in the neighborhood, who saw him daily play with their children . . . Twenty-five people told me there was not one trace of resemblance . . . All mothers compared photos of their children four years apart and the likenesses are identical. They can't understand it.

Surely, friends and family helped the Dunbars to write the letter off as a spiteful rumor from someone in town who didn't know them. But if there was any truth to this report about whispered sentiment in Opelousas, then the past three days had been far more than a simple homecoming. The celebration had been a collective effort to vanquish uncertainty from within the ranks. The ladies had done a fine job with their omnipresent little flags insisting "Robert," but the battle to come would be left to the men.

Chapter 8

Cover of sheet music for
"I Have Found My Child at Last, from the Finding of the Dunbar Child"
(words by Mrs. O. J. Chauvin, music by Harry Weston), 1913

THE LONGER JULIA Anderson waited at the Chadbourn depot, the more attention she attracted. Out at the Lawsons' and at the Walters place before that, she had been able to avoid the public eye. Only on infrequent trips to town did she face the scandalized stares and whispers of women, the laughter and lewd jeering of men and boys. For these excursions, she had learned to steel herself. But now, the details of her life were no longer just a subject of gossip, they were widely printed news. And the gawkers at the depot were emboldened.

Narrowly beating out the competition, the *New Orleans Item* had forced the Dunbar drama into its inevitable next chapter: paying Julia's way to Louisiana to see the boy for herself. For the first leg of her trip, she had been steered along by two of William Walters's relatives, his nephew by marriage, Boardman postmaster F. M. Stephens, and his sister Synthelia Williamson. They had urged Julia to do right by Walters, to do everything she could to identify the child as her son Bruce. But how could she know the boy until she saw him? And how could she do right by a man she barely trusted?

As if that wasn't pressure enough, now that she was alone and awaiting her next train, a man named Green broke from the glaring crowd and confronted her. He grilled Julia about details of her son Bruce's features and about the circumstances of his separation from her. When Green's hectoring got the best of Julia, she fought back, elaborating on her affidavit that she had a lock of Bruce's hair—it was blond, near white. But her defenses only gave Green room to badger her about supposed inconsistencies between her statements. Word on the street, he spat, was that she had been trying to give away Bruce for months before Walters took him. Word on the street was that she had murdered her latest child, strangled it to death. Before she knew it, Julia was in tears. At long last, her train arrived and she could escape, leaving Green to peddle his story to a stringer for the *Pic.*

As the *Item* would report, she "was annoyed considerably on the way across Georgia and the Carolinas," with Green and his accusations filling her head. Though this was likely the farthest she had ever traveled from home, the distance barely registered.

To meet her train in Montgomery, Alabama, Paul Thomson, the brother of the *Item's* publisher, had been dispatched from New Orleans. Guarding against expected competition, he transferred to the northbound train of the Atlantic Coast Line that she would arrive on, and traveled twenty miles out to meet her train early. When he returned through Montgomery with Julia in his custody, other reporters were there to swarm them. According to the *Atlanta Journal,* "Mr. Thomson declined to talk other than to say that the *Item* has gone to great expense to bring the woman to Louisiana."

The trip was just the beginning. In New Orleans, as *Item* editor Marshall Ballard negotiated with the Dunbars' family lawyer, John W. Lewis, over the terms of Julia's visit to Opelousas, the paper's finest talent was tapped to interview her as soon as she arrived. To play up the drama, editors chose three reporters when one would have sufficed, and offered them all the uncommon prestige of a byline: Martin Van, James Edmonds, and Ethel Hutson.

MISS HUTSON HAD worked anonymously at the *Item's* women's desk for over six months. Her sole recent foray into reportage, a story on a flare-up between the Tulane Era Club and its antisuffrage foes, had been rewritten by the city editor into a cartoonish battle of the sexes, full of fabrication. So the Julia Anderson interview should have been a welcome change.

But while this was the sordid human tragedy on which the *Item* had built its name, Miss Hutson herself did not fit the mold of a sob sister. Last year, for the Sunday *Pic,* she had researched and written two seven-column features, one investigating Mississippi levee plans in the wake of the 1912 floods, and another touting the dietary and economic potential of the South American root vegetable cassava. Since her arrival at the *Item,* she had covered education and sanitation, and penned an editorial on slang in schools. Notwithstanding the "light, feminine touch," which her proud father pointed out in her writing, Ethel's journalistic heart lay with more serious matters of policy and politics.

And in nearly every respect, her life was worlds apart from Julia Anderson's. The daughter of a peripatetic English professor, Ethel received an uncommonly full education, studying at Texas A&M and New York City's Pratt Institute for Art and Design. When her family settled in New Orleans, Ethel continued to reside with her parents, single and childless for her entire life. While she covered suffrage as a journalist, she was also an activist, working tirelessly as publicity chair for the city's Woman Suffrage Party.

Even without any details of Ethel Hutson's life, when Paul Thomson rushed Julia Anderson into the *Item*'s offices, the mere sight of a thirty-five-year-old female editor, with an assistant no less, must have struck her as remarkable. But after a few photographs, Julia was exhausted and needed to rest. For Ballard, getting her story that afternoon was as imperative as printing the first pictures, and since competitors would soon be swarming the *Item*'s doors, they had to move their subject fast or risk being trapped in the building. So, as the paper would later teasingly report, Julia "was then removed a short distance from the city" to "modern apartments," where she was seen by "immediate members of the *Item* staff and one or two of their relatives." Given these hints and all other evidence, the most logical conclusion is that Julia and her trio of interviewers traveled uptown to the booming suburb of Carrollton, to the side-by-side duplex on Pine Street where Ethel Hutson lived with her aging parents. Here they could speak comfortably and at length, and Julia could spend the night.

The Hutsons' modest home was overflowing with evidence of Ethel's many ongoing publishing collaborations with her father, Charles. And everywhere Julia would have looked, there was art: Ethel's watercolor irises and colorful glazed tiles, and also the work of Charles, who in his twilight years had become Ethel's pupil. His were landscapes, simple, vibrant pastels and oils from extended family campouts along the Gulf Coast of Mississippi: pine-lined sandy shores, railroad tracks curving over a marsh. For an anxious, travel-weary visitor, the images were a deep relief.

The interview began with all three *Item* reporters present. Julia spoke at length about William Walters, whom she bitterly resented but could barely see as a kidnapper, and answered painful questions about her children and their fathers. Eventually the conversation narrowed down to one with Ethel Hutson alone, a "long, quiet talk" that lasted well into the night. It might have been a strategy for the men to leave early, and, indeed, the *Item* would tout the gender angle in its lead the next day: "Woman Journalist Finds Frail Sister with Moral Ideas of Her Own." While Van and Edmonds wrote about Julia with sympathy, and Edmonds at least believed that the boy in Opelousas was indeed her son, the men would write of her condition as a "fallen woman" with a generic shorthand, borne of journalistic laziness or moral discomfort. Save Ethel Hutson, no reporter ever dared to find out precisely how Julia's "fall" had begun.

WHEN JULIA WAS a little girl growing up in Fair Bluff, townspeople would flock to the railroad station, dressed in their finest, just to watch the trains come in. As the pumper refilled the tender with water, passengers and crewmen stepped out to eat at the hotel, and buggies gathered up mail and traveling drummers to shuttle them over the Lumber River into Robeson County or down into South Carolina.

If young Julia was lucky enough to catch sight of this bustle, it was because she had been brought along for the ride to town with a wagon full of cotton, harvested from her father's rented acres, a mile or two northeast near Hinsons Crossroads. The 1880 census listed George Anderson as a laborer, but by 1900, he was a farmer, which suggests a move up from sharecropper to tenant farmer. The house and land were still rented, the debt was still insurmountable, but the tools and perhaps a mule were George's own. His wife, two years younger, was known by her nickname, Beady, more than her Christian name, Obedience. Julia was the fourth child she bore, at the older end of a line of offspring that would eventually number at least fifteen. In 1900 only two younger sons—one seventeen and one twelve—were officially recorded as farm laborers, but if a family expected to survive in the business of tobacco and cotton, every able-bodied child, male or female, would need to contribute.

Julia's formal schooling, if it was anything like most children of share-croppers and tenant farmers, was spotty. A "free school" opened in Fair Bluff in the late 1880s, and if George and Beady were able to spare her, Julia would have received, at most, only three months of education a year. Most of her schooling was likely at home, where the standard primer—for literature, grammar, and composition—was the family Bible.

In 1902 she was nineteen and unmarried. Not far down the road from the Andersons' rented parcel lived a land-owning widow, Adeline Floyd, who worked her farm with help from her youngest son, the only child still at home, twenty-seven-year-old Elisha. Other than geographic proximity and hints of a distinction in class, nothing is known about how the relationship between Lishy and Julia began. As later evidence would suggest, her understanding of his character was meager at the time it was decided that they marry. The wedding took place on a Thursday in March at the bride's home, with neighboring farmers recorded as witnesses. According to the reminiscence of one old sharecropper, farm weddings like this were simple affairs: "no wedding gowns as such, no floral decorations, no burning tapers, no singing, and few rings out in the sticks."

At Julia's wedding to Lishy, the most colorful element was the offici-ant. For the past several decades, the heavyset Rev. Moses Pridgen had preached the Gospel in one little wooden Baptist church after another, up and down this sandy, swampy Carolina borderland. Possessing the natural authority of his biblical namesake, Moses drew throngs to his revivals, his booming voice carrying out of the tent or church and well into fields and woods. In the early nineteen hundreds, Moses settled in Fair Bluff and ran a little grocery store, but his reputation remained larger than life. For the Andersons, it was certainly an honor to have him bless the union of their daughter.

But their pride did not last long. Reverend Pridgen tipped his hat and rode back into town, and the sole moment of brightness in the matri-mony of Julia Anderson and Elisha Floyd was over. She moved in with her new husband and his widowed mother, and exactly one day into their marriage, his true nature made itself known. It was Friday night, and the groom aimed a gun at his nineteen-year-old bride. Whether drunk, in a rage, or both, intending to kill, torment, or simply flaunt control, Lishy's motives remain a mystery. "He was crazy," Julia recalled flatly to Miss Hutson. "That was what the matter was with him."

Three shots echoed across the Floyd property. One met its mark. Julia felt the bullet rip through the skin of her foot, and Lishy stopped firing. Nine years later, she still bore the scar.

If Elisha used a gun on her the night after their wedding, it is unlikely that what she withstood for the next five months was any better. Finally, in the summer, Julia fled. The baby she was carrying did not survive. It is possible that Julia became pregnant before the wedding, which would explain the ceremony's apparent haste: in 1904, marriage with a preacher was a standard moral corrective. But there was no such redemption for a wife leaving her husband. She was expected to suffer through even the worst of circumstances. Her primary task, reflected in the very name of Julia's mother, was obedience. So while Julia's decision to flee may have kept her alive, it also set her down the path of moral ruination.

She did not return to live with her parents. Within a few years, George and Beady Anderson moved the rest of the family to Marion, South Carolina. There they joined the swelling ranks of poor Carolina whites who gave up the punishing, debt-ridden life of sharecropping or tenant farming for the hope of a brighter future—in the cotton mills. As her younger siblings toiled long hours to keep the family afloat (even eleven-year-old George Jr. was employed as a spinner), Julia found work waiting tables at a spacious new hotel seven miles west of Fair Bluff in the fast-growing lumber town of Cerro Gordo, North Carolina.

Sometime in late 1906 or early 1907, a traveling shoe salesman named James Cowan stepped off a train and lugged his sample cases over to the hotel. Phin Williams had just opened a shoe store in town, so Cerro Gordo was a new stop on Cowan's route. As Julia recalled, he passed through three times a week, always taking meals at the restaurant. She may not have been legally divorced from Elisha Floyd, but in the hungry eyes of a traveling salesman, so many weeks and miles from home, she was an available single woman. And for Julia, still scarred from the brutality of her marriage, this blue-eyed drummer promised what Lishy never had: intimacy, even if it was fleeting and false.

But that was not all James Cowan offered. Across the nation, from countryside to cities, women very much like Julia—escaping violent husbands, all alone, underpaid, and struggling to make ends meet—faced the same choice that she did. In Illinois in 1916, a former waitress testified before the State Senate Committee on Vice:

You wait on a man, and he smiles at you. You see the chance to get a tip, and you smile back. Next day he returns, and you try harder than ever to please him. Then right away he wants to make a date and offer you money and presents if you'll be a good fellow and go out with him. . . . For my work in the restaurant, I get three dollars a week and my meals and a few dimes each day in tips—just enough to pay my room rent and for my laundry. If I didn't pick up a little money on the side, I'd have to go naked.

While Julia did not address it directly when interviewed in 1913, she later would look back on her life in Cerro Gordo, and the true nature of her relationship with James Cowan, with unflinching honesty: "I was a woman in hard luck," she would admit. "[A]long that time in my life, it was that or worse. I had to live."

By February 1907, Julia was pregnant with James Cowan's child. When she couldn't hide it any longer, the pregnancy likely cost Julia her job, and she took refuge with her sister Katie and her new husband, a recently widowed tenant farmer. In mid-December, a black midwife was called for, and Julia gave birth to a son, Charles Bruce Anderson. He had watery blue eyes like his father and hair the color of straw.

Bastardy. North Carolina Criminal Code and Digest, chapter 8, section 253

When complaint is made on affidavit by one of the county commissioners . . . to any justice of the peace of the county in which the woman resides, that any single woman within his county is big with child, or delivered of a child, he may cause her to be brought before him . . . to be examined upon oath respecting the father; and if she shall refuse to declare the father, she shall pay a fine of five dollars and give a bond payable to the state with sufficient surety to keep such child from being chargeable to the county, otherwise she shall be committed to prison until she shall declare the same, or pay the fine aforesaid and give such bond.

In addition to the public shame of her pregnancy, it is probable (though no record survives) that Julia faced legal sanction under the laws of bastardy. The five dollars that James Cowan gave her, when their son was two, may have been reimbursement for her fine or payment for her silence, or both. She did not know where he lived, and she never heard from him again.

If she had remained silent about his name before, Julia could not afford to now. The stakes were too high. By the time she had arrived in New Orleans, three of the four city dailies had identified Bruce's father as James Cowan, Jim Cowan, or James Coward, a shoe drummer. His name had not been picked up by the wire services, but the names Julia and Bruce Anderson certainly had, appearing in papers across the country. The odds of the news not reaching the man in question seem slim. One thing is certain: he never stepped forward. "I don't know what he thinks about the case of the boy," Julia would later state. "I haven't hunted him up, and I have not asked him. What does a man care about a woman after he causes her ceaseless trouble? He left me to fight it out alone, and I have been fighting alone ever since."

Long into the evening, Ethel Hutson listened. Quite naturally, Julia's recollections focused on her years-long entanglement with the Walters family following Bruce's birth: the elderly Walters parents, for whom she worked as a sharecropper, housekeeper, and nurse; and the younger generation of Walters men, who had caused her little but trouble. Over the next year, this story would continue to emerge, in bits and pieces, in one news report or another. But in April 1913, Ethel Hutson's summation offered the public an insight into Julia Anderson's plight that was so far absent from all other coverage: "Just the usual story of brutal, selfish men taking advantage of the physical helplessness and dire poverty of the woman who had sinned once, and thereby forfeited her right to respect and decent treatment."

BEFORE ETHEL AND Julia had even finished talking, the *States* hit the streets, trumpeting Julia's arrival in New Orleans. The *Item* had been scooped. The article boasted leaked insider information and descriptions cobbled from earlier coverage, but its central selling point—a one-on-one interview with Julia Anderson herself—was a wholesale fabrication. The *Item* had taken the utmost care to sequester its subject from the competition, but there was no guard against fakery. The paper would decry the *States* with much outrage the next day, but by then, the copies had been sold.

In Opelousas, citizens devoured the *States'* "interview." "I'm going to see this boy," the fake Julia declared. "Nobody can stop me. And if he's my boy, I'm going to take him away with me." Upon a suggestion by the "reporter" that the people of Opelousas might attack her, "'Let them do anything,' she replied fiercely. 'If they don't treat me square, they'll be sorry.'" This was not just fakery, it was agitation.

And it worked. By midweek, the town was in an uproar over Julia's imminent arrival. Police were put "on the lookout," and one trickster even signed her name in a hotel register. The *Times-Democrat* reported that Percy Dunbar had consulted with his attorneys and intended to "hold" Julia as a material witness in the case against Walters. Then there were reports that the boy himself was "in danger." Percy "armed himself," arranged for friends to guard the house, and kept the boy sequestered in back. Archie was dispatched to chase down any suspicious strangers passing by. On the day of Julia's anticipated arrival, according to the ever-cheeky F. S. Tisdale of the *States*, businesses were closed and the streets were filled with excited citizens. "Nobody knew anything for sure, and everybody was guessing everything."

ON WEDNESDAY EVENING, under cloak of darkness, Julia sat across from James Edmonds in a train drawing room, its locked door rattled every few minutes by scouts from the *Item*'s competitors. Their pursuit of Julia out of New Orleans had spanned several hours and three train stations, punctuated by a minor car accident, a sweaty horse chase, and plenty of wrong turns. In a sleepless daze, Julia prayed that she would know if the boy in Opelousas was her son, but her ordeal thus far was taking its toll. "I wish it was over," Edmonds heard her murmur. "I wish it was over."

May 1, 1913

WHEN THE TRAIN reached New Iberia at two in the morning, Edmonds and Julia slipped off, unbeknownst to the scouts, who stayed on to Lafayette. The Dunbars' lawyer, John W. Lewis, was waiting to drive them the remaining forty miles to Opelousas in his grand red touring car. He took it fast through the prairie, and the speed gave Julia a second wind; for much of the ride, she found herself laughing and chattering. But it wasn't joy; it was nerves. Her anxiety was raw and mounting. As dawn broke, she realized the date: May 1, her twenty-ninth birthday.

At six o'clock Mr. Lewis crept his car down Court Street toward his house. Sited on an ample corner lot, the Lewis home announced its owner's status: a low, sprawling Victorian with a fat turret and a wraparound porch. Peering out into the breaking dawn light, Lewis and Edmonds saw right away that the front door was staked out by competing reporters, who had undoubtedly been waiting there all night. So they pulled up alongside the house, helped Julia out of the car, and hustled her into a side entrance as quickly as possible, locking the door behind them. The newspapermen noticed their presence too late, rattled at and banged on the door a few times, then plotted their next move.

Julia's eyes adjusted to the home's dim interior: it was spacious and elegant, with rooms and hallways spilling off in every direction. Mrs. Lewis was there to greet her, and she was likely the one to deliver the latest news to her husband. St. Landry district attorney R. Lee Garland had heard of the forthcoming proceedings and was insisting on being present; given that he would likely prosecute the kidnapping case against Walters, it only made sense. He wanted Judge Pavy to be present as well. Unfortunately, both men were finishing a term of court in Ville Platte, nearly twenty miles away, and would not return until later in the morning.

Julia's large frame sagged. The prospect of waiting, again, sapped the anxious energy right out of her. The Lewises could see how tired she was, so they offered her a daybed in the front parlor. Mrs. Lewis drew the blinds tightly, closed the door, and scurried off down the hall.

Julia lay down. In the morning light that filtered in around the blinds, she took in the parlor's fine furniture. She heard murmurings from elsewhere in the house and knew they were talking about her. Every now and then, there was a rapping at a door or a window from an indignant reporter shut outside. Sometimes an outer door would open briefly, and she could hear bursts of a crowd's chattering out in the yard. Mr. Lewis or some other man would bark out that Julia Anderson was not inside and then slam the door again. Even in the lulls, as much as she wanted to, Julia could barely close her eyes. She wondered how long it would be until they brought her the boy.

At eleven in the morning, she heard a commotion behind the hallway door, and then it swung open. Mrs. Lewis asked if she wanted breakfast. Julia stood up, and her head began to throb; she couldn't think of eating. Behind Mrs. Lewis, Julia could see that there were more men in the hallway, engaged now in a quiet discussion with Mr. Lewis. She saw Edmonds among them, a familiar face, and inched closer to ask when the boy would come. "Her eyes were red with weeping," Edmonds would recall, and "she looked years older." The men paused in their conversation when she reached the threshold.

Including Edmonds and Mr. Lewis, there were at least six altogether now. The new arrivals included Dr. Saizan, a physician for the Dunbar family; Dr. Haas, who had only days ago declared his certainty that the Dunbars did indeed have custody of their son; Dr. Charles Boagni; and Leon Dupre, a cashier for Opelousas National Bank. In later reports and court proceedings, these men would be referred to as "the committee."

Though Edmonds would report on their graciousness, Julia was not at ease. Her repeated question about the boy's arrival remained unanswered, and her understanding of what was to come was foggy. She mentioned her headache, and Dr. Saizan would later testify that he brought her some aspirin, which he had gotten from Mrs. Lewis.

Perhaps owing to Julia's mounting anxiety, the committee decided to get started in the parlor, even though Garland and Judge Pavy had not arrived. There is no transcript of what then transpired, but Edmonds's report describes it this way: "Kindly and in friendly, professional tones, they put her through a long, careful cross-examination." The subject was the attributes and appearance of her son, Bruce, and Edmonds listed the salient details of Julia's responses:

- Child perfectly formed. Small, round, dark blue eyes.
- No birth marks, save a peach mark above the right eye,
    which appeared at fruit time, but ceased to appear
    when the child was three and one-half years old.
- Mole above left knee and left hip. None on head or neck.
- Active, ruddy skin.
- Sharp, strong voice.
- No scars.

Julia answered confidently; the "leading questions did not lead her astray." Though Edmonds's reportage here is oddly dry, his choice of courtroom terminology—"cross-examination," "leading questions"—is telling. The committee included three physicians, but it was acting as a team of prosecutors.

They left her in the parlor and told her to wait, closing the door behind them. Julia heard an outer door open and another burst of crowd noise, and wondered if they were bringing the boy. But when no footsteps returned, she knew that a longer wait lay ahead.

It was, in fact, Percy Dunbar who had been admitted, along with his brother Archie; earlier, they had been summoned by phone. Like Julia,

Percy was asked questions by the committee about his son's physical appearance, with Edmonds on hand to dutifully record the responses:

- Head more round than long.
- Grayish blue eyes.
- Hair light brown.
- Black mole on lobe of left ear.
- Ears well shaped, not close to head.
- At times light limp.
- Voice is hoarse from adenoids.
- Strong and active.
- Not as stout for [his age] as when he left home.
- Mole on neck.
- No moles on legs.
- Some moles on back.

Although the brothers' answers about hoarseness and stoutness indicated a change in the child's appearance, the committee did not press these points. Edmonds's report mentions none of the prosecutorial techniques that they had used on Julia to try to steer her "astray." Thus, a central emerging question—whether these were details honestly recalled about Bobby Dunbar before he went missing, or whether they came from more recent inspections—was again buried. And the clinical tone of Edmonds's reportage—"the description of little Bobbie Dunbar was given"—served to keep it so.

At noon came another flurry of activity. A crowd of curious Opelousans had been gathering outside the Lewis home, and when Mr. Lewis again emerged to deny that Julia Anderson was present, competing newsmen who had in fact seen her enter called his bluff. The impatient question on everyone's tongue, of course, was when the Anderson woman would be allowed to see the boy. Cornered, Mr. Lewis sputtered that the identification would occur at two o'clock that afternoon, in public. A decoy party then left for the Dunbar home, but few were gullible enough to follow. By noon, Lessie Dunbar had arrived at the Lewises' with the boy Alonzo and John Lewis's six-year-old towheaded son, Seth, who were ushered to the back of the house to play.

In the front parlor, Julia faced another round of questioning, now with other reporters and Assistant District Attorney Edward P. Veazie present as well. The intent was to garner information from Julia about Walters, with talk of holding her as a material witness. "[B]ut the more she talked, the more the attorneys were impressed with the fact that she knew very little bearing on this case," the *Times-Democrat* reported. "Her distress was pitiful, and as the examination went on, it was decided that the test must be made soon, or the woman would be a mental wreck."

AT TWELVE FORTY-FIVE, the three boys were corralled into the dining room. Mrs. Lewis sat at the table with them, feeding them either cake or porridge, depending on which report one believed. As observers settled on their positions, there was a last-minute change of plans. By whom and for reasons unknown, the child in question was pulled from the room and taken back to the rear of the house, leaving only Seth and Alonzo at the table with Mrs. Lewis.

In the front parlor, Julia's hands were shaking around her coffee cup as she waited. She could hear movement and whispering in the dining room, but she could not glean its purpose. Finally, Mr. Lewis and Mr. Veazie entered and explained. *There would be multiple children in the dining room, and she was expected to identify her son from the group.*

Julia's face dropped.

Of course, she had heard the speculation that this would be the challenge she faced. But only now did she absorb it as reality. All morning, these men had been trying to tangle her in her memory and words, and now they were making her trial a physical one. As Mr. Lewis and Mr. Veazie escorted her into the hall, they were polite—gentle, even—but she had every reason to doubt their sincerity.

She entered the dining room and took stock of the scene. Percy Dunbar, reporters, and the committeemen were aligned against the far wall, watching her impassively. Seated at the dining room table, Mrs. Lewis studiously avoided her gaze, focusing instead on the two boys eating.

Julia could not afford to take offense at the setup. She had no choice now but to rise to their challenge and prove herself. She walked to the boys and took them in. According to the *Times-Democrat,* Julia ran her fingers through Seth Lewis's "silken hair," paused, then looked Alonzo over head to toe and said, "See them eyes. Them eyes are not mine." But later sworn eyewitness testimony indicates that Julia's rejection of both boys was, in fact, sweeping and based on an all-encompassing impression, not a single characteristic. With a wave of her hand, according to the testimony, Julia declared that neither child was hers. Her boy was not in the room.

A sharp hand clap rang out from somewhere near the dining room's far door. Julia's head jerked up. A man's voice—she could not tell whose—bellowed, "She failed to recognize the child!"

There were murmured reactions out in the hall and toward the kitchen. Dr. Haas glowered in the direction of the interruption, and the murmuring died down. But the damage had been done.

Julia turned back to the two boys in a panic. She searched their faces and picked apart their features. She tried, and tried again, to see her Bruce—in the older child, and then, more carefully, in the younger. But the condemnation rang loud in her ears: *She had failed to recognize the child.* How could she not have known him? Flooded with doubt, she began to cry.

Dr. Boagni hastened to correct for the interjection, assuring Julia that there would be other boys for her to look at. "Perhaps a dozen," he specified. That prospect was hardly a comfort. After an awkward pause, the committee left the room to confer in the hall. Mrs. Lewis ushered the boys out, and Julia was left in the dining room alone.

Dr. Saizan saw her crying. She was not hysterical, he would later testify, but "she looked like she was in distress." So he escorted her through the hall and back into the parlor, where she had waited before. "I locked the door and told [the other committeemen] I would leave her there until she regained her composure."

Neither Edmonds nor any other journalist present reported the last-minute removal of the child in question or the gloating interjection, though their significance was impossible to miss. Without them, Edmonds's version makes no sense:

> At 12:45 p.m. she failed to recognize two known children, Alonzo Dunbar and Seth Lewis. She partially collapsed. "People," she said piteously in her Carolina dialect, "my child ain't in this room."

All other men in the dining room, along with Mrs. Lewis and everyone else in the house, would remain publicly silent on these two particular wrinkles as well. Only a full year later, under the pressure of oath, would one of these men admit what had occurred, and a cascade of admissions—in compelled court testimony—would follow.

Given Haas's admonishing glower, it is likely that the interjection, and the fact that it might irrevocably taint any further testing of the Anderson woman, was discussed then and there. To make matters worse, an indignant Sheriff Marion Swords was finally allowed into the house, and he lit into the committee for keeping the proceedings so secret. Also muscling in were more reporters, leaving only Tisdale of the *States,* which had led the attacks on the *Item*'s secrecy, howling out on the porch. Percy Dunbar objected to the arrival of more reporters, and, in fact, wanted *all* press banned from the event to come: Julia's identification of the child in question. If true, this insistence suggests that it may have been Percy who was responsible for the child's last-minute removal earlier.

Regardless, it was a moment of professional crisis for Mr. Lewis. He had orchestrated this test, and now every aspect of it was being challenged. In either an impulsive rejection of Percy's suggestion or a panicked attempt to salvage the integrity of the proceedings, he took action, hoisting the mystery boy onto his shoulders and carrying him down the hall to the parlor. Confused and angry at being pulled from his playmates, the child fought Mr. Lewis, "his face . . . puckered with rage."

WEEPING IN THE PARLOR, Julia looked up when she heard the lock. The door swung open, and Mr. Lewis strode in with a writhing boy atop his shoulders. Behind and around him, other men hurried in: the full committee, Percy Dunbar, and the reporters. The door was locked again behind them.

Julia's swollen eyes were fixed on the boy, who fought Mr. Lewis even as he was set down on the floor. Beneath his tears and fury, this child seemed familiar. He looked like the child from the newspapers, the child that Walters said was Bruce. He could be Bruce; she felt hopeful that he could. And yet there was doubt. A year later, Mr. Dupre would testify that immediately after the hand clap and interjection, Julia's "statements and actions were very much more qualified." She knew this was not one of the two boys she had just seen and "failed" to recognize. Her thoughts turned and tangled trying to make sense of the committee's tactics, to find a method to their scheme. But her answer would come only by focusing on the boy.

She tried to stop crying. She looked squarely at him and called him "Bruce."

Whether too deep in his tantrum to hear, or not able to recognize the name, the boy did not respond. She took in his brand-new outfit—clothing she could never afford—then looked back to his face. "Bruce, speak to me."

She smiled at him. "Don't you know your ma?" one paper quoted.

At this, the boy looked scornfully at the big, crying woman and then turned back toward the hallway, where Lessie waited unseen.

Julia's tears flowed freely now. Edmonds's prose was terse: "She failed to express herself. She was crying like a child." When she leaned forward in her chair and reached for the boy, he slapped at her hands and twisted away.

Her head sank into her hands.

According to one account, she tried to coax him with money, alternating between an offer of pennies and a promise of "plenty of money." She turned to the committee and asked for help, or more information on the boy. They responded "as kindly as possible" that they could not answer any questions. "She would have to do her work alone."

So Julia did just that. She stood and extracted from her suitcase in the corner a "big, greenish orange" that she had bought on the train. Attempting a sly smile, she held it out for the boy and looked him in the eyes. Edmonds reported that he refused it at first. But again, Edmonds omitted what, by all other accounts, was a key detail of the subsequent exchange. The child smiled and, as he took the orange, clapped his hands.

Now Julia beamed in earnest: this was her proof. To the committee, she declared, "That's one of his old capers." Clapping for fruit apparently was a game that Julia and Bruce had played together.

The men were skeptical, so Julia pled her case. She wanted to act in fairness to the committee and to the Dunbars, she said, but also to herself. The clapping trick had made her more and more certain.

They remained impassive.

Whether prompted or not, she next examined the boy's feet. By now he was calm, and felt familiar enough to allow her to unbuckle and then remove his right sandal. She looked for a mole or a marking on his right foot that she remembered Bruce having, but apparently what she found did not make her any more certain.

She asked the men if this was the child that had been found with Walters. To her, there was no point in withholding this information; it would only help her confirm her instincts, her dawning recognition. Of course, the committeemen saw this only as proof that the child was a stranger to her. They refused to answer.

Again she broke down. "I can't just say."

The boy had been given a rubber ball to play with "as a 'pacifier,' " but now he took a quiet interest in Julia's weeping.

She called him Bruce. She asked him if he remembered his friend

Hovis Walters, if he remembered her, Julie, his mother. She called him Bruce again and again. But his attention returned to the ball. "Never once did he respond to the agonizing pleas," all the papers agreed.

The men watched her collapse back into the chair. At last, Mr. Lewis cleared his throat. She needed to examine the boy completely, he reminded her. There were other boys to be brought forward after this one.

She couldn't speak through her tears.

According to one paper, Lewis "cautioned her not to get excited or worried." It was an expression of concern as halfhearted as it was belated. Was she satisfied with her examination? he asked her. Could they move on?

She nodded yes. She said she wanted to be sure.

IN THE KITCHEN, there was whispered debate over which child to present next. By now at least five boys were in the Lewis home, being kept quiet with cake. In addition to the boy in question, Alonzo Dunbar and his own son Seth, Mr. Lewis had chosen Laurent Lacombe, the son of his legal secretary (and his wife's nephew), and the Dunbar boys' little cousin Robert Preston Dunbar Jr., son of Percy's brother. All were blond and hand-selected by Mr. Lewis. Doubtless, it was through the same prosecutor's cunning that had inspired this entire proceeding that Alonzo was chosen to be next. They took him into the parlor, now alone, smiling and unafraid.

Though all reports noted that Julia was immediately "struck" by the boy, none connected that reaction to the earlier incident in the dining room. Alonzo was one of the candidates Julia had "failed" to recognize, so it was natural that she would scrutinize him more carefully. She did want not to "fail" with him again. But when she tried again to connect him with her memory of Bruce, despite the fifteen months they had been apart, she could plainly see that this child was younger than Bruce by at least a year.

And yet he was smiling at her, so she engaged him, settling on a sunnier style of questioning, one more appropriate for a child this age. She asked his name. Was it Bruce? "What's your ma's name? Where's Julie? Who's this here?" With each question, she grew more animated and frantic.

Finally, in answer to her question about his name, he "looked wonderingly at the strange woman and lisped, 'Lonzo Dunbar,' in his sweetest tones."

If she had been in her right mind, Julia would have stopped there. But she persisted with her questions, and the men let her. Now, to every inquiry—about Hovis or Georgia, if she was his mother, if his name was Bruce—Alonzo answered yes. Most interpreted this as deliberate mischief, and if Julia looked up, she would have seen badly hidden smirks. Then the boy called her "old cock-caw" and repeated his real name, Alonzo Dunbar.

She looked from the boy to the men. Had they coached this child to fool her, to give a false name? He had said "Alonzo" but also "yes" to Bruce. He was the same child from the dining room, but she had not recognized him then. She guessed and second-guessed and second-guessed her second-guessing.

Bravely, she began her report to the committee: he was friendly; his eyes were not the same as Bruce's; and yet he answered to the name Bruce and was roughly Bruce's size. She wanted to do right, she said.

At their silence, she turned to the boy and kept trying, asking whatever came into her head. "Did your other papa give you bananas?" "Bruce, where's your aunt Dell?" Pleas for the boy to "talk a little bit," and, again, offers of money. When she opened her purse and handed him some change, Alonzo replied, "Thank you, dear, old cock-caw."

She scolded him for his rudeness.

She sputtered more questions and examined his foot. She barely knew what she was doing, much less why. There was something behind the men's blank stares, something behind this boy's tomfoolery—a secret, an unknowing—that chafed at her and kept her going. "He looks like my Bruce," she managed weakly, not sure if she believed it or not.

Finally, they led him out.

Laurent Lacombe was next, "dumb with fright at this strange face." Julia gamely tried to get him to speak, and at her question about where he lived, the boy responded, "By a church." Right away, she knew he was not hers, but whether compelled by a need to comfort him or by her delirious interpretation of the committee's expectations, Julia went through the motions of asking her standard questions. But the boy's babbling was indecipherable. She offered the men her assessment, because by now she knew this to be the routine: this boy's eyes were blue like Bruce's, but his hair was darker, and his skin was tender, as if kept out of the sun.

The next child was Robert Preston Dunbar Jr., held in the arms of Mrs. Lewis and even more terrified than Laurent Lacombe. As Julia examined him, the child did nothing but shriek, louder and louder, into her face, as if in terror of being handed off to her. Pulling back, she felt the boy's hysteria as her own. The parlor echoed with his screaming until Mrs. Lewis finally took him out.

After that, "the committee decided that the test had been sufficient." Julia was clearly hanging on by a thread, but it wasn't compassion that prompted the halt; instead of letting the woman rest, the men had more questions.

Veazie wanted to know more about Walters, about "what his notion [was] in taking children." Julia said she didn't know, but Veazie pressed, and as she struggled to answer, she felt her own mistrust of Walters flare up. She had heard a rumor that Walters once tried to steal his own children from his estranged wife, and another rumor that Walters's brother Frank had been involved in a kidnapping in Georgia. However she actually relayed these to Veazie, the *Times-Democrat* reported: "[S]he heard Walters and his brother were in the child stealing business." Julia stammered on that Walters had been mixed up in a murder trial in Georgia, but added hastily that he was proven innocent. Questioned about her husband, whether confused, lying in defense, misquoted, or thinking wishfully, Julia answered that Elisha Floyd had died last Christmas.

Before the inquisition could continue, there was a pounding at the locked hall door. District Attorney Garland and Judge Pavy were admitted, along with a gust of fresh air. Taking stock of the room and its occupants, Garland and Pavy quickly surmised the basics of what they had missed. They were livid, both at the secrecy of the test and the fact that Lewis had chosen to proceed without them. In addition to legal and ethical ramifications, for Pavy at least, there was the matter of human decency, which the committee seemed to have forgotten. Barely able to sit upright, the Anderson woman was shattered. And yet, even after they had put a halt to the brutal "tests," here the men were, still assaulting her with questions.

Just as Julia, in her repetitive spiral of babble to the boys, had been provoked by a need to recognize her son fully and to convince the committee of her recognition, the committee itself had been waging an unremitting campaign to convince itself, the public, and the woman herself that none of these boys was Bruce. Both Julia and the men were locked in an impossible battle to vanquish doubt.

Even when Pavy intervened, urging Julia to rest so that she could examine the child in question with a clear head, she resisted. She could not rest, she said. She wanted this thing settled now. But while that statement appeared to be a gauntlet thrown down before the committee, what came next was wholly different. One paper quoted her at length:

> This is the hardest thing I ever had to do, but it's been so long since I seen my Bruce that I can't take a look at a boy and say . . . There were no marks on my boy—not a blemish. He had two moles, as I remember, but his little toes were all straight . . . I must find my Bruce. I can't get no rest till I do.

At this, the men in the room pounced. They fell all over themselves with offers of aid and information, anything so that she could find her son. Without knowing it, Julia had surrendered. She had been gracious or weary enough to entertain, for a moment, their hypothesis that her child was still missing. It was a room half full of lawyers, and a moment was all they needed.

As soon as they all started talking, she realized what had happened. She started sobbing again.

Then Mrs. Dunbar entered the room, unannounced, the boy in question clutched in her arms. Julia looked up; the parlor went silent. Evidently, Lessie had been listening from the hall, a mute, unseen witness for the entire afternoon. And the test, unrelentingly inconclusive, had ravaged her almost as brutally as it had Julia.

Lessie leaned against a table to keep herself steady, and spoke. According to one report, her words were these: "Madam, this is my child, and I am its mother."

Julia searched Mrs. Dunbar's eyes.

But Lessie remained defiant. "I am Mrs. Dunbar. You have failed to identify him, and he is mine. Mine!"

Julia recoiled and grasped for the truth that she knew. She cried out for the boy in Lessie's arms. "Bruce," she begged over and over again. He held tight to Lessie and ignored her.

She pled for more time to coax the boy to remember her, bemoaning what she read to be his conscious, adamant rejection. "He won't recognize me one little bit."

Horrified at the turn of events, Judge Pavy, a towering and heavyset man, dropped to his knees—"forgetting his judicial dignity for the nonce"—to cajole the boy out of Lessie's arms. To ease him into more casual play with Julia, Pavy encouraged the boy to fill the rubber ball with water. Julia crouched to face the child as well. The committee stepped back, silenced and sidelined. Julia implored the boy as she had so many times already. For the judge, she recited all his qualities and features yet again.

Having heard Julia's wavering from the hall, Percy reentered. He suggested there were leads from his search for Bobby that might be helpful in Julia's quest for Bruce: letters, telegrams, and photos that he would be happy to share.

Then Julia turned to both Dunbars directly and assured them that she did not want to take their child; that she wanted only her Bruce. She alluded to Lessie's own initial doubts—"Your child has only been gone eight months, and you all ought to know it." So it would be only fair, she insisted, that she have some time with the boy herself, as they had.

But the accusation that she had not known her son proved too much for Lessie to take. She gathered up her Bobby and whisked him away, out of the parlor, out of the house, into a car, and home.

It was over.

Judge Pavy cleared the room. Then he and Garland sat down to speak with Julia directly. This was no longer an inquisition, and she gathered enough courage to ask the judge for another chance to see the child.

Mr. Lewis, the mastermind of the debacle, took this opportunity to rush out. He felt his task was complete, he would sputter a year later, and had outstanding court work in New Iberia. Edmonds had apparently dashed out to file his story, and before he returned, Mrs. Lewis would recall that she was alone with Julia in the house, during which time the two women spoke of the test. The details of this conversation would be a source of great contention.

By late afternoon, Pavy and Garland were calling on Julia at Florence Lass's boardinghouse, where Edmonds had found her a room. She would be given another chance, the judge and attorney assured her.

She was heard sobbing in her room throughout the night.

Chapter 9

SOLOMON WOULD HAVE SETTLED IT IN NO TIME.

T. A. Byrne, New Orleans *Daily Picayune*, May 4, 1913

IN THE MOST optimistic moments of her sleeplessness, Julia imagined that Bruce had not recognized her. It had been fifteen months, after all, and he was only a little boy, and the Dunbars had been calling him Bobby, filling his head with the idea that he was Bobby, for two solid weeks. She convinced herself that, by morning, without the other boys or the trickery, she could find a way to make him know her. Getting the Dunbars and the doctors and the lawyers to see it—that was another challenge altogether. But with Bruce, at least some small part of Bruce on her side, it might be possible.

Then there were the darker thoughts. She fixed her memory on the flickers of recognition that she thought she had seen, the traces of Bruce, in his clapping caper with the orange, in the way that he had eyed her sidelong, holding the ball, as she wept. He had known her in those moments. And yet he had hidden his knowing.

May 2, 1913

WHEN JULIA CAME downstairs at six thirty, Judge Pavy, District Attorney Garland, and the reporters were all waiting in the lobby. She steeled herself, told them she had slept well, and ate as much of her breakfast as she could. Then they all hurried the few blocks down Union Street to the Dunbar house. Fortunately, the crowds that had mobbed the streets the day before were still asleep.

Rather than entering the home, the men ferried Julia into the yard of a Dunbar neighbor, their family physician Dr. J. A. Haas. Here, they crowded into a garage with a small side window that looked out, through a hedge of roses, onto the Dunbars' yard next door. Julia pulled up a chair for herself, sat at the window with her hand against her cheek, and waited.

Percy and Lessie Dunbar knew they were there; Judge Pavy had alerted them that Julia should have a second chance, and they had had little choice but to agree.

Someone led the older boy out into the yard, along with his new pet goat, a welcome home present named Billy. Little Alonzo followed. The older boy, in his brand-new starched white rompers, tugged roughly at the rope around the goat's neck, then shoved the animal backward, humming a little tune.

Through the garage window, Julia studied his movements and features, again trying to join the image of this boy with her fifteen-month-old memory of Bruce.

From the Dunbars' porch, Lessie watched, too, pale and fraught. Standing at the front gate, Percy kept his own gaze fixed, whittling a wooden shingle to calm his nerves. For several minutes, the scene went on, the only sounds the boy's humming, the goat's weary bleat, and the steady rhythm of Percy's knife against wood.

Then someone in the garage coughed, and Alonzo spotted the faces through the hedge. "Hello!" he cried out. Julia smiled back feebly, bringing a handkerchief to her eyes.

Finally, she turned to the men behind her. She was ready. She asked them to bring the boy in so she could see him more closely.

"Which one?" retorted the St. Landry prosecutor.

They were still trying to trick her. "The one with the goat," she shot back.

There was a quick communication between the men in the garage and Percy Dunbar, who then nodded his assent to his cousin Harold

Fox. When Fox pulled the boy away from his goat and lifted him onto his shoulders, he didn't fight. En masse, the participants relocated to Dr. Haas's office next door, with Fox and the boy entering from one door and Julia from another.

As soon as she faced him, she raised her arms instinctively. "Come."

But the boy froze. According to the *States,* he tucked his head behind Mr. Fox's shoulder and yanked his hands behind his back. According to the *Item,* he laughed. No matter how he reacted precisely, his intentions were clear.

Sharp and sudden, the rejection took Julia's breath away.

She tried again, with more words of coaxing. But he still refused her.

Julia fought back tears. The possibility she had agonized over all night was now coming true. But she could not break down again; that would be the end of her. So she switched tactics: if she couldn't find her proof in his behavior, then she would find it on his body. She asked that the boy be taken into the doctor's inner office. Fox complied, and all the men shuffled in after her, watching mutely.

Fox sat the boy on the table, still holding him in his arms. According to the *Item,* "First the shoulders were bared. Then the little body." But when the boy felt her big gentle hands on the buttons of his rompers, by the *States'* account, he howled in protest. She managed to calm him, and soon he was naked from the waist up.

Julia stood back and took in his "fat, clean little body," looking for some distinctive mark that might trigger a memory. Hitting on a possibility, she reached in and pulled back his pants. There it was, she told the men: a mole on his left hip that she recalled.

The men appeared unimpressed.

So she moved on to the feet, which she knew had been the source of speculation and gossip for weeks. Pulling off the boy's shoes and white silk stockings, Julia had no clear idea of what she would see, or what she was supposed to be looking for.

Nonetheless, she studied the feet for a long while. The boy and the men watched her. As she would report momentarily to the *Times-Democrat,* the boy's toes "don't look to me like as they was anything the matter with them," save a sore on the left big toe from "wearing shoes what was too short for him."

This was how it was with the rest of him, too. There were markings and features, but none distinctive or decisive. She knew he was Bruce, but not by recognizing isolated parts of his body and patches of his skin.

And yet she knew that this was what they expected of her. She reached down and removed her own shoe and stocking, then pointed from her foot to the boy's and asked if the men did not see the resemblance. She did the same with their eyes. The "jury" looked from the woman to the boy again, and remained mute.

Julia was exasperated. They had sucked her into this same ploy yesterday and she would not let it happen again. Finally, she stepped back with the stocking dangling from her fingers, and announced, "Gentlemen . . . I believe from the bottom of my heart that this is my child."

The men absorbed her proclamation. Then prosecutor Garland shot back the expected question. "What proof" had she found on his body? Had she found any particular markings?

Julia shook her head no. She would not pretend that she had. Rather, she insisted, "[H]is actions and his general features are like Bruce's."

A question was lobbed from the crowd: "What about the scar on his foot?"

"Well, there ain't none big enough to recognize," the Associated Press quoted her as saying. "They are all little marks that might have been made by boils or scratches after he left me." It was a sound point: Bruce had been out of her care and in a wagon on the open road, where any number of minor accidents could have left their marks on his body.

From the back of the room, Percy Dunbar cleared his throat and challenged, "How about the mole behind his ear?"

Julia squinted over at Mr. Dunbar, his face tight with indignation. He wanted to know about a single tiny, well-hidden dot on the boy's skin. But she knew well enough that she would get nowhere challenging this hometown father in a room full of his friends and peers. She hadn't noticed the mole, she stammered; she hadn't looked for it.

Taking a cue from Percy's question, Judge Pavy reminded Julia that, unlike scars, moles were marks of *birth*. Further, he opined with a lawyer's talent for reductionist deduction, Julia had declared earlier that her boy tended to stay close to her side; on the contrary, this boy couldn't seem to sit still.

Any number of possible rebuttals crossed Julia's mind, but this man was a judge. How could she challenge a judge?

Julia turned to the boy himself—to the effort of coaxing Bruce out of his shell, finding some spark of recognition or hitting upon a shared memory. In what was fast becoming a repeat of the previous night's ordeal, she called him "Bruce" over and over again, reminded him of his sister, Bernice, and friends and relatives back home in North Carolina. She reached to take him in her arms.

The boy resisted. In the *Times-Democrat's* phrasing, "He turned a deaf ear repeatedly to her entreaties." In the *States* dispatch, "He made no sign of remembering the name." Painting a more overtly cruel picture, the *Item* reported that he "smiled and kicked," and the *Pic* observed that he "fought her and tried to get away, and would say nothing to show that he knew her or liked her in the least."

Like Julia herself, every curious reporter crammed into the little office was studying the boy's behavior and expressions for a glimmer of insight into his head and heart, and, of course, a decisive clue as to his identity. Most newsmen would opt to take the boy's actions at face value: he had rebuffed Julia Anderson because she was a stranger to him; therefore, he was likely Bobby Dunbar.

But their reports of his rejection offered another clue, one to which Julia herself was certainly attuned. The dominant commonality in all the descriptions was a sense of *determination* in the boy's spurning, a stark contrast to his tentative confusion and outbursts of friendliness the night before. An erasure of nuance. And the boy's guard was not up solely against Julia Anderson, either. It was up against the reporters themselves.

According to the *Item,* the boy begged Mr. Fox, "Come on, partner, let's go," and left Julia in tears for the second day in a row.

"There is one thing certain," Percy Dunbar told the *Times-Democrat* after Julia was taken back to her rooming house. "This is the last time my child is going to be examined. I am tired of this foolishness." The boy was his, and he would never relinquish him, "court or no court." As for Julia's child, who he insisted was still missing in Mississippi, Percy announced that he had already followed up on last night's offer to help with open leads from his own search. By the *Item's* estimation, though, the efforts seemed cursory and the clues "meager." According to the *States,* Percy returned to whittling on the porch, and as he listened to his wife insist that she would never let the boy go, regardless of what Julia Anderson said, he became downright menacing. With "a sinister light in his eyes," Mr. Dunbar interjected, "Somebody . . . is going to get their head shot off if this doesn't stop."

Most of Opelousas seemed to share the Dunbars' volatile exasperation. After last night's news of Julia's request for a "redo," impatience among the men in town had been running high, and there were even rumors that Julia had been threatened with violence. There was, and would always be, disagreement over this point. According to the *Pic*, Julia explicitly denied receiving any physical intimidation in a statement that revealed volumes: "I wasn't afraid that they would hurt me. Why should I have been afraid? No man would hit a woman when there is another man around." But in just two months, from a safe distance, Julia herself would write that unnamed Opelousans had threatened to kill her if she claimed the child, and she would repeat that for the rest of her life. Unquestionably, local sentiment was hostile to the "other mother," and she felt it. Running alongside the town's animosity was civic indignation, a defensive denial that Julia had been ill-treated in any way. That charge of mishandling, however, would only grow louder as yesterday's papers rolled in and the day wore on. Not a moment too soon, Julia's *Item* escort rushed her out of her rooming house and off to the depot, with his competitors right behind them.

Between the carriage and the train, Julia encountered a rare cluster of friendly faces: a group of local women who appeared sympathetic to her plight. "[T]hey broke the ostracism to which she has been subjected and introduced themselves and talked with her," Tisdale of the *States* reported. "Their names should be remembered, but they would not give them."

On the ride back to New Orleans, reporters mobbed Julia with questions. The "other mother" repeated her insistence that, while she did not claim to have "proof" in the form of specific traits that the boy was hers, "my heart says he's mine." When pressed, she mentioned that the boy had Bruce's cowlick, and she compared photographs of herself and the boy for the crowd. Near Harahan, a belligerent man approached to debate the matter of the boy's recognition, or lack thereof, and Julia grew upset. "It ain't natural fer him to know me with them all around and him not seeing me fer nigh on two year" was the *Times-Democrat's* phonetic quote of her retort. "Ef I could git with him for a spell, I bet he'd know me some." By the end of the trip, the crowd appeared to have grown sympathetic, and most of the reporters had become impressed with her conviction. Julia Anderson might be mistaken, but she was honest.

Arriving in New Orleans at around five thirty, Edmonds cleared a path through the inevitable crowd and ushered Julia into a taxi, hurrying her off to a nearby rooming house on the corner of Howard Avenue and Baronne Street. Reporters followed, grilling her about her next move, but she was too worn out to talk anymore.

In truth, Julia was not sure about her next move. For the past two days, she and everyone had expected her to go on now to Columbia to see Walters and meet with Dale and Rawls. But she was on the *Item*'s dime, so it was not her decision. Over the course of the trip to and from Opelousas, Edmonds's attitude toward her had shifted, Julia could tell, but she wasn't sure what to make of it. Someone from the paper would escort her down to the *Item* in the morning, he told her, and they would work things out then.

With the Friday-night city alive all around her, Julia lay awake again. "I tried to sleep, but just couldn't," she would recall to the *Item* the next day. "That baby face was before me; I heard his laugh, his cries. Oh, man. I wanted him." Replaying the events of Friday morning, her second encounter with the boy, Julia's mind snagged on his reaction. "[D]idn't his laugh seem queer?" she asked the next day. "Don't you think there was just a bit of recognition? It came to me so strong that I wanted to get him and run away."

FOR ALL THEIR rivalries and squabbling, the four dailies had been in agreement on Julia's first identification, at least in their headlines: "Anderson Woman Says Dunbar Lad Is Not Her Boy," "Fails After Repeated Tests to Recognize 'Bobbie' as Offspring," "By Her Decision, the Boy Remains as Robert Dunbar Jr.," and, typical of the *Item,* "Opelousas Half-Frenzied in Gratification, Joins Parents in Praising This Paper's Act." Julia had failed, plain and simple, the bold print barked.

But by the next day, in covering the "revision" of her identification, schisms opened up, the most gaping between the two afternoon dailies, the *States* and the *Item*. Central to all of the *States*' May 2 coverage—F. S. Tisdale's reportage, two editorials, and an interview with Thomas H. Agnew, superintendent of the Louisiana Society for the Prevention of Cruelty to Children—was an attack on the unfairness of the proceedings to Julia Anderson. The paper's indignation sprung more from being sidelined by its afternoon rival than from any principled sense of justice, but its defense of Julia was spirited and compelling nonetheless. All Agnew had to do was state the plain facts:

> From all indications . . . the woman was in a terrible state of mind when brought before the child. In the room with her were friends of the Dunbars, the Dunbar family, and paid attorneys of

the Dunbars. She had heard that she might expect violence if she claimed the child . . . The woman had traveled all night and was forced to choose from a group of children an infant she has not seen for some time.

Both the *Item* and the *States* weighed Julia's two identifications against those of Lessie Dunbar, noting the striking parallels but coming down on different sides of the issue of credibility. In its editorial, the *States* urged that the two mothers' reactions be judged as equivalent in both their doubt and certainty:

> To accept the fact that the child, be he Bruce Anderson or Robert Dunbar, repulsed [Julia's] pleading advances as conclusive evidence that he isn't hers is to forget that the same scene occurred when Mrs. Dunbar, a week before, went to Deputy Sheriff Wallace's home at Columbia. To dismiss her more reasonable opinion, 'I believe he is my boy,' expressed Friday, when, after a refreshing night's rest, she saw the child stripped, is to be utterly unfair.

Agnew—who had made no secret of his certainty that the boy was Bruce Anderson—observed pointedly that Mrs. Dunbar expressed doubt and hesitation with only *one* child to choose from.

The *Item*'s editorial, bemoaning the boy's lack of familiarity with either mother, nonetheless found Mrs. Dunbar's identification to be "much more positive." And, based on his own eyewitness accounts, James Edmonds voiced a surprising reversal of opinion: on the trip up, he had been convinced that the boy was Julia's. But after her initial Thursday "failure," Edmonds concluded, Julia "was self-hypnotized in the hours of her weakness . . . by her own aching, yearning for the recovery of her own son." Mistaken, but honestly so, deluding herself into recognition. While unkind, the latter observation made sense from a psychological perspective. And yet neither the *Item* nor any other paper dared suggest that the same diagnosis—maternal self-delusion—could be applied just as easily to Mrs. Dunbar.

Both afternoon dailies grappled with the implications of each likely possible reality: that the boy was Bobby or Bruce. The *States'* questions for the Dunbar side were far thornier than those for the Anderson side:

Suppose, for purposes of argument, that the boy is Robert Dunbar Jr.?

Answer these:

Where is Bruce Anderson? Why, if he had Robert in his possession, didn't Walters get out of this part of the country when he had a chance?

Why did he send Julia Anderson a picture of Robert Dunbar Jr.?

Why didn't Mrs. Dunbar identify the child as soon as she saw him?

If Bruce Anderson still is alive, and is not the boy at Opelousas, why hasn't some evidence turned up to show who has him now?

The *States* only glancingly considered the alternate hypothesis—Bruce's murder or accidental death—as improbabilities. Edmonds and the *Item* embraced them with open arms:

> Somewhere, somehow, Charles Bruce Anderson may have left Walters's company. A child-hungry family may have bought him from the tinker. He may have died. In a fit of the drunken rage which Julia Anderson has said Walters sometimes brought upon himself, the lad may have been killed.
>
> Cantwell Walters may have seen [Robert Dunbar], wandering about the picnic grounds, on the railroad, or perhaps in the hands of someone else who had picked him up. Walters may have noted . . . the general likeness of the lad to the one he had lost, and for which he would have to account to Julia Anderson, whom he had avoided and to whom he had not written for months. He may have felt the need for another little winner of kindness on his journeying.

Though the *States* and the *Item* would continue to stake out opposite positions as the case progressed, there was a limit to how far the *States* would take its pro-Walters stance: as much as it objected to Julia's treatment, Robert Ewing's daily was squeamish, if not revolted, when it came to the matter of her character. One of its editorials was entitled "Julia Has Forgotten":

> Animals don't forget, but this big, coarse country woman, several times a mother—she forgot. She cared little for her young. Children were only regrettable incidents in her life.
>
> There is no doubt that she is honest. She wants to help the

authorities. She wants to find her son, Bruce Anderson, but it is only a mild desire. She hopes her son isn't dead just as she hopes that the cotton crop will be good this year. Of true mother love, she has none.

Another *States* editorial suggested that, no matter the boy's true identity, Julia was as undeserving of custody as the prisoner: "No one, we are sure, would like to see an outcome that would take this child from a pleasant home and send him back to the wretched care of the old tinker or the poverty stricken and unmotherly woman of the mountains."

In its dismissal of Julia, the *States* was not alone. "The woman's mission is ended," the *Pic* spat, giving voice to a mob of disgusted citizenry eager to hustle the other mother offstage and back to North Carolina.

The boy was not her son. She was just an ancillary tragedy.

May 3, 1913

ON SATURDAY MORNING, Ethel Hutson greeted Julia at her New Orleans rooming house and walked her down to the *Item* office by way of St. Charles and Canal. Crowds recognized her as they went, with a cluster of boys straggling behind. Marshall Ballard usually left for Bay St. Louis, Mississippi, early on Saturday afternoons, so if he was in the office at all when the women arrived, he was itching to leave. Or he may have preferred to depart early, relegating to an underling the nasty job of delivering the news to Julia.

She would not be going to Columbia. The *Item* would cover her return trip and her expenses in New Orleans until her train left that day, and that was it.

Of course, Ballard needed to sugar up his decision, not just to Julia but also to readers. So on that Saturday morning, he dispatched George Benz, who had delivered a colorful account of his early-morning train ride from Mississippi with the Dunbars. Show the poor countrywoman around the big city, Ballard instructed Benz, and keep it light.

Julia would later reportedly write, "The *Item* newspaper would not let me go to Mississippi," which suggests there was argument over the matter. Benz's account failed to mention any reaction from Julia to the news at all, and even made the absurd claim that she was so dazzled by the sights, sounds, and tastes of New Orleans—along with an unlimited expense account—that she forgot about Bruce altogether.

The first activity that Saturday was a tour of the *Item*'s plant. According to Benz, Julia wasn't much interested in the administrative side of the operation. "[S]he wanted to see something that made a noise."

In the composing room, she gaped as the fingers of the Linotype operator darted across the board of blue, black, and white keys. Inside the giant Linotype machine, each tap triggered the drop of a matrix—a wee bar of metal with a single raised character on one edge. Thirteen matrices dropped, side by side, to form two words, with a single thin spaceband wedged between. They looked like a row of silver teeth. Once the line was complete, the operator pressed a lever, and the teeth rose up to align with a mold, into which a burst of molten lead was injected. The slug was cast. And a few seconds later, it was in the operator's hands. It was a standard prank to casually offer a scorching-hot slug to plant visitors, who invariably recoiled in shock and pain. Once the slug in Julia's palm had cooled, she was able to study it. Backward, it read: Julia Anderson.

Each slug was a headline or a line of type, the operator explained as he worked the machine. And once all the lines were stacked, spaced, and justified—into paragraphs, columns, and whole pages—the printing began. Once they had done their job, the slugs were melted back down into meaningless liquid, skimmed of dross, then re-formed into new slugs. New little pieces of the next day's story.

Seven more identical slugs had now been cast for Julia to take to the folks back home. Then, on with the tour: "Like a child," Benz observed, "she wanted to see more": from the stereotyping room, where she "leaned over machines, got hit in the face with bits of lead that rain from a reamer," to the press room, where she was given some choice *Item* clippings and a photo of herself.

After that, they headed out into New Orleans. On a ferry across the Mississippi, yellow and frothing from April's flood, Julia shuddered at the tangles of timber bursting up all around them. She bought a heap of molasses candy from a vendor and sucked it on the streetcar out to City Park. A quick rest back at the boardinghouse, and Benz hurried Julia off to the train, wearied, he would recall, by her incessant chattering. "I want you to know Julia Anderson ain't what she's painted by man," she told him as she boarded, "and God help you all."

Before the train had even crossed state lines, the buzz of molasses candy wore off. For the past four days of scrutiny and judgment, Julia had been anxious to retreat. But now that she was finally out of the public eye, alone with herself and headed back home, she wondered if she should have tried to stay, to make more of a fight, then and there, for Bruce. She reckoned with what was ahead: all the questions, how she would answer, more scorn from people in town. She worried over facing the Walters family. She wondered if she would still have her job at the Lawsons'. Her life had changed now in a way that it had never before. And all she had to show for it were some half-wrong newspaper clippings and a photo of herself, dandruff of lead shavings in her scalp, and eight dumb souvenir name slugs that weighted down her purse. All the other "Julia Andersons" had been melted back down.

Chapter 10

```
◆◆◆◆◆◆◆◆◆◆◆◆◆◆◆◆◆◆◆◆◆◆◆◆◆◆◆◆◆◆◆◆◆

  RAPIDES THEATER
  "The Most For A Dime All The Time."
  ─────────────────────────────────────
              TONIGHT
  BOBBY'S BABY (Drama)..........................Rex
  GOING FOR FATHER (Comedy).....................Eclair
  THE OCTOPUS (Comedy)..........................Eclair
  THE WHITE MAN'S FIREWATER.....................Nestor
           In Addition To Our Regular Programme
          We Will Give You Twenty-one Scenes Of

  THE   GREAT   DUNBAR   KIDNAPING   AT
               OPELOUSAS, LA.

                 FRIDAY
  ANIMATED WEEKLY
  AUNT KATY'S MISTAKE (Comedy)..................Imp
  PURE GOLD AND DROSS (Drama)...................Rex

                SATURDAY
  THE KNIGHTS OF RHODES.....Big Three Reel Ambrosia Feature

  10c ──────── NO  ADVANCE IN PRICES ──────── 10c

  WHEN YOU THINK OF PICTURES, THINK OF
         THE RAPIDES THEATRE
◆◆◆◆◆◆◆◆◆◆◆◆◆◆◆◆◆◆◆◆◆◆◆◆◆◆◆◆◆◆◆◆◆
```

Advertisement, Alexandria *Daily Town Talk,* May 8, 1913

ON MAY 3, 1913, political scandal erupted in Mississippi. After a months-long covert investigation, involving trips to England and a campaign of surveillance by Dan Lehon and the Burns Detective Agency, Governor Brewer ordered the arrest of the secretary of the board of prisons for massive embezzlement of profits from the penitentiary's cotton crop.

Before he and Lehon headed out to Parchman Farm to scour the prison's records, Brewer took stock of a far more trivial crisis: the Dunbar affair. Dale and Rawls, irate at the unfairness of Julia Anderson's test in Opelousas, asked the governor to insist that the Dunbars return to Mississippi with the child so that their Pearl River witnesses could finally see him. Barring that long-shot proposition, they asked for the governor's blessing in bringing their witnesses to New Orleans or Opelousas. Brewer approved of the plan, and although he assured the attorneys that he would take no action on the requisition before hearing their side, he stressed that he wanted the matter settled speedily.

When Dale suggested the plan to District Attorney Garland in Opelousas and received no response, he called his opponents' bluff—intimating that the Opelousans were not "sincere in their desire to solve the mystery"—and threatened to file for a writ of habeas corpus to have Walters released. Garland wired back tout de suite, "Will arrange for examination of Robert in New Orleans. Can't fix date. Will wire when."

As many in Opelousas saw it, solving the mystery was not as simple as letting the Bilbos and their neighbors see the boy. To Percy Dunbar especially, it seemed preposterous that Brewer would give so much weight to these few witnesses, when—as a glance at the past weeks' headlines would attest—dozens of others, from Louisiana and Mississippi, had come forward to challenge, if not shatter, Walters's emerging alibi. If Walters's witnesses were to be heard, so should St. Landry's. On May 5, the parish police jury voted to reappropriate $500 from its funds for witnesses and jurors to Garland for "gathering together the evidence necessary to be presented to the governor of Mississippi." The leaders of St. Landry were united behind the prosecution and around the Dunbars.

R. Lee Garland harkened from a long line of lawyers, including two grandfathers who served together on the state supreme court. As of 1913, he had been a prosecutor for seventeen years, well on his way to establishing, alongside Judge Benjamin Pavy, one of St. Landry's most enduring political dynasties. One memoirist recalled seeing Garland on the courthouse square, carrying on two simultaneous conversations in French and English, and on Sunday mornings, sharing drinks with Sheriff Swords (whom he otherwise abhorred) while standing back-to-back so that neither could—literally—observe the other's violation of the liquor law. A decade later, in a retrospective profile, Garland would recall that the Dunbar case was one of the most important of his career. And that it began shrouded in doubt: "Was it Bobby Dunbar who had been returned after all? The mother said it was, and that satisfied Garland."

But the prosecutor needed proof, of course, the most important being evidence to pin the criminal to the crime scene. Just after Walters's arrest, Percy had reported that his uncle Preston King had spotted a lame tramp on the tracks by Swayze Lake on the Sunday after Bobby went missing, and would easily recognize Walters as that man. But King's identification never happened, perhaps because he and Estorge left Jackson with no signed requisition to retrieve Walters from Columbia. But there is another likely reason why King's sighting had not been mentioned in the intervening weeks: in December, he had said that he saw *two* tramps near Swayze Lake *before* Bobby went missing, an encounter that was the basis for his failed attempt to identify the Marshall brothers. No matter that they could have been two different sightings, a shrewd lawyer like Garland would have been skeptical.

There were plenty of other local witnesses to consider, but before Garland took action on any lead at all, before the police jury even signed off on funding, Percy Dunbar seized the reins of the investigation himself. Leaving the prosecutor baffled, if not vexed, he traveled northwest to Alexandria and nearby Grant Parish. Here, citizens had come forward to righteously challenge a key tenet of Walters's early rumored alibi: the claim that, save his trip to New Orleans's Charity Hospital, he had never spent time in Louisiana in his life. These witnesses remembered Walters well, they had told the papers, and when Percy arrived, they told him in person. But if he had waited a day, he may have reconsidered the trip. On May 5 the *States* and the *Times-Democrat* published a lengthy chronicle of Walters's life in Louisiana, from 1907 to 1911, *as told by Walters himself*. He freely admitted to being in the state—he'd worked in a blacksmith shop and as a ferryman, he'd shattered his knee and been hospitalized—just not during this last year, when Bruce Anderson was in his custody. But like every lead that Percy poked at and stirred up, these witnesses were not done swarming and stinging.

In an apt coincidence, during Percy's stay in Alexandria, a local theater featured an extended run of *The Great Dunbar Kidnapping at Opelousas,* a twenty-one-scene newsreel. In the unlikely event that residents had wearied of the case, the moving picture, combined with the publicity of Percy's investigation, revived the thrill.

IN THE PRIVACY of their home, the Dunbars searched for clues to the boy's alleged abduction in his own memory. In late April, Percy and Lessie reported to the *Times-Democrat* a remarkable pair of spontaneous utterances by the child. While playing with Alonzo, he said "almost without any suggestion, 'A big man took me from the lake that day.'" His parents leapt at the statement and tried to draw out more detail, but the boy went mute. The next day, when Lessie refused his plea for a banana, he reportedly shot back, "My other papa found me on a railroad track. He was good to me, and I like him; he bought me some bananas and other goodies." Even taking into account the newspapers' penchant for cleaning up quotes, it was an odd response: a child's ploy to garner one adult's sympathy by playing her off another, awkwardly affixed to the offering of a detail he knew to be much coveted. Percy tried to follow up, this time opting for an "indirect" approach, but again the boy shut down.

On the Sunday evening after Percy's departure to Alexandria, the memory project continued. This time, when Lessie and a group of relatives circled back to the circumstances of Bobby's disappearance, instead of going silent, he began to link the fleeting recollections into a larger, cause-and-effect chain. "He said he had been picked up on a high railroad bridge and taken to some strange place," Lessie reported to the *Item* the next day, and "that he had cried when the man started to take off the rompers he was wearing and dressed him up in little trousers and a jacket. The only reason he submitted to the change," Lessie repeated his explanation, "was that he had been promised 'a heap of goodies.'" When asked if he ever tried to flee, the boy answered that he was afraid and that "always when he cried, he was promised more candy or bananas."

Changing clothes, now, was the event that linked tracks and treats. The purpose of the treat giving became more sinister: no longer just a salve for a crying child but now also a tool for silencing. And the fleetingly voiced affection for "Other Papa" had been supplanted fully by fear. Lessie was careful to note that Bobby was not coached "in filling out details or main points," but rather just responding to the adults' questions. The filling out he was now doing on his own.

And the very next day, it continued. As chronicled in the *Clarion*:

> Monday morning little Bobbie was telling his mother how he had cried when his ugly papa had taken his nice hat and suit off to put on some dirty clothes. After having ridden in a dirty freight train for a long ways he was taken out, when his clothes were changed and Walters promised him something good if he would cease his crying.

The mystery of the straw hat was solved, but beyond that, the boy now recalled multiple and repeated wardrobe changes. While he offered no more details on the "strange place" he had been taken, he did clarify the means and length of travel. And he enunciated a key quality of his ordeal: it had been dirty.

The boy also offered more pleasant recollections from his life before August 23. He recognized a vegetable peddler to be Carlo, their former ice man. He pointed out relatives in pictures on the wall. He remembered the goldfish in the courthouse square fountain, and by a cousin's account, he had even fallen in again. He called up Percy on the phone, one of his favorite old games, and, on April 28, finally called him "Daddy."

Another fond memory emerged during Percy's absence when Lessie and the boy braved an excursion downtown, where they were just as likely to be smiled at as whispered over. On East Landry Street, they passed by Winsberg's Clothier, Bienvenu's Drugs, then Bennett's Bargain Store, and the big horses of Dupre's Livery Stable just across the street. But it was the window of the Kandy Kitchen, a "high-class confectionary," that caught Bobby's eye and stopped him in his tracks. "Mamma, I know this place," he insisted. "I used to come here lots, long time ago."

"I HEARD THAT Bruce called Mrs. Dunbar 'Mamma,'" Walters told the listeners in his cell. "He would call any lady who was not too old 'Mamma,' and if a lady was too old, he would call her 'Grandma.' He called me 'Uncle Sam' at first, but lately he called me 'Papa.'"

For days now, reporters for the *Item*'s competitors had lingered in Columbia, anticipating a spark-filled reunion between Walters and Julia Anderson. After her initial "failure," the prisoner had lashed out to the press that she was lying or being bribed, prompting Dale and Rawls to scuttle further interviews. But they knew that nonengagement was not an effective long-term strategy; if reporters couldn't get words out of their client's mouth, they would put them in. So on Saturday, May 3, they ushered the most sympathetic journalist into the cell for a heavily stage-managed question-and-answer session. Young A. J. McMullen of the *States* did not disappoint. The first sentence of the "first authorized" interview with William Walters careened an inch shy of propaganda:

> When Walters was interrupted today to be given an opportunity to tell his story through the *States,* he had just laid aside his Bible and was engaged in writing a story of his wanderings that he is preparing for posthumous publication in the event of an untimely end to his declining years.

The most crucial task at hand was for Walters to walk the reporter through his movements during the summer of 1912. For this he was well prepared, wielding a sheaf of papers—letters, notes he had made for himself, loose receipts for work he had performed—to corroborate his chronology:

> On the third Saturday in July last . . . I was at Jeptha Bilbo's . . . with little Bruce. I fixed the Ford's Creek church organ and old grandfather clock. A few days later, I went to Charlie Myley's and did some repair work for him. On learning that measles had broken out there, I left Bruce with the Bilbos for about a week.

As to where he'd been in late August 1912, Walters replied that on the twentieth he had been in McNeill, Mississippi, where he had received a package at the post office, and expressed another to Reverend Meeks in New Augusta, Mississippi. When Walters reached the infamous August 23, McMullen cued his readers, "The little group that was gathered listened keenly to this part of his narrative":

> The morning of August 23, last year I went to young Mr. [J. S.] Thigpen's, who lives near the Whitesand church . . . I stayed there all day on August 23, 1912, and Bruce Anderson was with me. Also that night, which was Friday, I spent at Mr. Thigpen's [home]. Sunday I went to church with Bruce Anderson, and through part of the service I remained outside, where I could rest my knee, which had been giving me trouble. Several people talked to me and to little Bruce, who, by the way, was having the time of his life, as he did everywhere.

Leaving Bruce with the Bilbos in early September, Walters checked into New Orleans's Charity Hospital—bed 969, ward 69—under the care of Dr. Payne. Here, he said, "[T]hey found out I could play the zither harp, and they had me play for the patients. I like to play for the children, especially for those who had no one to look after them, for it made me think of little Bruce, whom I love."

Venturing into thornier territory, McMullen brought up Reverend W. E. Farr's report that, when he asked Walters about the traits of the two boys, Bobbie and Bruce, Walters had replied, "I must have got 'em mixed." As it spread through Columbia, this report was adding fuel to a rising fire of speculation that Walters had, in fact, stolen *both* boys.

"I must have said they got things mixed somehow," Walters responded carefully, indicating the Dunbars, not himself. And for emphasis: "You know I cannot harness the wheels of evolution, but the boy in Opelousas, no matter what they find, is Bruce Anderson."

When McMullen produced two photos—one of Bobby Dunbar before he went missing, and another of the child taken from Walters—the prisoner cried, "Can't you see . . . that there is not one iota of favor to Mr. Dunbar's boy? . . . Look at the hair of the Dunbar child, how it is trained up. I could never get Bruce's hair to stay like that, and I tried to. I always had to part it in the middle."

Out of indignation had come something like real tenderness.

For readers still dubious, McMullen offered his own observations: that Walters did not seem criminal and was not prone to curse, was well read, and was certain he could prove his innocence. McMullen wrote an even more opinionated opening paragraph, but his editor axed it before it went to print for fear that, as McMullen told Dale and Rawls, "someone would accuse us of undue prejudice."

The very next day, McMullen and the *States* were rewarded with a second exclusive. It called for a rough and muddy drive down into western Pearl River County, much the same route that had delayed the Bilbos' arrival in Columbia by nearly a day. But Mr. Rawls and his prized automobile made it through.

Not far from Spring Hill Baptist Church, the Goleman farmhouse was less than a year old. The previous October, according to Mr. Allen Goleman, Walters and Bruce had slept there for ten days while Goleman finished construction and Walters fixed their organ and some just-moved-in furniture. Most of the family's memories of the tinker and the boy were from before that, from their old home in Poplarville. The pair had stayed with them for brief stretches periodically, and they'd seen them in town, starting in July all the way up to just eight weeks past.

Mr. Goleman had already shared his memories of the pair in a letter to the *Times-Democrat* ten days ago. Between the boy and his guardian, he had observed a distinct mutual fondness. "[W]hen Walters would start off to do some work, and when he would tell the boy to stay with us, he would beg to be allowed to go with Walters." Things were not always so pleasant between the two, though. "He whipped the child several times while at my house, but under circumstances which I thought were justifiable. I would have done the same to one of my children."

When the lawyers brought out pictures, the Goleman children, all girls except for little Willie, clustered around to look. "Li'l Bruce," three-year-old Ruby lisped at the photo of the boy in question. And the others agreed.

Mrs. Goleman rattled off her own memories. At their Poplarville home, Walters would entertain them with his music, not on their out-of-whack organ but on an instrument of his own design, one that he had been building right there on their gallery. "I hear it was to have been patented as the 'New Era Harp,' and that it has two hundred eighty-seven strings," Mrs. Goleman told McMullen. "He used to get good music out of it." As for Bruce, Mrs. Goleman had not only dressed and bathed the boy but also made him clothes. "I remember making Bruce two dresses," she said. "One was a little blue one, and they tell me he had it on when the Dunbars took him."

The sentiment was no different among the crowd at the Bilbos. "That's Bruce up and down," one ten-year-old girl said as soon as the visitors brought out the photos.

Behind a high picket fence, the Bilbo home/boardinghouse looked far larger than it really was. A tallish box cabin with a peaked roof, it was surrounded on three sides by wide galleries, covered and railed in, on both first and second floors. While the interior might have been tight, the porches offered ample room for boarders and visitors to relax and socialize. The Bilbo place was a community center of sorts; Jeptha tended the post office and every week brought mail from Poplarville by mule. The couple ran a little store that offered coal oil and other necessities for sale or barter, Matilda's glass display case filled with "rick-rack and lace," and eventually a gravity-fed gasoline pump for automobiles. On maps as late as 1931, the spot was named Bilbo.

It was here that Walters had reportedly arrived, a sleeping boy in his arms, on the night of July 19, 1912. Matilda Bilbo recalled that event well: "I know it because we were putting up fruit and also because Walters fixed the organ in our church here, Ford's Creek Church." She pointed just up the road to the little wooden building with high windows. She and Jeptha had donated land for the church a decade ago, and during the week, it doubled as a schoolhouse.

When asked about markings on the boy's body, Matilda replied, "Bruce had a black speck that looked to me something like a tick mark," although she couldn't say where. As for oddities of the toes: "It seems to me one of them kinder crooks under."

Dale volleyed a rumor for her to shoot down: "Mr. Dunbar says you will not tell the truth because Walters promised to give the boy to you."

And shoot it down she did: "Walters would not give that child to anyone, and besides, I would not have it anyway. He had a pretty rough temper, and although he was brought up to a certain point, you could not teach him anything else, leastways, I couldn't." She even offered advice for the Opelousas parents: "They will have to teach Bruce to obey the word *Don't*. If the Dunbars pet him and give him his own way, he will get the place."

Mrs. Bilbo's most significant words were gentler. Sometime during the past weeks, as she and her family were piecing together their time with Bruce and Walters, this memory had burst forth. It would be a story she would tell for the rest of her life.

It was the evening of Sunday, September 8, 1912. Walters had just left for Charity Hospital, putting Bruce in the Bilbos' full-time care. They had been out fishing all afternoon, and by the time they got home, the boy was worn out. Mrs. Bilbo's daughter brought in a New Orleans newspaper and read it aloud as they ate supper. The boy sagged into Mrs. Bilbo and finally lay all the way down on the dining room bench with his head in her lap. Her daughter zeroed in on a story about a child from Louisiana, sixteen days missing. Robert Dunbar from Opelousas. The boy's eyes were drooping, if not closed, and, as McMullen made plain, "he did not give any indication of recognition."

Back at his Columbia hotel, McMullen typed up his story and called into the office. By now his editor was sure that Julia was not on her way and wanted McMullen back in New Orleans. McMullen left a copy of the story for the attorneys, then groggily climbed aboard the early-morning train. "Say 'au revoir' to Mr. Rawls for me," the young man wrote to Dale before he left. "I enjoyed my stay here immensely, and I will be back for the trial. Keep me posted on your plans, and I will help you from our end. Scoops would be doubly appreciated."

Thus began a long and fruitful friendship between reporter and attorneys, and a powerful symbiosis between legal and circulation strategies. With these two reports—along with a compelling three-day series of photographic portraits of the Mississippi witnesses, their environs, and even the Bilbos' dog Rambler, whom Bruce adored—the *States* unabashedly staked out its editorial position on the case, and its uniqueness among the four New Orleans dailies.

IN LESS THAN a week, District Attorney Garland struck back. Out of all the letters and telegrams that had inundated his cluttered office over the past weeks, he seized upon an affidavit from McComb City, Mississippi, as his most potent weapon. Three workers for the Illinois Central Railroad alleged that on December 18, 1912, they had seen an old man in the train depot with a boy who wore red high-top boots. To a crowd, the man had identified himself as W. C. Walters, said he was a detective who had just found the Dunbar boy, and planned to return him to Opelousas for a reward, presenting a photo of Robert Dunbar that was "an exact likeness of the child he had with him, and which corresponds in every regard with the published picture of said child in the different papers." Further, the affiants noted that they had studied Walters's published photo and were certain this was the same man. "Detective" Walters had been accompanied by a man and a woman, who were "with him very familiar but with others extremely reticent."

Although any licensed lawyer would have spotted weaknesses in the document—its reliance on newspaper photos and a months-old fleeting memory, the fact that December 18, 1912, had been the feverish height of the crippled-tramp roundup—Garland saw the lead as too promising to ignore. After a hasty stop in McComb, a town seized with turbulence from a violent two-year railroad strike, he and Veazie hustled their witnesses (the original three plus two more) over to Columbia for an in-person identification of Walters.

Immediately, it devolved into a sideshow for the press, the tiny courtroom stuffed with a rowdy audience of locals; the prisoner himself in the front row; and the witnesses, ushered in one by one to pick him out of the crowd. Disgusted but resigned, Dale and Rawls tried to toughen the task of the witnesses by finding seats in the crowd for two older gents who bore a passing resemblance to their client. Nonetheless, the McComb men fingered Walters easily, and with flourish. One man greeted the prisoner with a "Howdy" and an extended hand, and when Walters shook it, the crowd hooted giddily as if on cue, and the reporters credulously scribbled that the handshake was evidence of mutual recognition. The prisoner rose to debate two other witnesses, B. L. Morgan and Joe Johnson, prompting Sheriff Hathorn to force him into silence. To be sure that Walters was the man they had all seen wearing a "big white hat," the final witness requested that a big white hat be passed forward for Walters to don.

Most reports suggested that local sentiment, having cooled from its late-April lynch fever, took a prompt shift against Walters after the identification. Though the *States* tried to buck that narrative—impugning the McComb witnesses' truthfulness and pressing them to admit that they were strikebreakers—many Columbians did not seem to care. By Tuesday morning, two hundred residents had signed a petition urging Governor Brewer to grant the requisition to send Walters to Louisiana for trial.

After the Columbia fireworks, Garland and Veazie continued their investigation with more discretion, heading southeast to interview the accusers of Hub, then down the Pearl River, and east toward Poplarville. It was the more *unofficial* investigation, tactically and financially independent of Garland's efforts, that would garner the most startling headlines. Though Percy Dunbar's New Orleans relative Harold Fox had no training in detective work, he brought other assets to his Mississippi investigations: loyalty and availability. As a traveling salesman hawking Dr. Tichenor's Antiseptic, a family business, Fox could easily make time for a pressing family cause. Then there was Lee Hawes of the *Times-Democrat,* whose hunt dovetailed with Fox's. Since the case's start, these two men had forged a quiet alliance, but so far, little of the reporting attributable to Hawes had been dramatically slanted toward the Dunbars. That would soon change.

Tethered to Columbia by a full term of circuit court, Dale and Rawls were irate at the McComb witness circus and growing more rankled daily by the incursions of Louisiana "investigators." It is no surprise that the ugly local rumor made the news.

LESSIE DUNBAR'S SANITY had long been the subject of idle speculation. And Percy would be the first to admit that her mental health had weighed on him in the past months. But the latest gossip emanating from Mississippi was by far the cruelest: during his first trip to Columbia, Percy had confessed that his family doctor had urged him to find "some child to replace his own, otherwise it would affect Mrs. Dunbar's health seriously." It was not a case of mistaken identity, borne from grief. It was a premeditated scheme of replacement.

Just as enraging to Percy as the rumor was its alleged source: a Mississippi lawyer named T. R. Willoughby, who worked with Dale and Rawls. "I denounce such statement as false, as also the inference sought to be drawn from the same," Percy telegrammed to Willoughby (and the press), "and now request the name of your authority. For your information, I add that we have our boy safe and sound at home, and while the lawyer's art might save the guilty one, it can't take him from us."

That same day, what should have been more pleasant news arrived at the house on Union Street: an invitation from the New Orleans Sunshine Society to its annual May carnival that Saturday in New Orleans, with

Bobby as guest of honor. The Sunshine Society was a well-known charity for the "sick and poor," reminded the president, Mrs. Christian Schertz, and so the "world-famous" Bobby Dunbar's attendance would be a public service of sorts. As editor of the women's desk at the *Times-Democrat*, Mrs. Schertz knew her way around publicity. She followed this letter with a report to all the dailies announcing that she had made the invitation and expected a telegram response from the Dunbars "hourly." Then came a reassurance to wary readers that this was not a "vulgar publicity" stunt: the boy would not be onstage but rather just in the audience. The real attraction was the fairy carnival itself, a musical fantasia packed with "attractive" child performers, mostly girls—a dazzling spectacle that Mrs. Schertz promised would make Bobby's "childish elfin dreams" come true.

For Lessie, the invitation was less cause to smile than to panic. She was weak from the attacks on her claim to motherhood and on her mental well-being, in the newspapers and outside her own front door. Her instinct was to shutter the windows and hunker down with the boy she knew to be her son. Percy, meanwhile, was a man of the public, and that was where he fought for his family. And after the vicious Willoughby rumor, he must have yearned to jab back at the Columbia attorneys, who had been begging him to bring the boy to New Orleans for weeks. On Friday morning, he telegrammed this to Mrs. Schertz:

> Things may shape up so that we can come down,
> to leave here Friday or Saturday morning, either
> of which would put us in town in time for the
> entertainment. Mrs. Dunbar joins me in thanking
> the Sunshine Society for the invitation, which we
> all hope to accept.

It was not a "yes," of course, and Percy advised that their attendance was based on approval from District Attorney Garland, who was currently out investigating. Depending on the newspaper, this caveat was interpreted as either a formality or a stumbling block.

There was another factor at play, mentioned in passing amid Mrs. Schertz's blitzkrieg of persuasion and publicity in the New Orleans dailies: "As the little one is to have a minor operation performed, the Sunshiners are the more hopeful that the evident desire to attend the entertainment will cause the Dunbars to make every effort to be here on the eve of the necessary operation." Both Mrs. Schertz and her husband were well-connected pharmacists, and certainly knew Percy's New Orleans relatives, which might account for her insider medical knowledge. But precisely what "necessary operation" is not known. The most obvious possibility, adenoid removal, could be performed in Opelousas, and the Dunbars' better instincts were indeed to stay home. Or perhaps, worrying that the problem was acute, they were considering a New Orleans surgeon. As late as Saturday morning, it still wasn't clear what they were going to do.

When they first read the carnival report, Dale and Rawls had found it impossible to believe that the Dunbars would even entertain such an offer. But after some digging, Rawls would write, "our man in New Orleans had absolute accurate information that the Dunbars would have the child there on Saturday afternoon." So they did just what the *Item* and others had speculated; after all, this could be their only chance for the Bilbos to see the boy. Dale bolted down to New Orleans to arrange the details ahead of time, if such a thing were even possible. Would he try to meet the Dunbars at 7031 Freret? Or would he confront the family in the crowds at the Athenaeum, the banquet hall where the carnival would take place? From Columbia, Rawls enlisted his brother in Poplarville to send a car out to collect the old couple from their farm. They were irritated by the surprise; Mrs. Bilbo was tending a litter of newborn pigs and worried that they would starve if she was gone too long. But they couldn't turn down a chance to see Bruce. The driver rushed them to Orvisburg, one stop north of Poplarville on the New Orleans and Northeastern line, and got them on the train. During its brief stop in Poplarville, Rawls's brother met them and handed them $15 for the trip.

Also waiting at the Poplarville station were "citizen detective" Harold Fox and Lee Hawes of the *Times-Democrat,* both of whom were returning to New Orleans after their investigations. Their presence on the same train as the Bilbos may or may not have been a coincidence.

A third of the way into the journey, when the train stopped at Carriere, a station worker boarded and delivered a telegram to the Bilbos. The identification was off, the telegram said; the Dunbars would not be coming, and the Bilbos should not continue to New Orleans. The sender of the telegram is not known, although it certainly was not Dale or Rawls; a day later, they would protest to the *Item* that it was the work of "wiseacres," "someone without the authority or the right to do so."

As the train pulled out, Fox watched the old couple as they trudged down the platform, grousing and shaking their heads, with Lee Hawes tagging along after them.

This was their third false start, and they were fed up. "Walters is nothing to us," Mrs. Bilbo declared gruffly as they waited for a ride back home. "We want to see the Dunbars get their child back, and I do not intend to make any decisions until I see the child itself. The moment I look into the child's face, I can say whether it is Bruce Anderson or not." When or if that moment would come was anyone's guess.

A few hours later, a miniature bride ballerina fluttered across the Athenaeum stage, accompanied by an orchestral wedding march. Her little groom awaited, and bridesmaids, groomsmen, and flower girls swirled around them, with a "Little Minister" presiding over the flock. Marriage and Sunshine Happiness, the opening dance of the pageant, was under way. Backstage, a young couple stretched and primped for their upcoming pas de deux, and "winsome" Nanon Newman, already in costume as queen of the May, silently counted five full dances to go before she was crowned in Cupid's garden. Mrs. Christian Schertz took note of the overflowing crowd: she had done her job well.

Out in the audience, those who had thought it too vulgar to inquire in the lobby tried to focus on the children onstage, but they couldn't help casting sidelong glances in search of the elusive guest of honor.

DALE AND RAWLS were livid at their scheme being sabotaged, and not a little humiliated that it had been exposed. Meanwhile, Garland was now positively skittish about bringing the child to New Orleans, doubtless because of what he perceived as the Columbia duo's underhanded maneuvering. Beyond that, he had another fear: that "some newspaper would sue out a writ of habeas in New Orleans." The concern was not over witnesses seeing the boy; it was over the threat of a legal scheme to seek custody of the boy. And the fear was not so much his as it was Lessie Dunbar's:

> [R]esponding to a fear in every mother's breast, that something may happen to her child if carried away from her home, [she] absolutely . . . refuses to remove the child out of the Parish [and] nothing short of a court order, in my opinion, could take the child from her and carry it beyond the limits of this city.

In the Dunbars' eyes, the carnival invitation had tested Dale and Rawls, whether that had been its purpose or not. And the lawyers had shown their true colors. In the face of such subterfuge, no amount of reassurance from Garland would convince them that their boy was fully safe in their custody. When word of the scheme reached Opelousas, the family hastily packed for travel.

Watching Percy stalk through the house, locking doors and shuttering windows, the boy pointed to the six-shooter in his father's fist. He wanted to know if the gun was loaded—it was—and he worried aloud that Percy should unload it so that he wouldn't hurt anyone. Percy paid him no mind, but the boy demanded to hold the gun himself. When Percy gingerly handed the pistol over, the boy broke it open and emptied the cartridges with care. Percy was startled. He told the *Times-Democrat* a few days later: "Someone had evidently taught him about a pistol."

Amid all this talk of firearms came another surprise. "He asked me," Percy recounted, "what had become of the old black gun that shot my foot off." Whether or not the subject of Percy's missing leg had come up in the past few weeks is not known. Percy's inference now was that it had not, and that this was Bobby's own memory, returning.

The family shuttled out to Percy's parents' farm, several miles outside of Opelousas on the road to Washington. Down a long driveway, the house was safe and private, an ideal refuge from neighbors, lawyers, and reporters. Awaiting them on the wide front steps were Percy's parents, Robert and Madeline, his brother Wilmer, and, bearing the widest smile of all, Percy's younger sister Katie, eager for some playtime with her beloved long-lost nephew. In Katie's care, out here on the farm, the boy's memory of his former life would continue to blossom: both the carefree childhood before August 23 and the eight-month ordeal after. "He realizes that no one will whip him if he talks," Percy told a reporter, "and he is ready to tell what he knows."

Chapter 11

Map Showing Points Received in the Evidence

Illustration, *New Orleans Item,* April 19, 1914

PERCY DID NOT linger at his parents' farm. Harold Fox and Lee Hawes returned from their Mississippi investigations with leads too explosive for him to leave to Garland alone. Though presented as independent and carried by separate papers (Fox's by the *Item,* Hawes's by the *Times-Democrat*), the two accounts were published just a day apart, and their overall conclusion was identical.

The idea had been floated since April, once Walters's alibi began to find corroboration. It was not a simple question of mistaken identity, Bobby Dunbar or Bruce Anderson. In fact, *both* boys had been in Walters's custody over the past eight months. They had been swapped, the theory went. Sometime in late August, somewhere in Pearl River County, Bobby and Bruce had been exchanged.

For June and July, it was asserted, Walters had been moving steadily westward across the county with Bruce Anderson in tow. While his behavior may have appeared innocuous, in fact, Walters was "hanging about" in wait. In late August, west of the Bilbo place at a crossing of the Pearl River known as Cameron Ferry, the man and boy had been spotted taking up residence in an abandoned house and lingering at other ferry stations downstream. To some bystanders, they just looked lost, but as Hawes and Fox concluded, they were actually staking out the river crossings, awaiting a rendezvous with "confederates" from the western bank, with another boy.

This boy was Robert Dunbar, taken by one or more kidnappers at Swayze Lake, 150 miles west. They had traveled east by boxcar, through the Atchafalaya Basin to the west bank of the Mississippi, which they had crossed in a skiff with the mulatress, and headed into Baton Rouge. From there, they came by train to Covington, then traversed "out-of-the-way roads" forty-five miles northeast all the way to Cameron Ferry.

At the end of August, after a period of nine days, a man and a boy were seen finally emerging from the abandoned house. The boy, at least, was not the same one who had entered. This was not Bruce Anderson, but Robert Dunbar.

But before the swap was complete—before Bruce Anderson vanished—both men and both boys made a showing all together in early September in a restaurant in Poplarville. Both Fox and Hawes spoke with a waitress there named Katie Collins, who recalled the near-identical appearance not just of the two boys but also of the two men. Save that one appeared crippled and the other did not, the "rough-looking" fellows were so alike that she thought they might be brothers. As she approached to take their order, Miss Collins heard one of the boys called Bruce, but when she tried to talk to him, the lame man silenced him sharply.

Upon closer scrutiny of the lookalike boys, Miss Collins detected distinctions in their appearances as well. Based on her observations and those of witnesses near Purvis, Mississippi, where Walters had been spotted earlier in the summer of 1912 (before the alleged swap), Hawes put together this portrait of the boy thought to be Bruce Anderson: "Thin hair, almost white, left shoulder drooping, forehead covered with whitish fuzz, blue eyes, deep set, complexion chalky, showing evidence of hookworm disease, legs thin, and face emaciated."

Fox's version was identical, but with more detail about the shoulder: "His left shoulder was a little lower than the other and caused him to twitch occasionally. It might have been caused by a broken bone."

As for the second boy, Hawes obtained quite the opposite description from a Carriere farmer's wife: "Its hair, she says, was light and rather thick-growing, high on its forehead, with cowlick, mole on arm and neck."

Though virtually every witness recalled both boys, before and after, as having feet covered in sores or blisters, beyond that, the toes were different. In A. J. McMullen's earlier report, Matilda Bilbo had said of Bruce that one toe "kinder crooks under." But according to both Fox (who had interviewed her in Poplarville) and Hawes (who had interviewed her just after the aborted New Orleans trip), Matilda insisted that Bruce had a distinct "web" between two of his toes.

Once again, in dramatic contrast, all of Hawes's *post*-August witnesses recalled no such formation, no such web. And the toes of the child in the Dunbars' care, Fox reminded readers, were perfectly formed, aside from traces of a scar. This was Bobby.

WHILE THE *STATES* and the Columbia attorneys were quick to mock the "swap" publicity campaign, others were not so cynical. If two boys had been exchanged and one was in Opelousas, readers concluded, the other was still missing. From Natchez and Carriere, and from as far away as Florida, came a spree of breathless sightings, as well as imminent and almost recoveries, of little Bruce Anderson, the boy who had been swapped. But Harold Fox had a better idea of where to look, and his Opelousas cousin was eager to rejoin the search.

Now that there were officially *two* boys missing, Percy's long-held theory that there was more than one kidnapper was the only possible hypothesis. So convinced of an explicit link to last fall's hunt, he wrangled in Detective Berge from Mobile to accompany him and Harold Fox on their trip to Mississippi. In December, Percy and Berge had scoured the Alabama marshland in search of crippled tramps stashing Bobby in a shack. Now their destination was an abandoned house on the Pearl River, and as for their quarry, the headlines said it all: "Dunbars Seek 'Bruce.'" "If Bruce Anderson Is Found, Mystery Will Cease."

Before they made it to the swapping place at Cameron Ferry, there were interim stops. In Picayune, they obtained an affidavit claiming insider knowledge that Walters had kidnapped Bobby for revenge. In Poplarville, they heard a rumor that Walters had $10,000 in a Tylertown bank, stolen from a train. And before an awestruck crowd, Percy speculated wildly about the gang's motives: they exchanged children not just once early on but also multiple times over the next eight months "to prove an alibi . . . in case they should be caught."

According to this theory, then, every benign sighting of the man and the boy could be explained away by another swap.

The investigators' mission brought forth more than just "clues" from the community. Soon after their arrival in Picayune, a petition drive broke out demanding that Brewer grant extradition, with hundreds of signatures gathered in just hours. In Poplarville, a "fund for the prosecution of a search for Bruce Anderson" netted $33.50 from its citizens, and Percy was granted a personal audience with the fund's most famous contributor, Lieutenant Governor Theodore Bilbo. As the *Hattiesburg News* reported, Bilbo claimed to be "manifestly reticent," while at the same time "entirely favorable to the Dunbar theory of this remarkable case." Tipping the hand of his well-known political enmity, Bilbo even "volunteered the suggestion that the Columbia citizens petition should go to Governor Brewer."

Finally, on the morning of May 21, with Sheriff James A. Moody as their chauffeur, Percy, Fox, and Berge started out on what the *Item* called "a mysterious automobile mission to the interior of the Pearl River." At Cameron Ferry, readers imagined, somewhere amid the rot and detritus of that abandoned house, somewhere in the darkness, a clue—or maybe even a boy—would be found.

But at the end of the day, the detectives returned childless. Nevertheless, they soldiered on to Hattiesburg, to the vicinity of a sighting of *another* William C. Walters, with another man and multiple children in their custody. When first reported, it had been dismissed as the wrong Walters, plain and simple. But now Percy was desperate. Perhaps one of these children was the elusive Bruce Anderson.

IN OPELOUSAS, GARLAND looked on with irritation as Mississippi was taken by storm by Percy and the "swap." After concluding his own cross-state investigation, the prosecutor had been pressed by a reporter, "Are you positive that Walters was on this side of the river and that you can prove he was in Opelousas?" Garland's reply was measured but confident: "I will come pretty close to doing so."

But the central feature of the swap theory was that Walters had *not* been in Opelousas and had *not* actually seized Bobby Dunbar. That had been the work of confederates. As Garland well knew, extradition hinged on the conclusion that Walters, having committed the crime in Louisiana, was now a fugitive from justice across state lines. More importantly, once Walters eventually stood before a jury, he could never be convicted as a principal in a kidnapping if it were argued that he had been 150 miles away. At best, only a charge of accessory would stick.

So when Garland read Percy's interview with the *Pic,* deeming his effort to place Walters at the crime scene virtually irrelevant, he must have exploded: "The fact," Mr. Dunbar answered, "is this: we found my boy, Bobbie Dunbar, in Walters's possession. I don't know how he got there, but he is Bobbie Dunbar, and I am going to keep him . . . If you lost a horse, and found him in the possession of another man, no matter where he was, you would take your horse, wouldn't you? Whether the man stole the horse himself or got the horse from another, those details wouldn't interfere with the original ownership."

Of course, those details *would* matter for a charge of horse thievery. In dismissing the question of who took his son from Swayze Lake, Percy had lapsed into an unsolicited defense of why he took the boy from Columbia.

Meanwhile, Dale's and Rawls's reaction to the "swap" evolved from bemusement to rage. As they watched Dunbar, Fox, and any number of sheriffs and detectives plow through Pearl River County yet again, they had to fear that the case they were building was being destroyed. On May 22 they blanketed the press with a statement:

> From time immemorial, it has been considered bad tactics to apprise your adversary of your defense before the battle, and the wisdom underlying this rule of conduct may be again demonstrated. We have sat silently by, however, and seen so many false statements published in the columns of the public press regarding the movements of W. C. Walters that we feel that the public is entitled to know the real facts of his whereabouts on these dates.

With that, the Columbia attorneys unveiled the mother of all rebuttals. Over 2,800 words in length, the statement chronicled Walters's whereabouts, day by day, from August 18 to August 26, 1912, the period of Bobby's disappearance, and from December 15 to December 25, the time frame of the sighting in McComb. It was written by Walters, in first person, in prose stripped of emotion and flourish. Nearly each day's entry, each point of Walters's travels, was punctuated by a corroborative affidavit from one or more citizens. Most important were his activities on August 23, and in this, Ben Sones, from whose house he had left, and J. S. Thigpen, whose house he had traveled to and whose sewing machine he had repaired, offered compelling backup. Almost always, the affiants were careful to specify Walters's traveling companion: "he had with him at that time a little boy that he called Bruce."

Impatient readers' eyes may have glazed over at the detail. But for the more curious and open-minded, the chronology afforded an uncommonly vivid picture of the everyday life of a tinker, a man most people considered only for as long as he was on their porch, or in their employ, or up their road.

> On Dec. 16, 1912, I left Cotton Joe Stewart's . . . went by Tom Stewart's, who lives two and one half miles from Buck Branch Church, fixed organ on a credit, and eat dinner at Tom Stewart's. That evening I went to George Amacker's, eight miles from Poplarville . . . and one mile from Whitesand Church . . . [On] Dec. 17th, 1912. I worked at the home of George Amacker on his organ, eating all my meals there and spent that night there.

It took about two days for the old cripple to fix what machines were broken in a house, and two nights' rest. Meals were always part of the deal, he sometimes worked on credit, and he always welcomed referrals. He liked to pull off the road around supper, and never worked on Sundays. Telling details of his hosts' homes stood out in Walters's memory: at Amacker's, "his three grown daughters and a lady schoolteacher" were there, and "a Mrs. Mitchell coming after some hogs." And his trips and transactions in town were always well recollected:

> I got a shave while there, went into a store west of the depot, and got a box to pack a fiddle in.
>
> [I] traded the order out in Spier's store, and left the order with them. This is the same store where the man got his head shot off.

Only once did the corroborating affidavit tweak the version of events as Walters remembered them: Sunday, August 25, at Whitesand Church. By the tinker's recollection, "Bro. Holcomb preached at Whitesand

Church on that Sunday, and I played my harp and made a statement in public about fixing the organ. A good crowd was present, and all the people that were there will remember me and Bruce." Bro. Holcomb was not so politely bland:

> I preached at Whitesand Church on the 4th Sunday in August, 1912. Mr. Walters was there having just repaired the church organ. There was a little contention about the work. He insisted that the work was up to contract. He played his harp some, but none of this was in time of service. He made no speech from the stand . . . He had a little boy with him all the while.

To Percy Dunbar, the 2,800 words were a "hill of beans." Walters may have neutralized the December McComb witnesses, but he had left out the latter half of July, the month for which Fox and Hawes had just presented so much explosive detail. Aside from the obvious fact that the boy had disappeared in August, making it the more relevant month, there were other reasons for Walters's omission.

He *had* been working on his mid-July chronology, up to the moment that Dale and Rawls released this statement on August and December. This unpublished timeline is punctuated by Walters's suggestions to Deputy Lott to secure an affidavit or gather corroborating data—a work log for the blacksmith who shod his horses, or a grocery receipt. Trickling through these July notes are traces of hardship for him and Bruce, as well as the sympathy of strangers:

> I went to the Drug Store in Purvis and the boys made much over Bruce. I bought some medicine at this drug store . . .
> On the night of the 16th I went to the home of a negro named Galloway, who keeps Post Office at Odile, Miss. Galloway had a machine, clock, and perhaps an organ he wanted fixed. On the evening of the 16th about dark, I went up to Mr. Ham's and tried to get to stay all night. He couldn't take me, and it was a long ways to another white man's house. It was getting dark, and I took my blanket, and me and Bruce stayed on the gallery at the home of Galloway.

While Walters had the details for July down, he had virtually no affidavits. Postmaster Joseph Galloway had already taken quite a risk on his behalf back in late April, writing to the Columbia town marshal of Walters's visit to his house with the boy in July, insisting that the prisoner was therefore innocent. "Now, as I am a Negro, you know what I say wont do him any good, so I am just telling you so you wont help to mob him."

But plenty of white citizens, who *could* do Walters good, still had not done so under oath. In early May, the Golemans had been outspoken on Walters's behalf in the press, but once Percy Dunbar trumpeted his own interview with a young Goleman neighbor who insisted that the family had been "suspicious" of Walters at first, they seemed to go silent.

The most conspicuous absence of an affidavit came from the household the world knew best, where Walters said that he and the boy arrived on the evening of July 19. At the outset, Jeptha and Matilda Bilbo's identification of Bruce had been unequivocal. But over the past weeks, they had faced daily grillings by authorities, investigators, reporters, and neighbors. Harold Fox had come away from his visit to the Bilbos stating flatly that they were either mistaken or lying to protect Walters. When the *Item* interviewed Jeptha a few days later, he insisted that he had found an old postcard to help him verify his dates. And when Lee Hawes interviewed Matilda after she'd been tricked off the New Orleans–bound train, she told him, "I do not intend to make any decisions until I see the child itself." All of these details point to a newfound caution, a mounting worry that, before they signed their name to any statement, they had better be sure they were right.

That caution was not coming solely from within.

On May 24 Governor Brewer roared out a letter to Garland (and the newspapers): "[T]he report has been industriously circulated in Mississippi that if the witnesses from Mississippi should identify this as the same child in Opelousas that they will be immediately arrested for perjury and detained in jail there, and this, of course, intimidates and frightens the witnesses from here, and tends to the obstruction of justice and fair play." To Dale and Rawls, and now Brewer, it was obvious who the parties responsible for circulating this "report" were. Dunbar and Fox were not on a mission to find Bruce Anderson at all. They were on a crusade to spread misinformation, sow doubt, and suppress witnesses. And they were being assisted and abetted by Theodore Bilbo, who had—Brewer would not put it past him—browbeaten his own aunt and uncle into backing off from their initial certainty.

Brewer would never say so aloud. Instead in his letter, he took aim at Mr. Dunbar for an offense of which he was now more certain: taking the boy from Mississippi in the first place, though he knew the witnesses were on the way and had been "begg[ed]" to wait. And the governor laid down the gauntlet, finally issuing more than a suggestion: "I am going to require Mr. Dunbar to bring this child back to New Orleans, and in the presence of Dan S. Lehon, or John M. Parker, permit the witnesses from Mississippi to see the child . . . Both of the gentlemen mentioned are men of integrity and ability . . . and will give both sides a fair, impartial opportunity."

Exasperated with six weeks of delays, Brewer set a deadline: if the Dunbars did not comply "within fifteen days from this date," he would refuse extradition.

Percy's back was now to the wall. In New Orleans, having just badgered an innocent witness late into the night in what local police deemed a "fizzle" of a lead, and sensing rising skepticism over his entire two-week investigation, he hurled out his most hysterical conjecture yet. To the *Times-Democrat*, he insisted that Walters had not *one* double accomplice, but two or more, all traveling the country under versions of the same name. "They were all of similar appearance and were traveling as tinkers."

What's more, Percy charged, Walters had been unrelenting in his abuse of the boy. Witness after witness had told of whippings, from one farmer who saw several beatings in just a few hours, to a little girl who had seen Walters yank the boy by the hair and twist his head. The mistreatment was not just arbitrary, either. According to Percy, it was "for the purpose of intimidating the boy and making him accustomed to responding to the name of Bruce."

With this charge, Percy dove into the deepest mystery of all within the swap hypothesis: the eight-month-long shift and flux of the boy's identity, away from Bobby toward Bruce. Given his inability to recognize either Percy or Lessie at first, and his ongoing struggle to recall his former life, this shift had to have been the result of more than gentle coaxing. It was a rigorous campaign of erasure.

And it did not stop with his mind. Percy had long believed that the boy's hair had been dyed red, and had been fixated on the effacing of the toe scar, by conscious effort or wear of the elements. And there was the change in the boy's eyes, heretofore blamed on adenoids, squinting in the sun, or the harsh conditions of a vagabond life. Now Percy pointed the finger squarely at Walters.

According to the *States,* he asserted, "Dr. Hood, mayor of Poplar-ville . . . said that there was a drug that would have the effect of drawing the eyes together, just as belladonna widens them. He would not give me the name of the medicine but told me to find out whether the medicine Walters gave the boy was brown or yellowish."

This could be embellishment by the *States,* whose portrait of Percy was now careening toward open mockery. But it is just as easy to imagine Harold Fox, salesman of a popular homeopathic ointment, engaging a small-town doctor in speculation about the attributes and effects of various herbs and drugs.

According to multiple papers, witnesses saw Walters applying a substance to the boy's toes and legs that seemed to worsen their condition rather than improve it. From this, according to the *States,* Percy hypothesized that Walters had either been trying to remove Bobby's scar, or something far worse:

> Traces of what seem to be burns are appearing all over the little fellow's legs now. The scars that he had on his feet are dimmer and whiter. I was told that the scars from a fire burn were reddish, while a scar from an acid burn would be white. It is possible that Walters tried to make other scars on Robert's legs so as to confuse us when we tried to identify the boy.

But there was a simpler answer, and it was staring Percy, Fox, and all of the more sinister-minded witnesses right in the face. The "first boy" had been described repeatedly as appearing to have hookworm, a disease that was rampant in the rural South. In fact, a national hookworm pioneer was a native of Columbia, Mississippi. Tulane professor of medicine Dr. Charles C. Bass was a few years older than Hollis Rawls, and as he would eventually make known, a close follower of the Dunbar-Walters case. In 1903, four years into his practice as a country doctor in Marion County, Bass attended a conference of the American Medical Association, heard reports on a condition called hookworm "emerging" abroad, and connected them with a malady that he had noticed back home: "ground itch," characterized as a painful outbreak of itching, burning, and sores on the feet, made worse by constant scratching, and common in children. By one estimate, nearly 80 percent of Marion County residents suffered from ground itch. Bass purchased his first microscope, confirmed his suspicions, and began research at Johns Hopkins Hospital and in the field back home. His efforts culminated in a groundbreaking report and the popularization of a remarkably effective treatment.

His study focused unflinchingly on "the disposition of feces," the mode of transport of hookworm eggs, out of one body and, usually through bare feet, into another. Bass peered into broken-down privies, behind bushes and fences, down into the gully at the edge of town where country people flocked to heed the call. He observed differences in how men, women, and children chose their particular spots: "It is often possible to determine the number of children in a family by the number of piles of feces in the back yard." He noticed how egg-laden waste was spread wider by rainfall and washouts, and consumption by dogs or chickens. He shuddered as boys and girls splashed in puddles of manure and then shared bathwater with other children while their bare-handed mothers laundered their mud-caked dresses. He condemned the prevalence of bare feet, from children at play to adults removing their Sunday shoes to walk to church. Regardless of his disapproving tone, the world Bass described was, quite literally, the world in which these witnesses, and Walters and the boy, lived.

In his observations of ground itch, Bass offered gruesome, and relevant, details. From infected mud or water, squeezed between toes, the eggs enter the skin. Minutes after infection, stinging begins, and then itching. "Pinhead vesicles" appear and spread together, skin erupts, sheds in layers or is cut off with scissors, deep ulcers form under the toes, and "sticky exudate" clings to socks and bandages, and, significantly, *glues the toes together*. At the height of acute infections, "great swelling" is experienced, with swollen glands, red lines running up the leg, and fever.

These symptoms match precisely what everyone said of the boy. In addition to the prosecution's witnesses, Walters and Mrs. Bilbo had recalled that Bruce's toes had chronic swollen sores—what they called a "rising." "His foot 'riz up' considerable between the toes," Walters said in early May, "and I always had trouble with it." Mrs. Bilbo had said that the scar on the child's foot resulted from a swelling, from which he almost died while at her home in July.

In listing home remedies for ground itch, from mullein tea to fresh pine turpentine, Bass offered a host of benign possibilities for what Walters was seen applying to the boy's wounds. And among the effects of hookworm infection are symptoms that closely correspond to witness observations of "the first boy," thought to be Bruce Anderson. Sufferers became anemic, their faces pale or yellowish. They developed respiratory problems, and their growth was stunted. They were weak, listless, and easily exhausted, so much so that their condition was widely mocked as "the lazy disease." Yet the malady was reversible, and for treatment, Bass prescribed regular ingestion of powdered thymol, made palatable for children by mixing with simple syrup or goo of acacia. In his description of successful recovery is found a thorough and concise debunking of the prosecution's insistence that there were two very different boys:

> A child with 15 or 20 percent hemoglobin, pale, "tallow-faced," one-fourth, one-third, or even one-half under weight, undeveloped, dyspneic, and languid, can be seen to gain weight, height, and color almost daily, and often within two or three months be converted by a few doses of thymol into a red-faced, hardy, healthy-looking child.

The same child, sick in July and recovered by the fall. While neither Walters nor his witnesses ever named the child's condition as hookworm or ground itch, it is possible that it was an assumed condition, so pervasive that it made more sense to address it by its particular symptoms—a "rising of the toes"—rather than its whole. Perhaps more likely, the clinical terms were avoided because they carried with them an automatic stigma, not just for the infected child but for his environs (unsanitary, inhumane, poor) and his caregivers (lax, irresponsible, probably infected themselves). And if the adults around the boy were indeed infected (Walters himself would admit he was a hookworm sufferer), then they were certainly familiar with the classic hookworm stigma of indolence.

There were, however, two witnesses whose testimony the hookworm theory could not account for. Not just Katie Collins, the Poplarville waitress who had seen both men and both boys at the same time, but the boy himself. By mid-May, he finally remembered his double, Bruce Anderson. "A most important thing he told us was that there was another boy with Walters who fell out of the wagon and had to go on crutches," Percy told the *Times-Democrat*, underlining the story's significance. "That bears out the theory of two boys, and gives color to the swap theory." It also gave color to a key trait of the "other boy," as described by Fox: his shoulder, twitching and sagging, as if broken. It wasn't a simple case of hookworm, this memory proved. The other boy had been injured.

Later in the month, Bobby himself was recalling the exchange of names and identities as well. As the Dunbars retold it, his memory on this point was insistent: "The other little boy who fell out of the wagon way long time ago and hurt himself and had to wear crutches, was called Robbie, too. That was my name, and the other boy's name was not Robbie, but that was what they called him."

ON MAY 23, with Percy out stammering to reporters, the rest of his family tried to celebrate Bobby's fifth birthday as cheerfully as they could at his parents' farm. When Lessie cut the visit short and headed back into Opelousas, papers reported that she was well rested and feeling stronger, but nothing was further from the truth. She was not at all prepared for what awaited her.

From New Orleans came an anonymous profanity-laden note insisting that the Dunbars knew they had the wrong child and "ought to be filled with a load of buckshot." But the next letter was far worse, and from much closer to home. Weeks earlier, an unnamed, "prominent" woman in Lexington, Mississippi, had asked her "very dear friend" in Opelousas, Louisiana, to share her insider views on the Dunbar affair. By now most of Lexington was convinced that the boy was Bobby Dunbar. Not so, said the lady, who released her friend's letter to the *Lexington Advertiser* to prove her case:

> This Dunbar case is indeed a mystery. While I cannot understand how the mother could not identify her own child at first sight, I think that she really and truly believes that the child is hers. I could never have been so conservative.
>
> . . . For my part, I see no resemblance whatever between the two children, except in badness. The features of this child are absolutely different to what I remember of the lost child.

Up until this point, reading the letter in print, Lessie could have dismissed the writer as just another gossiping stranger in town. But then came this:

> I did not see the real Dunbar boy very often, for while I have known the mother since she was a child, we rarely visited. She came to my house with her boy just one week before he was lost. On that occasion, he was simply outrageous, and since I see this child, he also is outrageous. Apart from that, I see nothing in common; even the eyes are different—color and shape.
>
> Honestly, I do not think this is the same child, but as I say, a

mother should know her own child. I saw his mother attempt to dress him one afternoon, about a week ago, and he fought her like a tiger.

She told me with her own lips that he gave no sign whatever of recognizing any of the family, and never mentions one word of his past life. If you ask him a question, his lips are sealed.

A cousin of his father, a Mrs. Dunbar, from New Orleans, came in while I was at the Dunbar home. She never knew the child until he was brought from Mississippi to her home in New Orleans, but it appears she is the only one he will have anything to do with. On this occasion, he was screaming and fighting his mother. When she came in, he jumped up, rushed to her crying: "There is my 'dramma,' and I am going home with her, too." Immediately he ran to the dresser drawer, began pulling out his clothes and piled them in my daughter's lap. That was the only time he smiled the whole hour that we were there.

In my heart, I really believe that child was drowned—the real Dunbar child—but, as I say, the mother should know her child better than I.

Public opinion here is somewhat divided. A great many think as I do . . .

Do write me again real soon, and tell me something about the opinion of the Mississippi people regarding this Dunbar case. What do you think of it?

The letter was not reprinted in the New Orleans dailies. But though Lexington was nearly three hundred miles away, it made its way to Opelousas, where its contents and its writer's identity became the source of yet another round of wild speculation.

Lessie knew who wrote it right away, as did family and friends. In the Dunbars' family scrapbook, key passages of the *Advertiser*'s introduction to the letter are double underlined: "Some person at Opelousas whose identity has not thus far been revealed, writes a letter to a friend at Lexington Miss." What sort of confrontation resulted, if any, or when, is not known. But it would not be the last time the writer would speak.

Lessie could take easy umbrage at the letter's gossipy close and try to reason away the rest of its observations: it had been written May 5, well before Bobby had regained his memory; so much had happened since then, so many proofs. But the letter stabbed right through any armor she had. It erased all that had happened this past month, and yanked her back into a darkness she was frantically trying to flee.

ACROSS TWO STATES, citizens counted down the fifteen days on their calendars. The looming question, of course, was what would happen if the Dunbars did not cooperate with the governor's order? Would Brewer actually order Walters to be freed?

On day eight, Columbia citizens decided that they were not going to wait to find out. A. J. McMullen reported breathlessly that "a mob organized . . . to storm the jail," to either drag Walters to Louisiana, or to lynch him. Sheriff Hathorn preempted the siege by swearing in and arming fifteen deputies. When McMullen repeated the threat to Walters, the prisoner grinned. "Yes, I know it, and I keep my door locked."

On day eleven, shots rang out at the Jackson rail yards, followed by howling dogs and hollering men. Rumor was that Governor Brewer had ordered Walters to be brought to the capital, but the prisoner had escaped. The posse wound through the streets, drawing a parade of gawkers, then bolted into the Merchants' Bank building and up the stairs. Bursting into a third-floor office, the dogs pounced on the fugitive, who shot out the window and plummeted to the sidewalk, much to the spectators' horror. Upon closer inspection, the dead man was a dummy. The whole thing had been a stunt, orchestrated by the Boosters' Club as entertainment for its conventioneers.

On day thirteen, the *States'* campaign against Percy reached an ignoble climax, again via McMullen. "Dunbar Trying to Exploit Child," read the headline, followed by an explosive accusation, attributed to Dale: when the Dunbars first arrived in New Orleans from Columbia, Percy had negotiated with a vaudeville impresario "to obtain a contract to show 'Bobbie.'"

It was no secret that the Dunbars had been inundated with such pitches, and at the time, it was reported without controversy that they were "considering offers" for Percy and the boy to appear onstage together. Not unlike Jane Quick and her two daughters, who had recently recounted their escape from the *Titanic* on stages across Michigan, this would have been a straightforward attraction, the captivating retelling of a father's search and a kidnapped boy's recovery. But as the child's identity quickly became the focus of the case, the act would have been a carnivalesque curiosity, and the charge of exploitation more warranted. Now, over a month later, it was simply a cheap retroactive smearing.

Nonetheless, Percy's righteous rebuttal—"Neither my wife nor myself have ever directly or indirectly approached any person with the view of exhibiting our child, or of turning into gain the goodness of Providence in restoring him to us"—left no room for nuance and thus made matters worse. Dale doubled down, and the *States* pulled from its hat a signed statement from the vaudeville man himself, which detailed the late-April negotiations: after back-and-forth via phone and telegram, Mr. Dunbar had arrived at the showman's office, listened to his proposal, and suggested a $1,000 fee before taking the drastically lower counteroffer back home for him and his wife to contemplate.

In what can only be described as the height of hypocrisy, at the moment the "exploitation" scandal made headlines, the Columbia attorneys were privately angling to serve as intermediaries for a potential deal between Julia Anderson in North Carolina and a New Orleans movie man who had offered to help her recover Bruce—provided that the boy would be exhibited onscreen and that he (the movie man) would share in the profits. There was no moral high ground to take; everyone was strapped for cash, and everyone saw the child as a potential source of revenue.

On day fourteen, a brusque telegram from Garland to Governor Brewer was released to the press: the Dunbars had finally agreed to bring the boy to New Orleans on Saturday, June 7. Brewer's suggestion of either Dan Lehon or John M. Parker to oversee the identification left them with an easy choice. The former had said he thought the Dunbars were mistaken, and the latter was a political acquaintance, if not more, to John W. Lewis, their lawyer. After decades in the cotton business, Parker was one of New Orleans's most widely respected businessman, and a rising political star. Already known for taking on the entrenched corruption of the New Orleans Ring (an organization of Democratic power brokers), he had recently chaired the Louisiana campaign of his good friend, hunting buddy, and Bull Moose Party candidate for the White House, former president of the United States Theodore Roosevelt. The Dunbars couldn't have asked for anyone better.

A day before the hearing, the Opelousas camp released to the press a mass of affidavits that would also be presented to Mr. Parker to bolster its claim to the boy. None was more important than that of Katie Dunbar, Percy's schoolteacher sister, who had spent much of the past month with the boy. During that time, she had witnessed at least twenty instances in which the boy himself offered proof that he was Bobby Dunbar, now

Robert Clarence Dunbar.
Infant portrait, 1908.
(Courtesy of Anna Lee Dunbar)

Robert Clarence Dunbar
at approximately three
years old. On November 1,
1912, the William J. Burns
Detective Agency printed
this photograph on a reward
poster that was circulated
across the country.

Boy found in the custody of
William C. Walters, Marion
County, Mississippi, April 20,
1913. Pictured with Deputy
Sheriff Charles Day (driver's
seat) and unidentified others.
(New Orleans *Times-Democrat*)

William C. Walters. When
this first photograph of
the alleged kidnapper was
published in New Orleans
newspapers, reports of
recognition flooded in
from across two states.
(New Orleans *Daily States*)

Lessie Dunbar and the boy found in Mississippi. "Thousands gathered in front of the *Item* building while Mrs. Dunbar and the child she calls her own were posing exclusively for this newspaper." (*New Orleans Item,* April 23, 1913) (H. J. Harvey Photo, New Orleans)

Percy Dunbar and the boy, August 24, 1913. (H. J. Harvey Photo, New Orleans)

The boy claimed by the Dunbars and Lucille DeVerges. "Startled by Strange Events, Lad Confides in No One But His New Chum." (New Orleans *Daily States*, April 24, 1913)

On April 25, 1913, following a rain-soaked parade, a jubilant crowd gathered around the Dunbar home in Opelousas to welcome Bobby home.

The home of the Dunbar family lawyer John W. Lewis, where Julia's identification test was held. (New Orleans *Daily States*)

Julia Anderson upon her arrival in Opelousas, May 1, 1913. (New Orleans *Daily States*)

Members of the "committee" and other officials present for the identification test. *Left to right:* E. P. Veazie, Aaron Jacobs, Henry E. Estorge, Robert Harry, John W. Lewis, and Judge Benjamin H. Pavy. (New Orleans *Daily States*)

T. S. Dale and Hollis Rawls, attorneys for William C. Walters, arriving in New Orleans, June 7, 1913. (*New Orleans Item*)

New Orleans politician and businessman John M. Parker, arbiter appointed for the "Dunbar Investigation" in the Hotel Monteleone. (*New Orleans Item*)

Jeptha and Matilda Bilbo, witnesses for William C. Walters. (*New Orleans Item*)

Dunbar family, relatives, and attorneys at the Hotel Monteleone, June 7, 1913. *Standing, left to right:* Mrs. Christine Zernott, Mrs. F. M. Dunbar, Fred M. Dunbar, Mrs. John W. Lewis, Archie Dunbar, S. Harold Fox, and Mrs. S. H. Fox; *seated, left to right:* Mrs. William. B. Dunbar ("Grandma"), Mrs. C. P. Dunbar, "Bobby," and Benjamin F. Sherrouse. *(New Orleans Item)*

Attorney and witnesses and other Mississipians. *Top row, left to right:* Mrs. H. Allen Goleman with Ruby Goleman in her arms, Sheriff James A. Moody, Deputy Sheriff W. W. Lott, Homer Moody, and T. R. Willoughby and Hollis Rawls (attorneys for W. C. Walters); *seated, left to right:* Mrs. Rita Day, Mrs. George Bilbo, and Mrs. Willie Myley. (New Orleans *Times-Democrat*)

"It is well worth while to note the healthy, smiling face of the boy as compared with the strained, scared countenance of the child when he was taken from the keeping of Walters." (New Orleans *Item*, April 16, 1914) (Courtesy of Anna Lee Dunbar)

(Jacobs New Depot Company, Opelousas, LA)

ROBERT DUNBAR Jr.
Age 4yrs., 4 months, kidnapped August 23rd., 1912.
Swayze Lake near Opelousas, La. Found near Foxworth, Miss., April 21st., 1913.

recalled in her own baby-talk quotes. He remembered the Schell Canal Bridge ("I tossed this bridge a long time ago") and some cups ("Us div them to Eleanor, didn't us, Mamma, before I was lost?"). He asked his grandfather for a beloved old high chair and remembered his mother buying him watermelon. He noticed that Katie had changed the pictures in her locket during the time that he was missing. Spotting a ring on his mother's finger, he asked about *his* ring—his baby ring—that she'd taken off his finger the day he was lost.

And it was not just his former life that he remembered, either. Whenever possible, Katie prodded the boy about the eight months he had been gone. When she asked who fed him, he answered, "That old lady . . . That one that lived in the big house"—whom he called Grandma and who had "pictures of ladies and a safe in her kitchen." When Katie found him banging on a "little rubber" clenched between his teeth, making what he called "music," she asked pointedly, "Who plays music?" "The old bad man," he replied, who played so that "the mans div us moneys."

At supper one evening, Katie zeroed in on the "old bad man's" appearance. He had worn a "big white hat," the boy recalled, with "a ribbon on it like my new shoes." The same white hat that "Detective Walters" had sported at the McComb depot.

Katie brought up August 23, 1912, asking the child what he had done after shooting garfish. He told her he was sinking in a little boat, tied to a bigger boat, crossing a river. Asked what he did when the old bad man put him in the wagon, the boy explained, "We rode and rode and rode everywhere, and I seeped in the wagon." Along the way, the man fixed stoves and pianos, and the boy begged for lunch and sometimes sold pencils. When the boy was bad, the man tied him to a tree and whipped him. And to make him answer to the name Bruce, he whipped him even more.

In another recollection of Percy's cork leg, the boy was asked, "[D]o you remember when you were playing on the street in a ditch, and a man came and picked you up and took you in a store and put you on the counter? What did you tell him?" To which the boy responded, "An old black gun shot my other daddy's foot off." Of all Katie's questions, this was the most nakedly leading, the one that exposed—underneath the baby talk, behind the watermelon and the cups—how tactical this endeavor truly was.

And in the clearest indication of the family's sheer desperation to unlock the boy's memory of the past eight months, Katie wrote this:

At another time, I asked him to tell me a little story about what he did when he was gone so long, and he said: "I tant." I then told him: "You don't love your mamma, your daddy, your grandma, nor aunt because you won't tell us anything." He looked at me with a distressed look and said: "Aunt Tatie, I luves all of you. I tant tell you anything." "Why can't you, darling?" . . . "Tause he won't let me." "Who won't let you?" "The old bad man Walters. He whips me all the time."

Finally, Katie offered one of the boy's quiet memories of his phantom young companion. When she noticed him seated in the window alone, singing, she posed a peculiar question: "Who sings like that?" To which he responded, "The other little boy." "What other little boy?" she pressed. "The little boy with us."

Katie's compendium was overwhelming in its sheer number of "proofs," and in this, it was the perfect cap to a monthlong accumulation of clues, leads, rumors, and hypotheses. Out of beans, some might say, the Dunbars had made a hill.

For those not dazzled into submission before the mass, for those rare few who harbored little expectation that these proofs would deliver coherence and linearity to the case for Bobby Dunbar and against William Walters, one particular bean stood out.

It appeared in the *Hattiesburg News* in late May. Percy and Harold Fox had just emerged from a conference with local police and found themselves mobbed by a curious crowd. Question after question was volleyed at the pair so persistently that it took Percy, by his later recollection, hours to finish writing a short note home to Lessie. To the crowd, he detailed the evidence gathered thus far that convinced them the boy was their son, almost all of which would appear in Katie's affidavit and become canon.

Then, wearied and raw, and perhaps because he was in the midst of relaying it to Lessie in writing, Percy told of a new discovery. More than one recent witness recalled that the boy, while staying at their homes and eating at their tables, had asked for "taste" when he was hungry. This struck Percy as significant, he said, because that was exactly the word Bobby had used when Lessie nursed him. "He had learned to ask for 'taste,'" the *News* reported, "when he wanted milk from his mother's breast." Long after weaning, Bobby continued to use the word *taste* to mean "food," more generally.

The swarm must have gone still, if only for a moment. It was a revelation of unvarnished intimacy, startling not just for Percy Dunbar, speaking before a crowd, but for any man in any context. Of course, Lessie would bristle at its impropriety. And many other mothers might recognize the word *taste* as one that their own children used to mean breastfeeding. The story had no real value in the gathering up of a case, and it would never be repeated. Its significance was deeper.

Like most fathers of his day, Percy had been a witness to, more than a participant in, child rearing. Long before the word *taste* was repeated to and reinterpreted by him, its original meaning was something between Lessie and Bobby. Even if Percy didn't understand that, he had seen plainly that the word tugged at Lessie and was special to her.

In Hattiesburg, cornered by a mob that he himself had ginned up with expectation, feeling the weight of the imminent announcement of his case against Walters, and at least sensing how staggeringly insane that case might sound, some part of Percy wanted to take it all back. Not just the proofs and theories of the past month, but all that had happened the eight months before. The thing that Percy probably wanted the most, he and Lessie could no longer have: the simple but real pleasure and ache of parenthood.

The moment was forgotten in the tumble of events that followed. By early June, when the last spasm of resistance to Governor Brewer's demand had subsided and the family readied to bring the child to New Orleans, Percy was well armored again. He compiled the notes of his investigation, gathered his affidavits, rallied over forty friends, neighbors, and family members to swear in writing that the boy was Bobby Dunbar, and passed all of this along to Messrs. Garland, Lewis, and Veazie on the eve of their trip to New Orleans. He made his own bruised ego the subject of headlines again by issuing a blustering justification of his monthlong delay, and refusing to travel to New Orleans himself for fear that he might lose his temper with the Columbia attorneys. He ensured that his terrified wife would be surrounded by friends and relatives during the ordeal, and that the boy would be under the constant armed protection of Sheriff Swords.

In a fitting postscript, still another proof emerged on the entourage's train ride to New Orleans—quite by accident, according to John Lewis, who relayed the incident to the two afternoon dailies upon their arrival. The throngs that mobbed the carriage during its Baton Rouge stopover frayed Mrs. Dunbar's nerves to the point of physical illness, so Lewis took charge of the boy. To settle him, the attorney pulled him into his lap and told a story. Not just any story, either; the *States* described it as "the story of a little boy who had gone through the same adventures which have made Bobby a famous lad," and the *Item*'s summation was near identical: "The theme was that of the little fellow's own experience, but another, a fictitious boy, was named."

As the tale wound down, the boy's eyes were drooping, but he was alert enough to demand clarification on the ending. As Lewis recalled, he inquired sleepily, "And did the little boy's papa get him back just like my papa got me back?"

In Lewis's eager retelling, this was the key moment of his anecdote. The boy had recognized his own experiences in this thinly fictionalized version. Looked at from another angle, the incident had more complex implications. For most of the past month and a half, the boy's reported memories had been fleeting glimpses and impressions, temporally and geographically disparate, isolated and vague. The Dunbars had struggled to stitch these scraps together with the threads of causality and chronology. And today Lewis's story had made that process complete. He had gathered up all of the fragments and fitted them together into a satisfying narrative whole, one that the boy could make sense of, connect to personally, and invest in. Whether he knew it or not, Lewis had refashioned the prosecution's case into both bedtime story and memory.

For the boy, it was the end of a story whose telling began nine months earlier, in another warm lap. He had fallen asleep at the supper table, listening to Mrs. Bilbo and her daughter wondering how Bobby Dunbar had vanished. The boy today, before the train could rock him to sleep, needed to be sure that Bobby Dunbar had returned.

Chapter 12

Postcard of New Orleans, circa 1912 (Hotel Monteleone on right)
(A. L. Barnett, Detroit Publishing Co.)

ON THURSDAY AFTERNOON two jarring telegrams arrived in quick succession at the offices of the John M. Parker Company, 816 Union Street. First came a wire from John Lewis, sent from the Burnside depot sixty miles upriver, shortly after noon: "Coming on Frisco with Bobbie. Send seven passenger automobile rear end last sleeper."

Two hours later came this, from Governor Brewer:

> The Dunbars will be in New Orleans on Saturday
> morning to submit to an examination by Mississippi
> witness at your office. If satisfactory to you,
> I wish you would be present and see that the
> Mississippi witnesses are accorded a fair deal and
> would be glad to hear from you as to what you think
> about it afterwards. I do this on account of my
> confidence in your absolute fairness.

The telegrams reveal a startling truth: amid all the dramatic communications of the past week, no one had actually confirmed with Parker that he would serve as moderator. "I would unhesitatingly have declined," he would later grouse, "had it not been for the fact that these various witnesses and parties in interest were already on the way to New Orleans."

With no other choice, he wired Brewer back: "Will with pleasure comply."

BEFORE THE *ITEM*'s photographer had even raised his camera, the boy was posing, chin lifted, eyes focused on the lens. Restless from the train ride, he raced about the backyard of 7031 Freret Street, hurling himself into one little tableau after another, though when the cameraman tried to direct him, "Master Bobbie" balked. Finally, he was coaxed into a high swing, where he sat still and smiled patiently for as long as he could.

Inside and upstairs, Mrs. Dunbar lay on a bed, surrounded by a group of reporters. She was exhausted from the train ride, if not debilitated by a flare-up of kidney pain, but there was no ignoring the press. It was plain that the upcoming proceedings worried Lessie, but "God has been so good to us in giving us back our boy," she told the *Pic.* "There are too many good people in the world to let the evil overcome us, or to let him be taken away." She lamented that Governor Brewer "seems to cast the balance of favor on the side of the criminal," and had no kind words for Julia Anderson, who "was allowed to see Robbie four times" but had failed to identify him, and hadn't even kissed him when she'd left.

More than anything, Lessie was focused on her son's fear. Over the past month, although he had been steadily returning to himself, he still offered only indirect glimpses into the trauma of life with the "bad old man." He wears only rompers now, she said, and will tearfully reject any suggestion of a dress: the outfit forced upon him by Walters. When passing by a freight car, his aunt Katie had playfully invited the boy to jump in with her, and he had squealed in terror. This was how he had been kidnapped.

[A]lways when we are alone, he will tell me about how "the bad, dirty man" . . . took him from the railroad track. "Please, Mamma, don't let him take me away again. Please don't let him beat me," he will say . . . "Sh," he will say in a little terrified whisper, "don't let him hear you, or he'll come and get me and beat me again."

Being taken again, being beaten: in Lessie's telling, the boy was more than scared of it; he was fixated on it. This was not a surprise, given her own all-consuming worry that she might lose the boy, and her vocal aching over marks of abuse. As Lessie continued, an even more striking overlap between mother and boy emerged:

> [H]e had just finished his prayers, and I laid him on the pillow and was about to kiss him, when he said, "I just believe I ought to kill that dirty man Walters." I am so longing for the time to come when we won't have to talk about this miserable business anymore, and he can forget it all; those miserable eight months.

The mother wished Walters forgotten, erased from her son's mind, so that they might finally have peace. For the boy, whose remembering and imagining of Walters had become an obsession, the closest thing to forgetting was killing. It would not be the last time he wished it.

Mrs. Dunbar's dark talk came to an end when the boy himself leapt onto the bed to give her a hasty hug. As he climbed down, she asked him back up, first for a "peach kiss," and then, with cheeks comically inflated, a "puff kiss."

This was the first time reporters had seen the boy since May, and they scrutinized him hungrily. Although he still relied on baby talk, which was striking for a child his age, he was strong and healthy. The *Pic* reported that he had lost his sunburn and his eyes had even become "rounder," but the *Item*'s more realistic observation of a "slight puffiness under the eyes" is borne out by photos. In fact, although the *Item*'s account is not bylined, its nuance and painterly references suggest the pen of Ethel Hutson, who lived only a few blocks away: "Bobbie has a face a Raphael might have used for a cherub. His eyes are the deepest blue imaginable; his hair a tousled gold-brown that will not stay combed and at the least suggestion of wind rumples up in the artistic disorder."

The boy was rambunctious, sociable, and confident, and no adult could control him. That afternoon, he soared in the swing, nearly knocking Uncle Archie over; he chased chickens, climbed a fence and a pole, and frolicked with the collie. And while the *Pic* cooed over his "merry laughter" at a phonograph's music, the *Item* emphatically reported precisely the opposite: "One thing that will immediately strike the observer who meets the little boy of mystery for the first time is that he does not laugh aloud. He lacks that clear, ringing peal, the liquid joy of childhood."

As the boy played and reporters scribbled, legal maneuvering lurched into high gear. Hour by hour, telegram by telegram, the battling lawyers jockeyed to control the terms of Saturday's proceedings as much as they could, while at the same time accusing the other side of seeking too much control. Dale and Rawls launched a preemptive attack on the rumored proposal of a procession of boys for the witnesses to choose from, and the Opelousas camp (privately gunning for such a setup) shot back that Mr. Parker would conduct the test in any way he saw fit. To get early input into Parker's plan of action, Lewis sought him out as soon as he arrived on Thursday. But finding him already gone for the day, he showed up at Parker's office first thing Friday morning instead, bringing along Mrs. Dunbar and her relatives and friends. When rumors flared again that Dale and Rawls were plotting to seek custody of the child, Governor Brewer himself was forced to issue a last-minute wire to Garland: "You may rest confident that no habeas corpus proceedings or other civil action will be begun."

June 7, 1913

IN BOARDMAN, NORTH Carolina, Julia Anderson wrote to Mr. Dale. Just recently, she had met with a Walters cousin named Garland Brown, an attorney from nearby Whiteville. Julia told him the story of her trial in Opelousas and completed another affidavit attesting to her positive identification of Bruce. Brown had relayed to Julia all the news that Dale and Rawls had written to him: the witness/extradition standoff, and the possibility that the Mississippi attorneys might need Julia to appear in person at a potential hearing with Governor Brewer. But nothing of the upcoming proceedings in New Orleans.

In her letter, the mother of Bruce Anderson sounded desperate. "I no it is my child and I want it," she wrote. "I don't want the Dunbars to have the child." At the same time, she put her faith in the lawyers, trusting them to be just as loyal to her as they were to Walters: "I Put all confidence in you as I think you will Do all you can for myself and W. C. Walter . . . I am depending on you for the right thing and Believe you will do me wright."

Frantic and trusting, Julia was also oblivious: "Find out if you can if

Dunbar have got the Child with them. I have got a lock of the child Bruce hair. Would it be nessery for me to fetch it with me." She didn't know that the Dunbars had the boy.

In Louisiana, the fear of legal action to seek custody of the child had reared its head once again. Walters's lawyers and the governor of Mississippi had gone out of their way to take that option off the table. But the one person who mattered most in that decision was neither informed nor consulted. The one person who should have had a say in the matter didn't even know she had a voice.

ON SATURDAY MORNING, the motorman of the Carondelet streetcar idled in front of 7031 Freret Street so that passengers could get a good, long look at the lad in the white linen suit perched on the front steps. He babbled enthusiastically to the strangers, oblivious to the frantic call of a woman inside the house.

Finally, Mrs. Dunbar emerged, relieved to see the boy, but mortified to face the rubberneckers. Her eyes were dark, exhausted, and terrified. The day before, despite her optimistic front, Lessie had reportedly "broke[n] down several times" and had suffered "quite a spell of hysteria." This morning, with just hours before they were due down at Mr. Parker's, she was certainly much worse.

"Are you the mother?" the motorman inquired.

"Yes, I'm the mother."

The gawkers silently compared the two, until Lessie hustled the boy inside.

DOWNTOWN, THE MISSISSIPPI contingent had arrived. Stepping off the train were the Bilbos; the Golemans, with their two daughters; the Myleys, with their daughter Edna; Homer Moody, son of the Pearl River county sheriff; and Deputy W. W. Lott, who had spent the better part of yesterday rounding them all up. Tagging along were Sheriff Moody himself and a Bilbo relative, coming to New Orleans "not as a witness, but to have her eyes treated." These witnesses were dressed in their Sunday finest: the men in dark jackets and ties, or at least a fully buttoned collar; and the women in plain dresses or skirts topped with crisp white high-collared blouses. The most noticeable standout was Mrs. Goleman's hat, a simple straw affair, save the wind-blown riot of colorful blossoms that spilled down its brim.

Late last night, they had gathered at the Bilbo home and piled into a car to meet the four fifteen Northeastern in Poplarville. But the day's downpour had flooded an otherwise crossable creek, which required a detour. Mrs. Bilbo, who had "arisen from a sickbed" took the trip especially hard. She had two floating kidneys, and sitting upright or standing produced dreadful pain. Remarkably, the only advertised witness that was missing was Rambler, the Bilbos' fox terrier, who had been the boy's fast friend while he stayed there with Walters. They had hollered into the dark for the dog as they readied to leave the farm, but he remained true to his name. An elusive rabbit, they speculated, was a more pressing concern.

Joined by Dale, Rawls, and Sheriff Hathorn, the whole bunch made their way to the nearby Hotel Monteleone. At the edge of the French Quarter, the ten-story hotel, one of New Orleans's newest and finest, had become the unofficial waiting room / staging ground for participants in Saturday's proceedings. While the witnesses ate breakfast in the chandeliered dining room, Dale secured suites on the eighth floor for them all to congregate. For the Opelousas contingent and their supporters, Mr. Lewis had secured five connecting suites on the second floor. Meanwhile, the vast column-lined lobby was crowding with curiosity seekers and "interested parties" hoping for access to the afternoon's proceedings.

As the throngs spilled over to Union Street, Mr. Parker foresaw his cotton business grinding to a halt and Mrs. Dunbar suffering a gauntlet of gawkers. "This is going to be a private meeting," he barked to the crowd, "not a show!" What's more, its location would be kept secret, announced to invitees only a half hour in advance. The mob begrudgingly dispersed.

SHORTLY BEFORE TWO o'clock, fifty-two-year-old Abraham Oliveira tucked his legs under the delicate dressing table and got to work sharpening pencils. Under ordinary circumstances, the table would be stocked with the accoutrements of a young bride: combs and hairpins, perfume and jewelry boxes. But today it was a jumble of notebooks and pens. On a typical workday, Oliveira would be recording the proceedings of New Orleans's district court. But today he was the official stenographer for "the Dunbar Investigation," soon to begin in the luxury two-room bridal suite on the second floor of the Hotel Monteleone.

The bride's cheval mirror had been sidelined to make room for a mahogany table, and in place of flitting bridesmaids were at least a dozen sober-faced men, taking their seats and perspiring freely in spite of the fan: Mr. Parker; attorneys Lewis, Garland, and Veazie from Opelousas, and Dale, Rawls, and Willoughby from Columbia; Archie Dunbar; Harold Fox; and four reporters, one from each of New Orleans's daily papers, all bearing identical typewritten "passes," which Mr. Parker had addressed to their editors:

Dear Sir:
   One representative from your paper will be admitted to the hearing of testimony of the witnesses who have come from Mississippi for the purpose of identifying the "Dunbar Child."

Behind the closed sliding doors to the adjoining room, number 256, was the Dunbar Child himself, surrounded by family and friends and under the watch of his pale-faced mother, whose worry was betrayed by a constant "working of the fingers." With the venue change, the boy had been whisked into the hotel via the ladies' parlor, his face buried beneath the lapels of Harold Fox: a safeguard against premature sightings by Mississippi witnesses who might be lingering in the lobby.

By now the Mississippi witnesses were sequestered six floors above the bridal suite, sweltering in one of Mr. Dale's rooms. While the others reclined on the bedspreads and made languorous small talk, Jeptha Bilbo gazed out the window at a jumbled landscape of roofs, rippling with heat.

Meanwhile, strangers and acquaintances alike stalked the lobby and halls of the hotel, slipping under the bridal suite door notes that begged for admission. Private detectives kept watch, and a unit of New Orleans policemen, requested by Mr. Parker, kept order.

Finally, once a cotton wagon clattered by and the fan had been silenced, Mr. Parker began. He first read aloud Governor Brewer's telegram of June 5 and then offered some bristling caveats: he would have declined the governor's request if the Dunbars had not already been in transit; he "had never met or known any of the parties to this controversy" before; and he would serve impartially. In recapping the morning's legal negotiations for the record, he admitted: "I frankly stated that I had heard some rumors as to the credibility of the witnesses, and I desired to inform the attorneys of this fact; but I did not believe it would affect my judgment."

Without the fan, the air was deadly still. Wiping a handkerchief under his collar, Parker wrapped up his introduction by clarifying his intentions:

   I believe there is no question of the presence of the child who is introduced here today as having been at the various points named in Mississippi, from September until the time that it was recovered, and that in my judgment the essential feature to be developed [is] to prove the presence of this identical child in Mississippi *prior to* the twenty-third of August 1912, the time at which he disappeared.

His imprecise wording suggested favor to the Dunbars, but this was no time to quibble. Having tangled and postured for the better part of a month, the lawyers were ready to get on with it. In Oliveira's transcript, the action begins just three pages in, and while the reporters' accounts would heap on dramatic flourish, it is Oliveira's detached prose that best exposes the underlying absurdity of the affair:

> Mr. Parker leaves the room and brings in the child. Mr. Veazie stands by the child, who stands on a table. The child jumps into the arms of Mr. Lewis. The child plays ball with Mr. Parker.
>
> BY THE CHILD: Where is the man what gave me this ball? Where is the man?
>
> BY MR. LEWIS: There he is—Mr. Parker.
>
> Boy taken out of room.

During the ball playing, the first witness was brought in to observe the child: W. W. Lott. The deputy's testimony had been requested by Dale simply to confirm on record that this child today was the same child that had been taken from Walters in April, but Parker immediately veered, asking Lott repeatedly if he had seen the boy prior to August 23, 1912. Of course, he had not. For Dale and Rawls, it was an unsettling start.

A guard opened the hall door for the next witness to enter: old Jeptha Bilbo, spectacles on, slouch hat in his hands, took a seat front and center. Once again, the child was brought in from the adjacent room, this time in the arms of Mr. Veazie. The sliding door was left well cracked, revealing the "anxious faces of all the women" gathered in room 256, with Lessie positioned in front.

Upon the boy's entrance, by one account, Mr. Bilbo stood swiftly and voiced recognition. According to the transcript, it was Mr. Parker's question, "Mr. Bilbo, do you know this baby?" that prompted his affirmative reply.

"What is his name, Mr. Bilbo?"

"They called him Bruce."

Bilbo said that he'd first seen the boy on July 19, 1912, which prompted Parker to question how he came to recall such a particular date.

"We had a church organ out of fix, and we had a baptizing on the fourth Sunday in July, and got the old gentleman Walters to fix the organ, and he had the organ ready by the fourth Sunday in July."

Parker asked if this was the same boy with Walters, and Bilbo said yes. Parker asked about markings, if Bilbo had "any way or knowledge of knowing" the child, to which Bilbo responded plainly, "by looking in his face." The boy had stayed at his home, Bilbo testified, "all together . . . for about six weeks."

Mr. Parker turned to the boy, who was standing atop the mahogany table, oblivious to its varnish, playing ball with Mr. Veazie. "Do you know who this is, Bobbie?" Mr. Parker asked. However unintentional, his choice of moniker must have caused the Mississippi attorneys to bristle.

By more than one account, Bilbo repeated the name that he had used before: "Don't you know me, Bruce?"

Reports of the lad's reaction varied wildly. The *Times-Democrat* observed that he tucked his head into Veazie's shoulder. The *States'* correspondent reported that the boy "smiled in an uncertain way" and threw his hands around the attorney's neck. But in the *Item*'s version, the child "gazed straight at the elderly Mississippian and then smiled broadly." And the *Pic*'s reporter succumbed to folksy treacle: "Little Bobby Dunbar smiled back into the scarred and wrinkled face, in the depths of which there lurked gently kindness and the crowfoot marks of time, sunshine, rain and winds." When the boy spoke, his voice was described variously as "half frightened," a "stage whisper," and a "childish treble," and one witness suggested that he ventured toward Mr. Bilbo as he spoke. But all sources agreed, more or less, on the words the boy uttered.

The otherwise dialect-free transcript reads, "Dat's old Bilbo."

Mrs. Dunbar's face, according to the papers, was determinedly blank. She had readied herself for this moment; as she and her husband had repeated, they knew that the boy would likely recognize these witnesses. It was not his presence at the Bilbos' house that they were disputing; it was the dates he was there.

Dates were Mr. Parker's primary concern as well. Once the boy had been removed, Mr. Parker returned to that subject, and his questioning was dogged. He asked when Mr. Bilbo had last seen the boy, to which

Mr. Bilbo replied that he and Walters had stayed with them around Christmas. He asked again if this was the same boy that had stayed in July, to which Mr. Bilbo answered yes.

"Are you positive that the date was in July and not in August?" Mr. Parker persisted.

"Yes, it was July," Mr. Bilbo replied.

Mr. Parker forged on, unconvinced: "Are you a good hand at remembering dates, Mr. Bilbo?" And a few moments later: "What particular matter makes you remember that day and month?" After Mr. Bilbo repeated his explanation of the regular church meeting, Parker retorted, "After eight months, did that make such a particular impression upon your mind so as to identify the day and date?"

Parker brought back the child, who—as the exchange continued—scrambled on and off the table, dancing on it, gnawing the chain of his mother's card case. "Who else in the neighborhood saw this child besides your wife and yourself?" Parker asked.

"A whole lot—Homer Moody—he is out here, and on the twenty-ninth there was a whole crowd." And to Parker's persistent doubt, Bilbo explained, "I have seen him too many times to be mistaken. He knows me, too."

On this point, Parker conceded: "He said right away he knew you." The boy, perhaps prompted by the men's focus back on him, made a curious interjection. Mr. Oliveira recorded his words: "Oh, that bad man." Another paper filled in: "I don't want to go back to that bad man." And another paper went further, suggesting that "he seemed afraid, and asked if Mr. Bilbo had come to take him back to the old bad man, Walters."

Whatever its precise wording, the line had no cue. At the most obvious level, it confirmed that the boy had internalized Mr. and Mrs. Dunbars' dread of this event. Consciously or not, he saw causality, from his recognition of Mr. Bilbo today to a return to a life with Walters. But deeper than that, it almost reads as if "bad old man," this prominent new phrase in his lexicon, had become a means for the boy to garner comfort; to blunt uncomfortable questioning.

When the men turned back to the chronology impasse, Mr. Dale suggested that the timber cruiser Carl Bass might offer evidence to corroborate Bilbo's recollection. Bass had boarded at the Bilbos' while Walters and the boy were there; in Bass's work diary/date book, he had recorded the date of his stay as July 29, and had recently told as much to Mr. Bilbo and the Mississippi attorneys.

That nuance was lost on Mr. Parker, who took Dale's suggestion to mean that Mr. Bilbo had not recalled the dates on his own, but rather had sought out Bass and his records to help him remember. Just as rashly, Parker suggested that if Bass's stay had been on the twenty-ninth, then Bilbo's memory of Walters's stay with the boy on the nineteenth was a mistake or a contradiction. No one quite managed to explain that Walters and the boy could have been at the Bilbos on both dates.

Parker sent Mr. Bilbo back out into the hall with this: "I do not want the attorney to show me a date, but I want what you know, yourself, and not what you know from somebody else." Dale's interjection had backfired spectacularly. He had given Parker what Jeptha Bilbo, on his own, had not: a new cause for doubt.

Matilda Bilbo entered next, looking nervous. With her "readin'" glasses perched atop her head, she studied the boy through her "distance glasses" as he played. When Parker asked, she affirmed instantly that this was the boy she knew as Bruce Anderson.

But this time, the boy showed no overt signs of recognition. One paper reported that he smiled at Mrs. Bilbo silently; another reported that he recoiled when she reached for him. It was a remarkable contrast to his earlier reaction to Mr. Bilbo. An impartial observer would have assumed that if the boy recognized Jeptha, then he would certainly know Matilda, who had (it was not disputed) bathed, clothed, and fed him for weeks at a time, had tucked him in at night and tended him when sick. The boy's behavior seemed intentional.

And when he was "released" through the sliding doors to the next room, he ran straight into the arms of Lessie Dunbar, who had been observing every moment through the crack.

To Mr. Parker's first questions, Mrs. Bilbo reiterated what her husband had said: the first time she had seen the boy was the Friday before the third Sunday in July. "He was backwards and forwards," she elaborated, "and he stayed there for two months alone; he stayed there four weeks at one time to a day."

But when Parker pressed for dates of the boy's second visit, her anxiety mounted: "It was somewheres about the middle of September when Walters got back there—about the middle of October when he came back from the hospital—and I kept the child four weeks when Walters came—"

"Can't you remember the dates, Madam?" Parker interrupted.

"No sir," she responded, "I remember he got back on the twelfth—"

But Mr. Parker interrupted again, yanking her inexplicably back to

July: "How did it impress itself upon you as to the first day that you saw this child?"

Mrs. Bilbo told the story of church and the organ out of fix.

"We are not trying to mix you up, but we are trying to fix the date all we can, absolutely," Mr. Parker said, then leapt forward in time again: "You say you cannot tell what time in September he came back?"

She could not. All she knew was that Walters had returned sometime in September, left the child with her while he went to the hospital, where he had stayed for about a month. He had gotten out and returned by mid-October, she recalled, because "on October 12, he was at my house, and we went to a burying—"

"You identify that coming back because you say he went to a burying?" Mr. Parker stalled, to which Mrs. Bilbo politely responded, "Yes sir." At that point, Mr. Parker made yet another flailing attempt to expose her doubt by literally asking for the date she had just given: "You identify the burying—do you know what date that was?"

Mrs. Bilbo grew flustered: "All I know is the twelfth of October."

Though Mrs. Bilbo didn't explain it, twenty-five-year-old Delilah Ford Cothen, daughter of an old Ford's Creek family, had died on October 10. With the tombstone just yards from Mrs. Bilbo's home, she had good reason to recall the funeral date.

Mr. Parker pivoted back to July, grilling her yet again on how she could remember the date when the boy first came. "I told you as plain as I could," she insisted. When she noted that Walters had "cured the organ" on a Saturday, Parker interrupted: "What date of the month was Saturday?"

Her explanation that Jeptha had forgotten one of Walters's interim visits gave Parker an opening to question Matilda's memory as well: "Is there a possibility of your making a mistake in the month?" But she would not budge.

Finally, Parker explained his rationale: "Pardon my insistence," he said, but how could she pinpoint the date that Walters and the boy had first arrived in July, and yet remain uncertain about when they'd returned in September? She had told before and she told him again: there were events to remember the early date by, but none so specific for the later date.

He zeroed in on the duration of the boy's visits. She was precise on the first one, but the second she couldn't recall, and when he got to the third, she replied, "So many times I don't remember. I know he was there Christmas time, but I don't remember what time it was."

With that, Parker turned to the boy's physical traits: "[W]as [there] any peculiarity about the child's hands, or any peculiarity about the child's feet?"

"No more peculiarity than there is about lots of them," she answered. "Just a little web between his toes, and if you look, you will find it that way."

Parker was eager to oblige: "I wonder if we can show her the boy's feet."

The boy was brought back, but as soon as adult hands came near his feet, he began to kick and scream. "[I]t took two strong men" to remove the patent-leather shoes, then the short, blue-banded socks after that, the *Pic* reported, and Lessie was hurried in to pacify him with her touch.

Mrs. Bilbo switched glasses, took the boy's foot in her hand, and hoisted it close to her face. "This enabled 'Bobbie' to prove that he could yell as loud upside down as right side up," quipped the *Item*.

Mr. Parker asked where the web was, and Mrs. Bilbo twisted one foot, then pointed to two toes (reports did not specify which foot or toes). "There it is," she declared. "A score of heads" leaned in; Mr. Parker's was front and center.

"I don't see any web," he concluded flatly.

From the spectators in the adjacent room came a mocking laughter. As for Lessie's reaction, in particular, "It wasn't a laugh exactly," the *Item* observed. "It was more like a tired smile forced by the merriment of those present."

Mr. Oliveira's transcript omits spoken words and laughter, and instead includes a summary dictated then and there by Mr. Parker:

> The child's shoes were taken off, and its bare feet exhibited and examined, top and bottom by Mrs. Bilbo, and others in the room, and with the exception of a small scar on the great toe of the left foot, no apparent distinguishing marks or malformation were shown. Gentlemen, are you satisfied with this statement, as I have dictated it to the stenographer?

BY COUNSEL REPRESENTING ALL PARTIES: Yes sir.

As soon as the next witness, Charles Myley, entered room 255, he declared, "That's the boy." By one account, he did not even look at the child before he said it. In 256, Lessie laughed in disgust, then turned to a relative. "Did you notice that?" a reporter heard her say. Again, the boy "showed no signs of recognition."

Mr. Myley testified that he had first seen the boy in the care of Mr. Walters on the third Sunday in July at the Bilbos. The next Sunday, Myley had seen Walters and the boy again at the church meeting, and on the following Tuesday, the pair had come to their house and stayed.

When Parker pushed him on his dates, Myley tried to explain that he recalled the encounters as coinciding with a loan that he and his wife had taken out in Poplarville from the county's sixteenth sections fund. Just recently, Myley's wife had gone to the chancery clerk's office to verify the loan date as the Tuesday after that third Sunday, in the week prior to the church meeting. But Myley was muddy in his explanation and chronology, and Mr. Parker, mistakenly thinking that the first sighting and the loan had happened on the same day, scoffed, "Were you borrowing money on Sunday in the state of Mississippi?"

Later, Parker impugned the Myleys' record corroboration: "You do not know of your own knowledge what time it was?" He cast suspicion on Myley's certainty ("Mighty few people can remember a year afterwards") and directly after that complained that he wasn't certain enough ("You have not named a date to me except what you say was the third Sunday in July?").

Finally, Parker blurted in exasperation, "I am trying to get something that is going to satisfy me absolutely—not to the identity of this child, but as to the fact of whether or not you all are mistaken as to the times and dates. You understand?"

The exclamation laid bare a truth that by now had become increasingly apparent. It was not simply that Parker, as he had claimed earlier, had heard "rumors" questioning the witnesses' credibility, but could put them aside to judge impartially. In fact, those rumors were the foundation of Parker's entire approach. He was working from the assumption that the boy was Bobby Dunbar, and these witnesses were wrong.

"Hello, Bruce," Mrs. Myley said as she entered, in what—to the Dunbar camp—must have felt like a taunt. The boy looked up, "acting as though he had never seen her," and then turned back to his mother's purse, his latest toy.

At Parker's questions about markings or deformities, Mrs. Myley replied, "I noticed his peculiarity ways; I never noticed anything else." He asked specifically, "Anything the matter with the feet?" to which she answered, "No sir."

After the boy was removed, Mr. Parker plunged again into the task of ferreting out confusion. But Mrs. Myley had no patience for his badgering:

Q. Is there any chance, madam, of you making a mistake?
A. If there is, you got to show me where.
Q. Have you anything to identify your dates except that memorandum? Could it not have been the fourth Sunday in August?
A. No sir, it could not.
Q. You have no other way of placing your dates except that guesswork?
A. What guesswork?
Q. The dates?
A. You go to the clerk's office in Poplarville; I'm as positive as I am sitting in this chair that the child was at Jeptha Bilbo's when we borrowed the money.

Mr. Parker was facing a brick wall. He turned to Rawls and practically pled for help: "Have you looked at the records, Mr. Rawls? You know how it's possible to make a mistake?" Apparently now Parker was pinning his hopes on a hypothetical clerical error. Mr. Rawls did not respond.

So Parker probed in another direction: "Did you ever see any other child with old man Walters?" Mrs. Myley had not.

Finally stepping in to help, Dunbar attorney Lewis offered a question, which Mr. Parker read and took up with Mrs. Myley. Apparently, earlier today, she had been overheard by the Opelousas camp discussing this issue of webbed feet. "Did you not say this morning that you would know this child by his web foot because one of your children has a web foot?"

"No sir," she clarified. "My eldest girl has a foot with her toe next to the big toe—it seems like they start out to grow to themselves like they might incline to make a web toe; that is what I had reference to, and I said this child's foot was something like that."

Mrs. Myley had made this comparison before, to Harold Fox during his mid-May Mississippi investigatory trip. At the time, Fox misattributed the observation to Mrs. Bilbo and reported to the *Item* that she had called it a full-on web. Today, as Mr. Fox heard Mrs. Myley correct the record, he stayed silent.

Lewis found Mrs. Myley's answer notable for other reasons. After Mrs.

Bilbo's earlier "failure" to find the web, she had been excused, free to return to the room on the eighth floor where the other witnesses, including Mrs. Myley, were waiting. This was precisely the scenario that Lewis and his Opelousas colleagues, in their failed prehearing request for witness segregation, had sought to avoid: the sharing of information. Mrs. Myley, then, had come down to her own cross-examination "prepared," Lewis suspected. There was nothing irregular about the boy's feet, she had declared emphatically. And now, confronted with her morning statement, no matter how she strained to qualify and diminish the trait's significance, a spotlight had been shone on a discrepancy in her testimony, and quite possibly a weakness in her credibility as well.

But Mrs. Myley's rationale could have just as easily been benign. Her earlier discussion of toes that "might incline" to grow together may have been an attempt to differentiate this perfectly ordinary feature from a full-on web, which is what was being trumpeted as evidence of Mrs. Bilbo's misidentification. So, when Parker questioned her, the feature was not a peculiarity worth mentioning but rather a red herring to be avoided.

In fact, Mrs. Bilbo's earliest recollection of the child's toes seemed much closer to what Mrs. Myley was describing than a "web": "It seems to me one of [the toes] kinder crooks under," she had told A. J. McMullen.

The strongest evidence in favor of Mrs. Myley (and Mrs. Bilbo, too) comes from the unlikeliest, and most damning, of places: the Dunbars' own recorded observations. Within the catalog of traits that they had compiled for Governor Brewer back in late April, is this: "malformation of two little toes on left foot, the first phalanx of each turning inward slightly." This sounds strikingly similar to what Mrs. Myley said: "it seems like they start out to grow to themselves like they might incline to make a web toe."

The Dunbars' list was printed in three New Orleans papers. In the morning dailies, the couple discussed this particular trait at length, apart from the list. Parker himself may not have read these reports, but it is fair to assume that many others in the Monteleone bridal suite had. Of course, some may have glossed over the detail. Mrs. F. M. Dunbar and the Foxes, both in attendance that day, lived in the house where the list was drawn up, but even if they had been present, they, too, might have forgotten this specific "malformation."

But what of the person who had actually compiled the list and spoken of the trait? When Lessie heard Mrs. Myley's description through the cracked sliding doors, she must have known that this feature of the toes was one that she herself had seen and pointed to, twice or more, in the presence of a detective and reporters. She must have been reminded of that identification earlier in the proceedings as well. When Mr. Parker peered down at the foot with Mrs. Bilbo and saw no obvious webbing, when the room of observers around her laughed and she mustered a cursory smile, when Mr. Parker uttered this description aloud into the record—*"no apparent distinguishing marks or malformation"*—Lessie surely recalled *this* contradictory description of the very same boy, words that she herself heard, likely spoken aloud, and had a hand in putting to paper:*"malformation of two little toes on left foot."*

After Mrs. Myley's description, the *Item* reported, the boy "was not produced to be examined for this malformation, as his shoes and stocking had been removed when Mrs. Bilbo made her examination . . . and no such deformity had been discovered." So Mrs. Myley's more subtle and specific observation, then, had no chance of being verified. It was a crucial decision, to keep the boy's stockings on, and the record offers no indication of how it was made.

At approximately this point in the proceedings, Lessie was found to be weeping. She tried to stop herself, but the sobs "just 'leaked out.' " The other women circled in to soothe her. A short "intermission" was called when the Monteleone staff arrived bearing lemonade, ice water, and cigarettes, on the house.

MR. AND MRS. Goleman were the next two witnesses, both identifying the boy and delivering the same details they had been giving for months: they had seen Walters and the boy at the Bilbos in late July; then weeks later in Poplarville; again in October, when the pair stayed in their newly built home; and then finally, in Mrs. Goleman's words, "about four weeks before he was found." Neither recalled precise dates for the latter encounters, but they were certain of the first one. Since early July 1912, they had been hosting their "two little nieces and a nephew" visiting from Alabama. On that third Sunday before the church service, the Golemans, young relatives in tow, had offered Walters and the boy a ride out to the Bilbos'. The pair piled into the wagon with the children. The age of the nephew, the other boy in the wagon, was not reported.

Young Homer Moody recognized the boy easily and verified the Bilbos' dates. In July he had been boarding with the Bilbos and remembered Walters carrying the boy in asleep that first night. Homer "didn't pay any strict attention" to the boy, though they sometimes played together. But as the *Item* observed, today the lad "did not show the slightest inclination to resume these intimate relations with young Moody and contented himself with endeavoring to up-root Lawyer Veazie's iron gray mustache."

With the boy removed, Mr. Parker sought again to clear up what he called a "strong" "confusion of dates." Homer's winding response ended with a shock: "You know anything like that, you never pay close attention to it—to remember any certain date upon it. I never noticed much. Of course, when the old man came out there with the child, we were suspicious that something was wrong."

Parker pounced. "You were suspicious that there was something wrong?"

"Yes," fumbled Homer, "but we didn't have nothing to believe it by."

Mr. Veazie pushed, hoping to prove at last that these witnesses were wrong about the chronology: "Was there any discussion of the Dunbar child about that time?"

But Homer made clear, "Not at the time when I was out there; it arose after he was in that country several months."

Still, Homer's acknowledgment of suspicion was something that no other witness had voiced aloud that day. While accusations against Walters were common after the Dunbar child went missing, those at the Bilbos' had been wary *before*.

For Parker, this new wrinkle was irrelevant. Despite his best efforts, these witnesses, whom the *Pic* referred to as "plain backwoods country people of unblemished reputation," had been unwavering and unanimous in their certainty.

Parker had one more idea. Earlier, he had learned that Homer's father, Poplarville Sheriff James A. Moody, had accompanied the witnesses to New Orleans. As Parker told the lawyers, he knew Moody personally, "well," for twenty years now, and he wanted to summon the lawman to testify.

In addition to being the longtime county sheriff, Moody was one of south Mississippi's wealthiest citizens: owner of both a thriving commercial farm and "one of the largest and best arranged stores" in the state, according to the *Pic*'s column for traveling salesmen. In Parker's eyes, Moody was not a peer, but certainly of a different class than the other witnesses; a man he could trust and speak with frankly.

Dale and Rawls had not intended for the sheriff to testify, since they knew that he hadn't seen the boy prior to August 1912 and thus had no direct experience with the matter at hand. Nonetheless, they saw no reason to object. When the sheriff entered, Mr. Parker stood to shake his hand.

Moody recognized the boy, but said that the only time he had seen him had been December 24, 1912, "when he was passing." When Parker asked about suspicion of Walters's possession of the boy, Moody elaborated: "I heard that, and I sent a deputy of mine to investigate it, and they came back and said that they thought it was a mistake—that it was a different day when that child disappeared."

Then Sheriff Moody mentioned another investigation, more thorough and far less known: "I had my deputy Mr. Brooks, at Carriere, Mississippi, to make an investigation on the twenty-ninth of December, and I had him take a doctor with him, and they made an investigation, and they told me they were satisfied that it was not the child."

This was not what Mr. Parker wanted to hear. "What I am trying to get is facts," he replied, and then, taking pains to erase the sheriff's suggestion of mistaken identity: "Mrs. Dunbar is here with her little baby, and we want to find out all we can about it. Do you think those people are mixed in dates, those people who have testified here?"

The sheriff stood "straight and stiff as a soldier" before Mr. Parker. "Yes sir, it is possible," he said.

And with that, Parker drilled on.

Q. Do you think that these people would remember the particular day upon which this child came there first? I know you well; you are a public official?

A. Yes sir.

Q. Sheriff?

A. Yes sir.

Q. I have known you for twenty years have I not?

A. Yes sir.

Q. Do you think that these people would remember the particular day upon which this child came there first?

A. I should not think so.

Q. Do you not know plenty of your people who would be unwilling to accept a statement that that was July when they first saw this child there?

A. Yes, I would. I am sure; I could be mistaken about that.

Following this, the testimony of eight-year-old Edna Myley was but a colorful afterthought. She wore a little white dress, and when the boy was taken in and placed upon the table, she gazed up at him "intently." She recognized him as Bruce, whom she knew well. He "hung his head bashfully" and "showed every evidence of a young boy in the presence of his sweetheart," according to the *Item*. But when Mr. Parker asked if he knew the little girl, he "put his hands over his eyes and hid his face" and wouldn't answer.

With that, Mr. Parker was finished.

He dismissed the entire assembly without ceremony, stationed a "large blue bellboy" to stand guard at the door of 255, and then sequestered himself inside with Mr. Oliveira. He needed to review the transcript.

Chapter 13

W. K. Patrick, New Orleans *Times-Democrat,* June 7, 1913

M AMMA, IT WAS B RUCE, but he wouldn't look at me," Edna Myley reported when she returned to the ladies' parlor from the bridal suite upstairs. When a reporter asked her to describe the boy's reaction to her, she replied, "He just shrugged one shoulder like this," squirming her skinny frame to demonstrate.

The Myleys, Golemans, and Bilbos had been gathered here for some time after their questioning by Mr. Parker. But unlike Parker, with his suspicious demeanor and dry fixation on dates, the reporters in the lobby loved hearing these country witnesses talk. And what they wanted to talk about, most of all, was the child they knew as Bruce.

"Bruce what?" Mrs. Bilbo repeated the question. "We just called him Bruce. We knew he wasn't Walters's child, but with us he went under the name of Bruce Walters just the same." She went on about the boy, and despite the *Times-Democrat*'s exaggeration of her dialect, her feelings came through crystal clear:

> I'm just a fool about youngun, anyway, and when Walters first brung this here boy to our house, I just naturally picked him up and got to kissing and hugging him, and then I washed him and put on a new dress. Somebody said, "My goodness alive, Missus Bilbo, what fur air ye doing that?—why, you don't know nothing about what that child is." But I said, "I don't keer what he is, he's a human being, a child, and I jis' love him."

Sitting nearby, Jeptha Bilbo remembered the last time that he had seen Bruce before today: in Poplarville last February. As he and Matilda were loading up their wagon with supplies, a voice had squeaked "Bilbo! Bilbo!" from behind. They squinted and squinted, and finally spotted Walters and Bruce driving up in the wagon. After a brief reunion, the old man and the boy were on their way again. "I sorter like kids as well as the old lady, my wife," Jeptha said with a smile, "and I used to take this one on my knee and bounce him up and down a lot."

On the day of Walters's departure for Charity Hospital last fall, Mrs. Bilbo recalled, he gave her eighty cents to buy "candy and nuts and things" for Bruce, and told her to take good care of him while he was gone. The old man instructed her to not "let him get around any boy who cusses. I don't want him to learn to cuss." Then "he patted [Bruce] on the head and said, 'Bruce, you mind what Grandma Bilbo says.' "

But it was in her memory of the disputed "fourth Sunday in July" church service that Mrs. Bilbo inadvertently offered the most insight yet into her attachment to Bruce. The baptism that Sunday was for a baby in the Byrd family (Mrs. Bilbo's maiden name), likely a grandniece or grandnephew. "I dressed the baby in the clothes of our little dead baby and carried it there myself." In fact, though Matilda would never share it with strangers, six of the Bilbos' seven children were now dead: two boys who died in infancy; one whose death was unrecorded; a son, Jessie, who died at age eight; thirteen-year-old Joseph, who shot himself accidentally when climbing a fence; and Mittie, who'd died four years ago at twenty-seven. Only one daughter, Byrdie, survived, and she had left home for marriage in 1911. When Matilda told A. J. McMullen back in May that she wouldn't have taken Bruce even if Walters had offered, that was far from the truth.

It was not just to give dates and identify markings that the Bilbos had come here today. They had yearned to see a boy whom they knew and adored, despite his mischief and all the trouble he had brought to their lives. Even when their affections were not returned today, they still spoke of him fondly. But as they prepared to leave for the evening train back home, their words were suffused with nostalgia. Bruce was a boy they once knew, long ago. Like all their own children, he was now gone.

IN ROOM 256, Bobby was worn out. "I want my dinner," he moaned from the bed. Lying alongside him, Lessie fanned and petted the child anxiously, while someone ordered down for food.

But before dinner arrived, word came from next door: just fifteen minutes after the proceeding closed, John Lewis rushed in, fresh from a private consultation with Mr. Parker. "Let me hug something or somebody quick!" he exclaimed. He chose his wife, and the hug lifted her off her feet. To the room of family, friends, and reporters, Mr. Lewis announced, "Mr. Parker has just declared that he has not the slightest doubt that the child he saw today was the son of Mr. and Mrs. C. P. Dunbar."

It was not an official announcement yet, since apparently Parker was still meeting with Walters's counsel in the other room. But this inside scoop from Lewis was enough to bring an "audible sigh of relief" from the crowd gathered. Lessie clasped the boy close and kissed him on the lips. "I thought so all the time," she said. "Now I wonder what else they will ask."

She didn't have to wonder for long; reporters in the room began buzzing questions at her right away. Meanwhile, the frayed young boy, who neither understood nor cared why all the adults were talking and rejoicing, tugged at her arm. If he could not be fed, he wanted his mother's undivided attention some other way. He wanted his special song.

In 1848, the same year that he wrote his first hit, "Oh! Susanna," and a few years before "Camptown Races," Stephen Foster penned "Uncle Ned." By 1913, white mothers were still singing it to their children across the South. Mrs. Dunbar patted out the rhythm and sang to her boy, and the room grew quiet to listen:

Den lay down de shubble and de hoe
Hang up de fiddle and de bow:
No more work for poor Old Ned
He's gone where the good Niggas go.

When Lessie stopped singing, the boy was calm. "That was the song I sang to him," she explained, "before he was lost."

Some time later, they were playing quietly together on the bed when Garland and Veazie parted the giddy crowds and presented Joe Johnson of McComb, Mississippi. In mid-May, the attorneys had brought Johnson and four others to Columbia to identify "Detective Walters." A month later, still fixated on the case, Johnson "came all the way here to satisfy myself."

He recognized the lad right away and was eager to tell his mother the story directly. In a slight tweak of his earlier testimony, he said that when he and the other men confronted Walters at the depot in December, he had been "too slick for us," "outtalked" them by identifying himself as a Secret Service agent. In the presence of the mother, he might have wished he had done more.

There was another new twist today, too. Johnson had asked the boy his name, he told Lessie, to which "Walters said, 'Tell them your name is Bobbie Dunbar.'" It was a detail guaranteed to tug at the mother's heart. When Johnson lingered after the telling, Lessie smiled up at him and said, "I want to shake your hand again."

A tray of tea sandwiches finally arrived, but the boy rejected them with a scowl. Nibbling some herself, Lessie broke off a piece for the boy, who agreed to the ham but not the bread. Outside on the street, a crowd had gathered, and the boy was brought over to the French window to greet them. "[A]nchored by a friendly bellhop," reported the *Pic*, he stood behind the ornate cast-iron scroll balustrade, waving and calling hello to all the strangers. Lessie stood beside him, "bowing and smiling to let people know she was happy." Framed together, they posed: mother and son.

"I TRIED TO get to the very 'gizzards' of the thing," Mr. Parker told the *Item* on Saturday evening, having just wrapped up his report. "Acting in such a case is a thankless thing at the best, but I considered that I had a public duty." With that, he hurried off to catch the train out to his family's beachfront estate in Pass Christian, Mississippi.

Up in Jackson, the Western Union boys had been running all afternoon, back and forth from the telegram office two doors down to the Governor's Mansion, and rutting up the executive lawn on their bikes during breaks. On the Corinthian-columned circular front portico, another *Item* reporter lurked to witness the governor's wife open the incoming telegrams. Though Minnie Brewer had been following the case closely and "exhibited a lively interest" in the news of today's test, when asked her personal opinion on the matter, she "diplomatically refrained."

Her husband was only slightly more expansive. So far, although Governor Brewer had been given anxious advance reports from both sets of attorneys, and certainly had been telegrammed of the verdict by others, he still had not heard from Mr. Parker himself and would make no comment to the *Item* until he had. But before the actual telegram arrived, the *States*—in an effort to scoop the competition—rang the governor directly and read its copy of Parker's report aloud over the phone.

Written out by hand, it filled five full Day Letter forms. After noting that Oliveira's transcript would be sent separately, Parker assured the governor that he had listened carefully to all of the witnesses. Nevertheless, he had three central reasons to doubt their testimony.

First, there was the issue of memory. The witnesses "were forgetful of many dates," Parker wrote, twice offering the same quote—"about the third Sunday in July"—to indicate their vagueness. Elsewhere, he repeated, "Inability to remember correct dates, after a long lapse of time, is, to my mind, strongly evident throughout the whole proceeding, and I particularly invite your careful attention to the testimony of Mr. J. A. Moody . . . a gentleman whom I have well and favorably known for many years."

Next, there was the question of the toes: "In answer to my direct question . . . Mrs. Bilbo said two of his toes were slightly grown together, or web-footed," Parker recalled, but when the child's feet were displayed, aside from the little scar, "the feet were perfect." So, while Parker agreed that the boy presented today did stay with the Bilbos during and after Walters's hospital visit in September and October, this was not the same boy that the Bilbos had seen in July. That boy had webbed feet, and this boy did not.

Finally, there was the weight of opposing testimony, which Brewer would find nowhere in Oliveira's transcript. The child the Bilbos remembered from July, Parker opined, could not, "by any possibility be the same child identified by the mother who bore him, his father, the family doctor who brought him into the world, and by the many children who played with him, and by men and women of the highest integrity who have known him all his life." In his conclusion, Parker elaborated on this final factor, and again, he lapsed into tautology:

> After today, seeing for the first time the child, with its mother, relatives and friends . . . I make this as my report, with a full appreciation of the responsibility involved, that in my judgment the child exhibited today is Robbie Dunbar.

When the *States* reporter finished reading the telegram, Governor Brewer said flatly, "I will not make a statement until I have a full stenographic report of the testimony given at the hearing," and hung up the phone.

At 7031 Freret, where Mrs. Dunbar had returned with the boy, there was open rejoicing. In Opelousas, crowds flocked to the telegraph office and roared when the news came in. "I knew it all the time," Percy Dunbar exulted to the *Item*. "I knew any fair man would decide that way. I never knew before that a man could be too careful."

Inevitably, the opposing attorneys took their opinions to the press. There had been no witness "confusion," Dale and Rawls asserted, nor was it just these ten who remembered Walters from July: "a hundred other persons can be produced who will make the same statement." Mr. Parker had "misunderstood" his role, the attorneys carped, acting as prosecutor and judge, rather than moderator.

Lewis accused Dale and Rawls of "welching." Deriding the witnesses' method of fixing dates, he sniped, "I am a good Methodist, but for the life of me, I could not say when the last protracted meeting took place in our city—that is, whether it was July, August, or September." But when he claimed that Dale and Rawls had "practically dictated" the proceeding's terms, Lewis added hypocrisy atop his mockery.

Parker's insistence that he had "never met or known any of the parties to this controversy" notwithstanding, it was their prior (albeit lopsided) political and personal relationship that Lewis had exploited to ensure the Opelousas faction early access: both Friday's conference with Mrs. Dunbar, and another prehearing on Saturday with the boy himself (and no reporters or transcript). Though Lewis downplayed their significance, it was clear from Parker's telegram to Brewer that his encounters with Mrs. Dunbar and the boy had influenced him profoundly. Not just for the litany of proofs that she had proferred, either. As Rawls recalled on Sunday afternoon, based on seeing mother and child together, "Mr. Parker was frank enough to say to us before the meeting . . . that to brand the boy as an illegitimate child would be a crime."

This was a written statement from Walters's attorneys, printed in multiple papers, and neither Parker, Lewis, nor anyone else ever attempted to refute it. The sentiment had been voiced before, not just in parlor gossip but also on editorial pages: the child is better a Dunbar than a bastard, regardless of who actually birthed him. But Parker was no ordinary citizen or commentator. For him to say that legitimacy trumped identity meant that the entire proceeding to follow was a charade.

The final crack in the veneer of Parker's neutrality was the question of whom he did and did not trust. While he told Brewer that he felt the Mississippians were honestly mistaken, that wasn't the whole story, and everyone knew it. A year from now, he would recall, "When I was asked to judge, I stated [to the attorneys] that there were some people whose word I would not believe on oath." It was, of course, a thinly veiled reference to the Bilbo family, as Rawls pointed out in his written rebuttal. In 1912 Lieutenant Governor Theodore Bilbo had loudly opposed Parker's Bull Moose Party, and to a reformist like Parker, Bilbo's strong-arm, backroom politicking was anathema. Certainly, in mistrusting anyone who shared the Bilbo name, Parker was not alone among Louisianans or Mississippians. But this admission makes it clear that he was sugarcoating the depth of his bias when he announced that he had heard rumors about witness credibility but would judge impartially. Parker would not have believed Jeptha and Matilda Bilbo no matter what they said. "On the other hand," he would later recall, "I believed the Opelousas people worthy of highest credence, and understood the Dunbars to be reputable in every sense."

IN COLUMBIA, THE famous prisoner had little to say on the verdict for expectant reporters. Beyond the fact that he had not yet spoken to his attorneys, there was a private reason for William Walters's reticence: he had just received word that his father had passed away in North Carolina. James Pleasant had been infirm for two years, so the news was not a shock. But it must have, in conjunction with Parker's decision, brought Walters into closer emotional contact with the gravity of his circumstance. His father had died while he was in jail. Would he be free to see his mother before she went, too? And for Walters, there was the stab of remorse: his father's final days had been clouded with the ignominy of his son's imprisonment and worry over his fate. He had not died in peace.

PARKER HAD ONE day with his family in Pass Christian before traveling to New York for a week of business and Progressive Party politicking, and despite his public certitude, the Dunbar affair nagged at him throughout. To get to the bottom of the question of the webbed toes, he would later recall, he sought expert advice from "the highest medical surgeons of New Orleans." Not as a precursor to his decision (after all, it was rendered in minutes) but, more likely, as an after-the-fact covering of his bases. His specific question was "whether it would be possible to perform an operation that would separate a child's toes without a visible scar being left after a few months." A disturbing speculation, rarely voiced in print, but surely bandied about by those dark-minded tabloid addicts who recalled that the boy had required a "minor operation" in mid-May.

But dewebbing surgery was far messier than a simple snipping of the skin. Surgical experts of the era seldom recommended "operative interference" on webbed toes, owing to lengthy and encumbering recovery and the risk of nerve damage. Even dewebbing of fingers, one text warned, "is a severe operation, especially in little children." "They all told me positively no," Parker would report the experts' reply. "If an operation had been performed, the foot would have been red for some months, and the child would more than likely carry the scar for life."

Ruling out surgery, however, did not solve Parker's mystery of the discrepancy in identification; nor did his conclusion that the witnesses were mistaken, or lying, about their dates. There had to have been two boys, he was sure. And on Sunday afternoon, he found that theory confirmed under the most disturbing of circumstances.

Along the beach directly in front of Parker's commodious Pass Christian home, two young men overturned their sailboat, and while Parker's son John Jr. raced out to rescue one man, the other went under. As a morbid crowd gathered to watch the futile diving, a local grocery clerk approached Mr. Parker about the Dunbar verdict and mentioned a "clue" that Parker found revelatory: last fall, the clerk and several other Pass Christian residents had spotted a man resembling Walters and two boys, "very similar in appearance and very much alike," traveling in a covered wagon. For Parker, the news eclipsed the unfolding tragedy, and he raced inside to compose a telegram to Brewer:

> I leave for New York tonight and on my return
> will send you affidavits from a number of parties
> fully substantiating that Walters was here with two
> children whose resemblance was remarkable. Heard
> these statements tonight for the first time.

At eight o'clock, as the forty-hour flyer began its journey north, the young man's waterlogged corpse was finally brought to shore.

The next day, a journalist for the *Pic* dug a little deeper into Parker's report and interviewed the clerk, who admitted hearing the story from "another person," who had heard it from "still another person." This final witness was unable to confirm that the man had one or two children with him, or even if the man was Walters at all.

It was a thorough debunking, and Parker probably never read it. As soon as he returned from New York, he spent a full day rounding up "[t]welve or more" locals to confirm the clerk's original sighting of a man and near-twin boys, which he summarized via two more letters to Governor Brewer (tellingly, without the promised affidavits). The trio was headed toward Poplarville, Parker emphasized, and as he would later recall, witnesses noticed that "the two boys were barefoot, their little feet were red with cold, and they were shivering." With his logic now following a well-worn path, Parker promised Brewer, "I am going to use every effort at my command to endeavor to locate where [Walters] left the missing boy."

The 1913 Pass Christian accounts bore unmistakable echoes of reports from the fall of 1912: a lame tramp spotted along the Gulf Coast with "a small boy . . . whose little bare feet struggled, despite the cruel slag which cut them, to keep pace." But in 1912 the reported mode of travel was foot or train, and, as the *Pic* intimated, no one had mentioned a second boy. Even more fatally: William Walters was a recorded patient at Charity Hospital in New Orleans on the very days that these sightings had occurred.

Parker's "findings" didn't get much notice. Not from Brewer, who dashed off a politely pandering reply; not by the Opelousas legal team, who would mention them only in passing; and not by the press. But there is one hint that Parker may have persisted in his quest for "the missing boy," as he promised Brewer. In 1932 Bobby Dunbar himself would recall proudly, "John M. Parker, who was later governor of the state, was a great friend of my family and helped to look for me. He looked for days, I was told, and didn't stop until he fell down and was badly injured by a cypress knee which struck in his side." A generation into its retelling, the search for Bruce Anderson of 1913 had become the search for Bobby Dunbar of 1912. At least one fact was inherited accurately: Parker's efforts had failed.

ON JUNE 13 Jobie Sweeney, the thirteen-year-old son of a sawmill worker, stood before Marion County attorney T. R. Willoughby and swore to a jaw-dropping revelation. On Monday, April 21, he had been one of the hundreds of visitors to the Wallace farm, keen to see the mystery boy waiting in limbo for his identification as Bobby Dunbar. "[A]t all times when he would ask him if his name was Robert," Willoughby summarized Jobie's recollection, "his answer would be, 'No, my name Bruce,' and when ask[ed] if he had a little Brother named Alonzo, he would shake his head in the negative and say, 'No, got a little sister named Bernice.' "

Less than a week later, on a Tuesday night in the executive mansion in Jackson, Jobie's affidavit was among a massive sheaf that Rawls gamely presented, page by page, to a weary Governor Brewer. Looking on were Dale, the governor's wife, a young daughter, his secretary, a legal advisor, and a cluster of journalists. When the Columbia attorneys had boldly asserted that hundreds of Pearl River County citizens would corroborate the handful who had testified in New Orleans, they were barely exaggerating. Over the past six weeks, they had secured sworn statements from scores of others who recalled Walters and Bruce in the Poplarville area from July 1912, before Bobby Dunbar went missing, to well into the fall and winter. *The same boy.* They had affidavits from the Poplarville postmaster, another minister, and the clerk of Spring Hill Baptist Church, who confirmed the dates of its August services. The Pearl River statements drove home that Walters and the boy, while strangers at first, had become very much a part of these communities.

But as the evidence piled up, the governor and his advisors grew restless. Fearing that a decision had already been made, Dale took over from his younger colleague and began a direct appeal. If Brewer still believed that Walters was not in Louisiana at the time of Robert Dunbar's disappearance, then it was his solemn duty as executive of the state to refuse the requisition. If Walters was not a fugitive from justice, he should not be extradited. Arguing that Walters would never get a fair trial in Louisiana, Dale warned the governor, "I want you to remember that I said this. If the old man goes to Louisiana, an innocent man will be executed."

Brewer did not take such a possibility lightly. But it was the job of the courts, not the executive, to determine guilt or innocence, and with the cooling of tempers and a wave of high-powered reassurances, the governor now had grounds for at least reasonable hope of a fair trial across state lines. At the same time, Brewer's prolonged hesitation had become a source of political mockery in his own state and of colossal indignation in Louisiana. It was not just a rebuff of Parker's judgment; it was an all but open declaration that the citizenry of his sister state was nothing but a bloodthirsty mob, fundamentally incapable of administering true justice.

By eleven o'clock, the battle was over. As Brewer set about drafting a statement, Dale and Rawls made a last-ditch appeal for the governor to make public his true opinion on the question of Walters's innocence. Brewer obliged: "I have been of the opinion all the while that a mistake had been made, and I am now thoroughly convinced that the child now in the possession of the Dunbars is Bruce Anderson and that W. C. Walters is innocent."

But the advisors immediately objected that the statement was a flat contradiction of the requisition order and would create an unending legal mess for the governor. They asked the journalists to strike the draft from their reports, and all but one complied.

At eleven thirty the next morning, before a bevy of reporters, Brewer signed the requisition. According to the *States,* he quipped, "Solomon's task of settling that baby fuss between the two women was easy compared to what I was up against. Get that thing in the mail quick!" The *Item*'s version was catchier: "Solomon had a cinch."

But before Brewer had even dipped his pen in the ink, Dale and Rawls announced they would seek a writ of habeas corpus. And by the time Sheriff Swords and Henry E. Estorge arrived for the prisoner in Columbia on the morning of the twenty-first, the writ had been served, requiring Sheriff Hathorn to retain custody of Walters until a July 2 hearing. Swords presented Hathorn with the extradition order, Hathorn issued an official denial, and within hours, the Opelousas officials were on their way home again, empty-handed.

Amid the rote legal ceremony, out of view from the crowds, a noteworthy human drama did unfold. Columbia officials took the sheriff back to the jail for a meeting with the prisoner he would not yet be claiming. Up until now, Walters had read of Marion Swords as the Dunbars' menacing, gun-toting bodyguard during the New Orleans identification. And Swords, like most of the public, had been exposed to a vast array of impressions of William Walters: sinister child snatcher, lunatic hobo, simpleton zealot. When they came face-to-face, preconceptions washed away. The two men, just a few years apart in age, struck up easy conversation. The sheriff assured the prisoner that he would be well cared for when his inevitable extradition did occur, not just in transit but under Swords's care in the St. Landry Parish Jail. Walters appreciated the outreach, and insisted that he was, in fact, eager to come to Louisiana and face his accusers. He spoke at length of his innocence, and the sheriff listened.

When reporters asked about the conversation afterward, Swords initially felt it inappropriate to give details. But the impressions he did share were striking: "Walters does not seem to like his confinement there. He is a man who has wandered and hates inactivity. He is not as ignorant as some think . . . He is wiser than some of the curious who try to draw him out. He judges a man quickly and from all indications likes to talk to those who treat him square."

Returning the gentlemanly admiration, Walters opined, "Sheriff Swords . . . has the right spark in his heart, and I have no fear in accompanying him. I know a good man when I see him." To this, once he had gotten to New Orleans, Swords reflected, "I don't think he would give me much trouble if I did have him in my care," and then, icily back to business: "I expect to later."

Chapter 14

William C. Walters, 1913 (William Walters Defense File)

ON JULY 2 Judge A. E. Weathersby rose to the bench in Poplarville's sweltering, overstuffed courtroom. Peeling off his sweat-sopped coat, he announced that all those men with hole-free breeches and no pistols in their pockets were free to do the same. Walters entered dramatically, sporting a new suit and a fresh shave, and waving his handkerchief to get Sheriff Swords's attention. The reunited friends shook hands, and within minutes, the much-anticipated habeas hearing was under way.

When Walters himself was called to the stand, he told the story of "a man who has wandered" for the first time under oath, a narrative that included not only his travels in Louisiana, the dates of which were the hearing's central subject of dispute, but glimpses of his life before. Since his arrest, Walters and Julia Anderson had been telling this story in bits and pieces, and nine months hence, another voice would chime in: David Bledsoe, a childhood friend who had kept tabs on Walters, via letters and visits, for decades. Long before his movements were shrouded in the mystery of a kidnapping, William Cantwell Walters was a restless young man, eager for a future beyond Robeson County, North Carolina.

Q. How many brothers did you say you had?
A. [T]here was six boys and five girls.

Sixth in his line of siblings, Walters was weakened by rheumatism and hookworm since youth, which may have been what earned him the nickname "Cant," or at least helped it stick. He first left home as a teenager but didn't get far: just over the border to the Bayboro, South Carolina, farm of his friend and future brother-in-law Henry Bell. Walters worked there "about a year," according to Bledsoe, then returned home to farm alongside his own family. But there was another livelihood calling him, and thousands of other wandering fortune seekers, a business in his family for generations: turpentining.

For over a century, North Carolina had been the nation's leading producer of liquid turpentine and rosin, products distilled from the extracted resin of live pine trees. With an ever-growing number of industrial uses for these products, the vast belt of tall virgin long-leaf pine, stretching down the southern Atlantic Coast and westward along the Gulf, became a valuable but rapidly depleted commodity. Financed by and perpetually indebted to commissioning merchants known as "factors," turpentine operators bought or leased a stand of trees, set up camp, and corralled a sizable migratory workforce, usually African American, which itself remained in debt to the operators. With the industrialization of the trade, razor-thin profit margins encouraged sloppy practices—chipping too deep or wide into the tree, or too far up the trunk, notching multiple collection boxes into a single tree—which left the woods unable to heal and vulnerable to insects and wind. Having sliced one majestic forest to death, turpentiners simply packed up camp and moved on to another. "It was an army that recognized no loyalties of place or region," observed one historian, that "brought nothing to the forest but greed, left nothing behind but waste and destruction, and pocketed nothing but pennies."

Like other Walterses before him, William Cantwell may have first joined this itinerant army in North Carolina. Once the industry had marauded through that state, it moved southward into Georgia and Florida, where a skilled Tar Heel was a treasured asset. By the early 1880s, Walters was working in Montgomery County, Georgia, just south of Savannah.

Here he met Mary Alice Burch, the lovely daughter of a thriving Georgia farmer. In 1885 he shaved his mustache for what would be one of only two times in his adult life, and the couple wed in September at her father's home. Within a few years, they had two sons. But a turpentine camp was no place to raise a family, so Walters eased into the lumber business in the booming port city of Brunswick, then one of the nation's leading exporters of timber and rosin. For a while, Walters thrived just as Brunswick did. But when things fell apart for him, it was not the city's 1893 yellow fever epidemic, or the hurricane of the same year, or even the nationwide financial panic that his old friend David Bledsoe blamed. Walters went broke, Bledsoe insisted, because of "foolish business management."

On Christmas Eve 1895, life took another downward turn. At a country dance in Wayne County, not far inland from Brunswick, a fight broke out, a young man named Mumford Harrison was killed, and Walters was jailed for the crime. He insisted he was innocent, that he had only been a peacekeeper, and appealed to Bledsoe to find him a lawyer. Nonetheless, he remained behind bars for "some weeks," by his own estimate, becoming a jailhouse trusty: an inmate with special privileges, granted either because his jailers knew of his innocence or because he could be counted on as an informant against fellow inmates.

No matter that he had been exonerated, when Walters was released in the spring of 1896, he still faced financial ruin. Mary Alice was due with their third child in July, and tensions in their marriage were beginning to flare. Something seemed to shift in Walters. He was in his midthirties, a failure at all but siring children, and starting over from scratch. As Julia Anderson had heard, he "claimed to be crazy" and "went from bad to worse."

Indeed: Walters returned to what he knew best, an industry fast becoming reviled across the Southeast. In Florida at the century's turn, many greeted turpentiners with rage and alarm, yet their tide seemed inexorable. Walters was a part of that tide, uprooting his family to Escambia County, the westernmost county in the Florida panhandle (the same county where, twelve years hence, a crippled tramp and a small boy would be spotted on the tracks to Pensacola). It was 1900, several years before the state's real turpentining boom, before the industry depended on convict labor, and Escambia's forests were snatched up by larger interests. Walters worked a small operation, not far from the border town of Flomaton but still worlds away from Brunswick. He, Mary Alice, and their four children (their youngest, Nina, was two) lived in a rented home, likely a small cabin.

Here Walters's frustrations with life, with the world outside, found an outlet. As Bledsoe recalled to the press, he was plagued with suspicions of infidelity by Mary Alice. "I dare say they were not true," Bledsoe noted, "because she is a much better woman than he is a man." Stoked by whiskey, Walters's accusations grew louder, and his anger turned violent. According to Julia, who understood well, Mary Alice had no choice but to "quit him," returning to Georgia with the children and filing for divorce. Her accusations in court suggest that he was spinning out of control: she was the victim not just of his well-known penchant for profanity—he called her a "damn bitch," among other vulgarities unmentionable before a judge—but also physical abuse. He wielded a gun and threatened to kill her. He beat her with a stick and choked her. Walters failed to appear in court to address the charges, and the divorce was granted.

Mary Alice remarried in Ashford, Alabama, but as Bledsoe recalled, the relationship was short-lived. It was long rumored in Robeson County, North Carolina, that Walters tried to steal some or all of his children away from her, even that he'd locked them up in a barn, but Walters denied it. In 1913, that gossip was so darkened by the present charges against him that the truth is impossible to discern. Suddenly without family, without any fixed community, without a job or purpose, Walters was unmoored. He spent the next seven years in a dark, aimless exile, chasing work westward, from Arkansas to Texas, and finally back east to Louisiana.

By late summer of 1907, he seemed to have found tentative footing again. He was working for Industrial Lumber in the company town of Elizabeth, Calcasieu Parish, at home and with savings enough to settle and launch a business. He would build his own blacksmith shop. Just fifty-six miles southeast, newlyweds Percy and Lessie Dunbar had begun their own new life in Opelousas. Their first son had just been conceived.

On September 9 Walters's dream died early. He and a hired hand were unloading lumber to build his new shop when they lost control of the load, and it came crashing down on Walters's leg. His kneecap was shattered into three pieces. Though skilled at stabilizing the victims of industrial carnage, company physicians were not surgeons, and Walters was moved to a hospital in Shreveport, Louisiana. A doctor cut open his knee and drained the wound, then drilled holes into each of the patella fragments, threaded a metal wire through the holes, and pulled it taut, drawing the fragments together. After surgery, the leg was splinted, and Walters lay bedridden for months.

Even after his release, his leg was rigid, the knee barely bendable, and he was in constant pain. "I could hardly walk," he told the court in Poplarville. He made his way back south to Elizabeth, hoping to scrape some semblance of his dream back together. But his lumber was long gone, and so was his little buggy.

Up north, in Rapides Parish, he managed to recover the buggy, which "had been run away with and fixed up," and lingered in search of work. It is at this point in the Alexandria and Pineville chapter of Walters's Louisiana saga that discrepancies emerged in the retelling, between the prisoner's own memory and those of local witnesses.

Blacksmith A. J. McClendon recalled two visits by Walters, in 1908 and 1911, but he did not take the stand at the Poplarville hearing. Meanwhile, Walters himself swore that he had visited McClendon only once. As to the substance of their time together, the men were in agreement. When asked by Garland if he worked for McClendon, Walters's clipped response revealed volumes: "I stayed in the blacksmith shop with him. I couldn't do much." He had taken up assisting McClendon, with an eye toward starting his own shop once again. But in just a few weeks, he came to feel the full limits of his new handicap. Smithing required a physical strength and an ease and speed of movement that Walters no longer had. A lame blacksmith might find his place in the pantheon of Greek gods, but in mortal turn-of-the-century America, he was all but useless.

Walters was not one to wallow idle in despair; with one future foreclosed, he dreamed of another. It made sense that he would turn to his childhood friend from North Carolina for help in hatching his scheme. David Bledsoe was a well-known singing-school teacher and a writer of popular hymns, and Walters's dream was musical. He was designing a harp, he wrote Bledsoe from Louisiana, a giant contraption that he claimed would have "a thousand strings." As his friend grumbled later, "He has been trying to interest me in it for years, trying to get me to put money up so he could get it on the market. I don't take any stock in it and would not have anything to do with it."

Walters was undeterred. But building and marketing the harp would take time, and he was not so foolish as to expect a fortune overnight. He needed a new vocation, one more suited to his impairment. Over the years, he had developed a passable knack for fixing simple household machines, from clocks and sewing machines to devices closer to his passion, such as pianos and organs. With time and practice, he could turn that talent into a trade. But not in a town like Alexandria, where there was plenty of skilled competition already. Walters's best hope for work lay on the open road, where he could travel from one remote farm or tiny settlement to another, repair whatever things were broken, at his own leisurely pace, and move on before they broke again. He could work for room and board, and his buggy would be his toolbox.

In exchange for his treasured gold watch, Walters acquired from Mr. McClendon "a little old rake of a horse" to pull his reclaimed buggy through the parishes north of Rapides. Eventually, on the banks of the upper Little River, he found work for a Widow Wainwright running her ferry, and because the job required that he keep time, he traded in his horse and buggy for another watch. To supplement his income, he fished the river for white perch and trout and sold his catch to the kitchen of the brand-new Hotel Bentley in Alexandria. Nearby were the famously pungent healing waters of White Sulphur Springs, but if Walters partook, they failed him. While legend had it that cast-off canes and crutches piled up at the springs by the wagonload, Walters was still hobbling on a stick the following summer.

He left Wainwright's suddenly, and although some Pineville citizens rumored that one of the widow's skiffs disappeared along with him, Mrs. Wainwright herself never came forward to make such a charge. And while Garland took a stab at linking the Little River with the Atchafalaya, in an effort to nudge the defendant's water travels closer to Swayze Lake, the implied route would have taken Walters across the entire length of the state's largest freshwater lake, then down a crisscrossing network of rivers and barely connected bayous. It was at least two hundred miles of water— for a cripple in a skiff, an odyssey of epic proportions.

According to most witnesses, Walters actually ventured north. "He came to my home through direction of my neighbors," wrote R. L. Caldwell of Ouachita Parish in a letter just after Walters's arrest, "who told him that I have certain tools that he wanted the use of in making a stringed musical instrument; the instrument he made while here." From Ouachita, he moved on to nearby Jackson Parish, where witnesses recalled him mending clocks for the spring and summer, and boasting of his scheme to patent his harp. "[A]bout the last of 1910 or first of 1911," Walters swore on the stand, he left Louisiana for the last time and headed just over the border to the hospital in Vicksburg, Mississippi. Doctors may have reopened the knee, but they left at least one piece of the irritating wire inside him. Discharged, he traveled south to Dentville, where his renowned instrument was finally finished. The New Era Harp of a Thousand Strings, he called it, although the actual string count was 287.

Astoundingly, this was not the same instrument that Mrs. Goleman and her Pearl River County neighbors recalled from the fall of 1912. His first harp, he swore on the stand, he had left "at my old home in North Carolina." And it is in North Carolina, in the fall of 1911, that history caught up with Walters again. He would reunite with his aging parents, whom he had not seen in a decade or more. He would come to know the troubled young woman who cared for them and tended their fields, and he would meet her boy.

FOR THE POPLARVILLE habeas corpus hearing, Dale's sister and part-time legal secretary Sarah was cajoled into service as court stenographer for free, and her typed transcription runs ninety-nine pages. But legally speaking, the whole affair should have been a formality. "We can try this case in twenty-five minutes," Judge Weathersby had growled at its opening, announcing that no testimony on the vexing question of the boy's identity would be allowed. The only issue before them now was the narrow question of the writ. As if that had not hamstrung Dale and Rawls enough, when they began calling their witnesses—scores of Pearl River County residents who swore that Walters was in Mississippi at the time of Bobby's disappearance—Garland rose to object aggressively, and Weathersby soon concurred. "I don't think the question to prove an alibi is a question to be considered by me in the trial of this case," he declared. "If that was the law, there never would be an extradition on the face of the earth. Any man could live in a state long enough to make enough friends to prove an alibi."

Nevertheless, perhaps out of neighborliness, Weathersby allowed the Mississippians to speak, and irrespective of admissibility, they made quite a case. An express agent brought his records of Walters's package to Reverend Meeks on August 21: a boxed violin. Ben Alsbrooks recalled timbering dogwood behind the Soneses' place on August 22, and each time he came to the porch for water, Walters was there, the innards of broken clocks spread out before him. On Sunday, August 25, Emile Thigpen rode to Whitesand Church with Walters and the boy right beside him.

But it was the Louisiana witnesses who mattered most, and the bar for their testimony was far lower: all they had to do was offer the reasonable possibility that Walters had been in their state at or around the time of

Bobby's disappearance, leaving the issue of conflicting testimony to the Louisiana courts once Walters was extradited.

Railroad carpenter Frank Ansley swore that he first saw Walters standing by the tracks near Swayze Lake, as he was passing by rail, on Saturday, August 24, headed east on a work car, and on Sunday the twenty-fifth, headed west "on the back of a passenger train." Ansley's final encounter was more substantial: the same man appeared on Monday at his work site, curious if the Dunbar child had been found or if there were any reward.

Percy's uncle Preston King, whose Swayze Lake sightings had been speculated over for months, finally told the story himself. At dawn on Sunday, August 25, two days after Bobby went missing, King was alone by the railroad tracks when a tramp who he was sure was Walters approached, carrying a stick, and asked him if he were the sheriff. When King explained the search for the missing boy, the tramp said that he had heard about it, and agreed to keep a lookout on his way to Melville.

Under cross-examination, Dale pounded away at why neither witness had taken any action. Ansley insisted that there was nothing to hold the man on except "suspicion." King put it this way: "If I had thought for a moment that morning that the child was kidnapped, I would have taken charge of that gentleman." King's *earlier* Swayze Lake sighting—that he had seen and spoken at length with *two* men, *before* Bobby went missing—was not brought to light in court by the Columbia attorneys or in the newspapers. For this, Garland must have been relieved.

Witnesses from Rapides Parish—Albert Dantin, William Mallett, and Mrs. Lizzie McManus—all had slightly more sustained encounters with Walters, whom they had seen anywhere from 1910 to 1912. Like many who had come forward in the papers, Dantin and Mallett remembered Walters by his wagon: "W. C. Walters Stove Mender" was lettered across its canvas.

In a desperate bid to refute these witnesses, Walters was recalled to the stand. Ansley and King were certainly mistaken, he declared. He denied knowing Dantin, challenged Mallett's dates, and called Mrs. McManus "crazy." As for the emblazoned wagon, he stated flatly, "Never had anything of the kind in my life." And it wasn't just the wagon that didn't match, he insisted, it was the profession: W. C. Walters had never mended stoves.

Judge Weathersby's verdict was all but inevitable: the writ was vacated. Immediately and predictably, Dale and Rawls announced an appeal and asked for a stay of judgment. "For three minutes," the *Item* frothed, "Walters was in the custody of the state of Louisiana." When Weathersby granted the stay, the prisoner smirked at his friend Sheriff Swords and reportedly quipped, "Better luck next time."

Much to their opponents' disgust, Dale and Rawls insisted that they could not possibly ready their appeal before the close of the state supreme court's session in mid-July, so the case would have to wait until the court reconvened in the fall. "Keep Walters until we come for him in October," Garland sniped on his way back to Opelousas.

As Sheriff Moody escorted Walters to the depot for the return to Columbia, a small snarling woman shot out of the curious mob. Mrs. McManus of Pineville, whom the *Item* dubbed the "little widow," was still ired by Walters's testimony that she was insane. Prisoner and witness had traded glowers in the courtroom, but unrestrained and in the street, her tirade was so caustic that Walters fled into the depot's waiting room, at which point Mrs. McManus implored Moody to deputize her so she could drag Walters by the neck "all the way to the Louisiana line."

The two clearly had history. Walters had not denied it, although according to his testimony he had lunched only a few times in her restaurant during a single visit to the area. *Before* the hearing, Mrs. McManus had told reporters that Walters visited Pineville twice and had boarded with her for months. Under oath, she had grown circumspect, swearing only that he "worked in our town." It would not be the last time that she tailored her testimony, either. There was far more to the little widow than she wanted the public to know.

As Poplarville's other visitors made their exodus, it became apparent that there had been a surprising no-show: Julia Anderson. In the past month, Garland Brown (Walters's North Carolina cousin and Julia's de facto lawyer) had written Dale and Rawls, eagerly offering to escort her to Mississippi when needed. Notifying Brown of the hearing's date and time, Rawls suggested a rendezvous in either Columbia or Poplarville. In response, Brown had begun to hedge: he had a busy term in court, and it would be hard to pull away. Nevertheless, Julia's imminent arrival was trumpeted in Poplarville, and when she failed to appear, it was speculated that perhaps Brown had taken her to Columbia by mistake. In the coming weeks, Brown would write to apologize; he'd had every intention of coming, he claimed, but had fallen ill.

In terms of the hearing, Julia's absence did not matter. Since her testimony would relate to the "separate issue" of the child's identity, Judge Weathersby would have barred her from the stand. But in the court of public opinion, her presence would surely have made a deep impression, and Dale and Rawls were looking forward to conferring with her on strategy for the battles to come. Her absence was a profound disappointment.

But one person missed Julia for personal reasons.

Just before the hearing, Walters's youngest brother D.B. appeared unannounced in Poplarville, having traveled by covered wagon all the way from Florida. The *Item*'s description of D.B. as near identical to his brother—save his lack of a mustache, he had the same "shifting eyes, the peculiar way of talking, and the same nervous way of crossing and uncrossing his legs"—was carefully crafted to reignite speculation of a look-alike Walters Gang. Nevermind their thirteen-year difference in age. And because the reunion between the Walters brothers had occurred out of reporters' earshot, all sorts of guesswork had ensued as to D.B.'s motive for appearing. Perhaps Dale and Rawls would spring him as a surprise witness.

But D.B. did not testify. As the *Item* gossiped, "Julia Anderson did not arrive with . . . Garland Brown, from North Carolina, although D. B. Walters was at every incoming train expecting to meet them." At the hearing's close, D.B. announced that he would follow his brother to Columbia for a "consultation" with Dale and Rawls, and after that, he just might return to Pearl River County. "I like the people here," he told the *States*, "and the good grub they serve you."

As chipper as his presentation was, D.B. was adrift. He had made the long trip by wagon to support his brother, surely, but he had also come for Julia. And he would linger in the area less for legal "consultation," and more out of hope—vain hope—that she would finally appear. He and Julia shared both a daughter and an unresolved history.

Chapter 15

Julia Anderson, New Orleans *Times-Democrat*, May 1, 1913

ACCORDING TO FAMILY LORE, by the time their eleventh and final child came along, J. P. and Ailsie Walters had run out of names, so they called the boy Doctor Bunyon, after the physician who delivered him. In fact, Doctor was a common name in the extended Walters family. Some sources called him Doctor Brown (Ailsie's maiden name), and on official records, his name is listed as "Doctor B." or "D.B." with the middle name not spelled out. Everybody who knew him just called him Bunt.

In 1910 he was thirty-five and single, the last son still at home, and with the health of his eighty-year-old father on the decline, likely taking over the farm that he had worked his whole life. "They've got about three hundred acres, hill and bottom land together," recalled Julia Anderson, the unwed mother who had, sometime between 1908 and 1910, found her way into the Walterses' employ. "They are old folks . . . I lived with them, working in the house and making a crop on shares." Julia tended five acres of cotton, two and a half acres of corn, and some tobacco. In addition to her cropping, cooking, and housework, as the elder Walterses grew sicker and weaker, Julia was their caregiver.

Bunt knew Julia well. They worked alongside each other in the fields, ate meals together, and shared the same roof. Her illegitimate son, Bruce, was nearly two, and her past was no secret. Whether the relationship was romantic before it was sexual is unknown, but by summer 1910, Julia was pregnant again, and Bunt made no move to correct the situation with an offer of marriage. Making matters worse, around that time, he was indicted for assault with a deadly weapon, the details of the charge unknown.

In March 1911 Julia gave birth to a blue-eyed daughter, whom she named Dell Bernice. Now she had a newborn, a two-year-old, and an elderly couple to take care of. The situation was both scandalous and untenable, and everyone knew it.

Two months after Bernice was born, Bunt's older married sister Iredell Williamson came up for a visit from Eastman, Georgia. The previous July, she had returned to the family homestead for the whole month, during which time, while Julia was busy with household chores, she had dressed one-year-old Bruce and gotten to know him. He was "exceptionally bright," Iredell recalled in an affidavit, and on this second visit, she spent even more time with the boy. Bruce "had grown into an attractive child," Iredell observed, and though she had a house full of her own legitimate children back home, she found herself quite fond of this little blue-eyed unfortunate.

Julia could not help but notice the connection, and while it agonized her to imagine, she wondered if Bruce might be better off, even for just a while, with Iredell and her family. According to Iredell's affidavit, "at the suggestion of the said Julia Anderson, [I] came very near adopting the child." But in the end, she returned to Georgia without him.

After Iredell's departure, Julia's plight grew rapidly worse. She was penniless, in danger of losing her job, and utterly alone. In July 1911, just four months after giving birth to Bernice, scandal struck again: she was charged with fornication and adultery, alongside her codefendant and neighbor, McDorman Walters, James Pleasant Walters's forty-two-year-old nephew. It was not the first time that McDorman had faced these charges, nor would it be the last; he had both a wife and a long-standing mistress.

Fornication and adultery was a common and widely bandied charge in North Carolina at the turn of the century, and an indictment could be brought on the most circumstantial of evidence. The criteria for admissible charges tended to sanction suspicion of individuals who weren't in much position to fight back: a man and woman not married and of different races spotted riding in a buggy or eating at the same table; or a man and woman not married but spotted working together in the fields. So it is possible that Julia was wrongfully indicted, and no record of a conviction exists. Given all other evidence, however, a *Pic* stringer's report from late April 1913 provides a harsh but more realistic conclusion: "For years she has been a character . . . driven about, scoffed at and openly decried because of her prostitution."

Nonetheless, in the summer of 1911, Julia's feelings for Bunt Walters ran strong. As she would later confess to Bunt's brother Cant, she "loved [him] better than any man she had ever met." Bunt, however, was what a later Walters descendant would call a "rounder, a real rounder," known for boasting of the number of his sexual conquests. His feelings for Julia may have been different, or it may have been just her own wishful thinking when she told Ethel Hutson that he offered to marry and support her.

According to that same interview, the stumbling block to marriage was a moral one: Elisha Floyd—the husband who had shot her—was still alive. "I didn't think it was right to marry him when I had a man living," she had said. While noting Julia's religiosity elsewhere in her report, Miss Hutson found this stance on marriage peculiar, attributing it to Julia's "own standard of right and wrong." In fact, it was a commonly held tenet within devout Baptist communities of the era.

But by William Walters's later recollection, the real issue complicating matrimony with Bunt was that Julia's marriage to Elisha Floyd was not legally over. Divorced or not, Julia Anderson was not the Walters family's ideal wife for young Bunt. They encouraged him to propose to "a reputable farmer's daughter, whom he seemed to fancy," but that, too, was wishful thinking. The marriage imbroglio persisted for months, until, in the fall of 1911, the law came down on the unwed lovers again: Julia and Bunt were charged with fornication and adultery themselves. Considering that they lived under the same roof, the charges were likely to stick when brought into court.

No matter how fond he may have been of Julia, Bunt Walters couldn't face the prospect of serving jail time; when officers came to arrest them, he fled. Like James Cowan, Bunt skipped town and did not look back. So Julia was taken in without him, thrown in the county jail in Lumberton, with Bruce and Bernice in tow. Since her codefendant could not be located, Julia and her children were released after a half hour, and the charges were not pursued. But now she had even more scandal to contend with still.

★   ★   ★

EVER SINCE HER return from Opelousas, Julia had been tearing herself up with the same hindsight attacks: If it was really her child, why did she leave him with the Dunbars? Why didn't she stay and fight? And whenever she took up pen and paper, even though she was addressing lawyers she had never met, those last moments with Bruce were all she could talk about.

> Wilmington, NC
> July 5, 1913
> Mr T S Dale

Dear Sir

    I will take the time in riting you a few words in ansure to your Letter of Last week. was aful sorrow that W C Walters will half to bee turned over to La fore I don't have any ida that I will ever see my Deare baby any more. I have [moved] to Wilmington NC, and if you need me or want me to go, you will half to send heare fore me. I sure want to go. it is aful hard fore me, it seams Like it will nearly overcome me . . . I no it is my child and I want it . . . I would of sware to the child when I was out there but I was afraid that they would kill me . . . the People told me they would kill me and Bruce did Look so good to me but how my hart did ach to Just git him in my arms and get out of site with him. Well it brakes my hart. I now he is my child, and god noes he is, so Let me heare at once. I still Looking and wating on you.

> as ever your friend
> Julia Anderson

    tell Walters to still hold up fore me to be there when the trial is had

Wilmington was a bustling port city some seventy miles east of Julia's native Robeson and Columbus Counties, and she had moved there about a month earlier. The 1911–12 city directory lists her return address as the residence of a successful Russian dry goods merchant who had six children at home, the youngest an infant, so it is possible that Julia had come for domestic work and child care. She was not making much money, but life there was undoubtedly more tolerable than back home.

While Julia had mentioned threats in Opelousas before, her phrasing had never been so raw as it was in this letter—she used the word *kill* twice. A critic might accuse her of exaggerating her fear in retrospect, in an effort to justify her "passive" return home. But it is just as likely that now, only now, with two months and a thousand miles between her and

Opelousas, could she allow herself to feel the raw truth of all that had happened to her there: the thinly veiled mutterings of menace, the suffocating weight of disdain all around her. It had been more army than town, and its mission was to scare her away. That fantastical moment that she pined for, that break where she and Bruce could light out for freedom together, had never been there for her to seize.

JULIA'S TORMENT WOULD have been far worse had she known that just a week before she penned this letter, that same army had swelled its ranks and united in common purpose once again: a joyous affirmation that the boy she knew to be her son was in fact Bobby Dunbar. The nominal purpose of the celebration was the State Firemen's Association annual convention, a gathering of hook-and-ladder crews from every parish in Louisiana, but the return of the Dunbar boy gave the event its spirit. The Saturday courtbouillon and fish fry was held at Half Moon Lake, which, as the *Point Coupee Banner* felt compelled to spell out, was "near the spot made famous by the kidnapping of little Robert Dunbar, Lake Swayze." Enlivening that evening's elections, the firemen voted unanimously to make Bobby Dunbar a lifetime association member, dues paid in full. Then came Sunday's parade and tournament, for which thousands of visitors had arrived by train. Marching through town to the courthouse square, all the companies were preceded by their own brass band, and atop the Opelousas truck sat little Bobby, "flirting a small American flag"—appearing much happier in this spot than he had been in late April.

Soon Bobby Dunbar's homecoming had spread across the state. In mid-July, the Alexandria *Town Talk* announced that he would be an honored guest at upcoming "Alexandria Day," a grand civic tribute to the troops of Camp Stafford, the nearby training post for Louisiana's National Guard. During his stay, the merchants' association would graciously put up the boy and his family in the city's finest downtown hotel, the Bentley.

In the same edition that gossiped of the Dunbars' arrival came word that one of the Bentley's most notable guests would be checking out. "George" the much-beloved alligator who resided in the lobby's marble fountain, "who numbers among his friends some of the best known drummers in the South," was being shipped north to Kansas. Apparently George had outgrown the fountain and had taken to crawling out onto the lobby floor to visit with the public or to nest at the hotel manager's feet under his desk. So the manager had decided to gift the gator to a friend in Topeka, where George would live out the rest of his years in roomier quarters, in the pond of a city park. This may have truly been the full story, but it was a curious coincidence nonetheless: the Bentley's eviction of the alligator known for his affection for humans, just days before their welcome of the boy once feared to have been an alligator's prey.

On Thursday the seventeenth, a delegation of Alexandrians met the Dunbars—Percy, Lessie, Bobby, Alonzo, and Lessie's mother, Delia—and escorted them from train station to hotel, drawing a crowd as they went. Late the next morning, the official parade began. Nearly every store along its route was bedecked with flags and bunting, and directly opposite the town square, positioned in a prime viewing spot on the Bentley's loggia, stood Louisiana governor Luther Hall. First came the soldiers, 450 in all, headed up by the First Regiment Band. Ambulances, decorated cars, and the Lady Riders followed. O'Shee Coffee Company's colossal steam-spouting coffeepot was a big hit, even after it snagged on some wires. But the "center of attraction" was the magnificent Mother's Club Float, adorned with red roses and magnolias, packed with children, and, in the center of four giant white canopy-draped columns, Mrs. C. P. Dunbar and her long-lost son.

After an outdoor banquet for the soldiers, and an afternoon of horse races and free moving pictures, came the Opelousas-Alexandria amateur baseball game, for which little Bobby was invited to throw the first pitch. He "did it just as any other little American would," and apparently the throw was charmed: visitors trounced home, 7–1.

Sports rivalry aside, Alexandria loved Bobby Dunbar, and the feeling was mutual. "Mama, let's come here to live," the local paper boastfully quoted him, "They don't steal little boys here, and I like the people."

Kidnapping loomed large that day in the mind of the boy's father as well. With the town still reveling, Percy joined his family on a social call to the home of his aunt and uncle, but it was not long before he slipped off to meet his latest informant: Mr. A. Koenig, the German-Jewish umbrella man from New Orleans.

In April, Koenig had been one of the first to come forward with a Rapides-area sighting of Walters. Since this occurred in the winter of 1913, *after* Bobby disappeared, he was not needed at the Poplarville hearing. On top of that, he had stated emphatically that although he had seen Walters repeatedly in various locales, "I never saw him with a child." But now Koenig had availed himself of important new information, and invited Mr. Dunbar, via an article in the local paper on the eve of Alexandria Day, to a fact-finding rendezvous.

At the corner of Tenth and Scott Streets, Percy and the umbrella man stood before a large vacant lot. When the building next door had been a boardinghouse, the spillover guests and diners often hitched their horses there and camped in their wagons. In January, Koenig had been staying at the home of his sister and her family, on the other side of the boardinghouse, and had noticed Walters and his wagon tied up near the lot for more than a week. But the establishment had since closed, and its proprietress was nowhere to be found.

Instead Koenig took Percy next door to hear from his two nieces, twelve-year-old Ruby Greenstone and her nineteen-year-old sister, Regina. Together they told Mr. Dunbar what they had told their uncle just two days before: when he camped in the lot, Walters had not been alone. There was another man staying with him, whom the sisters and their uncle were inexplicably certain was Walters's brother D.B. Also, there were two little boys. Young Ruby, who often went over to play with the children of the boardinghouse's owner, saw these two lads regularly during that week, and she even spoke with them. Both she and her sister would know them anywhere.

Though he was in Alexandria at that moment, just a few blocks away, there is no report that the Dunbar boy and the Greenstone girls were brought face-to-face. Nevertheless, Percy wrapped up his Alexandria Day investigatory junket utterly convinced of the umbrella man's bold new claim: "W. C. Walters and his brother, Bobbie Dunbar, and Bruce Anderson—all four—were in Alexandria at one time." Percy would relate as much to District Attorney Garland, who would soon interview Koenig himself. The umbrella maker was now not just relevant to the case, but essential.

Days later, George the evicted hotel alligator, arrived in Topeka after a long journey north. As his crate was opened at the pond's shore, he lifted his head for a moment, then recoiled dramatically and expired. According to the Bentley's manager, his beloved former keeper, he'd probably died of grief.

WITH DEFENSE COSTS mounting through the summer, Dale and Rawls, who had long ago hocked Walters's horse and rig, begged his Carolina clan to contribute, but their financial response was well short of a trickle. Negotiating the sale of Walters's share in the Robeson homestead, the attorneys groused that it had been whittled down, via bloated percentages and made-up fees, to practically nothing. Meanwhile, Louisianans were showering money on his prosecution, with "Dunbar Funds" popping up all over the state in July, some established by local newspapers and some funneling their donations through the *Item*. In Opelousas, Jacobs News Depot ran a sale on Bobby Dunbar and W. C. Walters postal cards, the proceeds of which were intended for the boy himself. Featuring images of kidnapper and victim, along with the date and location of the latter's vanishing and the former's arrest, the cards garnered $5.65 in just a few days, so popular that two thousand more were ordered.

But Jacobs certainly was not selling out on Dunbar *news* like it used to. By midsummer, the afternoon dailies were grasping at straws to keep the story alive. When a desperate Massachusetts mother, whose estranged husband had made off with their three-year-old son in August 1912, became convinced that the boy in Opelousas was hers, the *States* gave a full column over to her sad delusion. The *Pic* merely scoffed: "Little Dunbar, if the farce continues, will have enough mammas to last him through several spans of life." From the *Item* came this shocker: "Bruce Anderson Is Buried," which turned out to be nothing but some short-lived gossip from a teenage girl.

The venerable Lyric Theater attempted to revive and cash in on Dunbar-Walters fever with a stage play, *The Tinker and the Boy: A Melodrama in Four Acts,* hurled together by a New Orleans criminal attorney and his brother, a newsman-cum-actor, who wisely chose to leave their names out of the playbill. Notwithstanding the remarkable transformations of its young female star, Aline Richter—from "Willie Barton" in act 1 at Swazye Lake, dirtied up as "Joe" in act 2 outside a Mississippi church, cleaned up again as "Willie" in act 3 rebuffing the pleas of "Maud Allison" from the Carolina hills, and, once and for all, "Willie" in act 4, as per judgment by "Mr. White"—the play was a thudding disappointment. It "starts in the air and stops there," complained the *States,* with "no hero, no villain, and no denouement. It sticks too close to the truth to be a melodrama. Comedy is furnished by the constable, whom you recognize as a comedian because he has that kind of whiskers." Worse than just a crass rehash, *The Tinker and the Boy* had managed to flatten the mystery of its underlying material, to suck the life out of its drama.

Finally, one or more impatient citizens took matters into their own hands, and penned the most lurid chapter in the Dunbar saga yet. The anonymous letters were addressed to Percy and mischievously signed

"Well Wisher." For at least a month, the writer had been promising valuable information in the kidnapping case, though for fear of "interference," he or she was reluctant to meet in person without a guarantee of confidentiality. Sheriff Swords suggested that Percy play along, if for no other reason than to "ferret" out this nameless tormentor, and Percy took his advice. In a preposterously simple cryptogram (A=1, B=2) that ran for three days in the *Item*'s "Special Notices" section, Percy responded: "I will be in New Orleans on August 6 and 7 at the Cosmopolitan Hotel, and would be glad to meet you if possible."

Inevitably, the *States* spotted, decoded, and printed the message in full, with mocking commentary, sending Percy and Swords into a bitter, public rage.

Days later, Well Wisher wrote Percy again, confirming their meeting but worrying that the publicity had now put him in grave danger with a certain other party. Next came a letter from that other party directly, whose moniker was far less sunny: "B. and H.," clearly intended to evoke "Black Hand," the Sicilian extortion racket that had kidnapped and murdered Walter Lamana in 1907.

"You are hereby warned not to make any attempt whatsoever to get into communication with [Well Wisher], or to try and secure the papers he holds," B. and H. intoned. "Failure to heed this warning will result disastrously for both you and your informer." Days later, they escalated the threat in a politely sinister letter directly to Lessie: "We may be criminals before the eyes of the world, but we are also human, and we know that by killing your husband and child we would also be practically killing you." It was not just Percy they would kill, but Bobby as well.

Despite their menace, B. and H.'s rationale for opposing Percy's meeting with Well Wisher was less than credible. The boy, they claimed, was a secret heir, willed a fortune in New Mexican gold mines by an old miser who believed him to be Bruce Anderson. Well Wisher was planning to offer the will to Mr. Dunbar, but B. and H. wanted the fortune for themselves. And in case *their own* threats were not deterrent enough, B. and H. went on, the will stipulated that if the boy did not live to the age of seven, the fortune would revert to Well Wisher. Which meant that Well Wisher had his own incentive to kill the boy. As fast as B. and H. plugged holes in their logic, a new leak sprung somewhere else, and they bullied away skepticism with two-bit snarls: *Do you think we are napping?*

Undeterred, Percy released all the letters to the press and headed to New Orleans with Sheriff Swords. "They can't bluff me," he wired the

Item, beelining to police headquarters to obtain a firearm permit, and finally explaining his curious determination: Well Wisher "tells me that he has information which will prove I have my boy and not Bruce Anderson." Though Percy himself long knew this fact, he still burned "to prove to the Doubting Thomases that they do not know what they are talking about." This was the same silver bullet Percy had been hunting for months.

When B. and H. got wind of his arrival, they unleashed their goriest threat yet, delivered, of course, to the *Item.* They had already killed Well Wisher, and no matter how much protection Mr. Dunbar enlisted—the police, the army; "let him dress up in a suit of mail"—if he showed up at the Cosmopolitan the next day, he would be dead, too.

> When the world reads Friday that C. P. Dunbar is no more—has been shot down like a dog—there will be a universal exclamation of, "What next in this case?" If the world only knew what the *real* facts in this case are . . . what motives prompted the kidnapping of Robert Dunbar . . . why Bruce Anderson is kept in seclusion . . . how many lives have been sacrificed, murders committed, how much suffering caused, it would gasp in astonishment that such things can happen nowadays. *And if it only knew what is yet going to happen* before the curtain falls on the Dunbar-Anderson-Walters case, *it would be astounded.*

To most objective witnesses, it had now become painfully obvious what would transpire that morning at the Cosmopolitan Hotel. And yet Percy arrived promptly at nine thirty, checked into room 307, and waited. Reporters, police, and detectives gathered in the lobby, and they waited, too. Sheriff Swords stalked the halls and cursed at F. S. Tisdale from the *States.* A motorcycle messenger boy buzzed in with an important letter for room 307 and then buzzed away just as fast. He was the only surprise that morning. He was the only arrival. No one else showed up, and nothing else happened. As Tisdale wrote, "[T]here was no cascade of gore down the stairway."

Percy did his best to downplay how seriously he had taken the letters, and the public lashed out at the cruel manipulation of the Dunbars. Most people blamed the newspapers, and Swords accused the *States* specifically. Hoping to gloss over its own dubious role in the affair, the *Item's* editorial agreed that the guilty party was "pounding a typewriter in some local newspaper office," and issued a bloodthirsty call for retribution "by St. Landry rawhide." In eight months, the likeliest suspects would strike again, but for this particular offense, they would go unpunished.

In Opelousas, with fear of sinister strangers gripping the household around him, it is no surprise that the boy's own mind would simultaneously darken. "Bobby's Memory Is Getting Clearer," read the report's headline, but the details, culled from an interview with Percy during the fizzled Cosmopolitan showdown, were not so happy. What Bobby was remembering were new details from his abduction. Not just that it had rained that night and he "got very wet," but before that, before even the kidnapping. "Daddy," Percy quoted his son, "if you had stayed close by me and hadn't ridden off on the horse, that old man Walters wouldn't have got me."

It was left unspoken, and probably unasked, how these memories emerged, whether in answer to questions or volunteered. In either case, it was clear that the horror of August 23, 1912 (the anniversary of which was fast approaching), had become a point of fixation for the Dunbar family and for Bobby himself. In collective conversation and in private thoughts, it was always with them.

As Percy went on to suggest, the boy's fears, which in early May had been focused on Walters, were now more generalized. He was scared of going anywhere in the dark. He was scared of being stolen again, not necessarily by the "bad old man," but by "someone." A person he didn't know. Anyone.

In the breezeless swelter of his cell, Walters savored a jawful of tobacco and scowled at the report about Bobby's memory. Friends and allies kept him up-to-date on the case with news clippings delivered by mail, and with nothing but time on his hands, he painstakingly transcribed the more noteworthy reports for his attorneys, line by line, on an endless supply of Sheriff Hathorn's stationery, mulling, questioning, and inserting bits of his own commentary alongside:

You no A Child can be taught to say any thing *But this Don't Look Real to Me.*

And the longer the prisoner considered the "memory" article, the stranger his doubts became:

Note Carefully

"Dady if you had stayed close by me and hadn't ridden off [on] the horse that old man walters wouldn't have got me."

And the Question Arises what should this mean unless He took his Own Child off for someone to get him and He on Horseback and Left the Little Fellow to Be taken.

It wasn't simply that Percy regretted leaving Bobby, and that his regret had tinged the boy's "memory." As Walters saw it, Percy had *intended* for the boy to be stolen and had inadvertently exposed that intention.

The tortured logic continued to flower, nourished by an unending supply of anger at his accuser. As for the overripe drama of Well Wisher and B. and H., Walters wrote, "I Believe CP Dunbar Has someone in New Orleans Doing this to try to Hold Public Sentiment." Still more wild-eyed, he contended that Percy "Belongs to the Black Hand" and "spirited his own Child Away," and also that "there is An organized Band of Criminals threw Miss and La And I beleave C P Dunbar is their Chief And it was A Plan they Had to take my Bruse and Put me out of the way and Put Him on the stag."

The fevered finger-pointing was borne of desperation. Though his lawyers kept him well stocked with tobacco and piano strings for his harp, they had just taken on another high-profile client—an alleged train robber—and until the state supreme court hearing, Walters was not a priority. On Sunday mornings when the heat wasn't too bad, he enjoyed the attention of curious Columbians who gathered on the jailhouse lawn for his sermons and music. But his public was bigger than Marion County, and as much as he itched to release a statement to the press—"If We Lie Still and say nothing, the world will say I am Guiltie," he fretted—Dale and Rawls forbade it, reminding him that the papers consistently ignored his words or twisted them into a mockery.

Walters was just as worried for his erstwhile young traveling companion. "When I Had Him, He would talk to anyone And tell anything He knew, and He has A Lot of Sense," Walters boasted wistfully to the attorneys, "But they have got the Poor Little Fellow Cowed." The Bruce that Walters knew would never have been scared of someone stealing him, as reports from Opelousas had claimed; he was never scared of the dark. These Dunbars belonged to "something bad," and Walters agonized over what they were doing to Bruce's mind. Since being in their care, "he has never seen any one that He loves like he Does me and her," meaning, of course, Julia. "[H]e Can't talk good about me and He wont talk [at all]." Walters was devastated to have become a target of the boy's fear, but beyond that, he ached over the past life that the boy was keeping inside. How long, Walters must have wondered, before that life was not just kept silent, but expunged?

WALTERS WAS NOT the only one with that fear. On August 22 Julia again wrote to Dale and Rawls from Wilmington. "I have findley stope getting any hearing from you at all," she cried, "I have rote 3 or 4 Letters to you and can not heare a word." She had no idea of Walters's fate and, startlingly, still didn't even know if the Dunbars "have my child." "[T]he Last hearing I got was June 23, and I do want to no so bad, it seams Like I will go crazy."

Rawls's response four days later was defensive: "We have written you a number of times since you say you received our last letter, and it must be due to the fact that you have been changing your address and the letters have gone astray." While it is impossible to know how complete the extant defense file is, the "number" of letters that it contains to Julia Anderson between June 23 and August 26 is zero.

That said, Rawls gave Julia a thorough update on the upcoming hearing before the state supreme court; on their rationale for keeping Walters out of Louisiana, where he would face "conviction and almost certain death"; and on the financial crisis that was crippling their ability to secure out-of-state witnesses.

And as for her son. "We are working hard on a plan to start proceedings to recover Bruce," Rawls promised, "but just at this time, we are not in a position to advise you definitely as to this. During September, however, we will want to take this matter up more fully with you." Offering no further details on that plan, he at last answered Julia's most pressing question:

> They have your child still in their possession, and the newspapers say that he is fine, healthy, and doing well.

Every single word of this sentence tore at her heart. The fact that the Dunbars still had Bruce was hard, but she expected it. And likely she could find some mother's comfort in the fact that he was healthy, much as she had when Walters wrote her of Bruce on their travels. But the rest of it, that her son was doing well with the Dunbars—coming from the newspapers, no less—that was the worst. Bruce was thriving in his new life, and everyone in the world knew it but her.

Julia wrote back immediately. The lawyers had given her a twig of hope, and now she was clawing at it. She proposed that "if I can get some where 75 ore a hundard Dolers would it bee all rite fore me to fix up and go out there . . . and see Walters and not Let none of the LA folks no any thing about it." She did not just want to be on hand for the trial, she wanted to come there, to Columbia, *as soon as possible*.

The hysteria and repetition in Julia's letter made it hard for the lawyers to absorb her words carefully, which they would soon come to regret. They did not write back.

IF THE ONE-YEAR anniversary of Bobby Dunbar's disappearance reignited tensions within Opelousas, the editors of the Lake Charles *American Press* offered a wry and affectionate salve, which the *St. Landry Clarion* happily reprinted. A reminder that this little boy was the town's hero, and they were united around him.

> Since Bobbie's return from Mississippi, the good old town has eaten, drunk, and breathed Bobbie. He is the Board of Trade, the annual parish fair, the condition of the cotton crop, the levee system and the corn and tomato clubs of St. Landry. Even Sheriff Marion Soward [*sic*], for the first time in his genial and spectacular career, is away back in the dust behind the distance pole.

When the Dunbars boarded the Labor Day excursion train to Baton Rouge, they must have hoped, for the day at least, that Bobby could be just like any other ordinary boy. Along with half of St. Landry Parish, they were headed to the state amateur baseball championship between Lutcher and Opelousas, which had gone undefeated the entire season. But Bobby was not going to pitch today, he was just going to cheer.

And yet, when they got to Baton Rouge, he was inevitably a celebrity. "The center of all eyes at the hotel and on the streets," burbled the *State Times Advocate*, and, in an echo of Rawls's report to Julia Anderson, "He appeared bright and happy."

Since his early August humiliation in New Orleans, Percy had lain low and stayed home, finally paying attention to selling real estate. But when curious reporters pressed, he couldn't resist a quick prediction: "I think we shall have Walters in a short time. The Supreme Court of Mississippi has to pass on the case, but I believe we have it won."

That day, though, in baseball, at least, Opelousas finally lost, 3–1.

IN THE HEYDAY of rail travel, the station matron was a fixture of most major depots in the United States. Her job was to keep the ladies' waiting areas clean and orderly, and to ensure the comfort of female travelers and their children. Up north in Chicago, in the vast and bustling passenger terminal of the Chicago and Northwestern Railway, a fleet of matrons was required—one for each of the ladies' waiting areas, the restroom, the ladies-and-childrens' apartment, the emigrant room, and the hospital—and a head matron watched over them all. In a station like this, given the segmented areas of purview, the shift changes, the presence of other terminal officials, and the constant chaos of arriving and departing passengers, it might be easy for a matron to overlook or pass off to someone else a lady who did not seem to be going anywhere.

Savannah's Union Station was grand from the street, with its twin Spanish Renaissance towers, but inside, its general waiting area for whites was just one octagonal rotunda, and its staff of matrons was correspondingly small. There may have been just one matron working. And still, it took her two days and nights to notice this woman's "peculiar actions," to notice that she was not sleeping or eating, and that her train never came.

On the morning of September 10, the matron notified the day officer of a loiterer, and together they approached the woman for questioning. In a matter of seconds, she burst into tears and began to speak freely. They recognized her story, and her name: she was Julia Anderson.

She had come from Barnesville, North Carolina, by way of Wilmington, she told them, and was on her way to Columbia, Mississippi, to testify at the trial of William Walters and to recover her son, Bruce. Her plan had been to work her way down, gradually, but her savings got her only as far as Savannah, where she'd promptly become stranded. And by now, fully unstrung.

Station officials called Associated Charities, and its secretary stepped in to help. She provided Julia, who had not eaten in days, with a meal and a proper place to rest. As proof that her travel had purpose, Julia presented a letter from an unknown New Orleans contractor, for whom she was apparently intending to work.

But the letter did not help the charity women find Julia travel fare, and so a call was placed to Columbia. Dale and Rawls were alarmed, defensive, and confused. Walters's trial would not be for months, they said, and they could not understand how Julia had gotten so mixed up about the dates (apparently forgetting their own offer to take up her cause in September). When the charity women asked if the lawyers could pay for the remainder of Julia's transportation, they reiterated that the trip would be premature. The women wondered if the lawyers might secure work for Julia in Columbia while she awaited the trial, and the lawyers apologized that they could not—that in their measured opinion, it was best for Julia to "stay with her people" until needed.

For two days, Julia remained in these kind women's care, resting, regaining her bearings, and trying to figure out just who "her people" were anymore. She told and retold all that had happened to her in the past two years, of going to Opelousas in May, and Walters traveling with Bruce before that. But there was more that mattered in Julia's story, before Walters took Bruce, details she probably did not share with the strangers.

Chapter 16

James Pleasant Walters Homestead, Robeson County, North Carolina
(Courtesy of Becky Bass Fain)

IT WAS NOVEMBER 1911. The bulk of the Walterses' cotton crop had been picked, loaded, and hauled off to the gin a month ago. After that, there was grading, tying, and bagging the dried tobacco. If croppers were in a rush, this became a community affair, a nighttime "tying party," with even the children chipping in. Bruce was three, perhaps too young to do any tying, but he certainly enjoyed the parched peanuts and the company of other youngsters.

Then it was back to cotton. The fields were still full of green bolls, the temperature was dropping, and as the local paper reported, "hands [were] scarce." All the way up to Thanksgiving, Julia was out there "scrapping," with J.P. and Ailsie, as infirm and aged as they were, working alongside her. With Bunt a fugitive from the law, and Julia's two children to manage, even if the Walterses' teenage grandson Jackson were on hand to lend his strength, it was not an efficient harvest.

Just as they finished loading it all into the cotton house, a strange wagon came bumping down the road, its progress marked by the everloudening tinkle and clang of pots and pans, hanging against the tent flaps. J.P. and Ailsie had not seen their son William Cantwell in at least a decade. From letters, they had heard bits and pieces: his jail time in Georgia, his divorce, his travels to Louisiana and Mississippi, and his time in the hospital. But it must have surprised them to see, in person, how much it all had aged him. Most apparent was his hobble. There was, Walters told them, wire in his knee still. What most struck Julia Anderson, who had never seen this Walters brother before in her life, were his eyes. "Cantwell Walters sure had vigrus eyes, theh ain't no gittin' round that," she would later recall.

Over Thanksgiving, the prodigal son regaled the household with tales of his travels, boasts of his burgeoning business as a fixer of musical instruments, and given half a chance, a song or two on his New Era Zither Harp. Between cooking, cleaning up, caring for Bernice, and running after Bruce, Julia caught snatches of the Walterses' conversations during those late-fall weeks. From what she could tell, Cant had money troubles. "He tried to get the old man to deed him his farm," she would later tell James Edmonds of the *Item*, "and promised to take care of the old folks if they would do that. They were too quick for him on that, though."

That was not all he tried, either. According to Julia, Walters offered to haul the bagged tobacco to market and then returned virtually empty-handed, offering Julia just ten cents' worth of snuff. In those days, croppers barely broke even on tobacco and often ended up deeper in debt, but Julia, who had worked hard for her share, suspected that Walters had skimmed her return. Sometime later, her mistrust was confirmed. Early one morning, with the rest of the house asleep, Walters woke Julia and demanded that she fix him breakfast; he had traveling to do that day and had to get out early. Julia groused that she "wasn't owing to get him breakfast before day," but finally agreed. Midway through fixing the meal, she glanced out the kitchen window and spotted, parked at the door of the cotton house, two carts full of the seed cotton they had harvested just before Thanksgiving. It dawned on her: Walters was preparing to make off with their cotton for himself.

She fed him his breakfast, and then woke J.P. as quickly and discreetly as she could. By the time they got outside, Walters had one cart hitched up and ready to go. "The old man and me just kept him from getting both carts," she recalled later. "He took away one of them." Sometime later, Walters returned, again with little in the way of profits, and for Julia, only "seven yards of ten-cent percale." The elder Walters were furious and demanded that their son "settle up." But he either denied there had been a profit or hedged on why it was not yet forthcoming, and the old folks—and Julia—were left to stew powerlessly. The homecoming had soured fast.

This was not the only source of tension between Walters and Julia. He had heard that his younger brother Bunt was the father of Bernice and assumed that Bunt had sired Bruce as well, an assumption Julia did not correct. Likely blaming Julia for Bunt's exile, Walters mistrusted the woman. In his words, he did not have "as good an opinion as I should have" of her. Perhaps sensing his mother's dislike for the newcomer, Bruce did not take to Walters at first, either.

Slowly but surely, though, the old man won over the boy. First with "candies and things," but most of all, with a banjo that Walters had crafted himself. The boy loved plucking and strumming it, and Walters loved being able to offer instruction. At night, when Bernice got fussy and loud, there was always a spot for Bruce under the covers with Walters. As his mother would recall, Bruce came to adore the tricky old tinker and "would follow him anywhere." Though her own mistrust still simmered, Julia did enjoy seeing her son so taken with the man. It gave her more time to tend to Bernice and the elder Walterses, but more than that, she was glad Bruce had a man to look up to. Around this time, Bruce began to call fifty-year-old William Cantwell by a name reflective of the tensions in their peculiar relationship: "Ugly Papa."

One night early in 1912, a true thaw occurred between the boy's mother and his ugly papa. An elderly neighbor was gravely ill, and both Julia and Walters went over to take care of him. The night he died, Walters would recall, "Julia proved to be an angel. Then I learned her real nature." With their newfound closeness, Julia also made a confession: "she loved his brother better than any man she had ever met." By Walters's later recollection, he made at least the overture of an attempt to bring the couple back together, to convince Julia to officially divorce so that Bunt could marry her. But by most indications, the whereabouts of the prospective groom, still a fugitive from the law, were unknown. It was not a plan that gained much traction.

For the elder Walterses, the turnabout between Julia and their son was cause for suspicion. Not of any romantic dalliance, but of a financial scheme. They still had not gotten to the bottom of the cotton matter, and now they suspected that Cant had secretly shared the pocketed profits with Julia. In this unseasonably cold winter—a ten-inch snowfall in mid-January—cabin fever took hold of J.P. and Ailsie, and they did not make life easy for those who lived under their roof.

Julia briefly fled to another live-in job, just down the road, taking Bruce and Bernice with her. At the home of Neal and Martha Stone, she was likely charged with standard domestic work as well as caring for the couple's two young daughters. With her own children in tow, she had her hands more than full.

Walters, who also was itching to leave his parents' home, approached Julia with an offer: he would take Bruce with him on a visit to his sister Hetty Bell in Bayboro, South Carolina, just across the border. Hetty and her husband had plenty of children already, but at least there would be a four-year-old son for Bruce to play with. Relatively speaking, the home was a stable one. And as Julia recalled, Walters promised that they would be gone only for a short while. With that reassurance, she agreed.

In early February, the snow was still thick on the ground, but the roads were passable. Bruce clambered into the wagon and Julia loaded in a small bundle of his clothes. Her May 1913 affidavit, corroborated by one from the Stones, depicts in clinical terms the good-bye that would haunt her for the rest of her life:

> That during the year 1912 she gave the body of her son, Bruce Anderson, to one W. C. Walters, a native of North Carolina, with the understanding that Walters was to take said child and return same to her upon her request. She further says . . . the child held by the Dunbars is the child she gave Walters in the presence of [Neal and Martha] Stone, and this was the last time she had seen Bruce Anderson until she saw him in possession of Dunbar.

A week into Walters's and Bruce's absence, temperatures dropped even further, to a decade low of six above zero. Another blizzard—twelve inches—blanketed Robeson County and the surrounding region. It was a crippling storm, shuttering churches, schools, business, and government, and it did not melt fast. From his sister's, Walters got word to Julia that he would be back with Bruce when the roads were clear.

In his extended absence, Julia knew that she could not leave J.P. and Ailsie untended, especially not in this punishing weather, so she returned with Bernice in tow. But during her stint back, the old couple's wrath became more brutal than ever, and the tension wasn't just over cotton. Sometime in these early months of 1912, Julia had become pregnant again. Julia herself would swear under oath in 1914 that the father was Bunt, which would mean that he had slipped back home sometime that winter. This possibility dovetails with Julia's confession to Walters, and Walters's matchmaking gestures as well. In the spring of 1913, however, Julia stated unequivocally that she had not seen Bunt after his July 1911 flight from arrest. It is conceivable she was covering for him.

A more unsettling possibility was reported in the spring of 1913 by a local stringer for the *Times-Democrat,* who identified the father as Dock Williamson, and again by the *Item*'s Ethel Hutson, who reported Julia's own confession a few days later: "She . . . told to one auditor alone, a woman like herself, the pitiful story of her betrayal first by a brother, and then by a brother-in-law, of the man who took away her eldest child." While two sisters of William Cantwell and D. B. Walters were married to Williamsons, who were stepbrothers, neither of them, nor any of their known brothers, was named Dock or Doctor. But there *was* a Dock Williamson in the Walters family: a *first cousin* to W.C. and D.B. He was a farmer in his early fifties, married with at least nine children, living nearby in Columbus County. It is certainly possible that Ethel Hutson inaccurately reported the man as a brother-in-law, or that Julia herself had not been sure.

Whatever the precipitating circumstances, Julia's February 1912 departure from the Walters farm was sudden. She was barefoot, wearing her only dress, and clutching a cold, hungry baby girl to her chest.

By March, she had found refuge eleven miles away in the booming tobacco town of Fairmont, North Carolina, living and working in the home of a livery manager, keeping house and taking care of the two young children, Mary and Memory. But her pregnancy did not remain secret, and that job lasted only a month. And although both the Stones and the elder Walterses knew where Julia was, when William Walters finally returned to his parents' farm with Bruce, he did not seek out Julia to return her son. Instead he took the boy to the homes of two other Walters sisters, one after another. Julia was struggling too hard to care for Bernice to register an objection, and if she had, it would not have mattered. She was in no position to take Bruce back. Her own words in 1913 suggest that she was aware of, and resigned to, Walters's true intentions. He was trying to find the boy, whom he believed to be his nephew, a better home:

He went down to Evergreen then, and tried to get [Gaston] Williamson, his brother-in-law, to take Bruce, but Williamson wouldn't do it. Late in March he left for Eastman, Ga., where he had another sister, Iredell Williamson, who had married another Williamson brother.

In the absence of letters from Walters, Julia did her best to keep up with him and Bruce through Iredell or other family connections. Once they left Eastman in April, they traveled farther south to Iron City, Georgia, home of Walters's childhood friend David Bledsoe, where another Walters nephew, Hovis, was visiting at the same time. Walters headed next toward Inverness, Florida, where Bunt was most recently known to be living. He was taking Bruce to the man he thought was his father.

While Bernice remained in the care of her mother, the one-year-old faced a future just as uncertain as that of her half brother, Bruce. Julia's life had utterly fallen apart. Though free of the Walterses' cruelty, she had also lost the shred of security that life with them had afforded. She could not find work, and she could not feed her daughter, and she had another child on the way. By late spring, Julia realized, she really had only one choice.

Ollie and Atlas Graves were a childless couple, forty-two and thirty-seven, respectively. Atlas was steadily employed as a laborer in a Lumberton cotton mill. They did not have much in the way of money, but they had more than Julia did. On July 16, 1912, their adoption of Bernice was made formal. It was an immeasurable heartbreak and a searing shame: Julia had failed as a mother with both of her children.

No surprise that she clung to small consolations. During the adoption proceedings, Julia and the Graveses settled on an informal agreement that she could see Bernice regularly and help out with her upbringing as she was able. Seeing the arrangement as fluid, provisional, and maybe even just temporary softened the loss for Julia, or at least eased her into it more gradually. And then there was the hope of the Graveses' potential as parents. It seemed to Julia that they were decent people who would give Bernice a childhood filled with love and affection. That, too, was a delusion.

And Julia had the baby inside her, due in the fall of 1912. That next chapter of her anguish was yet to come.

As she lingered in Savannah in October 1913, the losses of her children were more than just a weight on Julia's mind. They were what had motivated her decision to travel in the first place.

Although she had consented to parting with Bruce conditionally, and although she had accepted the reality that, for a time, he might be better off with Walters's sister, or with Walters himself, there had been no paper signing as there had been with Bernice. Bruce was still rightfully hers. But now that the Dunbars had him, because of her distance and the added layer of Walters's interim guardianship, Julia's claim to Bruce was deemed less authoritative and less urgent.

Up until now, she had relied on the wisdom of Walters's lawyers, trusting that they honored her custody of Bruce as the ultimate goal of their legal struggle for Walters. But as they told her to wait patiently all summer, she had grown uneasy. The longer she waited, the more forgotten she felt. In their Walters-centered vision of the case, she was almost an afterthought. Legally and morally, Julia worried that the longer she did not stand up and fight, the less weight her maternal claim would carry. If the boy had barely remembered her in May, how would he possibly know her after yet another interminable legal delay?

Coursing through these worries was indignation over the original injustice of the case: the Dunbars had taken her son, and their custody of him was not being challenged. Why should the attempt to right that wrong be held hostage to the fight for Walters? Regardless of whether Julia actually believed that a trial was imminent, she set out on her journey because she could no longer stand, or afford, to wait.

To be fair, Dale and Rawls had begun to take her claim more seriously, if only to speculate on how it might impact their defense of Walters. "It has occurred to us," Rawls wrote in late August, "that if Julia Anderson could institute Habeas Corpus proceedings for the recovery of her child in the Federal Courts of Louisiana, that this would have a bearing on the Walters case." But the attorneys were overwhelmed with other cases and were not being paid for their defense of Walters to begin with. Taking such a dramatic and complicated step, at this point, was not even a real consideration.

Two weeks later, Walters's nephew James Mac scrawled to the Columbia duo a call to greater urgency and moral clarity: "[I]f I have not bin misinformed, Mr C P Dunbar taken the child from Walters without due process of Law. So I don't see why Some steps cant be taken to recover the child under present condition. Walters is loosing out just a few more months and the child will be grown beyond identification by many who knew the child before Walters left NC with him. you See that 2 years makes a big difference in a growing child."

It was not just that the boy would no longer know his mother; after such a long delay, he might be unrecognizable to North Carolina witnesses as well. Further, Julia's right to claim parenthood was certainly on par with the Dunbars': "I can not See why Julia Anderson the mother of the child would not stand the same chance to Sue out papers for the recovery of the child as Mr Dunbar did to take the child from Walters. I think there Should be Some Steps taken at once."

This letter arrived in Columbia about the same time as the anxious call from the Savannah Associated Charities that Julia Anderson was stranded in the train station. Finally, the harried lawyers seemed to wake up. In response to James Mac, Rawls first blustered defensively that he and Dale would have taken legal steps back in April to stop the Dunbars from taking Bruce from Columbia, but they had been unsure of his true identity and concerned that such a move would lead to lynching. In any case, Rawls continued, while he agreed that fighting for custody of Bruce was an excellent idea and "would have already received our attention," he and Dale could not foot the bill. The proper party to take such an action would be Julia Anderson, with support from friends and neighbors. Suddenly breathless in his support of the strategy, Rawls wrote, "It is my personal opinion that a better move could not be made than to institute immediate Habeas Corpus proceedings in the Federal Courts at New Orleans for the recovery of the child."

Days later, the Walters relatives of Baxley, Georgia, who had stepped in to rescue Julia from her Savannah stranding, followed Rawls's advice. They brought Julia to a local attorney, Col. Vernon E. Padgett, whom they had already retained to help out with their brother's defense. Julia sat before Padgett and made her case in full, relaying her Opelousas ordeal and offering him photos to prove that the boy was Bruce. Padgett was impressed, not just with her argument ("She is a lady of reasonable intelligence," he wrote Dale and Rawls) but also with her conviction. "She seems to be very much in earnest and is very much effected over the Dunbars having her child. In fact she says that she will fight for the child as long as she lives."

When Dale and Rawls received this report from Julia's new legal counsel, they promised that the habeas issue will "have our immediate attention, as we propose to run it down thoroughly," inviting Padgett down to Columbia to coordinate strategy in person, and asking him to nail down the question of whether they would have "authority to secure Federal jurisdiction."

Padgett responded that, as he understood it, there was no question that they had the authority. The only matter still to be clarified was where and when the writ should be filed. It was Padgett's opinion that the filing should happen *before* Walters stood trial, and in Mississippi, so that the subsequent habeas hearing (for Bruce) would occur there, rendering the Mississippi witnesses more readily accessible.

Then Padgett got to the issue of legal costs. As Dale and Rawls knew well, there was no hidden fortune to be shaken free from the Walters family tree, and Julia was penniless. It was Padgett's hope, then, that they follow up on the offer made by a showman to Julia in the spring: somewhere around $1,500 for the exclusive right to Bruce Anderson's appearance in motion pictures once he was recovered. At the time, Julia had passed the matter off to Dale and Rawls, stressing that she did not want to do anything to jeopardize the case and that she most certainly would not give up custody of Bruce to a showman. Apparently she had been equally adamant on that point when she told Padgett of the offer. After conferring confidentially with an unspecified Walters brother, Padgett proposed to Dale and Rawls, "I think that we, as attorneys, could handle the matter aside from her, that we could manage her so as to comply with any agreement made with any party furnishing money for this litigation." In other words, the lawyers would negotiate the deal on their own, then force Julia to go along, regardless of her maternal objections.

As demeaning and manipulative as the scheme sounded, Padgett was the closest thing Julia Anderson had to a hero. Nothing ever came of the motion picture offer, but he did not abandon Julia's case. Instead he took her in to live with him and his wife as housekeeper and caretaker for their children, in exchange for legal fees. For the rest of the fall, Julia was able to work, doing what she did best. She relished the rambunctious company of two young boys who reminded her of Bruce. She felt accomplishment, and for the first time in this whole ordeal, a sense of purpose.

With Padgett pursuing the habeas approach, Julia's next public claim to Bruce would not be a defensive one, made in reaction to the Dunbars on their terms, but rather a claim that finally spoke with full throat the unvarnished truth: this child was her son, Bruce, and the Dunbars had taken him illegally. She was not so naïve as to feel confident of prevailing, but at least her voice would be heard.

IN EARLY OCTOBER, with the Mississippi State Supreme Court expected to hear his case at any moment, Walters again prevailed upon his attorneys to address the broader public. He had prepared a statement, he insisted, that was unlike all the others before it—all the others that the press had maligned as the "ravings of a lunatic" or "forty pages of foolscap."

At this point, the attorneys' path of least resistance was to agree. Wise to the papers' word-twisting ways, they sent Walters's statement in to all the New Orleans dailies with the demand that it be printed "exactly as he has prepared" it:

> [I]f the Supreme Court says that I must go to Opelousas for trial, I will go like a man, without a murmur . . . And if I am convicted and my life is taken for alleged crime of which I'm not guilty and know nothing of, who let me ask, who will be required to atone for my innocent blood? God will say who. God will repay in his own good way some day. I'm ready, I have suffered patiently a martyr to public sentiment and frenzied emotion. Though proud as the ancient Spartans by nature, a poor crippled beggar, I am made so by cruel circumstances. Living I yield to no spirit but the God spirit and the sweet music of the soul, such as is made from the harps of angels. Dying, I can look up through the ethereal blue of Heaven, thank God, and say my conscience is clear: the heart strings of weeping mothers bind not my withering limbs, and the crime of kidnapping stains not my humble threshold door.

For all Walters's and Julia's expectations of major developments in the fall, Dale and Rawls seemed to have lapsed back into the shopworn strategy of stalling. After they failed to file their perfected brief on time, the case was left off the supreme court's docket until December.

Neither the press nor the public paid much attention, for a different case was now center stage. On December 2, indictments were delivered against Lieutenant Governor Bilbo and State Senator G. A. Hobbs, for negotiating bribes in exchange for votes. The indictments were the culmination of a behind-the-scenes investigation that Governor Brewer and Dan Lehon had begun over a year ago, before the Dunbar-Walters case even existed, and they laid bare a long-known hatred between the governor and his lieutenant. After Hobbs's prompt acquittal, for which Brewer disgustedly blamed "agitators," Bilbo, though still under indictment, announced his candidacy for governor with a rowdy rally in Jackson.

On Monday, January 12, the Mississippi State Supreme Court handed down its highly unsurprising decision. In signing the requisition, Governor Brewer "makes a *prima facie* case in favor of the demanding state." The matter of contradictory evidence as to Walters's presence in Louisiana, presented at the hearing, "is not grounds for refusing extradition." For a fleeting moment, Dale and Rawls toyed with the possibility of an appeal to the United States Supreme Court, but their client overruled them. "Tell them I am waiting for them here," he thundered to the press, not nearly as biblical as he had been in the fall. "They can take my life, but they cannot eat me."

Chapter 17

Postcard of Opelousas jail (Jacobs News Depot Co.)

SHERIFF SWORDS HAD come for Walters twice before with handcuffs at the ready, first to Columbia and then to Poplarville, though he hadn't really expected to use them either time. On his third try, he fully intended to complete the task of extradition, but by now the two were on such friendly terms, handcuffs would be considered rude.

Walters had already cleared his cell, and his suitcase was bulging with socks, clippings, and his dog-eared Bible. The only thing left unpacked was his magnificent homemade harp, his second one, the fruit of nine months labor behind bars and almost a year before that. When Walters demonstrated the lovely sounds of its strings, the sheriff was so entranced that he could not refuse the prisoner's request to pay for its shipment to Opelousas.

On the morning of Walters's expected Sunday departure, the regular flock gathered at the jailhouse for a farewell sermon. But they found their preacher's barred pulpit vacant, for good: Swords had spirited his prisoner away on the predawn train. "W. C. Walters Left Us," the *Columbian* mourned cheekily, "Sunday morning, bright and early for Opelousas, La, where he is to be the guest of St. Landry Parish at Sheriff Swords's boarding bungalow, where 'gombo' the traditional Louisiana dish is cooked daily by the 'chef.' "

But before that, during their daylong New Orleans stopover, the sheriff welcomed his charge to Louisiana with another sort of local tradition. From the train station, Swords, Walters, and Deputy Lott, who had come along for fun, trolleyed over to the *Vieux Carré*. "I'm going to show you a good time," Swords announced to Walters, who replied with a grin: "My eyes are wide open."

After a late breakfast, their adventure took them to the Hotel Monteleone. Swords was a known regular here, and for Walters, there was satisfaction in visiting a spot so famously associated with his case. Plus, the hotel afforded a clean sight line from the lobby, where Swords and Lott could lounge about and chew the fat, to the lobby bar, where Walters could entertain the amassing crowds with a degree of freedom. His beverage of choice was whiskey with a beer chaser, neither of which he was "accustomed to" in the house of Hathorn.

Walters's oration started formally, with a written statement to the people of Louisiana. He had been assured high and low of a free trial, he read, and now it was time for the people to honor their promise. Specifically, he had recently petitioned the Opelousas Police Jury to help fund his witnesses' travel from out of state, and was awaiting a reply. It was a bold maneuver, holding St. Landry's feet to the fire so publicly.

But what choice did he have? Walters was in dire straits, he moaned theatrically. "I had a nice mule and buggy, a picture outfit, some tools, a one-fourth interest in a little farm in North Carolina, and a beautiful, sweet little boy. Now it is all gone. To the people of Louisiana, is it possible that you will do an innocent man this way?" He closed with an imprecation to read the Twenty-Fifth Psalm.

His appeal had immediate results, with "dozens" of listeners offering "financial support." But a far greater number—reporters, hotel guests, and curious citizens off the street; hundreds, by one report—lingered just for drinks and the show. Hour upon hour, Walters lectured more informally, offering stories of his life and travels, and quotes from Scripture and profane invective alike. If acquitted, he said, he would demand no less than $10,000 in damages; a few drinks later, it was $100,000.

As to a change of venue, he was adamant: "I want to be tried right in Opelousas, where the Dunbars live. There are people there who know that this thing has not been conducted fairly, and there are plenty of folks there who would not swear that the boy Dunbar took from me is his boy." Later and drunker, he made the same point more colorfully: "There's somethin' rotten up this creek, and God's goin' to bring it down in plain view and show them folk that think I'm guilty who's the really guilty fellows in this here case."

Bystanders shifted uncomfortably, and looked to Sheriff Swords to intervene. But while the officer did make it to his feet at one point, affording a glimpse of the "cartridge belt, supporting [his] coal-burning revolver," Swords did nothing to censor Walters's tirade. Rather, he stood back from the prisoner "with the modest air of a man who has something unusual to exhibit."

This late in his career, Swords had no patience for public expectations about how he should or should not behave. He had watched hundreds of men like Walters languish behind bars, their dignity eroding. This afternoon, in allowing Walters to make the drunken, angriest most of his brief few hours of freedom, the hardened old sheriff—in his own off-color way—was restoring a shard of the prisoner's humanity. The favor did not go unnoticed. Pausing his oratory for a moment, Walters nodded toward his keeper: "Sheriff Swords has treated me like a gentleman and a friend."

The mutual goodwill was still much in evidence when they reached Opelousas early the next morning. St. Landry's jailhouse was in wretched shape, and just two weeks before, the state health inspector had issued a withering report: trash hurriedly heaped in corners, broken heaters, and a bucket of week-old human excrement, all of this home to three crazy white men who belonged in the asylum, three preadolescent black boys who had tried to wreck a train, nine prisoners with lice, and one with a "skin eruption." And yet, as Walters settled in, all that bothered him was the heat. His cell was on the "cool" side, he worried politely, which might stiffen his bad leg in the night. Swords and his deputies got right on it.

He was rewarded handsomely for his agreeability (and his notoriety). Instead of one cell, Walters soon had a suite of three, including a separate "music room" for his harp and violin, with a window facing front, overlooking the tree-filled courtyard and the courthouse.

For a few weeks in Opelousas, Walters was nearly forgotten. When throngs gathered in public, it was for Mardi Gras or the municipal elections, or to witness the laying of creosote-soaked wooden blocks on Landry Street: Opelousas was finally getting pavement. Or, on the last Wednesday of February, to romp in the four inches of snow blanketing the courthouse square, the town's heaviest accumulation since 1899. With school cancelled, packs of children launched giddy snowball assaults on lawyers and clerks trudging into work until they finally gave in and joined the fun. "Many of the young generation had never seen snow," the *Clarion* smiled, "but it did not take them long to learn how to manipulate snowballs." For the old man shivering in his cell, four inches was but a dusting compared to the snowfall he had ridden through in North Carolina, two years ago almost to the day. He squinted through the bars and wondered if the boy who had been in his wagon was among the squealing children, and if he remembered that storm, too.

Walters first tried to draw the townspeople to his cell with words, forwarding a rather provocative letter to the *Clarion*: "I think that it is time for the good people of Opelousas, St. Landry Parish, and Louisiana, to get together to solve some of the mystery surrounding Opelousas and all Louisiana and Mississippi," he wrote with a wink and a nod. "I am willing to do my part in this." For all those who wanted the real story, Walters was happy to oblige, and for those in town who doubted the boy was Bobby Dunbar, he was all ears. And so he persisted, for the next two months, as both goodwill ambassador and gadfly.

Early on, the curiosity-seekers stood back from his window. Opelousas mothers shuttled their children to the edge of the yard, pointed up at Walters's bars and warned gravely of the perils of talking to strangers. But as soon as the giant wooden crate arrived from Columbia, and its cargo was unpacked and retuned, things began to change.

From a block away or more, they heard it. As often as a dozen times each day and into the night, on their way to work or home from school, in town for business or shopping, stepping out of a lunchroom, gathered by the courthouse for coffee, or sitting quietly on their porches, the music reached them.

If they dared draw closer, they were rewarded. The strumming of strings, tinny and primitive from a distance, opened into chords, rich with harmony. A soft, deep voice revealed its nuance: untrained but rarely out of tune, sometimes raspy from wear, and always brimming with emotion.

Walters's song, one listener observed "rose in strains in wildness and again fell into a cadence soft and full of heart appeal."

If his style of singing was "peculiar," Walters's repertoire of songs, at least those reported, was not. Townspeople would easily recognize the popular hymns and melodies, selected for their resonances with his current plight: "Jesus, Lover of My Soul," "Home Sweet Home," a John Henry Newman hymn called "Lead Kindly Light"—sung two years ago aboard the *Titanic*.

The tune that was his "standard," performed so often it soon became a joke, was Robert Lowry's excruciatingly mournful 1877 ode to the prodigal son:

> *Where is my wand'ring boy tonight—*
> *The boy of my tend'rest care,*
> *The boy that was once my joy and light,*
> *The child of my love and prayer?*

While *that* boy was kept well out of earshot, other children began visiting the jail yard, and not just for a maternal warning. "The little tots come to see me, and they have grown to like me," Walters reported one spring day, and as if on cue, a child popped to the front of the gathered crowd. "Hello, baby," he greeted brightly.

Once his music had drawn them in, Walters sparked up conversation, which—though he remained "unfailingly polite"—more often than not was one-sided: sermonizing, as he had done in Columbia, and as the trial grew nearer, anxious pleas for mercy from the court, from St. Landry, and from God.

Though Walters enjoyed it, attention in and of itself was not his primary purpose. His lawyers were in charge of his alibi, his witnesses, and the case for his innocence. But before St. Landry could believe he was innocent, its citizens had to see that he was *decent,* that he was *human.* As he wrote to Dale and Rawls in March, that was no small task:

> I Have worried And worried until My Brain is tired. I Have Sung and Played tunes And Been on my Feet until I am about Give out. All over I Have tried in my Ignorant simple way to Get the Good Peopple of Opelousas St Landry Parish & La Interested.

In the next sentence, he expressed cautious optimism that the effort was paying off: "Don't know Just How But what I think to Be some of the

Leading Citizens Has Assured me I should not Be Hurt," and further, that sentiment "stood about 10W to 1D."

Yet for all his confidence that the town was turning in his favor, Walters still burned with a greater need not just for acquittal but also for exposure of the full breadth of the injustice perpetrated upon him. The rotten thing was still fouling the waters from upstream—or, more precisely, up Union Street. Whether God would grant Walters's wish and finally wash it down for all to see, that question was far from answered.

"IF WALTERS MUST be tried in Louisiana, Opelousas is the place we prefer," Hollis Rawls had echoed his client after the high court defeat. "It is there that the people know Robert Dunbar, and we believe that they know that the boy now held by Mr. Dunbar is not the real Robert Dunbar."

Followers of the case might have questioned Mr. Rawls's rationale. After all, Opelousas had long ago welcomed the boy into its arms *as the real Robert Dunbar* and closed ranks against the one woman with the temerity to challenge its recognition. But by now, Dale and Rawls had sobered to the harsh truth: there was no greater guarantee of an impartial jury in any other parish. At least in St. Landry, they had been offered reassurance and assistance from Garland and Swords, men of the law and respected leaders, who would set an example for their citizenry.

Once Walters was extradited and Dale and Rawls made their stance on a venue known, a surge of collegial cooperation issued forth from Opelousas. Hearing that the trial was set for mid-February, the Columbia attorneys anxiously appealed to Garland for a continuance: they were due in federal court in Biloxi that very week and could not possibly corral their witnesses in such a short time. Garland readily agreed, and the date was pushed back to mid-April: even more time than they had asked for.

Then there was the task of navigating Louisiana law. While the state was well known, and unique in the nation, for its roots in French and Spanish Civil Law, this was not why its present criminal justice system was so peculiar to outsiders. Just prior to becoming a state, Louisiana's Crimes Act of 1805 had enshrined an Americanized version of English common law as the foundation for its criminal code. But for the next century, the system evolved via a willy-nilly accumulation of hastily written statutes to account for new offenses, revisions of punishment, and procedural reforms. Legislature by legislature, the morass of inconsistencies, contradictions, and redundancies grew thicker and more absurd. Shooting at a man, one reformer scolded in 1911, was a graver offense than actually shooting him with intent to murder. And if the most seasoned of Louisiana lawyers and judges found themselves consistently befuddled, outsiders like Dale and Rawls would be utterly lost.

So when Sheriff Swords suggested that "some young, reputable attorney of Opelousas" might assist with their case, they leapt at the offer, and the very next day, Judge Pavy wired back with his suggestion for an appointment. Neither Mississippi attorney had heard the name Edward Benjamin Dubuisson before, but the St. Landry lawyer had come highly recommended by Garland, which was more than enough for Dale and Rawls. "The court's appointment of this gentleman and your recommendation of him," they wrote in thanks, "voucher to us for his ability and competency."

Amid all the lawyerly goodwill and momentum toward trial, early February brought a nagging reminder to Dale and Rawls of the strategy—and the interests—that had been cast in the ditch. From Baxley, Georgia, Col. Vernon Padgett reported on his fund-raising efforts among Walters's friends and neighbors, and offered to help procure witnesses from the Carolinas and Georgia. But the bulk of his letter was devoted to the plan of filing a writ of habeas corpus for Bruce Anderson, which he had clearly been researching and preparing. Padgett was not the only one ready to move, either: "Mrs. Anderson is here," he reminded Dale and Rawls, "and is anxious to go to Louisiana and endeavor to recover her child."

Sensing unease in the Columbia attorneys' recent months of silence, Padgett reminded them of the strategy's merits. Taking the case up in a federal court, "as you know, would remove as far as possible the local prejudices in the case." What's more, if the habeas suit could be filed just before the criminal case, then the two teams of attorneys could work together and develop a unified strategy. By letter's end, Padgett was getting down to brass tacks, discussing ideal dates and venues for filing the writ.

Dale and Rawls read the letter, and considered their reply, with piercing regret. Looking back at the past nine months, they could see now that their strategy had never evolved beyond a myopic and entirely defensive battle against extradition. For this, they could blame busy schedules and a lack of resources, but in truth, the more aggressive step of a writ against the Dunbars, which could have changed the terms of the struggle entirely, was not something they had truly even *considered*. Back in the spring, when Garland and Brewer had speculated over this question of a writ, a threat that was impeding the Dunbars from allowing the boy to be seen by their witnesses, the Columbia attorneys had insisted that the option was not even on the table.

To be fair, they were Walters's lawyers, not Julia's, and their strategy had been to protect their client, not to recover the child. But over the months of their correspondence with Julia, amid repeated insistences that she merely stay home and wait, they mentioned recovery of her child only once, as a matter that *they* were intending to pursue.

It is impossible to underestimate how devastating their response to Padgett was, in both the short term and long term:

> As you know already, Walters is absolutely without funds or friends to make his defense at Opelousas, by failing to resist extradition further and going on to Opelousas of his own accord, it appears to some extent that he has made some few friends in Opelousas. At any rate, we are advised that there is a movement on foot to have the Police Jury of St. Landry Parish to make a small appropriation to assist him in bringing his witnesses to his trial. We are confident, therefore, that a habeas corpus proceeding now be for the recovery of the child, that this movement would result disastrously to Walters. The Parish would immediately withdraw its offer of assistance and leave Walters helpless and stranded, without the slightest hope of securing the attendance of any of his witnesses. In other words, we think this movement now would inflame public sentiment against him and make his conviction almost certain.
>
> We cannot help but feel that we are right in this proposition and that by far the better course would be for all of us to join hands in an effort to acquit Walters and then institute proceedings as outlined by you, for the recovery of the child.

Of course, Padgett had to trust the lawyers' judgment about "public sentiment." Nonetheless, he was stung, insulted, and exasperated. But the Georgia attorney's reaction was trivial compared to how his housekeeper would feel when he finally found words to tell her.

The St. Landry Police Jury briefly entertained a carte blanche approach to the matter of funding defense witnesses, and allowed as much to Dale and Rawls. But upon discovering that state law placed clear limits on their largesse, they bent the rules to save face: two dollars a day would be allocated for twelve defense witnesses, "and five cents per mile each way, from the boundary line of the State of Mississippi to the City of Opelousas," not to exceed $500. It was nearly quadruple the legal limit.

With a sigh of relief on that front, Dale and Rawls began the delicate task of locating local witnesses: those mysterious, nameless citizens who doubted that the boy was Bobby Dunbar. Facing countdown to trial, they recklessly broached the subject in their very first letter to their new local co-counsel, asking Mr. Dubuisson to investigate "in a quiet way" and report back. But they were naturally uneasy: could they truly rely on this man, whom they had never even met, to ferret out reluctant witnesses in his own community? As a backup, they hired a colleague and ally from Lake Charles, attorney Thomas Kleinpeter, to nose around among his own St. Landry contacts to locate secret skeptics. And they explicitly instructed Kleinpeter to keep his mission a secret from Dubuisson.

Neither lawyer left a paper trail of his searches. And while they may have found "plenty of folks there who would not swear" that the boy was Bobby Dunbar, as Walters had drunkenly boasted in the Monteleone, precisely which and how many people *would* swear that the boy was *not* Bobby Dunbar would be a mystery until well into the trial.

Kleinpeter was more than forthcoming on an ancillary aspect of his Opelousas investigation. Less than a month before trial, he wrote Dale and Rawls that he was convinced that an impartial jury could not be found in St. Landry Parish, and urged them to press for a change of venue. This must have startled the duo, who thought they had crossed that bridge already, and had just heard a rosier assessment from Dubuisson: local sentiment was "about equally divided." Eleven days later, the Lake Charles mole wrote again, far more insistent: "There is now a state of Astonishment bordering on protest that the State should or the Parish should furnish funds necessary to produce evidence to prove the innocence of the accused," advised Kleinpeter. "In my mind, this act settle[s] it . . . that it is intended to give no weight to such evidence, and is done simply to quiet a cry or fear of an unfair trial."

Suddenly nearly every reason Dale and Rawls had to feel hopeful about the coming trial had been called into question: not just confidence in their decision on a venue change, not just optimism about local sentiment, but also faith in the police jury's motives and trust in St. Landry authorities. They were not bending over backward for a fair trial; they were bending over backward for the *appearance* of one. For the past month, Walters had been writing to them that Mr. Dubuisson did not seem to be doing much work on the case, that he was not sure he trusted him, and that he had heard rumors that the judge's appointment of a local co-counsel had been a "trick." It had been easy for Dale and Rawls to dismiss all this as standard Walters paranoia—until now.

In the first full week of April, they wrapped up their session with the chancery clerk in Columbia and prepared for the extended journey across state and enemy lines. Along with suits and paperwork, both packed pistols. But for all the physical protection that the weapons offered, when Dale and Rawls boarded the train for Louisiana, they felt—legally speaking—as if they were headed into an ambush.

ON EASTER SUNDAY, the day before the trial was set to begin, excursion trains brought in out-of-towners by the hundreds, and the next day, that number was expected to reach a thousand at least. Hotels and rooming houses were booked solid; restaurants and cafés were doing brisk business. Along with its standard Creole fare, the Gem Restaurant promised out-of-towners "Specialty Dishes Served for the Dunbar-Walters Trial." To be sure, some had arrived on Sunday for the local baseball team's opening game. But most were there for the trial, and before and after the game, the crowds filled downtown. Two weeks back, the *Clarion* had scolded the police jury to get busy on the overgrown courthouse square with "a mowing machine, a rake, and a little taste," otherwise the trial spectators "will form an awful opinion of [St. Landry's] parochial pride." In the nick of time, the square had been cleaned up.

On Sunday the real attraction was over by the jail, where Walters's much-touted Easter sermon was just the first part of a well-oiled publicity machine. Today the showman and his audience were not separated by bars; to those curiosity seekers who drew particularly close, and seemed sympathetic, Walters extended an invitation up to his "suite," and soon the jailhouse became a kind of open house. Inside the cell awaited wonders far more thrilling than a sermon, which could be had for free, or if the visitors were so inclined, for a small contribution toward the prisoner's tobacco fund. Walters treated them to unlimited discussion of the case and full answers to any questions. He eagerly pointed them through his homemade "moving pictures," a giant poster on the wall adorned with cutouts of every newspaper photo he had gotten his hands on. His finger darting from the mystery boy to Julia Anderson, Walters insisted that, enlarged, the faces would be identical. By contrast, the photo of Lessie Dunbar bore no resemblance, nor did a photo of the undisputed Bobby Dunbar.

But most thrilling of all, in the suite's "music room," viewers finally could ogle, up close and in all its glory, the giant instrument that had lured them. Since 1912, Walters had been building this thing, and if asked, he could recall with ease when each part was added and where it came from, whether salvaged, plundered, or purchased new. Its frame was a wide, rough-hewn timber box, and the base of a tin tub served as its sounding board, fastened together with a motley array of screws, nails, and iron plugs. Walters had crafted the tuning key himself and, naturally, whittled his own picks. At a glance, the instrument's most prominent feature was the army of tuning pins dotted across its face, each one snugly wedged into its own hand-carved hole.

But precisely wound around each pin, and practically disappearing in the half tones of a century-old newspaper photo, was the instrument's most important and remarkable feature: its strings. Some reporters counted 287, while others counted only 260, but if either figure was anywhere near accurate, Walters's harp quite likely was (and is) a world record breaker. They were piano strings, old and new, arranged by thickness/pitch into partitioned sections, each section representing a chord. But perhaps most startling of all, there were two full rows, cross-strung at a right angle, one vertical, and on a lower tier, another horizontal, each tuned to a different scale. Thus, Walters could play any note with either hand, no lever shifting required.

Invariably, he offered his visitors an up-close demonstration, and the assessments from this vantage varied considerably: one journalist burbled that Walters could "get excellent music" from it, while another sneered that the sound was merely adequate, "considering the limitations of the instrument." Nearly everyone understood the harp's most pressing purpose: "With clumsy, weather-stained hands," one report lyricized, "he picks from its recesses appealing harmonies in vain endeavors to wring them straight to the heart of a child."

JUST BEFORE THE trial, Herman Seiferth, one of the *Pic*'s veteran reporters, made his way down the one side of Union Street that boasted a cement sidewalk. From a distance, the little house, with its shutters and doors closed tight, appeared "as if its occupants were absent." Instead when he knocked and was invited in, he found himself surrounded by the extended Dunbar family, including the Foxes and Mr. and Mrs. Fred Dunbar up from New Orleans, getting ready for dinner. Seiferth had met them before, during his coverage of the Dunbars' arrival in New Orleans a year ago. Lessie's greeting was polite, but a bit wary, and Percy—too agitated by interruptions and trial-related appointments to even sit and eat—was on his way out.

In the middle of them all were "a pair of chubby blonde boys," Alonzo and Bobby, fixated on a just-opened box of Easter candy. For a brief while, Seiferth was trusted alone with the boy. His questions started gently: would he share the candy with his brother? Of course, he would; "I love my brother." Further, the boy was eagerly anticipating his life's next big milestone: school.

But his strange and troubled past still tugged at him. "I saw Sheriff Womack," he offered unprompted. Then, because he had known a lot of sheriffs in his short life, and they tended to blend together: "He's the man who caught Walters."

Seiferth ventured a tricky question, asking, "Do you know Walters?" To this, "[t]he only response was a smile, a tiny bit wistful, and he said no more on the subject, nor was he asked."

As Percy readied to leave, Bobby begged to go with him. "I'll get my hat," he said, a distant echo of August 23, 1912. When "tenderly" refused, Bobby hollered out a warning. "Don't go near the jail, Papa. Walters has a pistol!"

After that, he was back to being just a boy again, chasing Alonzo out into the backyard, and Lessie came in to talk. The little mother looked like a different woman now, Seiferth observed. A year ago, she had weighed a mere 109 pounds, and now she was up to a healthy 151. And she was not the only changed one. Seiferth observed how much "sweeter" and "companionable" the boy now was, how much less "stubbornness" he exhibited, and how at home he seemed. In other words, "He is more like Alonzo."

Before he could put this all into words, Lessie did so herself. "Bobbie is so natural now . . . that I no longer realize that we ever parted."

Chapter 18

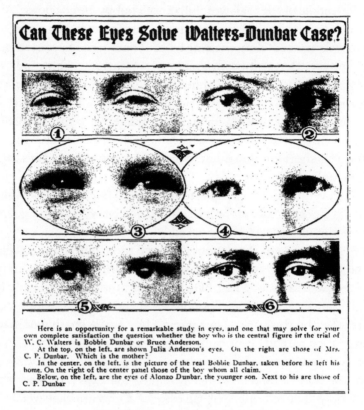

Can These Eyes Solve Walters-Dunbar Case?

Here is an opportunity for a remarkable study in eyes, and one that may solve for your own complete satisfaction the question whether the boy who is the central figure in the trial of W. C. Walters is Bobbie Dunbar or Bruce Anderson.

At the top, on the left, are shown Julia Anderson's eyes. On the right are those of Mrs. C. P. Dunbar. Which is the mother?

In the center, on the left, is the picture of the real Bobbie Dunbar, taken before he left his home. On the right of the center panel those of the boy whom all claim.

Below, on the left, are the eyes of Alonzo Dunbar, the younger son. Next to his are those of C. P. Dunbar

New Orleans Item, April 15, 1914

JULIA KNEW SHE was sick. She tried to mask it as she endured a lengthy late-night layover in New Orleans's Union Station, bouncing other waiting women's babies and snapping at aggressive reporters. Much was made over her "improved" appearance since last year, and her demeanor was certainly more confident. But something was wrong inside her body, and she was fighting it hard.

At least on this trip she was not alone. Traveling with her were three other defense witnesses: Walters's childhood friend David Bledsoe; Barnesville postal carrier Walter Murray; and the Walters's nephew by marriage, F. M. Stephens, who had ushered her to the train for her first trip a year prior. The men did their best to shield her from the press, and once in Opelousas, they escorted her through the morning drizzle to a boardinghouse.

The place, however, was full. Julia retreated to the porch, wondering what to do, pulling her raincoat tight against her trembling frame. The terror of her last visit came rushing back: *she was not wanted in this town.*

At last, a gentlemanly photographer gave her use of his room to rest and clean up, then she rejoined her fellow travelers for breakfast. Herman Seiferth followed along, and, perhaps owing to his colleague's act of kindness, she opened up. Their first reported exchange was actually her question to him. "Do you know what sustains me in my trials?" she asked. Hesitantly, Seiferth ventured that it might be the expectation of a reunion with her son.

Of course, that was Julia's greatest hope, but it was not hope that protected her or kept her alive. "It's God," she answered herself.

As word spread through town of her arrival, and her lack of a place to sleep, the manager of the Lacombe Hotel graciously offered "his best accommodation without cost." Before she went inside, Julia sat down on the porch, smoothed her hair, brought her hands to her lap with fingers interlaced, and gazed confidently, if not a bit warily, into the photographer's lens. It was her best picture yet, and Seiferth would report as much.

In her room, Julia had more words not just for Seiferth but also for the other reporters tagging along. She was eager to correct the record on her "failure" during her last visit to Opelousas, which had not been a failure at all. Asked if she would seek to recover her child, she diplomatically buried her heartbreak over the lawyers' change of strategy and replied, "All I am trying to do now is to save Walters's life."

A few hours later, she and her fellow East Coasters made their way over to the courthouse square. Built in 1886, the St. Landry Courthouse was grand from a distance, Spanish colonial in style, with a row of tall arched windows on two floors and capped with a looming corner tower. Up close and inside, it was a crumbling behemoth, an "eye-sore," according to a January 1914 edition of the *Clarion*, which wanted it demolished two full decades before it would be.

Julia and the men climbed the scuffed, creaking stairs and turned down a narrow hallway. Court was not in session, they knew; owing to the continued absence of several key witnesses, the defense had requested a one-day postponement, and then gathered the witnesses who *had* arrived for a strategy meeting. When she entered the courtroom, Julia saw a group of chattering Mississippians, from infants to elders, not one of whom she knew.

Then she spotted Walters. He turned rather casually, Mrs. Goleman's baby nestled in his arm, and when he noticed her, for a silent moment, all that had occurred between them rushed to the surface. Then they both smiled. Coming together, they embraced and kissed quickly and tried to talk in private. In most reports, the reunion appeared pointedly "casual," but in truth, they were less guarded against each other than against their observers. Julia was happy to finally see this old man again. He was her friend. No matter what had happened, she knew that he loved Bruce, and that two years ago, he had stepped in to save the boy. And now she was here to save Cant. Whether he could say so or not, he was sorry for his role in what had happened, and it did not matter if she fully forgave him. The heartbreak and injustice of losing Bruce was the glue of their reconciliation.

Then there were the ladies of Pearl River County: Mrs. Goleman, Mrs. Myley, and Mrs. Bilbo. There was no hesitation in their embrace of Bruce's mother. And the boy was all they could talk about: the last time they had seen him, dresses they had all made for him, how much he had grown. In this room that soon would be jammed with spectators and charged with life-or-death drama, where they soon would *all* be on trial, the Mississippians, Carolinians, and Georgian sprawled out and mingled, put up their feet, and defied its formality.

Just outside and across the courthouse square, a stern-faced cluster of men was headed toward the Lacombe Hotel. But not to see Julia. Civic rage was engulfing Opelousas, although these witnesses were not the offending interlopers.

ON APRIL 6, 1914, New Orleans's two morning dailies officially became one. The new paper's nameplate—the *Times-Democrat* splayed across the top in a fattened font, and then below and with some squinting, the *Daily Picayune*—reflected the less-than-equal nature of the merger. For several years now, the *Pic* had been hobbling along, according to one historian, "an overripe plum, ready to fall into the hands of anyone who wanted to shake the tree." The *Item*'s publisher James Thomson had tried first, with an offer barely shy of what the *Pic* would then accept, and far more than what it eventually settled for. His lowball quickly proved foolish. Though the *Item* had savored every chance to ridicule its rusty morning competitors, the new merged paper was no longer a thing to be sneezed at. The war for readership suddenly turned ferocious, and the opening battlefield was Opelousas, where the Dunbar-Walters saga was fast approaching its climax.

In advertising its upcoming coverage, the merged paper staked its position against sensation: "The *Times-Picayune* will publish the *news* of this case accurately and fairly, and . . . will not be overcome by hysteria." And in an insiders' swipe at the competition, the paper boasted "staff correspondents who are thoroughly familiar with the case."

Though only in his early twenties, Stanley Ray had fast distinguished himself as a savvy newsman at the *Times-Democrat,* and after the merger, would become managing editor. Beyond the newsroom, he spearheaded the fledgling Boy Scouts movement across three states, and transformed the *Times-Democrat*'s Doll and Toy Fund into one of the city's most successful charities.

His fifty-one-year-old partner, Herman Seiferth, was community-minded as well, organizing the city's Young Man's Hebrew Association and serving as director of the Jewish Children's Home. Well known for hard-hitting investigations into graft as well as columns on baseball, Seiferth eschewed "inaccuracy, overstatement, and yellow journalism," as one colleague would later extol, in favor of "those old-fashioned qualities of modesty, sincerity, truthfulness."

Such praise could never be uttered with a straight face for the duo's competition from the *Item,* a pair who were new to the Dunbar story and decidedly more colorful: Mignon Hall and Sam Blair.

The daughter of an Alabama Presbyterian minister, Mignon Hall was a precocious writing talent, landing her first reporting job for the *Birmingham News* at age sixteen. As she would recollect fondly, her editor often found her at work late into the night, and when he teased that she never went home, she chirped, "Oh, I'm going to have ten scoops tomorrow." A telling memory: from the start of her career, groundbreaking news was not something that Hall looked for on the street but something that she created in the wee hours of the night, alone with her typewriter.

From Birmingham, she was off to the New York *Evening Telegram,* then down to New Orleans for a stint at the *Item,* before being wooed away—at only twenty-five—by the Atlanta *Georgian* in early April 1913. Weeks after Hall joined the staff, the bludgeoned body of thirteen-year-old Mary Phagan had been found in the basement of the pencil factory where she worked, and the *Georgian* attacked the story with a ferocity that sent its competition, and all of Atlanta, reeling. It was a Hearst paper, after all. Day after day, the *Georgian* blasted tales of Mary and her alleged killer, Leo Frank, across its front pages, employing the same unholy blend of clever gumshoe reportage, rumor mongering, and florid fictionalization that marked the *Item*'s concurrent coverage of the Dunbar-Walters case. By the time of her return to the *Item*, Mignon Hall's teeth were cut.

Sam Blair was a year younger than Mignon Hall, and his rise in journalism was speedier: from an apprenticeship at the prestigious *Kansas City Star*, to the city desk of the *Chicago Inter-Urban*, and then to the *Item*, all just a year out of college. His first big *Item* story was President Woodrow Wilson's extended winter 1913 vacation in Pass Christian, for which he adopted a tone of cheeky mirth—profiling a pack of mopey girls who tried to donate their Christmas dolls to the president's daughters, or writing his entire report of Wilson's birthday as a stage play. Long after he had left the *Item* behind, Blair's career would continue to profit from this patented irreverence. In 1919, reporting for the *Chicago Herald and Examiner* from aboard the first transcontinental flight of Charles Lawson's world-famous airliner, Blair was bored to the point of dozing off, wondering aloud if a midair wedding might be arranged to spice up his story, or perhaps a mechanic could be brought before the world's first airborne jury for breaking a rule, then thrown overboard as punishment. Two years later, Blair scratched his itch for "news manufacture" with a sensational scoop in the story of Clara Smith Hamon, murderess on the lam. Blair's reportage boasted not just Clara's confession of the shooting of her oil-king lover, but also the explosive revelation of a secret will naming her as beneficiary, with a preposterously prescient stipulation that she would have to be acquitted to receive her fortune.

The will yarn bore an uncanny resemblance to another tale spawned seven years earlier in the Dunbar case: the phony gold-mine inheritance tale of B. and H. The initials—Blair and Hall—matched, too. Without a precise date for Blair's arrival and Hall's return to the *Item*, that ugliness cannot be pinned on them with certainty. But there is a mysterious quality to the duo's 1914 Opelousas dispatches that transcends a run-of-the-mill penchant for tabloid, unexplainable solely in the context of their careers. Nine months after the trial, Hall and Blair would be married. It would not last long, though. In 1920, after he had returned from World War I and become a syndicated star, she would be found back in her native Alabama, wandering among the 1,600 inmates of the Bryce Hospital for the Insane.

It is in this context that their coverage of the Dunbar-Walters story makes fullest sense: it resembles nothing more than mad young romance, with each report, like a love letter, more prattling and reckless than the last. They had been hired to write for the *Item,* but they were really writing for each other.

"Lost—A little boy with sunny hair and blue eyes, four years old" was the breathless opening of Hall's first dispatch on April 9, an endless chronicle of events in the case thus far, riddled with errors and fabrication.

> Mrs. Robert Dunbar's beautiful baby, who the day before had clung so closely about her skirts, played "big baseball" on the kitchen wall, stroked her soft cheek with one chubby finger and called her "pitty muvver," and climbed into her lap after a long day of play with baby lips almost too tired to say "B'ess papa and mamma and little brother," before they closed down to dreams, had disappeared from her, weirdly, strangely, suddenly.

"Opelousas is ready to explode into seven thousand atoms of intense excitement," Blair panted in return the next day. Column after column, day after day, they went on like this, Blair's bombast matched word for word by Hall's poesy.

There was greater purpose behind the duo's fluff: Ballard had dispatched them to Opelousas well before the competition as part of an all-out campaign to "prime the pump," to ensure that, when the trial began, the *Item* would be the public's go-to source. Heaped onto its pages was a slurry of gossip and speculation, stories that mattered less for their content and more for the space they took up. For example, in its first paragraph, an article headlined "Identity of Boy Could Be Fixed by Blood Tests, Says Experts [*sic*]," trumpeted a German psychologist's recent "discovery" of a serum reaction that could determine parentage. Then in the remaining five paragraphs, scientist after scientist threw cold water on the headline: the test was unproven, could not be developed in time to solve the Bruce-Bobby question, and would not be legally admissible. And the *Item* was not stopping with print, either. Cross-marketed heavily in the newspaper, the *Item Animated Weekly*'s newsreel coverage would be history's "first motion picture record of a criminal prosecution."

Before the trial even began, however, the *Item*'s juggernaut of tabloid supremacy backfired royally. While most Opelousans had long been tolerantly amused by the paper's fakery, Hall's and Blair's egregious early dispatches sparked rising local irritation. And the competitors' coverage was getting fuller, and better, by the day. By April 11, an army of correspondents had hit the ground in St. Landry, bearing a grudge against the *Item,* not just for its unrivaled circulation but also for its yearlong strong-arming on the Dunbar story.

The challengers' first major opening presented itself on Easter Sunday. It was on the *Item*'s front page that Hall and Blair took their paper "just one step too far," as Ray of the *Times-Picayune* crowed, "and broke the camel's back." Hall's story began:

> Mrs. C. P. Dunbar, mother of Bobbie Dunbar, child of whose disappearance a man's life hangs in jeopardy, issued Saturday night through the *Item* this appeal: "People of Opelousas: Do not hang W. C. Walters. I have suffered enough."

The context was an interview with the Dunbars at home on Saturday night, for which two competing reporters, the *Item*'s Hall and the *Times-Pic*'s Ray, were present. Lessie and the boy had just returned home from Ville Platte, where they had visited her girlhood teacher, Mother Melanie. In both reporters' versions, Percy expressed righteous support for the death penalty for Walters. In Ray's report, Lessie was hesitant on the question, but Mignon Hall ascribed to her a moral opposition: "I should not like to feel that we have been the cause of the taking of life which we cannot give."

The jump led readers to a bloated column by Blair, featuring three repetitions of Paul's ode to Christian love in 1 Corinthians 13, and loosely organized around a holiday theme. "The spirit of love to which all the world has dedicated Easter Sunday will rise upon Opelousas with the coming of to-morrow's sun." Blair offered his own "quote" of Lessie's plea for mercy and the report of a prayer from the boy to forgive the tinker.

When the Sunday *Item* made it to the Dunbar home Monday morning, Lessie, Percy, and other relatives scowled at what they read. Lessie did admit to saying "No" when asked if she wanted to see Walters hang, but that, apparently, was where the similarities between news and reality stopped. Later that morning, Archie Dunbar and Harold Fox spread word of the *Item*'s fakery through town, and the outrage mounted. It was not that the Dunbar camp was in favor of hanging, they were quick to note. It was that the phony plea for mercy could sway potential jurors, impact the trial's fairness, and thwart the administering of justice.

On Monday afternoon, a "committee" of leading citizens, including Drs. A. J. Bercier, A. J. Perrault, and Lawrence Daly, marched to the Lacombe Hotel for a word with Sam Blair. "[W]e came on a peaceful mission," Bercier insisted later, "to warn him" that while Opelousas had "received him here as a gentleman and treated him as such," the town "would not stand for any misrepresentation of facts." Blair delicately defended Miss Hall, insisting that she had merely reported Mrs. Dunbar's simple response to him (Blair), and he had added (in Bercier's words) "trimmings to make it sound sweeter."

That afternoon, the *Item* struck again. This time it was the movie men, eager to capture footage of the camera-shy Dunbars. First, the crew hid along the family's route from court to film Lessie "looking directly into the camera." Later, and trickier, they lurked outside the Dunbar home and "raised a hue and cry" to lure occupants out into the open, capturing a few seconds of Alonzo before being shooed down the street.

The gang that reconverged on the Lacombe that night numbered close to fifty, including Percy, and it was far from polite. "[H]ot words poured forth for a time" before the hotel manager defused the fray. The *States* dished out an alleged interview with one cornered newsman, who heard a menacing cry from the crowd—"Go'wn, Dunbar, get him!"—and knew it was time to skip town.

The eruption of Opelousas against the *Item* was circulation gold to the paper's competitors, who both led their next day's coverage with the story, and happily exposed other recent *Item* fakeries, too: an alleged interview with Rawls asserting that Walters was abandoning his claim to Bruce, and an elaborate tidbit from Mignon Hall about a "vision" that Walters had had of his own death, complete with a canoe ride through troubled waters and a mother calling him home. The *Item* made no attempt to defend the latter, but hit back hard against attacks on the former. Sadly for the paper, the counterattack made things worse: Mignon Hall wrote up an alleged statement from Dale attesting to the veracity of the interview's essence, *and then signed his name herself.* "*Item* Adds Forgery to Fakery," the *States* chortled.

In a frantic 1,500-word screed against its competitors entitled "2 Fakers and the Facts," the *Item*'s editors valiantly defended Blair and Hall, and boasted of higher circulation and quicker news, likening the morning daily to "cold hash made from hot roast beef." Their next attack on the *Times-Pic* was a schoolyard taunt, then a week later they grasped for mature admonishment: "It is . . . a matter of regret of the *Item* that the new combination of morning papers starts out by lending itself to a ridiculous attempt to discredit . . . [t]he *Item*'s staff . . . If it becomes a habit, it will call for punishment."

The assault on the *Item*'s credibility obviously made a dent in circulation. And the *Item*'s extended editorial tantrum (against the merged morning paper more than the *States*) betrayed just how immediately publisher James Thomson regretted not snatching up the *Pic* for himself. Already, the *Times-Picayune* was gaining ground in circulation, and in just one year, it would surpass the *Item* and ride its supremacy through the next decade.

In the shorter term, in Opelousas at least, revulsion for the paper persisted. On April 17 the *States* mocked that the *Item* was being given away for free, and the *Item* reported self-pityingly that its local distributor had been threatened with a knifing.

To Opelousans, the *Item* was a scapegoat. For a year, the town had been divided over the Dunbar matter, and even more so since Walters's campaign of jailhouse diplomacy. The committee's warning to Blair to "stick to the facts" was also a polite warning to citizens to stand by the Dunbars. As for the Lacombe mob, it was far easier for Opelousas to come together in an attack against meddling movie men, as a matter of civic pride, than to acknowledge tensions within. But that incident was only a release of steam. If the town hoped for a longer-lasting unity, it needed a truer enemy. And Blair, Hall, and the *Item*, stung by their own local vilification, were all too eager to help.

As WALTERS LIMPED from courthouse back to jail on Monday afternoon, accompanied by his specially deputized escort, Dr. George Stubbs, a friendly crowd amassed around him. The prisoner dutifully stopped to greet and chat with nearly every one. A patient Stubbs almost had him "home" when three women stepped forward. Walters, who could not resist a woman's attention, extended his hand to the first, and smiled. "I don't know you . . . but I'm glad to see you."

Just as quickly, the other two lurched closer, leering into his face:

"But you know me."

"And me. You stopped at my house for two days."

Walters's face darkened. He had been tricked like this before. Pivoting to the jail, he hissed, "I don't want to deal with the black hearted."

Behind him, prosecutors Garland and Veazie scurried up to the latter two women. Yes, they told the prosecutors, they were sure this was the man.

After midnight, the key to Walters's cell door turned in the lock. He shot up and squinted into the dim hall light. Into view staggered none other than his younger brother Bunt, who had gotten so disgustingly drunk on his train ride in that he claimed he must have been drugged.

He collapsed in the cell, and as Cant spent all night as "mother nurse," Bunt slurred the report of his journey: from Florida, he had stopped to round up witnesses in Perdido, Alabama, where Cant and Bruce had stayed for a week, but encountered nothing but "sickness and trouble" and so had arrived empty-handed.

The next day, after a visit from Dr. Littell and an oyster stew lunch with his brother, Bunt fashioned his crimson tie into a schoolboy knot and scuttled into court, where jury selection was under way. He skulked to the rail and stood like a forlorn child until his brother, who was already seated, spotted him. They whispered words, and then Bunt darted back out, down into the courthouse square, lost in the crowds.

Whether he headed to the Lacombe Hotel or not is unknown. On the question of a reunion with Julia, Cant would later profess ignorance. But this was the first and last anyone saw of Bunt Walters in Opelousas. The defendant, having noticed prosecutors' scrutiny of his brother, having heard the foolish gossip that Bunt was his "near double" kidnapping accomplice, sent him away to wait out the trial more safely in New Orleans.

Walters saved his brother more legal troubles, but his own were just beginning.

Chapter 19

Postcard of St. Landry Parish Court House (Jacobs News Depot Co.)

IT WAS IMPOSSIBLE for the crowd to miss the little boy perched on the sill of one of the courtroom's massive windows, especially during the tedium of voir dire, when attention tended to wander. He looked to be five or six, had blond hair, and was well dressed. Strangers naturally wondered aloud if it might be the famous Bobby. But when asked directly, the boy "confessed" that he was not; he was Bobby's cousin, George Kelt. The fact that all three New Orleans newspapers reported his presence, and the *States* called him Bobbie's "double," made clear that he was more than a spectator.

Tucked in the room's far front, by the door to Judge Pavy's chambers, was Mrs. Dunbar, flanked by two sisters. She was rigid, her face blank. Throughout the session, friends and neighbors waved, smiled, and stopped over to greet her, but she barely seemed to register their presence. Julia Anderson made a fleeting appearance "scarce ten feet" away, but Lessie did not turn. Most of her focus was on avoiding the sight of someone else: the mustached man who sat inside the semicircular bar, directly across the room from her. In an interview two days prior, Lessie had been quoted: "I could not think of any good of Walters, so I prefer to banish him from my mind." Today, that effort at banishment was physical.

Finding a jury for St. Landry Parish's most recent famous trial (and retrial) had been strenuous. In 1911 Mrs. Zee Runge McRee was charged with the murder of R. Lee Garland's nephew Allan, and Sheriff Swords had to hunt high and low for jurors, cornering men at political rallies, impersonating a poll tax collector, and watching in dismay as men fled stores when he drove up. It had taken nearly a full week for each trial.

Startlingly, the Walters jury took just a day and a half to assemble. Virtually every potential juror had read about the case, and many had been drawn to the jailhouse to hear Walters sing and sermonize, so there was no use wasting challenges on these grounds. Instead the men were asked about their ability to put aside what they'd heard and judge impartially, about their connections to the Dunbars, and about their feelings on capital punishment. In the end, both sides reported satisfaction with the chosen twelve: farmers and merchants, mostly, three from in or about Opelousas, and the rest from outlying communities. Intelligent, upstanding men, most married with children. Many knew the Dunbars and at least one knew them well.

Little scrutiny was given to the middle-aged, pockmarked Elijah Fisher, once an overseer of a rice plantation and now a city contractor, recently in charge of paving the streets. In the past twenty years, he had shot and killed four black men, most under vague and disputed circumstances, only one of which garnered him a conviction (and a swift pardon from the governor). In the sole clear-cut case, a fugitive robber unloaded both barrels of no. 6 shot into Fisher's face and body, prompting Fisher, then a deputy of Sheriff Swords's, to fire back. None of these killings was a secret to anyone in St. Landry Parish, and yet the press would get wind of two of them only after the Walters trial was over.

ON THE AFTERNOON of Wednesday, April 15, immediately after the last juror was seated, those reckless few who ventured to the aisle for a stretch were sent scrambling to reclaim their seats when Judge Pavy retook the stand.

In addition to Lessie and her relatives, there were an estimated eighty subpoenaed witnesses in attendance, all fretting that they might be evicted from the proceedings at the last minute. By law in Louisiana (and most other states as well), it was within the court's discretion to exclude witnesses from the audience of a trial, to prevent shaping, alteration, fabrication, or collusion of testimony. But after District Attorney Garland concluded his opening statement, the first state's witness was called right away, and there were eighty sighs of relief.

Jockeying for space at the press table, the journalists—from the New Orleans dailies, the national wire, and towns across two states—had little idea how historically crucial their work would become. Though a professional stenographer was present for the entire trial, her transcript, which must have been massive, remains elusive. After the courthouse finally succumbed to the wrecking ball in 1935, countless records that survived the transfer were destroyed by water damage in the new building's attic. The transcript may have gone missing long before that, too; like other courthouses of the era, St. Landry had a porous policy on files being checked out and returned. And any number of people would have been interested in this particular document, as the Walters trial would be chewed over on street corners and in saloons for decades.

At 4:50 p.m. Percy Dunbar took the stand. His testimony, as Seiferth and Ray heard it, was frank and complete, not at all grandstanding or "dramatic." "On the stand," they observed, "he was the same man that the townsfolk and the newspaper men have talked to daily on the streets and in his home."

In chronicling August 23, 1912, a day of unrelenting agony, Percy managed to remain collected and precise. He described the topography of Swayze Lake, the cabins, and the railroad tracks, and the deep mud of the shoreline that he had scoured on his hands and knees. He told of following baby tracks along the dusty path to the railroad, down the embankment, then back up to their terminus on the tracks. He told of the ever-widening search, the dynamite, the hat that was never found, and the test hat that was floated.

When Garland's questioning led to April 20, 1913, Percy delivered his answers just as straightforwardly, but there was a difference. "I knew the child the minute I saw him," he declared, a stark simplification of the contemporaneous record. His certainty stemmed from recognition of—as the *Item* quoted him—the boy's "features, head, and other marks of absolute identification of which I never had spoke except to one or two persons." To a question from Assistant DA Veazie, Percy responded with a burst of emotion: *"I wouldn't have him if he wasn't mine."*

It was time to bring the boy in for examination. Archie was tasked with retrieving him, but as he hurried out, Percy called from the stand, "Lessie, you go, too." During the wait, word of the boy's imminent appearance leaked out to the onlookers—massed in the hallways, courtyard, and streets—and "the already record-breaking crowd of women was augmented by fifty new arrivals."

WHILE THE CHILD would soon appear, he would not speak. Ever since the Salem witch trials of 1692, there had been deep skepticism in the United States over the reliability of children's testimony. In 1912 a six-year-old Utah boy took the stand to accuse a tramp of sodomy, after which the court fretted to the jury that since "children of his age are susceptible of impressions that are oftentimes of erroneous character," the testimony should be "examined with care and caution." In 1904 John Wigmore, in his definitive encyclopedia of the law of evidence, was less circumspect:

> Recognizing on the one hand the childish disposition to weave romances and to treat imagination for verity, and on the other the rooted ingenuousness of children and their tendency to speak straightforwardly what is in their minds, it must be concluded that the sensible way is to put the child upon the stand and let it tell its story for what it may seem to be worth.

In other words: yes, young children tend to make things up, but they are also inherently predisposed to tell the truth.

In the Walters case, later evidence points to behind-the-scenes pretrial tension around this subject, with the state hoping to allow the boy himself to take the stand to tell his by now well-known story of abduction. But in a case as unique as this, where the child's very identity was in question, so much time had passed, and charges of "coaching" had been at the root of the debate since the beginning, the defense clearly had the winning argument.

WITH ALL THE stirring at the back of the courtroom, only Ray of the *Times-Picayune* was careful enough to observe the silent drama gearing up in front. At the defense table, the prisoner chatted and chuckled with his attorneys, but with every new entrance, his eyes shot to the door. Walters was looking for the boy, whom he had called for in vain from his cell for months, whom he had not seen in person for almost a year to the day.

Finally, he appeared, in the arms of Mrs. Dunbar, who carried him through an awestruck crowd toward the bench. Walters studied the boy, top to bottom, and followed him as he was passed off from Mrs. Dunbar to attorney Lewis, who sat down with him just in front of the jury. At the front of the crowd, Mrs. Dunbar remained standing, hovering anxiously, her eyes never leaving the boy.

"Is this your son?" Mr. Lewis asked Mr. Dunbar.

"It is."

With that, Mr. Lewis passed the boy to Mr. Dunbar, who launched into an exhibition of scars and moles. The jurors stood up and crowded around the witness stand. Percy turned the young body every which way, coaxing its parts so that the men could better see, pointing out markings with practiced authority. The boy endured, though according to Ray, he "clung affectionately" to Percy throughout.

Sitting only a few feet away, the prisoner seemed oblivious to the particulars of what Mr. Dunbar said or pointed to. His focus remained on the child's face. "Fondness, eagerness, and a bit of apprehension ran successively through his eyes," Ray observed. "He seemed to be mentally pleading with the child." At some point, the boy was returned to Mr. Lewis, and Walters's gaze again followed him.

Settling into Lewis's lap and turning forward, the boy suddenly spotted Walters. "He looked him fully in the face with eyes that saw but seemingly failed to respond." And for almost a minute, theirs was a mutual fixed gaze, the prisoner and the boy.

Certain things about the old man were unfamiliar: he was groomed, trimmed, and clean. But his eyes demanded the boy to know him, and he did.

Walters had never left the boy's mind. During the year since he had seen him in the flesh, he had voiced recollections of him aloud, wondered about him, talked about him, and been told about him, caught glimpses of him in photos and likely had a chance to stare. His name for the man had shifted, from Other Papa or Ugly Papa to Mean Old Walters, and his mind's picture had likewise darkened. The old man had come to mean fear.

Yet now he was not afraid. Now in person, he saw the man as he had been, *before*. He saw Ugly Papa. This was neither imagination nor what he had come, over the past twelve months, to feel as memory.

But it didn't last. He broke the grip of the old man's gaze.

"Then he turned and looked at the man who had just sworn to be his father," Ray wrote: Percy Dunbar. He grabbed Mr. Lewis's neck and squirmed toward the jury box. Walters did not give up his gaze so easily, but by Ray's account, the boy never turned his way again.

When Dale stood for cross-examination, one of his first questions was, "Isn't it a fact you thought the boy was drowned?"

"Never thought so for a single moment," Percy shot back.

Dale pressed: "Are there not alligator holes in that lake and bayou?"

Yes, Percy answered, "[b]ut that idea is impossible, aside from all other evidence, because there was no traces left. An alligator crawls out on the bank to eat its food." With that, Percy launched into a rambling lesson on alligator behavior, based on a lifetime of experience, the particulars of which no paper felt worthy of quoting, but which begged the question: How did this father, who had never doubted that his son was alive, come to so carefully consider the possibility of his death? Was it solely in the context of fighting off the speculations of others, or had he—notwithstanding his insistence otherwise—wrestled with those thoughts himself?

Dale moved on to Columbia. He asked Mr. Dunbar to present the photographs sent to Opelousas in mid-April 1913, the photos that had convinced him and his wife that Percy should go see the boy in person. Dale allowed the jury to study the images and make the inevitable visual comparison with the boy sitting in Mr. Lewis's arms: aside from dress and aging, they were unmistakably the same. Thus loaded, Dale fired: "How long was it after you received these photographs before you left for Columbia?"

"Several days," Percy was forced to admit.

He had addressed questions about his delayed response before, explaining that with so many false leads, he did not want to get Lessie's hopes up again. But in that version of events, the tipping point from hesitation into action had been the photos' arrival. His response today, however, suggested that even after he had seen the pictures, he was unconvinced.

According to newspapers, Dale neither underlined Percy's response nor asked the obvious follow-up, trusting that these implications would not pass over the jury's heads.

Regarding Percy's first Columbia identification, he wondered aloud, "Didn't you say his eyes were different, and you couldn't find the scar on his toe?"

"I said his eyes were drawn more than my boy's eyes and I couldn't find the scar then."

"What was your idea in sending for your wife if you were sure of the identification?"

"I wanted her to corroborate me."

"Didn't you know your own child?"

"I wanted to be careful. A human life was at stake."

When asked if, at the Wallace property, he had heard reporters question Mrs. Dunbar if the boy was her child, Percy flatly said "No." When asked if Sheriff Hathorn had made a public statement that the Dunbars were not sure and wanted to see the child in the morning, the witness was somewhat more generous: "He may have; I don't recall it." As hard as Dale searched for a thread of doubt that he could tease out into something bigger, Percy Dunbar kept himself formidably defended.

Fast approaching supper, Dale introduced a new piece of evidence: a "postcard" from when Bobby first went missing, one of the thousands that flooded police stations across the country in the fall of 1912. It included a photo of Bobby at two, and a brief description that emphasized a visible scar on the big toe of the left foot.

It was not that Percy had a ready explanation that was surprising, it was the explanation itself: "My wife jumped on me several times about emphasizing that scar so much . . . It was caused by a burn when he was a baby, and in getting up the description, I remembered it distinctly and put it in. My wife told me the scars had become less distinct."

Dale pointed to the boy in Mr. Lewis's arms and asked, "Is this scar on this boy?" to which Percy responded: "Indistinctly, it can be seen."

With that, an hour-long adjournment for supper began. As Lessie ushered the boy out, Walters's gaze remained fixed on him, all the way up the aisle and into the crowd.

WHILE THE DUNBARS had often been asked about the scar and the discrepancy between description and appearance, Percy's latest explanation had never before been reported. Though not explicitly contradictory, it seemed to stand in tension with a more common response, one that Percy had repeated earlier in his testimony: the hypothesis that traveling around barefoot for months had caused the scar to wear off. In one explanation, the wearing off had happened *after* Bobby went missing; in the other, *before*. One was speculation sparked by confusion that the scar was now absent; the other was a rationale for why the scar's absence should not be confusing.

On April 25, 1913, Percy had offered the *Pic* the fullest explanation on record, which comes closest to reconciling the two explanations: after the burn, they had applied Unguentine, "and in eighteen months, the scar, which had extended to the instep, had disappeared, and it only extended to the base of the toe. Now, if that was possible for it to disappear that much in that time, it was possible for it to disappear from the toe altogether." The fading happened both before *and* after, Percy had said then.

But for the defense attorneys tonight, on their break, the significance of Percy's new testimony was not the scar itself but Percy's explanation of the description discrepancy. It was a momentous revelation, and they were already armed against it.

When Percy retook the stand, Dale zeroed back in. Percy explained that he had sent out a first public circular, then sometime after that, remembered the scar and added it in. No such early scar-free description exists, and the first extant description, published just a week after Bobby's disappearance, mentions the toe so prominently and in such great detail, that it seems unlikely that it was added in: "His left foot had been burned when he was a baby," the *Times-Democrat* had reported on August 30, 1912, "and the large toe shows a plain scar as a result and is somewhat smaller than the large toe on the right foot."

Percy might have been referring to the revised *second* circular, from November, the one printed five thousand times by the Burns Agency and sent to cities across the nation. Along with refining "light hair" to "hair light, but turning dark," that November circular simplified the description of the toe. But its essence remained the same, if not stronger: "Big toe on left foot badly scarred from burn when baby." And the changes were not just the work of the Burns Agency; as Dan Lehon himself had told the *States* in December 1912, "Before issuing the circulars, I received the permission of the citizens of Opelousas and Mr. Robert [sic] Dunbar to do so."

This would suggest that, at the time of the second circular's printing, Percy was aware of his wife's protest that the scar had faded, but he had overruled her. Indeed, he testified as much on the stand. With Lessie in the audience listening to every word, Percy swore that he had told her he was confident the scar remained visible.

On cue, Dale introduced two telegrams from December 30, 1912, the first from the Carriere, Mississippi, postmaster to Opelousas, noting that a "Suspicious man here name Walters cripple has little boy" who "might be Dunbar child." The sender requested a fuller description of Bobby Dunbar, to which Opelousas mayor E. L. Loeb responded, via telegram number two: "large round blue eyes light hair complexion fair Rosy Cheeks short thick neck big toe on left foot badly scarred from burn."

Dale and Rawls had obtained these telegrams less than two weeks earlier, along with an affidavit stating that Carriere officials "were unable to find any bad scar as mentioned in [E. L.] Loeb wire . . . or semblance of a scar near his big toe, or anywhere else on his foot, and therefore reached the conclusion that this child was not Bobbie Dunbar, and did not arrest or detain the said W. C. Walters, and let him go on his way."

The revelation must have taken jurors by surprise. Walters had been arrested before, with this very boy, but because no scar was found on the toe, he had been released. As the defense team saw it, the revelation challenged Percy's latest assertion that there had been too much focus on the scar. If that were the case, how, in December, could the incorrect description still be given out?

Mr. Dunbar responded that the description must have been copied from the circular, and Mr. Lewis hastened to point out that it was Mayor Loeb, not the Dunbars, who had sent the telegram. Defense opted to let the matter lie, for the moment.

As soon as he had a chance, Veazie took Percy off the defensive and inquired about any new markings on the boy. This was the father's cue to relate that he had found marks of a whip on the boy's legs and back. "Some of the scars are there yet." Percy swayed the jurymen further with desperate details of his eight-month search, which cost him every cent. Unprompted, he began to volunteer that "many people thought [I] was going mad," but was cut off by an objection.

As questioning persisted, Ray and other reporters gave up transcribing quotes and instead offered hasty summary. Despite their waning attention, one thing shines through in the record: attorneys on both sides remained fixed on the toe description. By the end of the night, it had been brought up a half dozen times, by Dale and more than once by the prosecutors themselves, trying to bat away the Loeb telegram. The defense had hit a nerve, and the state knew it.

ON THURSDAY AFTERNOON, Mignon Hall dashed off a florid editorial/recap of the first two days in court: "Mother Love Duel Obscures All Other Issues in Trial." While it contained "plenty of scoops," its angle was by no means an *Item* exclusive. When Julia Anderson arrived in court that morning, nearly every paper highlighted the silent drama unfolding with the two women's simultaneous presence.

Court was just starting when she appeared, and a sea of heads turned. She managed a tight smile and was eventually escorted up to the bar. According to Seiferth of the *Times-Picayune*, Lessie Dunbar "allowed" the other mother "to pass her without even looking up." But McMullen of the *States* saw something else—"A fleeting glance, one of contempt and scorn,

and the other expressionless, passed between the contending mothers"—
though he neglected to specify which mother exhibited which reaction.

Once inside the inner circle, Julia stood, maintaining a fixed smile for
all those who stared at her, but clearly at sea as to where she should sit.
This had happened to her two days ago as well. Though the ladies of
Opelousas had been polite enough, she had been crammed into the rear
of the court: allowed in, but certainly not welcomed. After sitting out and
stewing through the prior day's proceedings, Julia had resolved not to suc-
cumb so easily to the ladies' polite shunning.

She stood, smiling and waiting in front of them all, until finally, someone came to her aid. A wedge of a spot was made for her, at the far end of
the enclosure by the jury, on a bench between two hulking men: Wallace
Dunbar, last witness of the night before, and John Oge, first witness of
the morning.

It was during these two men's testimony, and that of Paul Mizzi, that
prosecutors reminded the jurymen that they also could rise and interro-
gate the witnesses, inevitably prompting a ponderous spate of grandiose
and overly picky questions. Finally, the state brought the case to Columbia. Deputy "Big Partner" Day began the chronicle of those events, but
the real stir came with the recollections of Dr. Anderson, whose wife had
been instrumental in alerting the Dunbars of the boy to begin with, who
had driven Percy to meet the boy, and who had been with the couple in
the Wallace cabin when Lessie first saw him. As Anderson told of that
event, and of Lessie's reluctance to leave the child behind for the night, he
began to tear up.

But as Columbians, Dale and Rawls well knew that there was more
to the story of Walters's arrest, and they were both itching to pounce.
Indeed, both of them did, in succession, battering a fuller story out of
the good doctor, piece by piece. They forced him to acknowledge that
Walters had been around Hub for some time before the arrest, though
he refused to shed light on whether Walters had been fleeing or not
when tracked down at Newsom. Similarly, Anderson admitted that he
had heard, but had no direct knowledge, that a "citizens' committee" had
banded together to confront Walters and examine the boy in early April,
but found no reason to pursue the matter further.

That would have been bad enough. But the very next day, the doctor
admitted, Walters himself had come to his office, of his own accord, and
insisted that the doctor examine the child for the scar. The *States'* account
of Anderson's recollection was spare and to the point:

"You looked for a badly scarred foot, did you not?"

"Yes."

"Did you find it?"

"No."

"You let the child go?"

"Yes."

It was a damning confession, which Anderson struggled to qualify: the foot was filthy and calloused, and though he did not find a scar, he did find a red mark. Asked what he had said to Walters afterward, Anderson chose his words carefully: "I did say that I failed to find the scar mentioned in the description advertised," quoted the *Item,* "and that I was not sure that the description tallied with that of the boy with Walters."

It was not the wrong boy. It was the wrong description. The misworded circular did far more than explain away Anderson's inaction; it helped square the revelation of his examination with the prosecutors' charge of Walters's guilt. If he were in fact the boy's kidnapper, why would he have so willingly flaunted the child for examination? Only if Walters himself knew that the description was inaccurate might he credibly be so cavalier. Still, that was a lot to ask a reasonable jury to accept, and prosecutors were probably eager, by then, for the doctor to leave the stand.

But the defense had more well-aimed darts to throw. Had the doctor not heard Mrs. Dunbar say that his eyes were "squint," while Bobby's were "big" and "wide open"? The doctor admitted so. Had Walters himself not supplied Anderson's wife with the photos sent to the Dunbars? The doctor did not know. When, in response to juror Elijah Fisher's question about Walters's line of business, Anderson testified, "I heard he was a stove mender," Dale was on his feet again: "As a matter of fact, don't you know he was not; don't you know he was fixing organs and pianos?"

"I have heard that too, but can't say of my knowledge" was the doctor's familiar refrain.

WHEN WORD RIPPLED through the crowd that Lessie would testify next, as Seiferth politely reported, "[A] hint [was] dropped that it would be best if Julia remained away from the crowded courtroom when Mrs. Dunbar bared her mother's heart to the jury. The advice was well meant, and Julia followed it, though in none too good grace." As "the other mother" stalked off to the Lacombe, a gaggle of reporters scurried along. She was a mother, too, Julia said, and she knew her child as well as Mrs.

Dunbar. She rattled off her own angry list of traits, then let her temper get the better of her decency: she was not the kind of mother who would carry her son out to "the marshes to drown."

Mignon Hall's version of this rant formed the explosive centerpiece of her "Dueling Mother Love" story the next day. In it, she reported that Julia Anderson had disputed one key element of Percy's testimony: the scar on the boy's eye had not come from a sewing machine, as Mr. Dunbar testified, but from a splinter, when he had been in Julia's care. "It isn't true," Hall reported Julia's objection, "Bruce got that scar on his little eye when he was at home with me. He was crawling around on the floor when [he] stuck a splinter in his little face. I distinctly remember that day."

Julia had never said any such thing before. In fact, quite the opposite: she had said that she did not know the cause of particular "boils or scratches." Indeed, only days after his April 1913 arrest, Walters recalled that the scar was from a falling window sash at his sister's in Eastman, Georgia. Hall's embellishment bomb did plenty of damage the day it was printed, but its full detonation was yet to come.

THE ROOM SILENCED as Lessie stepped forward. At every court appearance she had made thus far, reporters detailed her fashion flair, but for her testimony today, she had gone to a startling extreme. Her tea-gown was lilac gray with overskirts, blue blossoms trimmed and sprouted from her hat, and her face was as geisha white as the gloves that ran up her arms. She bypassed the clerk's desk, where prior witnesses had been sworn in, and instead, as Ray observed, stood "proudly erect upon the witness stand, with hand raised high above her head as if to emphasize the oath she took."

As she sat in the witness chair, plainly wracked with anxiety, a protective huddle formed around her inside the bar. A chair was brought for Percy to sit at her side, the state's attorneys edged near, defense attorneys closed in on their side, and even Judge Pavy half stood and hovered. Then Mr. Veazie, a family friend, began the questioning.

He took her back to Swayze Lake, and while her husband's testimony of this day had been dry, and the men before her had even found room to laugh in the retelling, Lessie's memory was utterly different. In wrenching detail, she relived the terror of losing her son, from the moment she first asked after him, through the running, calling, crying, and collapsing. Someone found footprints, and she was sent for.

They were "Robert's, I know them," she answered Veazie. "They led to the railroad tracks. I knew he was gone."

In short order, Veazie had gotten her to Columbia, and her recollections now were virtually identical to Percy's. Her voice sped up and grew louder: "I knew him the minute I saw him . . . I whispered to my husband, and he urged me to keep quiet."

Tears overcame her, and they spread to the crowd.

Lessie told of the Lamptons, the bath, and the sandals. The boy was cowed, she said; even when they returned to Opelousas, he was terrified of everyone. And as the sobs welled up again, she recalled, as Percy had, that there were whip marks on Bobby's back.

Through her tears, she saw that Mr. Veazie was presenting her with a ring. She took it, rubbed it affectionately, and held her fan up to her face so that she could kiss it in private. It was Bobby's baby ring, she told the jury, and when he returned home, he had asked after it, begged for it, and she allowed him to wear it.

Arthur Collins, the mustached old farmer in the jury box, chimed in with his second question on this subject: was she sure he was her child?

"I would not have taken him and kept him if he was not mine."

She told of his markings and the burned toe: a severe burn that "had mostly disappeared," though when he goes barefoot, the burn spot still becomes red. Lessie affirmed that she had told Percy he had emphasized it too much. "[B]ut he had printed the cards and distributed many," Ray summarized, "so he didn't change it." Upon prompting by Mr. Lewis, she elaborated that Percy had not consulted her and that he was not "a close observer." It was she alone who bathed the boy, "never trusting the task to another," and thus, she who knew the burn had faded.

Veazie asked about the scar on his eye, and she told about the sewing machine. He asked about behavioral proofs, and she had plenty. Most unforgettable was his happiness to be home: according to Ray, he hugged her and declared, "You are my good mother. Walters told me you were dead, and my papa threw [you] into a creek."

WITH THAT, THE state had nothing further, but before Veazie had settled back into his chair, forty-nine-year-old Edward B. Dubuisson was on his feet, at the witness stand, and "engaged in the gentlest sort of colloquy" with Mrs. Dunbar. The Mississippi attorneys had wisely chosen Dubuisson, a trusted and revered Opelousan, to cross-examine the mother. His was a sympathetic presence, and to those who had never seen him in court, he may have even seemed frail or silly, the rubber tube of his ear trumpet trained on Lessie to catch her words. The device was not a gimmick that Dubuisson intentionally exploited—he was far too smart for that, and he really couldn't hear without it—but it had a conveniently disarming effect nonetheless.

"Mrs. Dunbar, you are the one woman in the world most affected by the loss of this boy," McMullen heard him say, "but we must ask you a few questions."

Lessie cut short her crying and braced herself. She knew Dubuisson's reputation, and certainly something of his career. After Virginia Military Institute and Tulane Law School, he had served as St. Landry's district attorney and was a member of the state constitutional conventions of 1898 and 1913. Like everyone in Opelousas, Lessie had read the reports of his politely brutal cross-examination of the twice-tried murderess Mrs. McRee. From Dubuisson, brevity was the best that Lessie could hope for.

Why was she so certain that the footprints at Swayze Lake were her son's? he asked first. She knew Bobby's footprints well, she answered. She had seen them in the sand, where he had run to play after getting wet in the fountain. As soon as she saw them on the dusty path, Ray paraphrased, "she was willing to lay down her life" that they were her son's.

Mr. Dubuisson paused. Her conviction was compelling, but she had studiously avoided the question. It was not *if* she had known the footprint, but *why*.

He asked if her sons, like most boys, liked to throw off their shoes and go barefoot in the summer. She allowed that they did, and still do from time to time. Was the scar from the burn still visible on his bare foot at Swayze Lake? "He had it then nearly three years, and it had not disappeared, although faint," Ray summarized.

Dubuisson turned predictably to the reward circular. Was she not, he asked, the person most impacted by her son's vanishing? She was. Was there anyone with "more interest in his disappearance and recovery?" There was no one. *Then why did she allow the erroneous circular to go out?*

Her answer, as reported by Ray, came in several parts: "She said her husband thought to spare her worry, and did not consult her, nor did she know what he was going to send out."

Dubuisson then lifted a copy of the hometown newspaper, the *Clarion*, published a week after Bobby went missing, and read the relevant excerpt: "Left foot had been burned when a baby and shows scar on big toe, which is somewhat smaller than big toe on right foot." He let her absorb the words before he spoke again.

Lessie's eyes darted to the paper. At the end of the August 31 article, although Dubuisson did not point it out, was his own name, among other town leaders, offering $25 toward the $1,000 reward fund for the recovery of little Robert. In that awful time of 1912, Mr. Dubuisson had been on her side. The whole parish had united around them.

Dubuisson looked up and asked the inevitable question. He wanted an explanation for the Dunbars' emphasis on the burn, "at the tragedy's inception."

Ray (who in four years would be taking stenography for Governor John M. Parker) carefully summarized Lessie's responses. His report, the only surviving record, suggests a quiet but all-out scramble: "Mrs. Dunbar replied that she may have seen the paper or had some part of it read to her. She did not remember if she had seen that issue or called any attention to the story. She was so distressed at the time that she did not take much note of such things. She could not even recall if she had read it since. If she had seen it at the time, she would have called her husband's attention, although she does not even know if he had the article inserted."

And when Dubuisson returned to the "later circulars," "she repeated the delay in showing them to her, and said she knew they had already spent more than their means. Mr. Dunbar was alone in New Orleans at the time, and it was when he returned that she cautioned him that he had laid too much stress on the burn."

As for the late-December Loeb telegrams, months after she had flagged the error, "She said her husband never showed her any such message then."

Dubuisson and his colleagues had nothing further.

Lewis leapt to the rescue with an anxious redirect. He coaxed out of her that Mr. Dunbar did not share materials related to the search with her "for the sake of her mind's ease"—not the first time this point had been made.

Lessie sat, still and stunned for a moment. Her trial was over.

As she stood, Percy bolted to her side to assist. The lawyers and audience parted so that he could usher her through to the exit, but instead they paused. Percy wanted her to go home to recuperate, away from the gaping throngs. But female friends and relatives in the audience invited Lessie to sit with them. The couple stood at an impasse before the audience, until finally, Percy gave in and released Lessie to the women, then resumed his spot behind the state's attorneys.

In her dispatch for the *Item,* Mignon Hall characterized Lessie's cross-examination as "lenient" and offered no details, misattributing it to Dale and Rawls. Had she bothered to listen, she may have reported otherwise. Mr. Dubuisson, before an audience of Dunbar relatives and friends, before a jury of neighbors, acquaintances, and lifelong parish natives, had come as close as he possibly could—as close as anyone would come in these proceedings—to calling this weeping mother a liar.

But it was Lessie's visible emotion on the stand, not any details about scars or circulars, that stuck with spectators, reporters, and jurors. This was a mother who loved her son and lived for him, who had been scarred by his loss, made just barely whole again by his recovery. And when court reconvened, the state brought to the stand an army to back her up: relative after relative, friend after friend, to swear that this child was Lessie Dunbar's natural-born son. After Katie Dunbar gave details of her affidavit in person, so many witnesses swore to the Dunbars' claim that the papers just offered a list:

> Miss Maud Taylor, intimate friend of the family; his aunts, Miss[es] Douce and Rowena Whitley; Miss Maude Estorge, daughter of H. E. Estorge, partner of Mr. Dunbar; Miss Thelma Dupre, a [niece] . . . Miss[es] Mamie and Clyde Lawler, playmates; Mrs. Frank Shute, a close friend of Mrs. Dunbar . . . each in turn swore positively to identification.

Christine Zernott, a New Orleans cousin, swore that the boy remembered a pair of socks he had loaned to her son before he was lost. Percy's brother Archie, who had lived with the Dunbars since before Bobby went missing, listed a variety of confirming marks. Lessie's sister Mary Dupre recalled that when the boy came to her house after his return, he asked after the little toy gun that he kept there. To "test" him, she told him to fetch it, and he beelined to its old spot and brought it out for her.

She cocked it, and he started off. She asked him what he was going to do, and he answered. "Aunt Mary, I'm going to shoot a nigger." He went out in front of the house, pointed the gun toward the Methodist church, and pulled the trigger.

This was apparently one of Bobby's old routines.

As witness after witness took the stand, defense attorneys offered little cross-examination, allowing a wave of certainty to build and wash over the jury. Then Mayor Loeb took the stand.

Loeb was popular and widely respected, and his testimony was calculated to put an official Opelousas seal on the identification of Bobby

Dunbar. He had known Bobby well before his disappearance, he told the jury, and was certain that this was the same boy. Attempting to defuse an inevitable line of attack, prosecutors introduced a telegram the mayor had sent to Poplarville during the search, in which he had stated that Bobby had a badly scarred left big toe. As expected, Mayor Loeb confirmed that he had copied the description from a reward circular, not from any direct conversation with the Dunbars. The defense pounced. Had the mayor been alone when he sent the message? No, he had not, he was forced to admit. He had been accompanied to the telegram office by none other than Archie Dunbar.

The defense asked pointedly about other telegrams related to the search that the mayor might have had a hand in, to which he replied non-committally that he would "endeavor to look them up." And with that, the mayor hurried off the stand.

While newspapers did not specify the date of this particular telegram, it likely was one from September 1912, when Archie was known to have been in contact with the Poplarville sheriff while Percy was off on his search. In either case, the burning question of that *December* telegram lingered unanswered after Loeb left the stand: if Lessie had indeed flagged the toe description as inaccurate, why—*four months into the search*—had a correction or clarification not made its way to Mayor Loeb, who was playing a key role in search-related communications?

Mayor Loeb, of course, was not the one to answer that question.

IN THE DUNBARS' family scrapbook, passed down from Lessie Dunbar to later generations, is a photo of an unidentified toddler. The boy is standing, wearing a dress, and though his hair appears darker, his eyes and mouth bear an arguable resemblance to other infant photos of Bobby Dunbar. But in this photo, unlike any others, both of the child's bare feet are visible. On the left foot, the big toe appears oddly curved, misshapen, and unmistakably smaller than its counterpart on the right. It is possible that this is a photo of another child, mailed to the Dunbars during their search because of its match to the reward poster description. It is also possible that this photo is Bobby Dunbar. In any case, it was never made public.

Chapter 20

Trist Wood, *New Orleans Item,* April 20, 1914

WILLIAM WALTERS'S PATH from jail to courthouse was no longer a place for hellos and handshaking. Just a few days into the testimony, it was becoming a gauntlet of hecklers, muscling for a front-row spot to sling an outraged insult into the limping prisoner's face, or, barring that, at his back. Once he was gone, the unruly crowd was left behind and stuck outside, day after day. And so they loitered and roamed the square, looking for something, anything to keep their blood running or just to pass the time.

Fresh off the fair and carnival circuit, or up from the tourist haunts of the *Vieux Carré,* a market moved in. Corn doctors laid out their hammers and knives and ointments, and got to work on all the aching feet. Postcard writers boasted perfect penmanship, and hordes lined up to dictate greetings from the world-famous Walters trial to everyone they knew. Fire tongs, vanilla-scented envelopes, and souvenir photos of Bobby Dunbar were peddled, and there were even some piteous sideshows: a two-headed calf, a half-human/half-arachnid named Spido. But what most kept the crowds lingering was the regular trickle of news from inside the courthouse.

In the latter half of day two of the trial, having established the boy as Bobby and chronicled his disappearance and recovery, the state at last got down to linking the defendant to the crime. Over the course of the next few days, it produced a parade of eyewitnesses who placed Walters in Louisiana before August 23, 1912, and in the vicinity of Swayze Lake on and around that day. From there witnesses told of sightings across southern Mississippi, kidnapped child in tow, throughout the fall and winter. Their accounts grew ever stranger, and the alleged movements and machinations of the defendant grew ever murkier. Each session brought a new, outlandish twist, and had the audience crowding deeper and deeper into the aisles.

To place Walters in Louisiana well before the disappearance of Bobby Dunbar, Deputy Mallett, who had testified at the habeas hearing in Poplarville, returned to the stand in Opelousas to repeat his controversial memory of a wagon with "W. C. Walters Stove Mender" painted on its canvas. Originally, Mallett had sworn in an affidavit that Walters was a stove mender in 1912. In Poplarville, seeing Walters face-to-face, he had added another memory, of Walters as a clock fixer. Now, on the stand in Opelousas, he added yet another sighting and profession still: a repairer of sewing machines, in 1909.

Then came Mrs. Lizzie McManus. It had been almost a year since "the little widow" had sparred angrily with Walters at Poplarville, and, like Mallett, she had been revising. In light of Walters's objections, she tweaked the dates she had seen Walters, dropped any claim that he had boarded in her home, and begrudgingly acknowledged that he had merely eaten at her restaurant. But she now threw in that he had also camped on her land. And when Walters left Pineville to go off mending stoves, "[h]e wanted my son to go with him, but I told my boy Mr. Walters was not the kind of man he ought to go away with." Her boy, jurors were led to infer, could have been Walters's first victim.

In fact, Mrs. McManus was not a little widow at all, nor was her son a child. Her husband, William, was two years into a life sentence at the Angola prison farm, for stalking and gunning down Judge Emmett Walker, the mayor of Pineville, who had had the temerity to fine William and Lizzie's son Robert—a grown man—for "shooting into a crowd of Negro hay riders."

If it were known that Mr. McManus was in prison, questions might have arisen about his wife's motivations for offering (and tailoring) testimony. Garland must have been relieved when she received no cross-examination.

HAVING ESTABLISHED WALTERS'S history in and familiarity with these parts of Louisiana, prosecutors now brought him closer and closer to Swayze Lake on August 23, 1912. As Walters looked on in contempt, W. O. Stogner from Tylertown, Mississippi, reiterated the explosive claim he'd made in a June 1913 affidavit and again at the habeas hearing: while staying at Stogner's home just prior to his final arrest, the defendant had confessed that he had been in St. Landry Parish at the time of Bobby's disappearance, but had not taken the boy. A year ago, though, Stogner had told this story to the *Pic* a little differently: Walters had mentioned being arrested and released in the Dunbar investigation, but said *nothing* about being in St. Landry.

When Mrs. E. W. Nix of New Roads, Louisiana, took the stand, the prisoner's sneer grew even more pronounced. Her mammoth hat was tilted over her face at a preposterous angle, but those familiar angry eyes flashed bright from the shadow of its brim. She was one of the "black hearts" who had tried to trick him with a handshake by the jail.

In August 1912 Mrs. Nix had been living in Port Barre, halfway between Opelousas and Swayze Lake. On the morning of the twenty-third, she peered out her window to spot a strange man leaning over her front fence, in the very act of snatching her little son. Mrs. Nix barked out, and the man released the boy, who scampered inside. When she asked what the man had wanted, her son replied that he had said he was fond of children and wanted to go fishing. "[I] told him not to talk to tramps," quoted the *Item*.

Had Mrs. Nix stopped there, her testimony would have been sufficient. But in the glow of center stage, she had much more to tell. After "the guilty party" (as she referred to Walters) had failed to abduct her boy in the front yard, he knocked on her back door, asking for something to eat. Astonishingly, Mrs. Nix allowed him in, thus furnishing her with the following observations: he limped up the stairs, explained that he had just come from Charity Hospital, volunteered to fix her stove, peppered her with religious ravings, inquired about her son's webbed toe, and asked directions to the Swayze Lake–bound O.G. Railroad. The defense did not dignify the witness with a cross-examination, but it probably should have made the effort. The next day, even the most evenhanded of reporters, Herman Seiferth, opined without a hint of irony, "Mrs. Nix's description of the rambling religious faker fits his former pose like a glove."

From here, prosecutors took Walters to the site of the alleged kidnapping. Frank Ansley repeated his Swayze Lake sighting from the habeas hearing—a reward-curious hobo on his way to Charity Hospital—and Preston King did the same. But with key alterations. Whereas Ansley had sworn last year that he first saw the tramp on Saturday, August 24, after Bobby went missing, today on the stand, he said he had seen the man the morning of the twenty-third, hours *before* Bobby disappeared. A bit more subtly, King now swore that when he saw the tramp at dawn on Sunday the twenty-fifth, the man told him that he had spent the night before in a boxcar, just down the tracks at Williamson Spur. As the *Times-Picayune* quoted him: "I asked where he was from, and he said he had slept in a boxcar about three-quarters of a mile down the road." In Poplarville, his testimony had been precisely the opposite:

> Q. He didn't tell you anything about where he was from?
> A. No, sir. I didn't ask him. Ask[ed] him where he was going.
>   I remarked, "Why don't you wait and catch a train?" and
>   he said to me you could ride the train, but they would put
>   [someone like] me off.

Neither witness apparently faced cross-examination. But why would King now need to "remember" this new detail of Walters's sleeping at Williamson Spur, two nights after the alleged kidnapping? "For some time there had been an undercurrent of rumor that Walters had an accomplice around the Swayze Lake neighborhood," reported Lee Hawes, now writing for the *Item*, another kidnapper to keep the boy hidden while "he was going up and down the O. and G. tracks from [Williamson] Spur to Melville trying to establish 'a getaway.' "

According to the state's chronology, after Walters's fleeting appearances in the vicinity of Swayze Lake from August 23 to 26, he was next seen between thirteen and twenty days later, and 160-odd miles east, across the Atchafalaya Basin, across the Pearl River, in Poplarville, Mississippi.

When Poplarville restauranteur Katie Collins took the stand to fill in the details, most casual followers were aware of the broad strokes of what she was promised to say. In May 1913 her account had been widely publicized, and more recently, the papers were touting it in the buildup to trial: Miss Collins, they exclaimed, had witnessed the all-important "swap"— two near-identical men exchanging two near-identical boys—right there in her own Poplarville roadhouse. Today, hearing the details for the very first time and straight from the source, the crowd sat riveted in their seats.

On that early-September Saturday, Miss Collins began, her widowed sister was cooking, and she was helping out as a waitress. As she approached the table and chatted with the two men and two boys seated there, she could not help noticing not just how dirty they all were but also how alike both pairs appeared. Of the two men, one was a bit stouter and darker haired than the other, and this was the man she now knew to be Walters. As for the boys, there was perhaps a few months difference in their ages, and one was sickly and quiet while the other was healthy and active: this latter was the child she had just seen in court, the boy the Dunbars claimed as Bobby. When she first approached to take their order, the healthy boy was standing in his seat, and Walters told him to sit down. He obeyed, and Mrs. Collins observed—both in May 1913 and now—that the lad positively cowered from the man. On the stand today, she added a flourish, "It was the same expression that was in the eyes of the little boy when he was looking at Walters in this courtroom the other evening." At some point, though she did not specify when or why, the four left the restaurant in a hurry.

As clear and consistent as Miss Collins was on those bare points, on the question of how she came to be interested in this ill-behaved child to begin with, there emerged roughly two versions of the story, both attributed to her at various times and yet largely irreconcilable. In earlier retellings, Miss Collins's interest was piqued because Walters called him Bruce, which—as the *Item* would later explain—was her nephew's name. She tried to engage the boy, but the man "resented" her attempts and "spoke gruffly" to the boy. In the other version, to which she swore on the stand, the man told the boy to sit down (but did not utter his name). It was only when she drew near and asked, that the man ordered the boy to tell her his name was Bruce.

The latter version was clearly the more damning. Dale did his best to force an admission that Walters had, in fact, called the boy "Bruce" *before* she asked, but Miss Collins would have none of it: "He did not call him Bruce . . . Only when I asked what the boy's name was."

She knew what was at stake. It would not do to simply report the restaurant sighting and the name Bruce, or to acknowledge the more innocuous possibility that the boy had become tongue-tied when spoken to by a stranger and required some prompting from his guardian to answer. This moment at the table in the restaurant had now been loaded with so much more. It was the much-ballyhooed "swapping place," or as close to it as the prosecution could get, the nexus of an exchange of bodies, names, and identities: the healthy, active Bobby Dunbar, kidnapped and forced to take over the life of the sickly, injured Bruce Anderson.

And yet Katie Collins's testimony threatened to crumble under scrutiny. Why had Walters commanded Bobby to assume Bruce's name, *with Bruce sitting right there at the table with them?* Would he not have worried that Bruce would object and compromise the ruse? One might also wonder why it was so crucial for Bobby to be known as Bruce, right then in the restaurant with a passing stranger, to whom the children appeared virtually identical anyway. But this, of course, might lead one to wonder how the two men could be so certain of Bruce's eventual demise that they were crafty enough to kidnap Bobby as a replacement in advance, and then why they were so brazen as to bandy the two boys about in public together. While the state needed the "swap" hypothesis to resonate as plausible, the last thing it could afford was for the jurors to venture into this sort of speculation, to linger too long and think too hard about the bigger picture. The state needed the swap to stick in the jury's gut but not in its head.

As Miss Collins left the stand, few in the audience seemed to notice that her testimony had included not a single word of an actual physical exchange. Nonetheless, to reinforce that inference, the state called Eliza Loveless, a Pearl River County nurse with a nervous countenance and her hair bundled up in a snood. On or about August 19, she testified, while caring for a sick woman in the area, she had seen a man who looked like Walters and a boy who looked like the child in question, first at the home of Levy Holleman and then, a day or two later, on the Bilbos' porch. The pair, she remembered, were indeed called Walters and Bruce, just as Holleman, Bilbo, and dozens of others had sworn before and were scheduled to swear again. But they were all wrong, Miss Loveless insisted: that man and the boy were not the two she had seen here in Opelousas, and she had proof. Though the man fixed all kinds of musical instruments, he did not have a limp. The boy was sickly, withdrawn, and (this she noticed because he was barefoot) he had webbed toes.

Two months later, in October, Miss Loveless had seen the pair again, only this time they were slightly different. In fact, although they, too, went by the names Walters and Bruce, and everyone else around her assumed they were the same duo as before, she felt sure that they were not. This second Walters did have a limp, she said, and, seeing the defendant in court today, she was certain it was him. The boy was rambunctious and unruly, but (this she knew because she had bathed him in December) had no webbed foot. She was certain this was the boy she had seen in Opelousas.

At last, prosecutors had found a witness to verify firsthand what John M. Parker had speculated to Governor Brewer: the Bruce of summer was not the Bruce of fall.

But that was not all that Miss Loveless had solved. Even with two different boys, there had remained the thorny problem of the timing of his abductor's movements. How could Walters plausibly have been in Mississippi so soon before he was alleged to have appeared at Swayze Lake? He wasn't, Miss Loveless's testimony allowed prosecutors to suggest. That had been his nonlimping double. *"Two boys by the name of Bruce? Two men by the name of Walters?"* Lewis handily summed up for the jury, at once acknowledging how absurd it sounded, but also assuring the members that in all seriousness, he believed it, and so should they.

The defendant himself had been chortling, softly but visibly, throughout Miss Loveless's time on the stand. And his lawyers wore wide, determined grins to telegraph their ridicule and disbelief. But as Ray observed, "[T]he jury was watching the witness," not them, "and taking in every word."

WALTERS WAS NEXT spotted on December 18, 1912, in the guise of a "detective" and with a young boy, seventy-five miles northwest of Poplarville at the McComb City depot. When strikebreaker Joe Johnson took the stand to repeat the story he had told in the Columbia courtroom and to Mrs. Dunbar in the Hotel Monteleone, Dale cross-examined with an aggressive accusation. Had Johnson not been heard bragging that "as long as Dunbar and Fox hauled him around in automobiles, he could be counted on"? Johnson squealed that he had never laid eyes on Mr. Dunbar until this past Sunday (which did not entirely answer the question), and others in the McComb delegation, including B. L. Morgan, backed him up. But once again, they all omitted a key point from their April 1913 affidavit: "There were with Walters at the time another man and woman who were with him very familiar, but with others exceedingly reticent." Today's revised version fit the prosecution's latest rule-of-thumb hypothesis a little better: one boy with one man; two boys with two men.

If the state had presented these witnesses in such a neat, chronological order, it would have risked too much scrutiny upon the causal and temporal links between all of these alleged sightings. Why had Walters told

Mrs. Nix he was coming out of the hospital in late August 1912, then told Ansley he was on his way in? If he had forced Bobby to call himself Bruce in Katie Collins's restaurant in September, why did "Detective" Walters eagerly identify the boy as Bobby Dunbar to Johnson, Morgan, and others in December? Was the motive for kidnapping ransom, as the McComb and Swayze Lake witnesses suggested, or, as Mrs. Nix and Mrs. McManus seemed to hint, some deranged need for companionship? And of course, in the end, what was the real motive behind the "swap"?

These accounts did not add up. So prosecutors had simply jumbled the witnesses over a period of two and a half days, scattering and shuffling their testimony in an effort to dazzle the jury with their plentitude and dizzy them into belief.

And when a last-minute opportunity for showmanship and one-upsmanship presented itself, they leapt. On Thursday, April 16, the defense finally herded two of its much-hyped witnesses into Opelousas: a pair of wandering stove menders named Linder and Edwards, who had worked throughout St. Landry and surrounding parishes, often with Linder's young son in tow, and whom, the defense believed, Louisiana witnesses had mistaken for Walters and his cohort. The pair had been sub-poenaed twice, delaying the trial, and once they arrived, Linder was irked by all the fuss. And in fact he bore little if any resemblance to Walters.

The news narrative, naturally, was that one of the defense's chief lines of defense—mistaken identity—had imploded. The "double" was not a double at all. Never mind the subtleties: Dale, Rawls, and Dubuisson had never said the men were actual doubles, just that Linder had been *mistaken* for Walters, and their travels had roughly overlapped.

Nevertheless, the state seized the potential of the "double" debacle and on Friday morning snatched Linder as *its* witness. The *Item*, which had been flogging the lack of resemblance for days, reported that as Linder weaved through the overflowing crowds up to the stand, the audience's eyes shifted from his face (clean shaven) to Walters (mustached) and broke out into grins. After allowing the jury to take in the sight of the "nondouble," prosecutors asked Linder about his movements in the Opelousas area. None of which, the prosecution hoped the jury would infer, corresponded with the dates and places that previous witnesses had seen Walters.

The defense was unprepared. In cross-examination, Dubuisson asked if Linder recalled recently being approached by a sheriff, who had asked if he had ever been mistaken for Walters. Linder did recall such a conversation, yes. But when Dubuisson pressed, according to the *States,* "Linder used an ear trumpet and seemed to develop a sudden inability to hear questions . . . Attorney Dubuisson, himself hard of hearing, found great difficulty in making the witness understand." The *Item* focused not on Linder's avoidance but on the crowd's belly laughs as both witness and attorney simultaneously adjusted their hearing aids.

But as successfully distracting as he was, the state's purpose in calling Linder was not merely theatrics. Many of the witnesses whose testimony the defense had hoped to challenge with Linder and Edwards—Mr. Koenig the traveling umbrella man, chief among them—*had not even taken the stand yet.* It was a preemptive straw-man debunking of the entire mistaken-identity defense.

"As the proofs tighten guilt around the prisoner, feeling is beginning to unbosom itself with new force," the *States* observed. "In various parts of the courtroom, imprecations were hurled on the prisoner." And there was plenty of nonprofane invective being slung at Walters as well. Jeering, aggressive laughter, outbursts of rage and cheering, and waves of applause punctuated the testimony with more and more frequency.

Perhaps the free-for-all was inevitable, considering the crowd's size. One thousand people now filled a courtroom with a capacity of three hundred, squeezed into every possible inch of standing, seating, or crouching room, up and down the aisles, outside and inside the rail. On Thursday night, a crowd of ladies overtook the reporters' table and used it as a bench. On Friday morning, laying the groundwork for an appeal, Dubuisson complained to Judge Pavy that he "could not stand it." Of particular objection was the proximity of such hostile observers to the jury box itself: *six inches away.*

Yet Pavy allowed the trial to continue all morning. Beneath the courtroom, one floor down, "directly under the greatest massing of Opelousas femininity," the door to the assessor's office became dislodged from its hinges. When court reconvened in the afternoon, deputies had to beat a path to get Walters to the bar. After his own struggle to reach the front, attorney Lewis was forced to climb and hurdle the rail to get to his seat at the state's table. Finally, Judge Pavy, too, had had enough:

"His ire seemed to rise like a suddenly swelling wave," Seiferth wrote. "His towering form rose above the tide, and at 2:55 he announced that he could not continue the trial, as there was no room for the lawyers or the jury."

To prove he was serious, he sent the jury back into sequester at the

Lacombe Hotel, and for a full hour, attempted in vain to winnow down the crowds to an acceptable level. Finally, with a sidelong glance at Dubuisson, Pavy adjourned until the morning and stalked off the bench.

As ejected audience members spilled into the courthouse square, an impromptu sideshow broke out to mollify them. An ancient farmer from Avoyelles Parish, renowned for his ability to float motionless down the bayou while hunting alligators, leapt into the fountain for a free demonstration.

And when Walters was finally escorted out, the flocks of hecklers swooped in to have their daily fun. As awful as they were, the prisoner was more shaken by the past two days' barrage of witnesses than the taunts he faced while walking back to his cell. "They are all lying about me," he moaned darkly, and for once, had little else to say.

Elsewhere in the crowd, the *Item* found Percy Dunbar. "Walters is as good as hanged," he boasted, echoing the giddy sentiments of the vast majority around him.

OVERNIGHT, PLACARDS WENT up all over town, in large black type banning the public, including "special deputies, from inside the bar of the courtroom."

When the trial resumed, the state called its final witness, carefully chosen to return its case to its strongest point: that before he went missing and after he had been found, the boy was the same. Dr. Frank Shute had known Bobby Dunbar since birth. Guided by prosecutors, he recalled specific markings on the boy's body, each of which he had treated before Bobby disappeared and observed after he had returned: the burn scar on his toe; a scar below the right eye; a "malformation" of Bobby's "person" for which he had advised an operation prior to the boy's disappearance.

With that, the boy was brought into the court. It was a clever lawyers' technique: after reciting the specific markings from memory, Shute could now "find" them on the boy's body, and point them out for the jury to see. He could prove himself correct. So dramatic was the effect of the doctor's confirmation that it was easy to overlook that he had "found" these markings before, when the boy was brought from Mississippi.

The child's face was pale and impassive. He remained still while being handed off from his mother to Mr. Lewis and then seated upon the table, and he even stayed still while his shoe and sock were removed and Dr. Shute pointed to his big left toe.

"Here is the burn scar," the *Item* quoted him, his finger tracing a "delicate blue line."

"Make no comment," Judge Pavy ordered as the jurors moved in close to study the scar below the boy's eye. Nonetheless, under their scrutiny, he started to squirm. He turned for reassurance to his father, sitting close, or his mother, poised at the edge of her seat just inside the bar. His back was to the defense table, but if he'd glanced in that direction, he would have seen that Walters uncharacteristically averted his eyes, too.

Before he knew it, the doctor's hands were on his clothes, loosening the belt of his immaculate white duck sailor suit, and unfastening the shorts. He gripped the edges of the table and leaned back.

The doctor spread the boy's legs and pointed to his genitals. *"Long before the time of the kidnapping,"* the *Item* quoted Shute, *"I examined this skin overgrowth, and . . . advised an operation to correct the situation. The operation never was made . . . This condition still exists."*

The judge and the jurymen made hasty inspection as the doctor spoke, and the boy felt three hundred stares searing into his back.

TWO PAIRS OF anxious glassy eyes, side by side, peered through the pen's flimsy rails to greet and unsettle an unending parade of onlookers. Most people paused only a moment to gape back at the two-headed calf; a few kind children lingered to try to pet or feed it. All day long, its little jail was filled with squeals of disgust or moans of pity.

Being dead and stuffed, the calf was oblivious.

While fake two-headed calves were known to crop up in sideshows and state fairs, bicephaly was a common enough veterinary mutation that it was not hard to find the real thing. The little four-eyed creature penned in the empty shop by the Opelousas courthouse square was likely a genuine, unfortunate freak of nature.

The same could not be said for Spido, housed nearby. No reporter was foolish enough to pay a dime and venture inside, but if he had, he probably would have seen a version of Professor Roltair's famous turn-of-the-century Spider Woman or a male version of Spidora, a curiosity in state fairs for decades to come. A real moving and blinking head greeted customers when they entered, but in place of a human torso and legs was the giant body of a spider, complete with furry, crawling legs and surrounded by a lattice web. It was an illusion, made possible by hidden mirrors built into the booth itself and a pillar-framed staircase to disguise the man's body.

Though plenty of old-fashioned folk stalked away from Spido muttering over "fakery" and bemoaning a rip-off, whether it was "real or fake" was not truly the point. This was a more modern sort of curiosity, one whose elaborate construction was cause for astonishment rather than credulity. Noted one review of Spider Woman and the other mirrored gimmicks of Roltair's show: "As Professor Roltair is prouder of his brilliant optical effects than any trick, however clever, he has no objection to the trick being exposed." Craning their necks to the stall's ceiling, to its dark rear recesses, looking for the mirrors, the lights, some sign of Spido's hidden human body, customers did not ask, "How can this be real?" but rather, "How did they do it?"

On the afternoon of Saturday, April 18, when the lucky few hundred poured out of the courthouse, mulling over the examination of the Mystery Boy and the state's just-concluded case for Walters's guilt—two look-alike boys and two look-alike kidnappers!—many took the newspapers' cues and debated the matter as a two-headed-calf sort of spectacle, a freakish sideshow: Is He Bobby or Bruce? Those whose hearts stirred for the Dunbars, particularly their friends and neighbors, certainly *yearned* to see it this way, as a genuine conundrum of nature, a dark and real mystery. But dispassionate observers knew better. They marveled or jeered at the case against Walters not for its truth or untruth, but for the cunning—or shoddiness—of its construction.

Offering fodder for that ongoing debate was the boy himself, redressed and recovered, on the way with his family over to Shute's Drug Store to convene with relatives for dinner. For the brief duration of their walk, the *Times-Pic*'s Seiferth and Ray muscled out the competition for an exclusive. They opened by asking if the boy had recognized Walters in court today, to which he nodded and said, "Yes, he had a big mustache."

"Then suddenly, without question or prompting," the boy offered new details on a shocking story that he had told before. Ray and Seiferth quoted him:

"Walters was inside playing the piano. I was in the wagon holding the horse. The horse got scared. The other little boy fell out of the wagon."

When they asked which other boy, he stayed mum, so they tried again: what happened to this other boy?

"They took Bruce to the graveyard."

He had finally said it aloud: Bruce Anderson was dead.

But just as abruptly, the boy moved on to other topics, and the reporters could not steer him back.

Finally, they asked if he wanted to return to Walters.

"I want to cut his head off" was his immediate reply before he wriggled free and ran off after his mother.

Lurking nearby was Mignon Hall, who snatched Ray and Seiferth's real interview, altered some details, added her patented baby talk ("And one day he felled off and it hurted him"), and made it her own, scooping the competition by a full half day.

This latest revelation—the death of Bruce Anderson—was already well embedded in the public imagination. It was the inevitable conclusion to the prosecution's theory of a swap, and the final chapter in a story that Bobby had been telling for a year: the other boy who fell off the wagon and was forced to travel on crutches. Mignon Hall's account went to great lengths to downplay the significance of today's telling, including reports from Dunbar friends and family—real or fabricated is unknown—that Bobby had been speaking of Bruce's death in private for months, so often that they had grown weary of it. They had not publicized it for fear of being accused of "coaching."

For contrast and "balance," the *Item* offered this incredulous response from Julia: "How could Bruce be dead when that's him telling the story himself?"

From the prosecution's standpoint, the fatal flaw with the boy's memory was that it was not admissible in court. Mignon Hall and the *Item* knew this all too well, and they were already at work on a solution.

Chapter 21

Trist Wood, *New Orleans Item,* April 20, 1914

DURING THE BRIEF recess at the close of the state's case, Walters sat alone at the defense table, staring ahead. The attorneys clustered for a conference with the judge, and behind him, the ladies whispered their daily gossip. But Walters wasn't even trying to eavesdrop. "His eye has lost its cunning glare" was the snide observation of Rudolph Ramelli from the *States*. "He has dropped the haughty air that long characterized him as a man confident of himself."

Last night, he had returned to his cell and sat alone in the dark, listening to the merry honking of the Opelousas Town Band's Friday-evening concert, wafting over from the courthouse square. He had heard that the jurors were honored guests, kept separate from the crowds on their own special bench. For all he knew, the judge and the lawyers were there, too.

But Walters wanted none of it.

He missed the company of his fleeting cellmate. For all Bunt's foolishness, he offered the comfort of family. Julia would have been a welcome visitor, too, but her illness had worsened and she was now bedridden over at the Lacombe.

Instead a captain of the New Orleans Salvation Army, making his rounds among the parish jails, stopped in to do some ministering. He was a fine diversion, this stranger, and Walters liked him enough to invite him to the trial the next morning. But when reporters popped in for their nightly dose of colorful anecdotes, Walters shooed them away.

According to Lee Hawes of the *Item,* the prisoner's heavy silence had a specific root. Rumor was that he had received threats, not the run-of-the-mill violence of his twice-daily tongue-lashings, but rather something written that had gotten him scared. In a few weeks, Walters would explain: it was "a postcard bearing the picture of an oak tree with the inscription 'suicide' under it."

And though he would claim indifference to this attack, it did seem to have touched a nerve. Seiferth detected despair: "Walters still eats heartily and sleeps well, and says God will pull him through, but that is mostly in the morning. Night finds the shadows lengthened and the darkness dense."

For the past two and a half days, he had witnessed a carnival of mendacity, witness after witness looking him in the eye and swearing on the Bible to the cruelest of lies. He had been no stranger to liars in his lifetime, and for the past year, had watched dozens of them slink forth with some outlandish new sighting or claim. But to see them in person, arrayed against him en masse, had finally taken its toll. The conspiracy that he had worried over and warned about had taken full form, and it was a terrifying monstrosity.

He had now been advised by the court—for his own safety—to stay away from his cell window, particularly at night, and not to stand in the light. In the eyes of this hateful populace, he was once again a coldhearted child snatcher, now even more cunning than they had imagined. The "suicide" postcard could have come from any of them; they all wanted to see him die.

And the papers were in on it, too. Even those more sympathetic reporters seemed to have lost their heads, salivating over this nonsensical swap, blinded to the telltale signs of a shoddy frame-up. The reporters who were not just innocently duped were as black hearted as the likes of Mrs. Nix and McManus—the ones in the pocket of the Dunbars, the ones hell-bent on seeing him hang.

Walters pulled his chair back from the defense table and stood. He turned to the reporters, and saw them rising from their table inside the bar for a stretch, already planning for lunch. They noticed the prisoner coming their way and gathered around for a comment. He might have smiled to greet them, but it was not heartfelt.

"I have been lied about," the prisoner opened, according to the *Item*. And then, according to the *States*: "I want to get the names of some of you reporters, so that when I get up to the glory land, *I* can testify against *you*."

They gaped back at him. Then, just a second later, their eyes darted down to their pads and they scribbled their notes.

THE DEFENSE OPENED weakly. Through no fault of their own, the first two witnesses, Deputy Lott and Sheriff Hathorn from Columbia, failed to make a much-needed splash. Lott recalled that Percy, upon meeting Dr. Anderson's auto, admitted that the boy's eyes were more drawn than Bobby's were. Then Hathorn testified that the Dunbars had taken twenty minutes alone with the boy at the Wallace cabin, and still needed more time the next day. But the Dunbars had already explained away both points, and neither officer seemed eager to impugn the couple further. Both did offer strong exculpatory testimony for Walters: Lott recalled that the old man had become so fed up with being stopped and questioned that he suggested Lott take the boy to the Dunbars directly to claim as theirs or not; and Hathorn noted that Walters, after initially being released, had made no attempt to flee. But if the newspapers were any indication, these stories made little impression on the jury: "Many believed that the officers from across the state line had important disclosures," opined the *States*, "and their testimony was disappointing."

The officers' testimony was not the only cause for panic on the parts of Dale, Rawls, and Dubuisson. The three attorneys didn't know who would testify next. Julia Anderson was in bed with a high fever. Now, apparently, Mrs. Bilbo was sick, too, and their other witnesses were "scattered about town." Dubuisson's associate counsel had made a formal request to the citizenry of Opelousas for donations toward the effort to bring more of Walters's witnesses to the trial. But that had been just last night. At eleven thirty, defense requested and received a three-hour reprieve, during which time it quickly reached the best—and only—possible conclusion about what to do next. The lawyers would put Walters on the stand right away.

Julia Anderson, in Opelousas on the eve of
the Walters trial. (New Orleans *Times-Picayune*)

"Two Views of Bobbie Dunbar; in Normal Attire
and in Rags." (New Orleans *Times-Democrat*, June 7, 1913)

Percy, Bobby, Alonzo, and Lessie Dunbar. "Four Happy Dunbars Home Again," first published in late April 1913 and reprinted on the eve of the Walters trial. (*New Orleans Item*)

"On his thousand-string, hand-made harp, W. C. Walters plays for the crowds that daily gather in the jail yard under his cell window at Opelousas. It gives good music and helps to drive dull care and troubles out the steel-barred windows, says the accused tinker." (New Orleans *Daily States*, April 12, 1914)

W. C. WALTERS Addressing Crowd From Cell.

William C. Walters in the Opelousas Jail.
(New Orleans *Daily States*)

"The photo on the left is that sent out by the Dunbars on circulars at the time the Dunbar child disappeared. The one on the right is the boy now held by the Dunbars as their child, taken from Walters. The defense contends the photos are mute evidence that the boy held by the Dunbars is not the lost child. Study the features closely—what do you think? Is the one on the right Bobbie or Bruce Anderson?" (New Orleans *Daily States*, April 12, 1914)

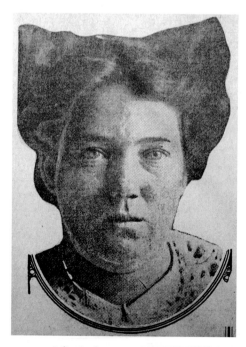

Julia Anderson. (*New Orleans Item*)

Trial souvenir.

Advertisement for the "Two Reel Feature of Dunbar-Walters Trial." A mustached Walters sits beside his attorneys in an overcrowded courtroom.

Julia Anderson Rawls and Ollie Rawls, date unknown.
(Courtesy of Jewel Rawls Tarver)

Alonzo, Lessie, and Bobby Dunbar, Gulf Coast Military Academy, 1923–24. (Courtesy of Anna Lee Dunbar)

Alonzo, Percy, and Bobby Dunbar, circa late 1920s. (Courtesy of Anna Lee Dunbar)

Wedding announcement of Bobby Dunbar and Marjorie Byars. (New Orleans *Times-Picayune,* May 12, 1935)

Bobby Dunbar Sr. with Bob Dunbar Jr., 1936.

Top row, left to right: Marjorie, Bobby Sr., Imelda, Bobby Jr. holding Ronnie; *lower row, left to right:* Margaret, Marie, and Robbie. Bob Jr. and Imelda's youngest child, Swin, were not yet born. (Courtesy of Elizabeth Dunbar)

If the prisoner had felt powerless coming off his confrontation with the press, this announcement had the opposite effect. Walters had been ready and waiting for this chance—to set the record straight, in person and under oath—for a year. His testimony in Poplarville had been constricted by the parameters of a habeas case, and he had left the stand frustrated. Today his spirits lifted, and his heart felt unburdened before he even uttered a word.

When he rose for swearing in, the Saturday-afternoon crowd, still removing their hats and rustling their lunches, was stunned into silence.

"Whose boy is this child under discussion?"

"That's my boy—rather Julia Anderson's boy" were Walters's first words, according to the *States*. "She is the mother of it."

As he recounted his history with Bruce, of getting to know him and Julia in North Carolina, Walters found his voice right away, quavering with emotion. "I would tell it all if I had time to. I would enjoy it." But as true as this was, his attorneys—who knew his long-windedness all too well—hurried him along to the matter of his itinerary, cautioning him to go easy on the details and detours.

He complied, and day after day, month after month, town after town, and state after state, he traced his 1912 movements with confident precision. Even under cross-examination, this itinerary was unwavering.

From his sister's in Eastman, where Bruce's eye was scarred by window glass, to Bledsoe's in Georgia in May 1912. And then—as Julia had suspected—into Florida, to visit his brother Bunt in Ocala, possibly to leave the boy there. But flooding in the northern part of the state blocked his way. Instead Walters lingered in Tallahassee, and eventually—in the early summer—headed east to Mobile for an operation. Soon thereafter, he was in Mississippi, where the details of his travels had been told so many times before.

To back up his account of August, his attorneys wielded documentary evidence. They had a signed money order from Poplarville on August 7 (the same date as one of Deputy Mallett's alleged sightings), and the express package receipt from McNeill on August 20. At the latter, the courtroom filled with murmurs of surprise. *Three days before he had allegedly been spotted at Swayze Lake, he was 160 miles east.*

His attorneys rattled off the highlights of other witnesses' testimony against him—Collins, McManus, Mallett, Nix, and the men from McComb—and Walters denied each and every accusation, flatly.

This certainly was not good enough for prosecutors. "Can you give any plausible explanation as to why certain witnesses . . . should perjure themselves to convict you?" Lewis challenged. But this was met with an immediate objection. Instead, he demanded a fuller explanation, witness by witness, and Walters obliged.

Of Miss Collins, he did admit that he had eaten soup at her restaurant on a Saturday. Of Nurse Eliza Loveless, he knew her from the Bilbos, but "all I noticed was her peculiar conduct." Of W. O. Stogner, he was seething to correct the record: "Mr. Stogner and [his] wife and children begged me for the little boy. I had done some work on credit for them, and when I came back to collect, they were much put out when I wouldn't give them my little boy." Of "Widow" McManus from Pineville, he denied virtually all of her charges. "You look and see if Mrs. McManus was not out of business in 1912 . . . I don't believe she was in business there—or worse."

More than once, having no other explanation for his accusers' testimony, Walters simply dismissed them as "crazy." Veazie took this and ran: "Is he crazy?" "You think Miss Collins must be crazy too?" "I believe you said that they're all crazy?"

A driving rain marked the dinner break, and the crowd, save the women and girls who had packed their meals and saved their seats, returned spattered or sopped. Two full hours of cross-examination ensued.

Prosecutors did their best to tinge Walters's time in Charity Hospital with suspicion. In late September when the search for Bobby Dunbar was hot, perhaps a hospital bed was a safe place to hide. Or perhaps the boys had been switched when he was gone. The state also sought to impugn brother D.B., suggesting that he had skipped town so suddenly because he feared that Katie Collins might identify him as the "double." Defense protested that Walters's brother was not the one on trial, which did not entirely erase jurors' suspicions, but silenced the prosecutors.

Garland wanted to know how Walters was so precise about his movements, about where he worked and had supper, without the benefit of a daybook. "Ask God that," the defendant spat. When the prosecutor tried to tangle him on dates, Walters's response was derisive: Saturday was the eighteenth, Sunday the nineteenth, and Monday the twentieth, and if Garland needed any more clarification, maybe he should just look at a calendar. At this, "Judge Pavy called the witness to order."

Inevitably, the charge of physical abuse was raised. First, by bringing up the recollection of a Carriere farmer's wife who had long ago been discredited:

"Did you beat that little boy one night after they had been making cane syrup when he wanted to get up? I ask you: Didn't you beat the boy?"

"I did slap him, but nobody never could say I beat the boy."

And more generally:

"That child found with you had whip marks on his back. Did you whip the child?"

"Yes, I whipped him sometimes. I never put any scars on his body."

While prosecutors struggled mightily to portray Walters's relationship with the boy in a nefarious light, his responses did precisely the opposite. He loved the boy deeply, he said more than once. At Lewis's question about Julia, Bruce, and their relationship to the Walters family, the defendant's clear-eyed explanation must have startled those who were at all prone to believe him:

"I intended to adopt her boy, Bruce, and educate him, and to leave him what property I could."

This was not what Lewis wanted to hear. "Didn't you make any investigation of the child's parentage? Did you ever inquire from Julia who the father of that child was?"

"I learned it was born out of wedlock." Walters grimaced. "I didn't make any inquiry as to the father."

"Now, why did you want to adopt Julia Anderson's kid when you have four living of your own flesh and blood?" Veazie hit back.

It must have hurt; by every indication, Walters was estranged from his children.

Nevertheless, when Walters left the stand an hour shy of midnight, it was not his weakness or his belligerence that stood out. To all but those who would never be convinced, Walters's affection for this child shone through, and his guardianship made sense in a new way. Over panicked objections by the prosecutors, the defense had been able to introduce a letter from Julia to Walters, written March 1, 1913, before he was arrested. In addition to the letter's heartbreak, it mentioned Walters's family and corroborated his dates of travel. If jurors were inclined to see it, the letter made a case not just for his innocence, but for his humanity. Prosecutors had done their best to fight against that, and they had more fight in them still, but for tonight, Walters felt he had won. Unburdened and unbroken, he marched out of the courtroom and savored his walk through the cleansing rain.

The question of juror Collins, which he had swatted away, was now just a fleeting irritation: "Can you tell us, Mr. Walters, if you were not in Louisiana in 1912, how you came to have Bobbie Dunbar in your possession?"

To Walters's pleasant surprise, it seemed as if journalists *had* heeded his warning: there was little, if any, gross mangling of his testimony, and most papers characterized his ordeal on the stand as strong and unwavering. His stern, dignified portrait made the front page of the Sunday *States*, "Walters, Hard Grilled, Sticks to His Story" emblazoned over the masthead.

For Opelousans, the defendant's tears, and his heartfelt and credible testimony, revived a collective conscience that had been trampled almost to death by the mob of prosecution witnesses. How could the parish sanction the execution of a man that so many now felt to be innocent? St. Landry, as represented by twelve of its citizens, faced an impossible choice between justice for a stranger or allegiance to neighbors. Life for an old man or happiness for a family and future for a boy.

LIKE THE PARADE of St. Landry residents who took the stand to identify the boy as Bobby, in a period of two days, at least eight witnesses came forward from Mississippi to insist that he was Bruce, whom many had seen both before *and* after August 23, 1912. All of them were well known and had provided affidavits before: the Golemans, the Myleys, the Thigpens, Jeptha Bilbo, Bass, Amacker, Alsbrooks, as well as the two Baptist ministers, Reverend Holcomb and Reverend J. Q. Sones, son of another witness, Ben. Once again, they were a formidable force, offering confident memories, precise dates, documentary proof, a clear fondness for the boy, winning country charm, and deep religious conviction.

Prosecutors struggled to destroy them, insisting that their dates were *too* certain, resurrecting the webbed-toe canard whenever possible, and picking at work diaries and scars like buzzards on a carcass. In its cross-examination of Jeptha Bilbo, the state pushed hard to establish that his homestead, so close to the Pearl River and the Louisiana border, was the ideal spot for a kidnappers' lair and a swapping of boys. Soon enough, prosecutors were joined by the jury, some of whom appeared to have made up their minds. When Reverend Sones said that he had seen Walters and the boy on August 21, juror Soileau wanted to know, "Could a man get from [there] to Opelousas by the twenty-third?" When Emile Thigpen could not be shaken on his memory of Walters and Bruce staying at his home on the night of August 24, one juror insisted that although Thigpen said he remembered the child's playfulness, he had never had a chance to observe the child at play in Opelousas to make a comparison. Ergo, Thigpen's claim was bogus.

Meanwhile, the boy himself had been frolicking throughout the courtroom for long stints during all these witnesses' testimony. Every now and then, when instructed by his mother, he sat still by the witness stand, so that he could be officially identified. But for the most part, the courtroom was his playground.

During his moments of stillness, Seiferth and Ray observed, "Walters tried his hypnotizing look, and it lingered long, but to the child he is no more an actual personality, but a memory of terror, and he returned no sign of recognition or interest."

Fighting, and losing, against what it knew to be an accumulation of ironclad evidence, the prosecution resorted to cheap gimmicks. When the defense did not call the boy in for Mr. Goleman to identify, on cross-examination John Lewis darted out of the courtroom, ostensibly to retrieve the boy, but instead returned with his cousin and "double," little George Kelt.

"No, that don't look much like him" was Goleman's dry rebuff, according to Seiferth and Ray.

George was terrified by the ordeal, and it fell to the boy himself, once he had been successfully identified by Goleman, to comfort his cousin, take his hand, and lead him scampering out.

FOR JULIA ANDERSON to sit in a court of law, in Opelousas no less, and hear one Pearl River County witness after another insist that this child was her son Bruce, this would have been an experience of supreme, public affirmation. But she was not there.

Her fever still ran high, and Dr. Saizan had been called to her room twice. On Monday, April 20, she fainted, managed to eat a bit of supper, but soon thereafter took a sharp turn for the worse. As Opelousans packed the Princess Theater just yards away, howling at the first moving pictures of the Dunbar-Walters trial, Julia thrashed in her bed, suffering sweats and chills, surges of abdominal pain and hallucinations. At two thirty that morning, Dale was awoken and rushed to Julia's room, where he sat awake at her bedside, nursing her through the night. The next morning, he was relieved by a professional. That evening's session of court was cancelled due to her inability to testify, and Dr. Saizan returned to her room carrying his surgical kit.

While the doctor did not publicly report the condition that he had discovered (and he may not have been able to offer a full diagnosis), it would be known later that Julia suffered from pancreatitis. He did report that she had an abscess and was dangerously close to peritonitis, meaning that the infectious contents of the abscess would spill into the peritoneal cavity. Under the circumstances, this could be fatal.

The surgery, he would later report to the *States,* "was a very severe one and very painful." Almost certainly, it involved cutting open her abdomen and draining the abscess. The procedure offered only "temporary relief," he said, and once Julia had stabilized, another, larger surgery was "compulsory," in a hospital in New Orleans.

Once he had finished, the nurse and Mrs. Myley were there to clean up and change the sheets, to surround Julia's bed with flowers from anonymous supporters, and apply cool towels to her forehead. If she awoke from her delirium, Mrs. Myley could tell her of their triumphs in court.

WALTERS'S RELATIVES HAD sent letters and affidavits, but it had been difficult for them to contribute to his fight financially. Unsurprisingly, then, no one from his immediate family in North Carolina had come to testify or, aside from Bunt, to appear in support. Instead the Walterses had pooled their resources to pay for Julia's trip, which was paramount, and for the two witnesses who stood the best chance of surviving a charge that would most certainly be leveled at them from the prosecution: that they had come solely to protect one of their own.

Walter Murray was the rural postal carrier who had delivered mail to the Walters farm for years. He had known Julia since she arrived to work there, he testified, and had known William Cantwell Walters since his fall 1911 homecoming. And he knew Bruce, who raced out to the road daily to collect the mail from him, accompanied—more likely trailed—by the elder James Pleasant.

When the boy was ushered into the court, Murray recognized him immediately: this was Bruce Anderson, he declared, adding "or there are two just alike," according to the *Times-Picayune* (or "and mighty like him," according to the *States*). Jurors and audience alike sat up straight.

It was Murray who had delivered a letter to the Walters home in the spring of 1913, from their son in Mississippi. At J.P.'s request, the carrier had opened the letter and read it aloud. Also enclosed were some photographs of Bruce and a note for Julia, which—before they reached her—were turned over to P. W. Johnson of the Marion County *Star,* stringer for the *New Orleans States.*

Since Murray had signed a detailed affidavit in April 1913, the prosecutors had few openings to challenge him on his facts. Instead they assaulted his credibility, turning assets—the immediacy of his recognition and, as predicted, the fact that he'd traveled so far to testify—into liabilities. "Remarkable man," Lewis sneered in response to Murray's insistence that he knew the child right away, an aside that earned the attorney a rebuke from Judge Pavy. As base as their tactics were, they worked, and within minutes, the jurors themselves were piling on with smug outrage of their own. "Don't you think that Mrs. Dunbar would be in a better position to recognize this child than you would be?" jabbed Elijah Fisher, prompting Dubuisson to rise in objection and Pavy to readily sustain.

F. M. Stephens, whose wife was Walters's niece, fared better, answering questions with the boy sitting, silent but agreeable, in his lap. He had known W. C. Walters for thirty years, and Julia Anderson as long as she had been in the employ of his parents. Every month, Stephens and his wife visited the elder Walterses, and Stephens had played with Bruce often. With relative ease, he parried jurors' quizzing about which side the boy's cowlick was on (left, but he could not be sure) and whether the boy looked sickly (no).

The latter question must have unsettled Dale, Rawls, and Dubuisson considerably, and Garland's questioning of both Murray and Stephens only worsened their fear. It was sharper and more specific than his colleagues' petty badgering; he wanted to know about the defendant's brother Frank. All it took was a few pointed questions:

"Did you ever see Frank Walters and W. C. Walters at their father's house at the same time?" (Neither could say he had.)

"They look alike, don't they?" (Both admitted family resemblance.)

"As a matter of fact, are they not twin brothers?" (Neither would go so far.)

And with that, the jurors were off and running with double/swap questions of their own. It did not help matters that both witnesses admitted to hearing rumors that W. C. Walters had stolen the Anderson child, or that brother Frank, in addition to owning a farm, also was a traveling stove mender.

Then came the third and final East Coast witness who had been able and willing to make the trip on behalf of Walters: his friend since boyhood, composer and singing-school instructor David L. Bledsoe of Iron City, Georgia. Found in *Bledsoe's Catechism on Music: Two Hundred and Eighty Concised, Pointed Questions and Answers,* his loving but firm little instructional for educators of children and beginners alike, is this no-nonsense insight that only a natural teacher would know to say:

> What are the greatest and most important lessons to be learned in the study of music? 1st. That music appeals only to the sense of hearing. 2nd. That the things [symbols] we can see are not real, but signs and indications of things that are real.

As soon as Bledsoe heard of Walters's arrest back in April 1913, he wrote to his friend in jail. He, his wife, and four others signed a joint affidavit on April 28 asserting that Walters had stayed in his home in the spring of 1912 with a boy they knew as Bruce. This May visit had always been a key point in Walters's own version of his itinerary southward from North Carolina. Just days before the trial, Bledsoe had released to all the newspapers a written account of his own colorful, lifelong association with Walters. "[R]eputed to be wealthy," according to the *Times-Picayune,* Bledsoe left a sick wife and daughter and other young children at home in Georgia to come testify. He could be safely described as Walters's best and most eagerly anticipated character witness.

On the stand, he first ran into trouble when it arose that he had helped Walters find a lawyer for the 1896 murder of Mumford Harrison. The state also impugned Bledsoe for saying, before the trial, that he would not be sure that he knew the boy until he had seen him in person. Whereas Murray had been too sure, now Bledsoe was not sure enough.

It grew worse when the boy himself was brought forward. He had been present in the courtroom already, and Judge Pavy beckoned him to sit at the foot of the witness stand. Bledsoe's eyes turned to the boy, and he soon recognized him as Bruce, although he acknowledged that he'd grown.

The prosecutors showed no mercy. They knew Bledsoe was going blind in one eye, and he was up on the stand without his glasses. They held a newspaper in front of him, which he could not read. They asked him to discern the color of Mr. Dubuisson's suit, which he could not. According to the *Item,* they asked the color of Dubuisson's hair, to which he answered with self-deprecating humor, "I can't find the hair."

But the moment most devastating of all to Bledsoe—and Walters—came when Bledsoe asked to hear the boy speak. As he would later testify, he recalled from May that Bruce Anderson's voice had a peculiarly "musical" quality.

John Lewis was all too happy to oblige. He asked the boy his name, and Bledsoe listened closely.

Music appeals only to the sense of hearing.

"Robert Dunbar."

Chapter 22

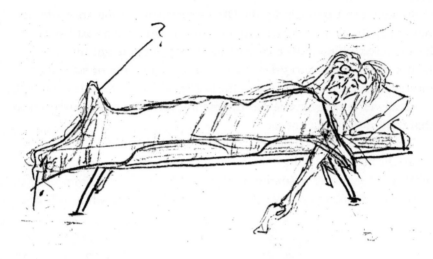

Unsigned sketch in the Dunbar family scrapbook

JULIA'S EYES DARTED from Judge Pavy to all the other men standing around her cot. She clutched her bedding and braced herself. They hoisted her up and carried her into the hall as gently as they could, but every step was agony. It was only yesterday—*less than twenty-four hours earlier*—that Dr. Saizan had cut open her abdomen.

The men paused at the top of the stairs and maneuvered for descent. Mrs. Myley hung back, clutching a vase of flowers. She had been a loyal nurse, but even if her hands were not full, there was nothing she could do for Julia now.

They took the first step. The cot heaved, and pain jolted through her body, coursing equally with the terror of tipping and tumbling. Step after step, the men's breath grew labored. She saw the strain in their arms and shoulders, and heard it in the clipped, grunted commands that they volleyed across her body. She clung to the sheet, even as it slid from her legs.

Finally, she was flat and steady and could breathe again. They carried her into the Lacombe's little parlor and set her down at the front of a cluster of chairs. Mrs. Myley placed the vase at the head of the cot where she could see it—St. Joseph's lilies, from "A Sympathizer" in New Orleans—

then smoothed the sheet over her legs again. Julia inhaled the spicy aroma and marveled at the blooms, a streak of white down the splayed throat of each vibrant red petal.

Judge Pavy called for the jurymen to enter, then the attorneys and reporters after that, along with four Dunbar relatives: the Foxes and Dunbars from New Orleans. Percy and Lessie Dunbar were not among them. Julia craned her neck to greet the crowd and saw a sea of staring faces, pitying or blank.

Cant was leaning over her, smiling gently. He reassured her with words that the reporters did not catch.

Then Judge Pavy stepped in close and swore her in.

To the porters peeking in from the lobby, it must have been a freakish picture: the audience of somber-faced men, the lilies, the big man in robes sermonizing over the prone figure, covered in a sheet as white as its face. This wasn't a trial, it was a wake.

Standing beside Julia, Dale began his examination, coaxing out the story of her life in simple, dry questions. He knew that she had barely recovered from the operation, and it was quite conceivable she was under medication for pain. His questions may have been an effort to determine, or to demonstrate, that she was competent to testify. "What is your name?" "How old are you?" "Were you ever married?" "How many children have you?"

Her voice came out so weakly that the jurors in the back row stood and moved in closer to hear. Though she tried to answer just as matter-of-factly as Dale asked, the shame and sadness rose in her with every new detail. Elisha and her first child dead; Jim Cowan and Bruce; Bunt and Bernice—and her last baby dead, too. As hard as she tried to look only at Dale, it was impossible to ignore the frenetic scratching of the reporters and now the court stenographer, too, making it official and permanent.

They turned to the subject of William Cantwell Walters, and she told of meeting him at his parents' house and of letting him take Bruce to his sister's in South Carolina, but just for a while. She remembered watching Bruce pull away in the wagon, then later hearing that they had returned. Walters had looked for her, she'd heard, but had then left with Bruce again. Over the months, she had heard from them by letter, but never received a photo.

When asked about the boy's feet, she replied that they were just like hers. They requested to see her foot, and she extended it out from under the sheet. As the jury moved in to study it, she kept her eyes on the ceiling.

They drooped and closed, and she pulled them open again, then they drooped and closed again.

Then someone said to bring in the boy, and she was suddenly alert. *He was here.* He had been here all along, somewhere in the hotel with her.

Shortly, there was a commotion at the door, and a parting of the wall of men, and then he was there, at her side, just feet away.

She pulled herself up in bed and took him in. He was so much older.

He stared at her, wide eyed and stunned.

Though she had agonized over this meeting earlier, now, in the moment, her mind had no room for worry over his reaction to her ghastly appearance. He was so beautiful, standing there so close.

"Whose boy is this?" Dale finally asked.

She pulled herself up higher and spread her arms. "That's my boy," she rasped. "Come here, darling. Kiss your mama, baby."

She could not wait for him to respond. She reached out with every bit of strength she could muster, took him in her arms, and pulled him close. She kissed him, and relished the feel and the smell of him.

He was hers.

Lost in the embrace, she didn't notice his stiffness. Then she felt him tugging and twisting. When he finally got free, she could see his face. "More startled than he has appeared in any of the examinations," observed Ray.

For a moment, she thought she had seen it in his eyes and felt it in his body—recognition of her, need for her—but now she was a stranger. Worse, it hit her again that she looked like a living corpse. And that everyone in the tiny parlor was watching her. And the reporters were scribbling more loudly than ever.

She called for him again.

But he darted away behind Mr. Garland's chair. And while the papers offered no procedural explanation, he was then dismissed.

She strained to watch him race out of the parlor, and wondered if that was the last sight of him, the last touch of him, she would ever have.

THE BOY SCAMPERED down the hallway, past a row of closed doors. At the last one, he burst into a room full of waiting Dunbar family and friends, a reporter, and on the bed at the center of it all, Mrs. Dunbar, prone and overcome with strain, like the woman in the parlor that he had just fled. He was keen to report all that had happened, and she, more than anyone, was keen to hear.

Julia Anderson had kissed him, he allowed, but he did not kiss her back.

From the reporter came the most impolite and important question: "Is Julia your mamma?"

The boy glanced at Mrs. Dunbar and saw in her face the familiar tightness. She was used to these trick questions, and so was he. "No, here's my mamma," he answered.

The reporter pressed on: "Who's Julia Anderson?"

"She's a jumping jack," the boy shot back.

There must have been a few smirks across the room, but Mrs. Dunbar was quick to scold, "You mustn't say such things, they're naughty."

By way of response, he announced that he was hungry.

IN THE PARLOR, Julia and the small gathered audience studied the faces of the jurymen as they reviewed the faces in two photographs. Closing his direct examination, Dale had introduced the photos into evidence: one, of Bobby Dunbar before he went missing, and another, of the boy that the jury had seen just moments before. Dale's obvious intention was to highlight their differences. While they took ample time to scrutinize them, alone and side by side, much to their observers' chagrin, the jurors remained poker-faced.

The state began its cross-examination. Did Julia not say, back in April or May, that Walters and his brother Frank were "never in any other business than kidnapping children"? Did she not say, at the supper table of her boardinghouse in Opelousas in May, that the Walters in North Carolina had told her to identify the boy as Bruce, whether he was or not? Did she not say, in the Lewis home, that she had not recognized the boy the first time she saw him?

It was a barrage of the most inflammatory of reported quotes, all from a time when the dailies were first clamoring for access and angling for an edge, a time of rampant fakery. Certainly, in the prosecutors' effort to glean the raw, original story from a revised and rehearsed one, there were parallels to the interrogation of the Dunbars by Dale and Dubuisson. But what was distinct to the state's evolving approach with Julia was an utter lack of restraint. To override jurors' pity for her illness, they had to hammer the impression that she was a wanton liar.

Still, Julia held her own. When she felt it was warranted, a flat-out denial was all she gave, with no attending clarification. But on the matter of her May 1913 ordeal in the Lewis home, she was aching to correct the record, in vivid detail. If the prosecutors had expected her to be ashamed of her "inability" to recognize the boy as her son Bruce, they were badly mistaken. She detailed her wearying travel, and insisted that, when she arrived at the Lewises', she was in no condition to undergo such a grueling trial.

Mr. Lewis, still defensive about his own role in that event one year later, bristled at her response. "Were you treated with kindness and consideration at my home?" McMullen quoted him.

"In some ways I was, and in some ways I was not."

"Did you hear any threats?"

"Yes, I did."

"In my home or after you left my home?"

"After I left your home."

Asked why she had not voiced recognition at first, in the Lewis dining room, according to McMullen, she issued a barbed retort: "If the child was there, then I did not recognize it." By now she well knew the child had not been there.

Just as they had a year ago, prosecutors tried to trip Julia up on the question of markings. She had not mentioned any particular existing moles, scars, or birthmarks on the child's body that she could point to as proof, they charged, but rather than clarifying the point she had made at the time, that she knew the boy by "general features and actions" (which seemed, in this court, to be the flimsiest of proof), Julia merely sputtered denial that she had said anything like it, plain and simple.

The jury brought up a more reasonable line of inquiry: the scar above his right eye, which had been brought up by the Dunbars in their testimony a few days prior. Had Julia, last year or now, mentioned the eye scar, and did she, then or now, know of its origin? She had not mentioned the scar, she said emphatically, because she did not know where it came from. Bruce got the scar after he had left her, while he was in Walters's care.

At this point, McMullen, Ray, and Seiferth must have raised their eyebrows in the direction of their two young competitors from the *Item*, which had reported its exclusive account of Julia's "splinter" story days before. In his report on today's testimony, Blair would trumpet the discrepancy between Hall's earlier interview and Julia's sworn statement, twice, using it to assail her credibility: "She readily denied every statement previously assigned to her that in any way conflicted with her intention of testimony at the present time." But for Julia to have lied about a matter that she knew she would be asked about in court, or even worse, the opposite, would have been astonishingly foolish. The question was not whether the *Item* had faked the splinter detail but what kind of fakery it truly was.

Blair's earlier dispatch on the splinter provides the clear answer: *"Although not yet brought out in testimony,"* he had written, *"Julia Anderson also will swear an oath about this scar."* The splinter was a deliberately planted fabrication, which would, inevitably, contradict Julia's later sworn statement. Just as B. and H. had manipulated Percy Dunbar into armed confrontation at the Cosmopolitan Hotel the summer before, giving the *Item* a week's worth of juicy drama, Blair and Hall laid a trap for Julia Anderson's testimony, pointed to it for readers to see, and then they sprung it, assaulting her credibility in a craven attempt to regain their own.

In his redirect, Dubuisson tried to cut through the mole/scar minutiae, and asked if Julia could be mistaken that the boy she'd seen was Bruce. "If that ain't my child, he's never been born on this earth," Ray and Seiferth quoted her reply. And when the state returned to its assertion that she had "failed" the first time, Julia's weakened voice was tight with defiant anger: "I recognized him the second time, and I think I done as well as Mrs. Dunbar."

But while Julia might have beaten back Lewis's and Veazie's assault on her identification, Garland came at her from another front: her character. He forced her to repeat the damning details of her history, laying particular emphasis on the fathers of her children. He wanted names and dates of birth, and he did not shy away from her children that died, either. Though his tone and most of his questions were not reported, Ray and Seiferth observed, the grilling left Julia "abashed."

Garland brought a piece of paper down to Julia's cot and asked her to examine it. It was the letter she had written to Walters, entered into evidence by the defense a few days ago, the date of which was under dispute. Garland's theory was that it had been written March 1, 1912, then altered to read 1913. But the defense insisted it was written in 1913. Today from her cot, Julia confirmed that it was 1913, without a doubt. She knew the letter well.

Garland pointed to the mention of a "Frank" in the letter, and asked who that was. He was, of course, William Cantwell's eldest brother, and Garland's question was part of the prosecutors' push to suggest that the Walters brothers—any or all of them—were near doubles and part of a kidnapping gang.

But for Julia, hearing the name Frank and staring at this letter, in her own hand, shot her back into one of the darkest times of her life.

* * *

SHE HAD KNOWN Frank long before March 1913. He was the oldest of the Walters brothers. For over a decade, he had been running his own poultry farm in Barnesville, but in recent years, his son James Mac had taken over the business. To make ends meet, Frank, like his younger brother, had taken to the road, mending stoves and doing odd jobs. Cant, seven years younger, had embraced itinerancy much earlier in his life. For Frank, in his late fifties, this was a difficult and humiliating downward turn.

Frank was also a widower. When his wife died in 1901, he was left as the sole parent of their youngest child, an infant daughter named Laura Vincy. Help raising the girl came from Frank's sisters and parents, especially during the more recent years, when he was gone from home for stretches at a time.

Unlike Laura Vincy, unlike his brothers, Frank had no soft spot for Julia Anderson. She had brought one bastard child into his parents' home, and then had another after that, which had gotten Bunt chased out of town. To Frank, it was a step in the right direction that she had sent the boy off with Cant and given up the girl, but by the summer of 1912, here she was, back at the farm and pregnant again.

In April 1913 Ethel Hutson asked the obvious question: Why had Julia returned? "They're mean people, from the cradle up," Julia admitted, "and time and time again I've left 'em and vowed I wouldn't go back. But every time I did, when they sent for me . . . [s]eemed like I couldn't be contented away from 'em." The Walters farm was probably her only refuge, and her bond with the old couple was certainly unhealthy. But Miss Hutson saw something else:

> She turned a face that shone the look you see in the eyes of an artist talking about paintings, a physician about the science of medicine, or a priest telling of salvation. Her blue eyes were filled with the light of enthusiasm.
> "That's what I can do best, you see—what I love to do—care for old people, and sick people."

In July, when Bernice's adoption was made official, Julia's fourth pregnancy was six months in and showing. She spent that summer alone, cropping and caring for the elder Walterses, and getting rest for her and her baby when she could.

In the third week of September, Vincy, who had just turned thirteen, came over to her grandparents' farm. She had received a letter from her uncle Cant, she told Julia, but since she couldn't read too well, she needed Julia's help.

The return address was Charity Hospital, New Orleans. Walters had been there for some time, he wrote Vincy, getting a wire removed from his knee. He asked where Julia was, and if Vincy could pass a note along to her (which he enclosed) and get her to write. This was the first time he had written Julia since February, although no other details of these letters are known. After transcribing Vincy's dictated reply, Julia wrote her own. They put both letters into the same envelope and mailed them off.

In October, another letter came to Vincy from Walters, now in Poplarville, Mississippi. "[H]e said a fine old lady took care of Bruce while Cantwell was in the hospital. He wrote a few words to me, wanted to know Bruce's full name, and his age. He said he hadn't heard from me." This struck Julia as preposterous: "[I]f Cantwell got [Vincy's] letters, he got mine." Frustrated, anxious, and powerless, "I sat right down that Sunday morning, early in October," and wrote Walters about Bruce: his full name, birthday, and even the truth about his parentage: "the son of James Cowan, that I hadn't seen in two years."

To Walters, this must have come as a shock. Unbeknownst to Julia, he had returned from Charity Hospital to the news that Poplarville authorities had paid a visit to the "fine old lady" following up on a rumor that the boy was Bobby Dunbar. That suspicion was put to rest, but only for the moment. For months, Walters would be grilled on this question of where the boy came from. And now he could no longer claim that Bruce was his nephew. He had no ready answer at all.

A few weeks later, on October 23, Julia gave birth at the Walters farm. It was a baby boy.

Over the holidays especially, he kept her mind off Bruce. Walters still had not written to tell her what his plans were, or when he would bring back the boy. Whenever she stopped to count it up—that he'd had Bruce with him for nearly a year—her stomach knotted. She was missing her son's life. She would never have agreed to let him take Bruce for so long, and yet, what could she do but wait?

As if sensing her worry and outrage, Walters wrote in early February 1913, again from Poplarville. "Bruce is as fat as a pig and is the sweetest thing I ever saw," Julia recalled his fond report. What's more, the day before Christmas, Bruce had spoken his mother's name for the first time since they had left North Carolina. "[W]hile they were in a store buying candies, fruits, and things," Julia went on, "Bruce had said he wished his mamma had some of these good things." When Walters asked Bruce who his mother was, he used the name he had back at home, what everyone else did: "She's Julia." As warm as the story was, one interpretation carried an obvious sting: he had not spoken of her in nearly a year. More overtly agitating, Walters went on to mention that "he was about to get into some trouble"—of what sort he did not specify (likely his first encounter with Deputy Lott). At the time, Julia didn't think much of it, considering "he was always getting into some trouble somewhere."

On February 27, whatever fragile optimism the letter may have given her was shattered. Just five months old, her baby son died. The cause of death remains shrouded in mystery, but at the time there were rumors of foul play. The most detailed account of the event comes from a North Carolina stringer's report published in the New Orleans *Pic* of April 27, 1913, more reliable as a document of the vicious Robeson County gossip mill than for the actual details of the death:

> The child was killed in bed, and the woman buried it the next morning before the coroner could investigate. The body was dug up, and the child was found to have died of strangulation. The woman claimed it was smothered. She was never prosecuted.

Strangulation was not the worst method of murder alleged. Frank Walters claimed that he had seen Julia insert a needle into the baby's ear to kill it, a story that was passed down for generations in his family.

Indeed, it was Frank who seemed to have publicized the death among the neighbors and led the charge of foul play: within a week, he had circulated a petition to have the matter investigated. As reported in the local news on March 3, the county coroner was called out to the Walters farm, "but he found no evidence to indicate that an inquest was necessary." Four weeks later, the coroner's published requests for reimbursements bear this report out: he charged "$21.40 over body of Charley House," "$19.70 over body at Pembroke," and only "$6.20 over infant child of Julia Anderson."

Frank's accusation was not just borne from his mistrust of Julia. Exactly two years prior, according to court records, he had been indicted on a charge of attempt to poison. As Julia told a reporter in 1913, he had put match heads in a jar of peach jam and given it to "them Arnett folks down by Lumberton way." As quaint as it might sound, in 1911 this was no innocent prank: white phosphorous matches were poisonous, and accidental deaths, especially among children, were so rampant that a campaign was under way to ban the matches nationwide. Frank pled guilty; if he could imagine Julia capable of killing, it was only because he was.

Nevertheless, the story had spread across the county and taken on a life of its own. By several accounts, the ongoing controversy caused a "rupture" in the Walters family, with some defending Julia against Frank and others, finally, fed up with the trouble that she always seemed to bring.

Julia knew she had to go, once and for all.

After she had moved out, but while Frank's crusade against her was still under way, Julia poured her heart out to Walters. A year later, her letter would be in the hands of the Opelousas district attorney, waved over her cot like an accusation, passed among the jury and reporters, and read by the world.

> Barnesville, N.C.
> March 1, 1913.
> To Mr. W. C. Walters:
>
> Deare Sur:
>
> I will ansure yours at hand today glad to heare from you and Bruce glad to no you were getting along so well. I am not myself. I am in lott of truble. Frank come home from Georgia and started to cutting up, and I left and I moved Wednesday, and my baby died Thursday and buried today, and I have got nobody now but myself and in lott of truble and not a bit of money, and I don't know what I will do. no one to care fore me nor to help me on a big det and nothing to pay with and what will I do. Will youre papa is so he can get out to the road and steer about hope he will soon able to go to the bluff again well. Cant Darwin paid the det off and made money I don't know where he is nore what he is doing him [and] Conner is both gone well no news to rite at the present.
>
> I want you to send me yours an Bruce pictur so I can see it one more time I have rote you 5 or 6 times and sent you Bruces age twice. He was fore years old the 18th of December Burneace is gone to Chadborn and I haven't no one well I will close rite to me as often as you can and send me youre and Bruce pictur and tell him I love him still tell him to all ways love his mama well I will close rite soon to youre friend Julia

Though her wait for photographs was in vain, for nearly two full months after the death of her baby, Julia was able to take solace in the fact that she still had Bruce. Walters offered no indication of when or if he would return, and that was agony, but she still could hope and imagine that a reunion with her son was possible. After all, even though he was seven hundred miles away and had been gone from her for over a year, Bruce had still remembered her at Christmas. And if Walters gave her boy the message like she'd asked—"tell him I love him still tell him to all ways love his mama"—she would be alive in his mind still.

"I'VE DONE SEEN Julia Anderson once," the boy complained, stomping down the Lacombe Hotel's first-floor hallway on his way back into the spotlight of the trial.

When he entered the parlor, he stole a glance her way. She was still on her cot and her eyes, again, were on him as soon as he appeared. Looking away, his eyes snagged at the lower edges of her bedding, where her foot, her big bare foot, was purposefully extended.

Before he knew it, his own shoes were being removed. Then, amid some deliberation by his handlers, he was coaxed to sit at the bottom of her cot, then worked into position so that his little foot, and Julia Anderson's big foot were side by side.

The defense pointed out what the *Times-Picayune* called "a slight web between the second and third toes of the woman and a similar peculiarity between the second and third toes of the child," what the *Item* called proof that "Julia Anderson and Bobbie's were broad between the toes as Julia Anderson had stated," and what the *States,* playing it safe, called "a peculiarity about two of her toes represented . . . as identical to the boy's."

One by one, the jurors stepped forward and knelt down to examine for themselves. According to the *Item,* all of them touched both feet, turning them and easing them as close together as their owners would allow.

The boy had long ago learned to stay still for these examinations. But this one was especially trying. For his foot to be at a juryman's eye level, he had to lean back, into the bedding and closer to the rest of Julia Anderson's body. She and the sheet were hot, they reeked of fever sweat, and looking up, her foot next to his was monstrous.

Julia could see the boy's discomfort, and it pained her, but there was nothing she could do. And yet, the sight of their feet together, mother and son, was an undeniable pleasure, pure and innocent.

Quick to thwart the suggestion of a hereditary similarity, prosecutors hurried in Alonzo Dunbar and placed his bare foot alongside the boy's for the jury to study. Ray and Seiferth called the boys "barefoot double[s]," this comparison a stronger one than the first, with Julia, though no other reporter was so bold in their conclusions. "What the speculation of the jurors was could not be guessed," Blair observed.

After they were finished with the feet, Bruce was led up to the head of her cot to stand beside her. The jury was called in close to look now at their faces, side by side. Both woman and boy did what anyone would do, finding themselves in such an alien situation: they kept their faces as blank as possible, trying to look through or beyond the jurors, whose eyes squinted into theirs and darted back and forth, from his to hers.

His face was so close to hers. She yearned, more than anything, to squeeze him tight against her. Only in Hall and Blair's version of this moment of strained intimacy did she take action on the yearning: as the boy drew his lips up in between his teeth, "in childish fashion," and his breath quickened . . . from beneath the sheet, Julia's hand emerged, found the boy's, and clutched it.

He let her hold it.

But as soon as prosecutors called an end to the scrutiny, he yanked it away and was escorted out by Mr. Lewis.

With her testimony over, the officials, jury, and spectators filed out, and Walters shook her hand warmly. Seiferth, Ray, Blair, and Hall lingered with the witness.

Her eyes filled with tears. In the *Item,* they were tears of regret that she hadn't been allowed more time with him. In the *Times-Picayune,* they were more like tears of joy at his recognition of her, and their moments of physical intimacy. "Recollections commenced to flow," Ray and Seiferth observed, "and her version of the kiss almost bore the glory of delightful vision."

"He kissed me," she said, weeping. "I called my son to me, and he came . . . He knew his mother."

Two hours after the ordeal had begun, the Dunbars hurried Bobby out of the hotel with little patience for reporters, and refilled his heart and mind with the simple pleasures of childhood: devouring his promised ice cream and gliding along in an automobile on the newly paved streets. The intoxicating tang of creosote erased the stench of Julia's illness. With the wind on his cheek, her kiss disappeared.

*　*　*

WHEN THEY FIRST left North Carolina in the wagon, Walters later recalled, Bruce had been homesick. It was not so much the place of home that he missed, the Walterses' farm or the Stones', because place had never been the same. If home was anything to the boy, it was his mother, Julia. The woman who fed and bathed him, who sewed his clothes and told him stories, the woman who held him in bed through cold nights and thunderstorms, who cut and cherished a lock of his hair.

No matter how Julia and Walters explained the trip, Bruce could not understand. Julia told him she loved him, yet she was keeping Bernice and sending him away. She told him he would be fed, watched over, and cared for at Walters's sisters, yet they did not stay in either home for long. She told him they would only be apart for a while, yet when they returned to the Walterses' farm, Julia wasn't there.

He must have hardened to abandonment. As they traveled south on the wagon through the spring flooding, he grew fearless of night and thunder and the cold, wet unknown. The wagon became his home, Walters became his home, and Julia was a painful memory.

In the houses along the way, there were mothers aplenty to take her place. In April in Eastman, Georgia, Walters's sister Iredell cared for him for three full weeks while Walters tinkered his way around the county, and for months afterward, Bruce always had words for her to add to Walters's letters. In May, in Iron City, Georgia, Nettie Bledsoe bathed and fed him alongside her own children. She took him to church on Sunday, and would later recall—in a letter to his mother—how polite and sociable he was, "how sweet he looked when he would hug his papa's neck, as he called him, and clasp his little hands and say his prayer and then go to bed." When Walters and Bruce headed off toward a hospital for Walters's knee, the boy hurled his arms around Mrs. Bledsoe and promised to return. In Tallahassee, Florida, there was Mrs. Crump, who had lost two children and longed to raise Bruce as her own—a possibility that Walters, worried over surviving surgery, took quite seriously. Near Mobile, there were old Mrs. Duck and Mrs. Cochran, and when Walters made it out of the hospital alive and was able to travel again, there were all the mothers of Pearl River County, Mississippi. Mrs. Holden allowed the boy, for over a week, to sleep between her and her husband.

And of course, Mrs. Bilbo, who had lost so many children of her own.

He knew he was different than the other children, the children who lived in the homes, whom the mothers kept. But he also knew, in these mothers' eyes, that he was special. Their affection for him was boundless, unhardened by the ordinary grind of the life they had with their others.

It was easy, then, for his real mother, sad and weary Julia, to go forgotten for long stretches at a time. Walters read her letters aloud, reminding him how much she loved him. And Bruce may very well have thought of her at Christmastime 1912, as Walters had assured her in his letter. In early April 1913, when Walters finally got around to honoring her request for photographs, he readied his "picture outfit," positioned Bruce barefoot on a stool, and reminded him that the images would be for his mother. But when Bruce stared into the lens—over a year into their separation, a full quarter of his chaotic young life—it was difficult for him to imagine who exactly that was.

Chapter 23

Evidence, *State of Louisiana v. Walters* (Courtesy of the
St. Landry Parish Archives, St. Landry Clerk of Court)

TWO DAYS BEFORE the trial's close, Deputy Sheriff A. L. Andrus set
out onto the streets of Opelousas with eleven summonses in hand, tracking down witnesses for the defense. His exceptionally detailed return
notes, from this expedition and an earlier one the prior week, reflect both
the difficulty of his task and the rigor with which he was expected to carry
it out: whereas virtually every local state witness had been successfully
tracked down and served, Andrus met with defense witnesses who "could
not be found," or were "about from the city," and was forced to deliver the
summonses to a coworker or a relative, whom he was careful to name.
All witnesses were required to appear in court "instanter," meaning that
same day, a last-minute rush not borne of lack of preparation. It was in
the defense's best interests to leave as little time as possible between sum-
monsing and witness stand.

One of the first to testify was J. A. Rowe, an assistant railroad foreman
and an acquaintance of Percy Dunbar. In August 1912 he had been in
the work crew overseen by the prosecution's most consistent and reliable
Swayze Lake witness, Frank Ansley. While Rowe remembered the same

tramp who asked about the boy and the reward on Monday, he was positive it was not Walters: "The man was taller, slenderer, and thinner than the defendant, and did not limp," the *Times-Picayune* summarized his testimony. Another defense witness, N. L. White, had arrived to the Swayze Lake search on Friday evening and, because of his familiarity with the terrain, was put in charge. During the search, he, too, had encountered a hungry tramp he swore was not Walters.

But it was what happened before that sighting that made White's testimony unique. As part of familiarizing him with the search's progress, apparently he had been shown the footprints earlier identified as Bobby's. As reported by the *Times-Picayune*, "Bobbie's track was identified by the burn on his toe forcing a deeper impression, he testified. Mrs. Dunbar also produced sandals to measure the footprints . . . The peculiar deformity of the type was noticeable, the witness said." The scar was so prominent at the time of Bobby's disappearance that it was visible in his footprint. In fact, it was the print's *defining characteristic.*

Though E. K. Eastham had just taken Percy Dunbar's seat as alderman, there was nothing but goodwill between the two men. So it must have been painful for Eastham to now take the stand. Having worked on the railway's construction, Eastham was familiar with the Lakes region: it was dotted with gator-filled bayous and thick with vegetation, and while it was possible for a man to flee through this country with a child, Eastham deemed such a scenario "improbable." Again, this was not the meat of what Eastham had to say. As a member of the search party, he had examined the footprints. While the *Times-Picayune* reported that he knew there were "peculiarities" but could not recall them exactly, the *Item*'s account offers a more specific detail: the markings were "as though one toe was bent far under the plane of the foot."

It is these two men's testimony that comes closest to explaining why the boy's prints were "unmistakable" as Bobby's. While Dr. Daly said that he had relied on their size relative to another child's, Mrs. Dunbar had had a more instantaneous way to know they were her son's, a uniqueness other than their size. Precisely what this uniqueness was, of course, she had not said.

Then came the neighbors.

Before Bobby went missing, "prominent" cotton man Jesse Barnett had lived next door to the Dunbars, and his backyard chickens had often drawn the little boy over for a visit. Barnett knew Bobby well, he swore, and ever since his "return," he had been utterly unable to recognize him as the child he knew before. It was the eyes, he stressed, that were impossibly different.

The jurors leaned forward in their seats.

The prosecutors could not let this stand. They presented Barnett with two photos of the boy in question, one barefoot in "rags" before the Dunbars claimed him, and one after, in a spiffier getup. They did look different, Barnett admitted. And when asked if he had noticed any markings besides the eyes, Barnett admitted that he had not.

Prosecutors had a stickier time with the women. Another former neighbor, Fannie Bowden, "knew Bobbie quite well" and could not reconcile her memory of him with the boy that the Dunbars brought home. The best prosecutors could do was to expose that she was related to Jesse Barnett, a hinted accusation of collusion. Never mind, of course, that the vast majority of the state's own witnesses were related to one another as well.

Mrs. W. B. Robert, a former backyard Dunbar neighbor, could not recognize the child as Bobby either, although she'd had a chance to see him often since his "return." At the close of her direct examination, the defense attorneys, having done their homework well, pointed out a scar on her forehead, and she handily explained that it was from a burn when she was a baby. It had never faded.

Cumulatively, the witnesses were a powerful force. For the first time, local doubt was not just whispered or rumored, it was sworn to with honest conviction: this boy was not Bobby Dunbar. Though the *Item* downplayed the Opelousans' testimony as "not vital to the case," the jury was plainly startled. As the Crowley *Daily Signal* observed, "[T]hey sat up wide awake for the first time in several days." These weren't Mississippi strangers, these were upstanding St. Landry citizens, many whom the jury knew personally. They were neighbors, as much as the Dunbars.

And no Opelousan promised more dramatic testimony than Mrs. Douce Mornhingveg, wife of a well-known local jeweler, and Lessie Dunbar's third cousin. They had known each other since childhood, and Douce had seen Bobby just before he went missing.

"I ask you, Mrs. Mornhingveg, if you were able to identify the boy as the Bobbie Dunbar you knew before the child was lost?" asked Mr. Dale.

"No."

"You knew him well?"

"Yes, very well." When the defense led the witness into her planned testimony—the story of an event that occurred when Mrs. Dunbar brought the boy for a visit in late April or early May of 1913—the state cut her off with an objection, most likely on the grounds of hearsay. Prosecutors knew what she had to say, and they fought to silence her aggressively.

Judge Pavy sustained the objection.

By this time, however, it was not just prosecutors who knew her story. For a year, all of Opelousas had been atwitter over it. Douce was the unnamed letter writer of May 1913 who had recalled the boy's utter lack of recognition of Mrs. Dunbar, and whose gossip-hungry friend had passed her report on to a newspaper. Until today, her name had never been made public.

Since they could not get the story from her letter into the record, the defense had to rely on its witness to reiterate, adamantly, that she could not recognize the boy as Bobby. The cross-examination must have been as fierce as decorum would allow, but the *Times-Picayune,* the only paper to report it at all, mentioned just two details. When asked about the burned foot, she remembered Dr. Shute taking care of it when the boy was a baby; a juror wanted to know if she had noticed the scar later. She had not.

Despite the blockage of her most sensational testimony, the *States* observed that Mrs. Mornhingveg "proved to be the strongest witness that has yet been produced to controvert the evidence given in support of Bobbie's identification."

No reporter observed her third cousin in attendance.

But the boy himself most certainly was. At the opening of the Thursday-morning session, he had darted to his traditional "perch," where he sat obediently as witness after witness looked down at him and swore that he was not Bobby Dunbar.

THE OPELOUSAS DOUBTERS worsened an unease that had been building in the district attorney's mind all week. It began in earnest at the crack of dawn on Sunday morning, when Garland was awoken by a rapping at his front door. There stood an anxious umbrella maker, who had arrived in Opelousas with his nieces, scheduled to take the stand against Walters as one of the prosecution's star rebuttal witnesses. But Koenig had a confession: having seen stove mender Linder face-to-face at the trial for the first time, he was now convinced that, indeed, this was the man he had seen in Alexandria, after all. Not Walters. As for the children his nieces had seen, these were "strangers in town for the carnival," he supposed. Garland wearily accepted the man's sincerest apologies, and a shamefaced Koenig shuffled out of town as quickly as he could.

Since then, Garland's case had only weakened. On Wednesday morning, a cluster of his most prized witnesses, the men from McComb, were brutally discredited by one of their own brothers. Defense witness Dee Morgan swore that he had been at the McComb depot with his brother B.L. when the mysterious man and little boy arrived on a freight train. The pair lingered in the area, and though Dee remained in the depot "all the time," he never heard any word, from the man or boy, about being a detective or Bobby Dunbar. What's more, the man looked utterly unlike Walters.

But Dee had offered more than fraternal contradiction. After news of Walters's April 1913 arrest reached McComb, B. L. Morgan and the other witnesses "made four successive affidavits," each one an alteration of the last. When Dee was asked to join in, he refused "because he did not know the man and wouldn't swear against him after seeing him only once." In fact, Dee finally announced, *they had made it all up*. His brother and the other men had decided to turn this nonsighting into something else: the detective bit, the Bobby Dunbar bit, the resemblance to Walters, all of it they had agreed to create, later and together. And for little other reason than a lark—as Ray and Seiferth put it, "going to Opelousas, with all their expenses paid."

By week's end, the air was thick with talk of acquittal or mistrial. In the *Times-Picayune,* Seiferth and Ray took stock of Garland's case, as he himself must have, too: "The State has shown that Bobbie Dunbar disappeared," they began. "But the State has not produced a consistent chain of evidence to show how Walters got the child. . . . Why Walters, a lame man, would have gone into the wild country in the first place, how he chanced on the child, and then was able to escape unseen, has never been explained."

It is unsurprising that the state's rebuttal was ferocious. In a matter of days, prosecutors rounded up two fresh McComb witnesses to swear that Dee Morgan was a dishonorable drinker, but that his brother and the other state witnesses were, by contrast, fine and credible men. Prosecutors produced two ministers of their own, from Beauregard Parish, who recalled that in midsummer of 1912, they had briefly encountered Walters and another, near-identical man, complete with the "W. C. Walters" wagon.

Then came Mrs. M. E. Sloan, of New Roads, Louisiana, second of the leering "black hearts" who had fingered Walters at the beginning of the trial. On the stand, she even repeated her same line: "You remember staying at my house, don't you?" The defendant's response was now more composed; he shook his head with a weary smile. In January 1912 Mrs. Sloan swore that Walters, another man named Whit-something—she couldn't recall—and a mysterious little sickly boy who was not Bobby Dunbar had rented out her "company room," where they had stunk up the place with their cooking and burned a hole in the floor. She had the courtroom roaring with her feisty spark, and when Dale angrily demanded the names of the "fifty" others she claimed would corroborate her tale, she rattled them off faster than he could scribble.

The most righteous state rebuttal came from John W. Lewis, who recused himself as counsel long enough to take the stand as a witness, to describe the May 1913 identification in his home and challenge Julia Anderson's charge that it had been unfair.

Dale begged to differ. "Frankly, wasn't the whole thing staged as a trap for the poor woman?" he countered.

Lewis spat back, "Any such insinuation is false." And to corroborate himself, he called to the stand members of the "committee" itself: Dr. Boagni and Dr. Haas, the Dunbars' neighbor who had been the committee's leader. Both swore that while Julia was tired and nervous, that was not the cause of her failure. The fact that there were just two boys in the dining room when she entered (neither of whom was the one in question), not to mention the infamous hand clap and exclamation ("She has failed to identify the child!")—these were details that Lewis did his best to sweep under the rug.

Hastily moving on to the next phase of his counterattack on Julia Anderson, he called his own wife to the stand. Mrs. Lewis proudly repeated that Julia had been given every courtesy in her home, from a quiet room where she could sleep to black coffee and food when she had awoken. Julia herself had even told Mrs. Lewis that "she had been treated better than ever in the world."

Then, after the test and after Mr. Lewis was gone, Mrs. Lewis and Julia were alone in the house for a time. The hostess asked the weary, defeated North Carolina woman about the child, if she had recognized him as her son Bruce.

And what was her answer, the prosecutors wanted to know.

Mrs. Lewis was a good wife. Her husband's honor and integrity had been challenged by a woman who, as Mrs. Lewis saw it, had no such virtues herself. She let her indignation rise and carry her through the most flagrant lie of the entire trial.

"I am an honest woman," Mrs. Lewis said that Julia told her, "and before God that is not my child. My child was web-footed."

Julia Anderson's statements about her son's feet, from *before* she saw the boy in Opelousas and for the entire year *afterward*, had been consistent and unwavering. Dunbar defenders had certainly sought to lump her in with the Mississippi witnesses as erroneously identifying a web on Bruce's toes, but Julia herself had *never* made such a claim. Mrs. Lewis's story was so bold and convenient, it must have raised eyebrows at the defense table, if not elsewhere in the audience. And yet, not a single word of cross-examination was uttered. It was not just the sheer force of her righteousness that rendered the defense mute, however. As the wife of an esteemed legal colleague, as a member of the Lacombe and Lewis families in St. Landry Parish, this witness was virtually unassailable.

And how much easier for Mrs. Lewis to lie, with the one person who could challenge her well out of earshot, lying in a hotel bed with her abdomen sliced open.

Without a doubt, however, the most powerful possible surprise witness in the state's arsenal of rebuttal was—by the time it sought to unveil him before the jury—not a surprise to anyone in town. For the past two days, he was all anyone in Opelousas could talk about.

IN THE EARLY-MORNING hours of Wednesday, April 22, Mark A. Cowart had been ushered by the *Item*'s Sam Blair and Mignon Hall into the office of John W. Lewis for a conference with Lewis, Garland, and Veazie. Cowart wore a heavy dark suit and a bowler. His face was long and gaunt and ended in a point with a scruffy gray beard. Behind his spectacles, one eye was shot through with blood. He was a farm laborer and livestock man from Baxterville, Mississippi, and his story would become the *Item*'s climactic bid to "own" the Dunbar story again. Plastered across its front page that afternoon was this headline:

"Witness Found by *Item* Says 'Bobbie' Was with Walters."

According to Cowart, in February and March 1913, Walters and the boy had stayed at the home that he and his wife shared with Mr. and Mrs. George Burt, roughly halfway between Poplarville and Columbia. Hired by Burt to do assorted "odd work" about the place, Walters lingered there with the boy for nine days, during which time their hosts grew suspicious. Who was this man traveling the countryside with a child?

More than that, like so many of the witnesses that Harold Fox and Lee Hawes had dug up in May 1913, Cowart observed that the boy was terrified of the old man, utterly in his thrall. The boy was filthy, but Walters refused to allow the wives to clothe or bathe him, which led the hosts to conclude, though they had never seen any abuse, that he was hiding "the marks of the beatings . . . on the little body." One day, the boy darted off to take a ride with the ladies, but Walters stopped him, as Cowart remembered, barking, "You never can go with them or anybody else unless I go, too, or if you do, you'll catch it!"

At one point, Cowart questioned Walters about his background. They were from North Carolina, Walters said, but when asked if that was where the boy's mother was, he hedged, then muttered "No," and hurriedly changed the subject.

Finally, one evening while Walters curried his horse outside, Cowart had his chance to speak with the boy alone, inside by the fire. His opening gambit, he recalled, was this: "Kid, you're a nice little boy, and you've got a pretty name. The best friend I ever had was named Bruce."

To this, Cowart observed, the boy had something he wished to say but couldn't. Cowart assured him that he need not fear: "Your papa is out in the yard, Bruce." The boy went to the window to see for himself, then returned "stealthily" and confessed:

> "Yes, Bruce is my name now, but it's my new name. I've got an old name, too."
>
> Bewildered, Cowart asked what his old name was, and after another peek out the window, the boy murmured, "It's Bobbie."

At that time, as Cowart told the listeners gathered in Lewis's office, he had not heard of Bobby Dunbar, so the boy's next secret didn't resonate: "That's my new papa," the child said of Walters out the window. "I've got another papa away off who is a good papa. And I got a mamma, too. She isn't here; she's away off." Nevertheless, the confessions were alarming enough for Cowart to urge George Burt that they corner Walters at gunpoint, rope him to his wagon, and get to the bottom of the matter. "But George said that he believed we'd better not," Cowart recalled with regret, "as we didn't have any proof, and Walters might sue us for damages." And so, reluctantly, they let the man and the boy go on their way.

Later the pair returned for just a night, and when Walters repeatedly asked to be paid for the work he had done, Burt refused, on the grounds that "he had not done enough more than to pay for the board he and the boy had consumed."

By this point in Cowart's narrative, a prosecutor should have had a sinking feeling. In February 1913 Cowart had somehow missed the news of Bobby Dunbar, and in spite of his grave worry, he had done nothing to alert authorities. What's more, there had been an altercation over wages, which could be pointed to as a motive for cooking up a tale.

But Cowart had a ready answer for the first of those concerns—"[W]e only got the papers about every other week. You see, we live in the center of Mississippi pine woods"—which also answered the next burning question: Why had he come forward only now? The intricacy of Cowart's answer was remarkable:

[W]hen I heard Walters had been arrested and the boy . . . returned to the Dunbars, I figured that that was all that was needed . . . I knew that he must be guilty from what the boy had said to me, so I just went on with my work, and didn't pay much attention.

Then, several weeks ago, I had to go to New Orleans to get treatment . . . I was in a barber shop . . . when I picked up a paper and read about this trial. My eyes are poor, and I don't see so very well. So, as I was reading about some witnesses who testified as to where Walters had been, I saw where one of them had testified that Walters had been in Alabama in February. I thought that the year in which this was said to be was 1913, but I understand now that there was a mistake likely; that was supposed to be 1912.

But anyway, I just jumped up and said, "Well, here's a yarn. It looks as though they are trying to save him by a yarn. Walters was with me in February."

The *Item* heard about me and sent me here. I want to do my duty. Then I want to go back to New Orleans and get fixed up.

In case that explanation was apt to make listeners—or later, readers—jump up and cry "yarn," the next attendee of this early-morning meeting was ushered into Lewis's office: the boy himself. "That's the little fellow," Mignon Hall quoted the red-eyed man, who then asked the child if he remembered him. The boy nodded. "We stopped at your house," Blair reported his reply. And then began a long chat between Cowart and the boy, with attorneys listening in.

Afterward, Blair escorted Cowart over to identify Walters in person during his walk from jail to courthouse. First Blair extended his own hand to shake, then Cowart did the same. He looked familiar to Walters, but also "sneaking." In mid-handshake, the prisoner realized that, yet again, he was being tricked. He jerked his arm back and raised it violently, but the man held on, so Walters yanked downward until the grip was finally released. "Who are you?" Walters demanded. "Where are you from!"

In court two days later, Walters returned to the stand and admitted freely that he now remembered Cowart and that he had fixed George Burt's organ. Lewis teasingly grilled Walters about the handshake gone awry, to which the prisoner shot back, "Let a man come up like a gentleman, not like he did."

IF COWART'S STORY came before the jury, it meant that Walters was as good as hanged, so when it came to the matter of putting Cowart himself on the stand, three full hours of all-out legal war broke out in the courtroom. Voices were raised, righteous speeches were made, and caustic barbs hurled, volumes of case law were slung onto tables, their pages ripped through and jabbed at. The defense called Cowart's testimony "the rankest kind of hearsay." But Cowart was what Garland and his team, what Percy Dunbar and every Dunbar sympathizer in the world had been looking for, this entire past year: insight into the dark eight months of Walters's campaign to transform the boy's identity. More simply, he offered sworn testimony that the boy had called himself "Bobby."

Remarkably, it was during this debate that for the first time on record, the lawyers argued over the issue of the boy's memory and the admissibility of his words. "The boy is not qualified to testify," Rawls insisted. "His age forbids him from recognizing the solemnity of the oath. If it were otherwise, the boy himself would be the best witness of what he said to Cowart." On the contrary, Lewis insisted, the boy's statement to Cowart had been given "in the very camp of the defense" "at a time when the child was under the sole control of Walters, so there could not be any suspicion of coercion or fabrication." According to the *States*, Garland took that even further. Regardless of time or place, "Bobbie Dunbar's age was such as to preclude the possibility of falsehood. His age was the age when nature speaks by instinct, and finds expression for things evoluting in the mind."

In youth was a purity of truth, Garland insisted. A child cannot make things up.

After recess, when the jury was seated, Judge Pavy returned to the bench, quoted aloud case law, and ruled against the state on the matter of Cowart. Garland sank back in his seat. His last-ditch scramble had failed.

But in the court of local public opinion, his battle had been won, hands down. All Opelousas had needed was this extra nudge toward certainty, and the *Item*'s Blair and Hall—reviled for their fakery just two weeks ago—had provided it. The esteemed Opelousan Gilbert L. Dupre, who had spoken on the Dunbar matter back in 1913, wrote to the *Item* that, on top of all the other evidence, Cowart's "startling testimony" made it "sufficient to convict . . . beyond a reasonable doubt."

On the other hand, the *Item* would wait two weeks to print another letter, dated April 24, far less agreeable to its efforts: "[A]s I have been a patron of your paper for years," wrote W. Childs of Church Point, "I beg to say that since the trial began, in my estimation, the *Item* has gone down 70 degrees. In [this] case you have not only been a prosecutor but a persecutor."

THE COWART AFFAIR was not just the nadir of a newspaper's integrity or the apex of a prosecutor's desperation. The boy's crack-of-dawn chat with the bloody-eyed stranger marked the crystallization of a yearlong shift in his young mind. The experience was practically buried within the infantile embellishments of Mignon Hall's account:

[I]n a minute, a little boy was in an "old dad's lap," and they were talking all about feeding the cows, and the high fence . . . and how he talked to "old dad" while Walters was currying his big bay horse, named "Charley."

They spoke of a time when Bobbie was sitting in Walters's old wagon just before they left old dad's house, and how Bobbie had offered him some crackers he was munching as he sat on the high seat.

"Do you remember the crackers?" laughed old dad.

"Ugh-huh," grunted Bobbie. "I was awful cold."

"Do you remember how you talked to old Mrs. Burt and what you told her about the little boy that was with you and what happened to him?"

Bobbie nodded his head up and down. He remembered it all.

And then old dad went on to explain to the attorneys that he had declared that the "other little boy that used to be with them" fell off the wagon and broke his leg and he hopped on crutches, just like he told folks here.

Bobbie had also declared that he wished he had some crutches, too. But he said the little boy was gone, and he didn't know where he was.

Bobby had remembered the little boy on crutches for nearly a year. Finally, though, here was *someone else* who remembered him. No matter that Cowart was telling the lawyers what the boy had allegedly told him or Mrs. Burt in the past, none of those tenses or conditionals registered or mattered to Bobby himself. Cowart was a man he knew, cows and crackers were things he knew. They gave him a bridge to what he didn't *quite* know, what he had said aloud before but had not been quite able to see or to feel. The other boy was no longer a glimpse, a half memory, a question, or a bedtime story. It was something much closer to a fact.

And Bobby himself brought plenty of lived experience to the table, too. During his travels with Walters, there had been scores of boys—undeniably real boys—that Bruce had known, played, and traveled with. Walters's sister Hetty Bell had two boys, Johnnie and Coy, who would have been seven or eight during Bruce's stay there. Iredell had seven-year-old Isham, and the Bledsoes had four-year-old John. There was another boy at the Cochrans in Mobile, and other boys at the Hollemans, the Golemans, the Amackers, and the Thigpens in Pearl River County. Many of these boys rode with Bruce and Walters in the wagon, interminable miles to and from town or church that, in a young child's memory, would seem like an epic journey. Any one of them could have fallen from the wagon, especially with no adult supervision, and any one of them could have had crutches.

What of the death and funeral so recently blurted out to Seiferth and Ray? The boy had at least one true memory to draw on. Mrs. Bilbo had fixed the date of Walters's return from Charity Hospital as coinciding with a "burying" they had all attended—Delilah Ford Cothen, who had died October 10, 1912—in the Ford's Creek Cemetery, a stone's throw from the Bilbo home. Later in their trip, in mid-December, four-year-old Freddie Stockstill died and was buried near Picayune, perhaps ten miles away from where Walters swore he and the boy had been staying. In all those months of travel and churchgoing, there certainly could have been other burials for the boy to call up in his mind.

But finally, what to make of Cowart's claim that Bruce had called himself Bobby? It could have been last-minute fabrication, plain and simple. But considering the boy's reality during those eight months, there was another possibility as well.

HE FIRST HEARD the name in September, after a day of fishing, falling asleep on Mrs. Bilbo's lap as she read the newspaper. Robert Dunbar, a little boy over in Louisiana, lost and far from his family. It would have been easy for Bruce to feel an inkling of kinship. He had not seen his own mother in eight months and Walters, the closest man he ever had to a father, had just left for the hospital in New Orleans. Just days after that Sunday, Homer Moody and the other adults at the Bilbo place began to scrutinize him and whisper. When officials arrived, he heard the name again—Robert Dunbar—this time directed at him. The men studied his features, and compared them with the writing on a paper; they pulled up his dirty foot and studied his toe. Bruce's foot had long been the subject of adult attention—Walters applying ointment, Mrs. Bilbo tutting over his sores during his sickness—but this attention was different. They were looking for a scar, he heard them say. Robert Dunbar had a scar.

With each new community, each new home, there was the same suspicion. Everywhere Bruce and Walters went, the name Robert Dunbar was on everyone's lips, along with stares and pointed fingers in his direction. In Carriere, a deputy and two other men confronted Walters and the boy, armed with a warrant for Walters's arrest and a telegram from the mayor of Opelousas. As Walters groused, the men compared the boy to the telegram, feature by feature. He was not the Dunbar child. The next month, a reward-hungry young George Baylis caught up with the pair stopped on a roadside, where the boy was tormenting a salamander and the old man was cheering him on. Though Walters accurately predicted that Baylis would soon be disappointed, the man insisted on examining the boy and, by one report, compared him to a photo from the news or a reward poster. So, at least this once, Bruce himself gazed at the blurred baby picture of the famous Robert Dunbar.

At the Stewarts' home in January, Mrs. Stewart and her grown son Otis recalled an encounter very much like Cowart's, when out of Walters's earshot, the boy confessed that his name was "Little Robert." District Attorney Garland himself had heard this story from the Stewarts in May 1913 but had not called them to testify, likely because he anticipated the same hearsay objection raised against Cowart. And probably for another reason: it would have been odd for the real Bobby Dunbar to refer to himself as "Little Robert," though this was certainly the moniker Bruce would have heard from inquiring strangers, reading from newspapers, telegrams, and reward posters.

No matter what truth there was to Cowart's story, then, its essence was not at all implausible. By February and March, when he and Walters stayed at the Cowart home, Bruce knew exactly who Bobby Dunbar was. This other boy lost from home and family materialized in his consciousness at the same time that his memories of his own home, and of his own mother, were fading.

He may very well have begun to wonder if all of the strangers' speculation was correct. Perhaps he *could* be Bobby Dunbar, after all. And how could Bruce Anderson not *wish* to be the Bobby Dunbar these strangers wanted him to be? The boy with parents who would do and give anything to have him back.

Two months after the visit with Cowart, in early April, came the final wave of strangers' scrutiny. Walters and Bruce had pulled in for the night at a farmhouse and were in bed when the men charged. Bruce may not have seen the angry confrontation, but he certainly heard it. The next day, when the men came after Walters again, Bruce could not have missed the fear rippling beneath the old man's indignation.

Walters hustled the boy into Columbia, where he made his case to Dr. Anderson, Deputy Day, and anyone in a position of authority who would listen. In a bid to end the harassment for good, he issued a bold challenge to Deputy Lott: if this boy is Robert Dunbar, take him to Opelousas and let the parents see him for themselves.

Standing at his side, Bruce probably heard the words differently than Walters had intended.

It was two weeks shy of the Dunbars' arrival in Columbia. Bruce would fight them like strangers when they came, then struggle, moment by moment, test by test, memory by memory, to become their son.

But well before he even saw them, some part of him was ready. When Walters readied his picture outfit and told him that the photo was for his mother, some part of Bruce imagined Mrs. Dunbar.

HAD HE BEEN in court for the closing arguments of the defense, Bobby would have heard his newly accumulated self unraveled. Mercifully, he was kept at home.

E. B. Dubuisson, the only defense attorney who could get away with such a thing, held up two photographs before the jury—Bobby Dunbar as an infant and the boy in question—and cast all delicacy aside: "Some members of this jury know the Dunbar family. Look at this picture. It is Dunbar all over. It has the Dunbar eyes. Look at this other picture, the child that was found. There is nothing of the Dunbar about it. You never saw a Dunbar with eyes like that."

Some jurymen leaned forward for yet another look at the photos, but few eyes dared to look at the real, live Dunbars for comparison. They were sitting separately as they had done for the entire trial, Percy on his regular perch behind the state's table, and Lessie, in the audience, surrounded by relatives and friends.

On a softer note, Dubuisson began with sympathy and ended with realism: "My heart goes out to Mr. and Mrs. Dunbar . . . I hope from the bottom of my heart that the child they now have is their own son. But the circumstances in this case are very much against it."

And then, with a nod to Shakespeare, Dubuisson delicately suggested what the long, futile search for their son had wrought upon the heart and mind, not just of Lessie but of Percy as well. "There are times . . . when a mother's identification becomes poorest of all; times when an idea has become an obsession and the wish is father to the thought."

Mrs. Dunbar's body was rigid and her face, drained of color and determinedly blank.

This was not the harshest verdict delivered against the Dunbars. From other quarters, Dubuisson's conclusion—that they had made an honest mistake—was met with scorn and impatience. Just days earlier, Dale and Rawls had received a handwritten letter from Dr. Charles C. Bass, the Marion County hookworm expert from Tulane University, who had nothing but blistering anger toward "[a] father and mother whose conscience permits them to conjure up the fancy that some other child is their own.

"As for the Dunbars, they are not entitled to sympathy or quarter. If they are mentally unbalanced sufficiently to allow them to make the effort they have to destroy an innocent man, they are a source of danger to others and should be restrained as we do others who try to destroy life or property. The child should be restored to W. C. Walters from whom he was kidnapped."

Bruce had been kidnapped, and his kidnappers were deranged, treacherous, and amoral. The Dunbars were the criminals, not Walters, and in their custody, the child was in peril.

* * *

DURING THE STATE'S close, Walters shook his head gravely to signal his repudiation of the charges being leveled against him. The three attorneys pointed righteously at him, but he did not waver. His only flinch came when Lewis approached and shook his fist directly in his face.

Veazie wrangled in D. B. or Frank Walters as a coconspirator, and pointed to the testimony of Loveless and Collins—of a sickly boy "near the point of death"—to answer the question of the "other boy's" fate. Garland, so hoarse that Dubuisson had to point his ear trumpet into his face to hear, insisted that the utterly seamless nature of Walters's alibi belied just how meticulously it had been faked.

Lewis flung caustic derision in every direction. To the Mississippi witnesses, whom he accused of collusion and cover-up, and to one family in particular, whose name had been in the news for months, synonymous with corruption. In addition to his gubernatorial campaign, Mississippi's lieutenant governor, the so-called Piny Woods Statesman, was facing trial on charges of bribery. "The Bilbo home; yes, back there in the piny woods," Lewis growled, "back there where anything might be under cover." How convenient that so much of Walters's alibi hinged on Bilbo; how convenient that it was Bilbo who had rushed to New Orleans in his defense. And, really, "What does Bilbo do for a living?"

Lewis again lashed out at the invalid in the Lacombe: "Try this case, gentlemen, but do not try it on a basis of Julia Anderson against Mrs. Dunbar—their names should not be mentioned in the same breath."

As for the accused, he did his best to inflame: "He put marks on that child's back that it took weeks of a mother's tender care to efface—that's what Walters did. Gentlemen, a death verdict is not too severe in this case. The sentence should be death."

Walters had prepared a speech of his own to deliver to the jury, but was predictably denied. As the twelve men shuffled out to deliberate, he could only hope that, instead of these monstrous lies, they would recall his final appearance on the stand three days earlier, when he had read aloud two letters he had sent to North Carolina in early April 1913, prior to his arrest. Prosecutors insisted these were "manufactured evidence," but Walters hoped that jurors would conclude otherwise.

BRUCE POSED BAREFOOT, standing in the dirt and on the little stool, as Walters captured his image with his "picture outfit," twice at least. Then, because Julia had asked, Walters endeavored to take a photo of himself, too. "I had a man help me," he explained to the court. "He pressed the bulb when I told him to, after I had arranged things."

A few days later, Walters was on his way to the post office when Deputy Day approached, knowing of Walters's camera and asking for a photo of Bruce to send to the Dunbars. Walters, who hoped he had defused suspicion by standing up to the "citizens' committee," was exasperated. He ripped open the envelope in his hand, insisted that Day read the letters—one to his parents and one to Julia—and gave him two of the photos of Bruce. Then he mailed off the letters, and remaining photos, to North Carolina.

April 8, 1913

Dear Father and Mother: I will write you a few lines which leave me as well as usual . . . we have been Having Lots of Rain But Have Been Severrel nice Sunshining Days and the mornings are Very cool. How Long Did [Frank] stay with you all . . . Write to me at Foxworth Miss. I will send you one of my pictures, also one for Vinita. Will put in some for Julia if she is not staying with you. Git it to her. I have decided to Buy me a Place out There and try the Poltry Business. I would be glad if you would sell out or rint out and come Live with me. Your son as ever, W. C. Walters.

And the letter enclosed alongside:

this is for Julia

I will try after much delay to write you a few lines. I guess you began to think I would not write. But about the time I got your letter I had ordered me A Picture outfit and Been trying to Get A good Picture of Him to send to you But I find it A Hard matter. But I will Send the Best I have. Bruce appears to Love me Better and Better All the time. I Have Been Given some trouble about Him on account of A Child lost about His Age. But you need not Be uneasy about Him. He is one of the Happiest Little Boys you Ever Saw. So write to me soon and all the News as Ever.

your Friend W C Walters write Foxworth Miss

On the corner of the envelope containing these letters was scrawled "Missent." After a delay in the Barnesville mail, it reached the Walters farm after Julia had fled for the last time. So she never read the letter or saw the photos of Bruce for which she had been begging. Meanwhile, the two photos that Walters gave to Day successfully reached the Dunbars in Opelousas, the first images they ever saw of the boy they would claim as Bobby.

AFTER THE JURORS left, Walters strolled over to the press table, smiling and passing out prayer chain letters. Musing on his plans after his antici-pated release, he imagined that he would first visit Julia in Charity Hospi-tal. Then he would return to Pearl River County and take up the life that he had hoped for in his letter a year ago: starting up a farm. Or maybe he would go onstage, but then again, he might go to Washington to secure some patents on his latest musical imaginations, described in one report as "a key by which musical instruments could be made multi-toned . . . [and] a music chart by which anyone could learn to play in a few hours."

His aura of confidence was undermined only by the raw, bloody scrapes up and down his neck. This morning, he had refused to leave his cell until he'd gotten a shave. He would not hear his fate improperly groomed. When the barber finally arrived, his work had been brusque.

Chapter 24

V. Morel, "Justice Weighs Pleas in Fight of Mothers,"
New Orleans Item, April 14, 1914

ON THE SUNDAY before jurors began deliberation, Father John Engber-ink of the St. Landry Catholic Church issued a plea to his flock for peace and restraint upon delivery of the verdict. Barring that, extra riflemen were kept at the ready around the jail. Worrying how easy it would be for a knife or a gun to emerge from within Walters's court-to-jail gauntlet, McMullen called it "a more or less open boast" that the prisoner didn't stand a chance in the event of acquittal or mistrial. To this speculation, "Sheriff Swords points significantly to a large leather belt filled with soft-nosed cartridges."

During the anxious wait for a verdict, the crowd migrated across the street from the courthouse, where they could see, through the windows of its front office, the silent pantomime of the jurors' deliberation. Little if anything could be gleaned.

What they would soon know was this: on the first vote, nine jurors, one after the other, rendered Walters guilty without capital punishment. Much to the shock of the nine, the remaining three voted for death. Hours later, the three were down to one: Elijah Fisher, who had administered his own brand of justice four times in his life with the scars on his face to prove it, saw no cause for mercy. They argued with him and begged, as a group and one-on-one, but Fisher stood his ground: Walters should die.

At 4:55, six hours after deliberations had begun, the courthouse bell tolled and the crowds poured into the already overstuffed building to hear the verdict. In the courtroom, they barely noticed when the defendant himself was escorted in. His gait was confident and his expression sober.

Foreman George Caillouet of Port Barre stood. Walters was guilty, he announced, but he would not hang. Elijah Fisher had finally been broken. Less because his fellow jurors had persuaded him, he would later insist, and more because of fear of mistrial.

Walters absorbed the words, expressionless.

Before the crowd could cheer, a lady in the audience fainted and slumped to the floor, and after panicked attempts to revive her, she was carried out in the arms of Deputy Chachere.

Outside in the courtyard, hundreds of upturned faces watched Mignon Hall's hand slip out from an open window, and drop a sheet of paper into the air. In the moments leading up to the verdict, she'd been spotted clutching three sheets, marked with each possible verdict. The single page fluttered down, down, down, into the outstretched arms of a young boy whom she'd enlisted to stand below. He held it up, and the crowd erupted, swarming Percy Dunbar, who had been waiting among them.

Moments later, when Judge Pavy gave his gavel its final whack, a similar pandemonium overtook the courtroom, with the crowds surrounding the jurors to shake their hands in congratulation and appreciation. Twelve smiles of relief broke out, and the jurors let the crowd carry them out, down the stairs, and into the square, to fete them as heroes.

Meanwhile, Dr. Stubbs, Deputy Andrus, and Sheriff Swords, their expressions grave, surrounded the limping Walters and practically dragged him back to the safety of the jail. "A verdict like that don't bother me!" he cried to the *Times-Picayune*. "God and the law will not let an innocent man suffer!" The lawmen placed him in the "bullpen," an interior cell with other prisoners, but away from any windows. He was denied his violin and harp.

Opelousas rejoiced.

On Union Street, crowds inundated the Dunbar home, and the phone never stopped ringing. In a flurry of handshaking, backslapping, and tearful embraces, Percy beamed. Having searched for his son for eight months and fought for him for a year after that, it was all finally over. He felt "ten years younger," he told reporters. For now, he would savor his elation, but wanted nothing more than to get back to work, to return his family's life to normal.

Elsewhere in the crowd, Lessie was plainly exhausted. To all of her well-wishers, she "smiled sadly, but sweetly." She had little to say beyond that she was satisfied with the verdict, and she was happy.

Bobby, although not quite sure what all the excitement was about, enjoyed it nonetheless. When telegrams arrived at the door, he raced them to his parents. Whenever he could, he answered the phone. When his mother swept him up in her embrace, he relished her warmth and her kisses.

And, alone in the exultant, ever-milling crowd, he enjoyed a simple boyhood pleasure. He snatched an orange from the kitchen and asked a distracted adult for a knife, one of his favorite toys. Bobby crouched amid all the legs and sliced into the fruit, giving the task his full attention. He jammed one piece between his lips and sucked its juice as he cut up the rest. Almost a year ago exactly, in the Lewis home, he had clapped his hands at the sight of an orange, but today, the fruit was no longer a "test," and the hand that had offered it was that of a ghost.

Two days after she saw the boy in the parlor of the Lacombe Hotel, Julia had lain in her bed, recovering, and wondered aloud if there were another way for this to end. Her erstwhile roommate Matilda Bilbo, too dangerously infirm to testify, had just been rushed home by her husband, and so it was with Herman Seiferth that Julia shared her speculation. "In the beginning," she told him, "I would have been willing to compromise, I would have consented to Mrs. Dunbar keeping the child half the time, and [I] would have worked in Mrs. Dunbar's house in order to be near the boy." She'd never suggested such a thing, she admitted, but only because she hadn't been given the opportunity. It was a strange and seductive fantasy, a leftover from her delirium, and Julia knew it to be untenable. What would the child's name be? Which woman would he call mother?

On the eve of the verdict, Julia had arrived at Charity Hospital, helped through the trip by Dale, who remained at her side. When reporters asked for a comment, she "smiled weakly" and referred them to the lawyer instead.

When news of the verdict reached her the next day, she would not speak at all.

* * *

"IT IS NEEDLESS to say that the verdict is a disappointment," Dubuisson announced to the press, "although it was not entirely unexpected. On the evidence, Walters should have been acquitted, [but] that was too much to expect in view of the public sentiment here. Walters was found with a child whom Mr. and Mrs. Dunbar claimed as their own. From these facts, the public condemned Walters as the kidnaper [sic] of the child."

Weak, circumstantial evidence had not mattered. The contradictions of the swap theory had not mattered. For the jurors, in the end, out of the two full weeks of testimony, it was this single sentence, from John Lewis's closing argument, that resonated most when they came to rendering their verdict: *"You cannot say, 'I believe this is the Dunbar child, but believe this man is innocent.'"* Finding Walters not guilty, even if they felt the evidence warranted such a verdict, would have been an unimaginable betrayal to Percy and Lessie Dunbar. It would have placed a legal imprimatur on doubt over the identity of their son.

But the battle over the fate of William Walters was far from decided. When Dubuisson said the verdict had been "not entirely unexpected," that was an understatement. Throughout the trial, though he had often sat silent, leaning into his ear trumpet with an enigmatic smile across his face, he had been working perhaps harder than any attorney in the courtroom. With stern precision, Dubuisson had reserved exceptions on key points of the conduct of the trial, and out of court and late into the night, he brought the full force of his intellect into the sculpting of a formidable appeal. He had been planning for the inevitability of this verdict before the trial even began. In mid-May, he made his case public with a request for a new trial, and when Judge Pavy huffily denied that request, he immediately appealed to the state supreme court.

His first point had been hotly debated throughout the trial: the statute under which Walters had been indicted was, in fact, unconstitutional. Act No. 271 of 1910 had been hurried through the legislature in the wake of the kidnapping and murder of Walter Lamana, intended to amend an earlier statute to make kidnapping a crime punishable by death. In fact, Dubuisson (and others) argued, the act amended the *wrong* kidnapping law, and thus was fatally defective in title. Walters had never been *legally* indicted. As explosive as the claim was, critics scoffed that it was based on a convolution and mangling of legal logic.

The same could not be said of at least one of Dubuisson's other bills of exception: an attack on his dear friend Judge Pavy's instructions to the jury regarding the distinction between the "principal" and "accessory" to a crime. In his original order, Pavy had literally rewritten the law, and when Dubuisson had pointed the error out to him, Pavy not only refused to correct it, but redoubled, removing all traces of "presence" (at or near the scene of the crime) from the jury's understanding of the definition of "principal." As Dubuisson saw it, Pavy's instructions were "erroneous in law and calculated to mislead and confuse the jury." If the state had not shown that Walters was at Swayze Lake, with these instructions, the jury could find him guilty anyway.

Meanwhile, Dale and Rawls did everything they could from Mississippi, mustering up evidence to destroy the McComb tale, the last-minute reverends, and black-hearted Mrs. Sloan. And after much sleuthing, they obtained an affidavit from William Winningham, who recalled stopping for dinner in a Poplarville restaurant with his six-year-old son in September 1913. At another table, they had spotted the organ mender they knew from Reverend Sones's Chapel and the little boy in his care. The four had chatted as they ate, then gone their separate ways. *This is all that Katie Collins had seen.*

The most significant element of Dubuisson's mid-May campaign did not make it into the appeal: his exposure of the truth of what had happened inside the Lewis home on May 1, 1913. "Owing to my infirmity of being deaf or hard of hearing," he insisted, he had missed the hurried mention of these events during rebuttal. So when Dale and Rawls brought it to his attention that the child had been removed from the dining room just before Julia entered, it came as a shock. Indignantly, Dubuisson forced virtually every man involved—the committee, Veazie, and Garland himself—to revisit this event yet again, under oath, in far greater detail than they had done at the trial, in far greater detail than they ever would have wanted. And on this go-round, a transcript of their words would survive.

It was Assistant District Attorney Veazie himself who had clapped his hands and exclaimed, "She has failed to identify the child!" In his own defense, Veazie sputtered to Dubuisson that he had just arrived, and he had not known that there were only two children in the room. None of the men revealed, nor did Dubuisson ask, *who* had actually removed the boy from the room to begin with, but significantly, the only key participant not to testify was John Lewis himself.

Though Veazie insisted to Dubuisson that the moment was insignificant, nothing could be further from the truth. It was this moment that had led to Julia's anguished spiral of doubt. It was this moment that had led to the conclusion that she "failed," a conclusion that spread like wild-fire through the press and public opinion, becoming accepted, incontro-vertible fact, so entrenched that even this exposure of its falsehood would not erase it from accepted history.

Julia had not failed.

HAVING RECUPERATED BY early May, Julia fled Charity Hospital abruptly, as reported with ominous restraint in the *Item*, "after voicing a strong objection to undergoing an operation she was advised to have." She made her way up to Columbia, where she met with Dale and Rawls and discussed the appeal-in-progress. They also discussed the recovery of her son, a possibility that the lawyers knew to be increasingly remote.

From Columbia, Julia traveled southeast, retracing backward the route Walters and Bruce had taken a year before. At the Bilbos, she was welcomed with open arms. Still recovering, Matilda had a gift for Julia that she had forgotten to proffer during her illness in Opelousas: the baby clothes for Bruce that she had supplied Walters with during their forays from home. No doubt, these were the little slips she had sewn for her own children, almost all of whom were now dead. For Julia, they were a bittersweet treasure. Together, Matilda and Julia healed in the sharing of loss. They worshipped side by side and always spoke of Bruce. Their friendship blossomed.

ONCE THE SUPREME court appeal was filed, Walters's existence in the St. Landry prison grew dramatically more tense. A new jailhouse trusty appeared, whom Walters suspected of being a stool pigeon for "the Dun-bar camp" and stealing donations left for him by supporters. When Wal-ters confronted the man, he responded with a resounding punch to the eye, made stronger by the ring of keys clenched in his fist. It was plain to Sheriff Swords that Walters's future in Opelousas would only get worse from here.

In the dead of night, he whisked the black-eyed prisoner onto the train to New Orleans, where he would be safer kept in the parish prison. By nine o'clock the next morning, Swords and Walters were guzzling their last beer together at a saloon across from the depot. Two years later, Swords would only narrowly win reelection, in no small part because the Pavy-Garland political dynasty felt that the sheriff's conduct had become reckless, unprofessional, and an embarrassment to the parish. A few months into his fifth term, on the hunt for a bloodthirsty "half-breed desperado," Swords would be gunned down in a cornfield, his death and funeral making front pages across the state.

ON THE AFTERNOON of Monday, June 29, 1914, Walters peered through the grating of his massive iron cell door and recognized a friendly face: A. J. McMullen of the *States,* the first journalist to give him a respectful jail-house interview in Columbia, in April of last year. McMullen was beaming, and Walters could tell right away that he had news.

The Louisiana Supreme Court, he announced, had just released its decision:

> It is therefore ordered that Act No. 271 of 1910 be declared unconstitutional, null and void, and it is further ordered that the verdict and sentence against the accused be set aside, and that he be discharged from further prosecution under said statute.

Walters sat still and absorbed the news. McMullen's glee was so plain that it crowded out any spontaneous reaction that the prisoner might have had. Instead he stayed cool and responded, "I am glad to hear it, but I expected nothing else. I was always confident that I would be vindicated."

McMullen did not point out that the ruling hinged on a technicality, not exoneration. Instead he asked what the prisoner planned to do, if he was released right away.

Now that the possibility was real, Walters was filled with a strange sort of dread. In jail for the past fourteen months, he had been taken care of, kept safe, fed, and warm. "I really don't know what I will do now," he replied. "If they turn me out . . . I will face a very cold world . . . I have only a nickel and [that] belongs to the iceman, for he trusted me with a nickel's worth of ice yesterday."

And what of the boy?

Walters thought of Bruce, whom he had seen in court and called for from jail. He thought of Percy and Lessie Dunbar, whom he had pled with, then denounced and despised, and then finally, to a degree, pitied. Fourteen months of feeling swirled up into his answer, but he managed, again, to deliver it with serenity:

> They tried to have me murdered by trying to prove that I kidnapped the boy, and if they had succeeded in having the extreme

penalty pronounced on me they would have been my murderers. But I will forgive them if they return my boy to me.

UP IN POPLARVILLE, outside the courthouse, the mood on Wednesday, July 1, was giddy. It was "sort'a celebration" of the supreme court decision, Julia told a reporter, grinning at the quiet, gangly farmer at her side, surrounded by courthouse officials and a local reverend. But her happiness that day was not really about Walters at all.

Once she had made it up to Mississippi, the people of Pearl River County welcomed her into their community. The Bilbos, Golemans, and Myleys, witnesses who had cared for and grown fond of her son, now did the same for her. As she got on her feet, she found hope in this life among the last people to know her son Bruce as Bruce.

Living nearby was Ann Elizabeth Rawls, the recently widowed aunt of Walters's lawyer Hollis Rawls. When she grew gravely ill, Julia moved into Mrs. Rawls's farmhouse to cook, clean, and nurse. As at the Walters farm, Julia's charge here had a grown son: James Oliver Rawls, Hollis's first cousin. "Ollie" was five years younger than Julia, ran the family farm, and had never been married. Like Bunt before him in North Carolina, he watched Julia come alive as she did her job and found her place. She filled a void in this household left by his father's death and his mother's illness: she offered Ollie companionship, conversation, and vitality. In just weeks, he knew that she belonged here even once his mother got better.

As he told the story from the Poplarville courthouse steps, "he admitted that he 'popped' the question only a couple of days ago and that Julia hesitated, blushed, and said something about the suddenness of it all."

It was sudden, and an outsider would have every reason to worry that once again, Julia had fallen into something that would soon go bad. But Ollie was no Lishy Floyd, and Julia's second wedding was followed not by a shotgun rampage and a stillborn child but by some shopping in town with her groom, then a drive back out to the farm to carry on with the afternoon.

Before they drove off, Julia Anderson Rawls answered a final, obvious question from reporters. "She expects to make a still harder fight to get the boy she claims is Bruce, now that she has a home."

What steps Julia took toward that end, in her Columbia meeting with Dale and Rawls earlier in the summer or after that, are unknown. Nearly a century later, two of Julia's proud and reverent children from her marriage to Ollie, Hollis Rawls and Jewel Tarver, would remember that Julia did everything she could do legally to get Bruce back. But as much as it anguished her, though she knew she would mourn him for a lifetime, her decision to fight the Dunbars no further was less a legal one than an emotional one.

> *And they brought a sword before the king.*
> *And the king said, Divide the living child in two, and give half to the one, and half to the other.*
> *Then spake the woman whose the living child was unto the king, for her bowels yearned upon her son, and she said, O my lord, give her the living child, and in no wise slay it.*

As King Solomon understood, the true mother was the mother that thought of her child more than herself, who would rather suffer injustice and unending grief than see the child die. If Julia had kept fighting, the sword of Solomon would have cleaved the boy, forever, half into Bruce and half into Bobby, doomed to endure a lifetime of crippling doubt about who he truly was. By letting him be Bobby, she gave him a chance at a life that was whole.

Two weeks earlier, in mid-June, the *Item* tried to resurrect the Dunbar mystery one last time, by ginning up another crank letter scare, this one promising that the real Bobby Dunbar was, in fact, still in the hands of kidnappers, and that half of his hand had been cut off. An *Item* reporter tracked Lessie down at her sister's house in New Orleans to deliver the news.

She began to cry. And not just because of the scare. Earlier in the day, she and Bobby had been down on Canal Street, where they had been pointed at and whispered over everywhere they went. As the *Item* reported, "she was of the opinion that forever their lives would be disturbed" by this sort of publicity and malice, and "despaired of ever again living happily." "It is a shame that now that courts in Opelousas have settled the question of Bobby's identity," she lamented, "that it should be brought up again and again."

While waiting for his verdict in Opelousas, Walters had made a similar prediction: "Even if convicted, I would not change places with the Dunbars. They have acquired a life [of] trouble never ending."

But Walters was not telling Lessie anything she did not already know.

How could she reasonably expect her life to return to normal? The doubt would never go away on the streets and it would never stop eating at her. And she must have feared that it would poison her marriage, if that process had not begun already. If she and Percy caught each other's eye for too long, they would surely see it.

But she would not let Bobby see it, or hear it, or feel it. Her fight to come—like Julia's surrender—would be for Bobby to simply be Bobby. While she wept to the *Item* reporter, her son was over at the DeVergeses' house, playing with his beloved cousin and confidante Lucille. When he returned, Lessie would greet him with a smile.

THREE DAYS LATER, on Saturday, June 20, Bobby pressed himself against the rails on the rear deck of the steamer *Fairhope*, gazing eagerly across the ashen surface of Lake Pontchartrain to the receding line of New Orleans on the horizon. The chug of the engine filled his ears, the sun was on his face, and fishy air in his nostrils.

In two hours, the *Fairhope* would dock across the lake at Mandeville, where, under the oaks of Jackson Park, a picnic awaited Bobby, Alonzo, Lessie, and all the Texas Oil Company employees who had invited them as guests on their annual chartered excursion. There would be a band and dancing, and adults ogling him and ruffling his hair—all the tedious routines of another summer celebration.

But right now, they were almost in the middle of the lake, the most thrilling part of the voyage. New Orleans had finally disappeared, and if Bobby raced from stern to bow, he could not yet see anything ahead.

Chapter 25

Postcard, *New Orleans Item*

ON THE MORNING of Tuesday February 23, 1915, Walters stepped through his open cell door, wearing his finest suit and carrying his boxed-up harp under his arm. Down the long hallways, he shook all the hands extended through the bars, both white and black. "Be good fellows," he cautioned, "and don't do anything that will reflect on the prison."

For the past nine months, Walters had befriended these men, wearied them with his lecturing and soothed them with his harp. He had worshipped and sung with them in the prison chapel, and battled them in tobacco-spitting contests and tournaments of *fan-tan,* the Chinese game of chance.

All the while, beyond the prison walls, his case had dragged on. Following the supreme court's June decision, the state had filed for a rehearing before the full court. In November, the justices reversed their ruling on the question of the kidnapping law's constitutionality, but then took up Dubuisson's remaining bills of exception, which they had heretofore not considered. On Dubuisson's charge related to jury instructions, the high court agreed that Judge Pavy's instructions had been "so worded that they might well have misled the jury to convict the accused of being a principal in the second degree upon evidence of his guilt as an accessory." The case was remanded for a new trial, but after much prodding by Dale, Rawls, and Dubuisson, Garland finally admitted in public that "[i]t is doubtful if we will ever be able to try Walters again . . . The first trial cost the parish of St. Landry eight thousand dollars and broke us flat." They were not only lacking money for a retrial but also the appetite. Now that the Dunbars had their child safe and secure, for all practical purposes, justice had been done.

Walters descended three flights of the grim iron staircase, and waited as the final double steel doors opened at last. As the sunlight hit his eyes, he accepted the best wishes of a jailer, posed for photographs, and fielded a volley of questions from gathered reporters about his plans for the future.

"When I get ready to move, the spirits will guide me," the *Item* quoted him.

His first stop was to Pearl River County for a reunion with Julia, now happily married and six months pregnant. When Walters cropped up again, broke and stranded in Carriere with Brother Holcomb (the minister who had testified on his behalf), Dale and Rawls steered him back down to New Orleans and into a deal with a vaudeville showman. The attorneys had tried and failed to sell their story as a magazine serial for *Collier's* or the *Saturday Evening Post*; they had traveled seven hundred miles to showcase a fund-raiser in Robeson County, North Carolina, that actually sank them further in debt. Dale and Rawls still hoped that a career onstage for Walters might mean they would finally get paid.

By late April, Walters was signed up for a limited theatrical engagement along the Gulf Coast. In Pass Christian, then Biloxi, and finally at the Gulfport Opera House, he limped onstage and narrated the details of his story night after night, singing and plucking out his favorite melodies on the 287 strings of his famous harp. Audiences came "for mere curiosity rather than anything else," scoffed the *Times-Picayune,* adding that the old man was long-winded and merely repeated what the newspapers had beaten to death already.

Two weeks later, Walters was back in New Orleans to drum up business with a moving pictures operation. But when he took to the streets to tell his story, amassing a crowd on the corner of Canal and Rampart Streets with photos of his long-lost Bruce Anderson and angry taunts at the Dunbars, a police detective swooped in and arrested him for disturbing the peace. At his arraignment, he could not possibly scrape together the $25 fine, and so was remanded, again, to the parish prison for thirty days. On his arrest record, his occupation was listed as "lecturer."

Upon his next release, that career had vanished, and Walters headed eastward to resume his life as a tinker. A black New Orleans songster named Richard "Rabbit" Brown bade him farewell by immortalizing him in music. On the streets outside "sporting houses," on trains to and from Baton Rouge, and while rowing tourists out into Lake Pontchartrain, Brown sang "The Mystery of the Dunbars' Child" in his plaintive, rough-hewn twang for a decade or more to come:

> He says I know God wouldn't have me punished for a Crime that I
> didn't do
> I hope and trust each and everyone someday'll find out that I'm true.

JUST AS MYSTERIOUSLY as his wagon had appeared on the horizon of his parents' farm back in 1911 after a decade-long absence, Walters next wandered back into view at the Surrency, Georgia, farmstead of his ailing brother Radford, who lived with his daughter and grandchildren. To this day, both Barbara Moore and Jean Cooper remember in vivid and loving detail their great-uncle Cant's periodic visits, which typically stretched for weeks at a time.

Their mother tended to roll her eyes at Cant's arrivals, hoping aloud that his horses wouldn't eat up all their hay. Rad's reaction was different. On Cant's first return, the brothers hugged and danced together. On later visits, when Rad was too sick to rise from his bed beside the fireplace, he would perk up and order the children to fix supper and pile on more wood.

The whole family would huddle together and shell peanuts while listening to the brothers catch up. Invariably, right from the start, the conversation would turn to the kidnapping, with Cant's indignation rising fresh with each telling. To lighten the mood, Uncle Cant took up his harp or fiddle, and all those who were able would rise for a little jig. Cant always brought the girls trinkets from his travels, and for Rad, he had a concoction of roots to ease the suffering when his asthma was bad.

During the light of day, the girls would climb up into Cant's wagon and study its contents: a decent bed, "every imaginable pot," a store of dry goods and meat, and a live chicken or two in a crate. While it was not the same wagon, it was easy for the girls to imagine what the traveling life must have been like for Uncle Cant and this little boy named Bruce that he so fondly recollected.

Rad's family always speculated over Cant's motivations in traveling with the boy and how he'd gotten mixed up in the Dunbar affair. Cant himself allowed that Bruce opened doors: the ladies fawned over him; fed, bathed, and dressed him; and their husbands were more inclined to welcome and employ his caretaker. Privately, Barbara and Jean's mother suspected that Cant may have offered the boy to the Dunbars, hoping for a reward. One night, Barbara remembers, as Rad was lying by the fire sleepily listening to his brother retell the story, his eyes shot open, and he barked impatiently, "Well, what the hell *did* you want with the boy in the first place?!"

Outraged, Cant stood up, stalked out of the house, hitched up his horses, and took off. According to Barbara, that was the last time they ever saw him.

From Surrency, Cant headed to Atlanta to the home of his grown son Bill, a married and successful businessman. When Cant drove up to Bill's fine Peachtree Street home with his ancient horse and buggy and his baggy, threadbare clothes, Bill's wife was none too pleased. In bustling Atlanta especially, he was a relic of a bygone era. Cant soon wore out his welcome, with Bill's wife at least. For his part, Bill tried to convince his father to settle down; he even arranged a place for him to stay. But whether Cant was aware of the tension around his visit or not, he was not the type to stay put. Soon enough, he was on the road again.

In the late 1930s, Walters was working in a family's home in the Florida panhandle, north of Tallahassee just over the Georgia line, when a thick splinter pierced his arm and lodged beneath the skin. It festered there, the infection becoming so worrisome that the family tried to bring him to a doctor. But Walters, a "great believer in home healing," according to his great-niece Jean Cooper, assured them that, in time, the splinter would work its way out. Instead he died of blood poisoning.

In 1930, Cant reached out one final time to his young traveling companion from 1912 and 1913. From somewhere in Alabama, he wrote a letter to Opelousas lawyer Alex Robertson, who had been E. B. Dubuisson's associate during the trial. As Robertson would recall, Cant asked "what Bobby looked like" and "what kind of a man Bobby had grown up to be." A response would come from Opelousas, two years later, via the Associated Press.

AS UNSETTLED AS Walters's life remained, Julia Anderson's was quite the opposite. Cant never bought his land or started his poultry business, but for the rest of Julia's life, home was a farm in the woods, eighteen miles northwest of Poplarville, where she and Ollie raised seven children: Horace, Mattie, Ollie Mae, Wertner (aka Mut), Hollis, Jewel, and Virginia. Ollie was a seasonal timber worker, hired to look after tracts of virgin pine and haul logs with his team of oxen. So it was Julia who was largely in charge of the family farm, working alongside and overseeing the children. "She didn't do too much going but to church," her daughter Jewel recalled.

Early into her new life in Mississippi, Julia's role in the Ford's Creek community began to shift. No longer were neighbors taking care of her; she was now the one taking care of her neighbors. Julia became a nursemaid for the elderly and infirm, and if no doctor could be found, she even was known to deliver babies. Her skills as a seamstress were renowned, and folks from miles away would bring over catalog photos of their desired clothing, which Julia would cut, sew, and tailor without a pattern.

But above all else, Julia was a loving and selfless parent to her children. Her new family gave her a second chance at motherhood, and she seized it. After long days of farming, she relished being surrounded by her children, reading aloud to them the latest westerns of Zane Grey. She crocheted booties for the girls' dolls, using twine torn from flour sacks and broom straw instead of crotchet needles. Not only did Julia keep her children fed and decently dressed, even in the poorest of times, she gave them a life governed by her own deeply felt sense of morality. She taught them to be compassionate and accepting, humble and honest. Nearly eighty years after Jewel stole an extra egg from a neighbor and her mother caught her in the act, she remembers the shame, and the lesson Julia gave her as a result, as if it were yesterday.

Growing up, Julia's children always knew they had a brother Bruce and a sister Bernice. She spoke of her lost children with affection, but also with a plain and primal sadness. When Jewel was a young girl, she remembers a missionary couple stopping at the Rawls farm, and when they announced where they were headed—Opelousas, Louisiana—Julia grew emotional. She had a son there, she told them; a son she had lost years ago. Giving them a photograph to identify the boy, Julia asked them to look for him. The couple took the photo, but apparently did not report back. As Julia's granddaughter Linda would understand, years later, the only photograph that Julia could have had was of the boy at age five or six, at the latest. But by that time, Bobby Dunbar was a grown man. "In her mind's eye," Linda believes, "he still was that child." To Julia, Bruce was frozen in these boyhood photos, frozen in the moment when she lost him.

Given Julia's enduring and quiet anguish, its sheer intractability, the final major chapter in her life, which began in the early 1930s, was not at all surprising. Her son Hollis remembers how it started: like so many, Julia was drawn to the sound of beautiful singing at a roadside tent revival. And when she herself stepped into the meeting, she found herself enveloped by an intense spirit of love and joy. It was not long into the revival before Julia felt and heeded the call. She walked to the front of the crowd, where the hands of Spirit-filled women were laid upon her, their prayers began, and the electrifying power of God coursed through her trembling body. For virtually everyone who joined this nascent movement of Pentecostalism, "conversion" was a profound and unforgettable experience, involving admission of and repentance for sins, baptism of the Holy Spirit, and often the miracle of healing or speaking in tongues.

For Julia, the experience of embracing a true Christian lifestyle was not just about giving up her persistent snuff habit or abandoning Zane Grey in favor of the Bible. It was a process she had begun as early as 1913, as she struggled to piece together her life in the face of losing all her children. For the twenty years since, she had reckoned with the consequences of her early moral failings, but had not come to full peace. Life in Mississippi had given her a second chance at community, marriage, and family. Now, finally and fully, she felt redeemed in the eyes of God.

In 1939, when word came that her mother, Beady, had died back home in North Carolina, the Rawls were so strapped for money that they had to sell a mule to pay for Julia's train ride up to the funeral. One of her younger sisters who still lived in North Carolina knew the Graves, the couple that had adopted Bernice, and arranged the reunion between mother and daughter. When Julia entered the small millworkers' home in Lumberton, she stood face-to-face with a beautiful young woman with bluish-gray eyes.

Three-quarters of a century later, Bernice Graves Hardee remembered this moment vividly. She knew this woman in the doorway instantly. The old pain she had felt from when she first learned she had been adopted, the sting of a mother's rejection, surged up, and for a moment, she resisted acknowledging Julia. Yet this was the reunion that Bernice, too, had prayed about for years. At last, she spoke. "I said 'You are my mother, and I know it.'" And mother and daughter embraced, Julia's body heaving against Bernice's, sobbing.

Julia spent that night in Bernice's home, in her bed with her daughter. "I never slurred her or questioned anything," Bernice later recalled. Alone together, they talked and talked. Julia told Bernice of her life in Mississippi, Ollie and her children. Bernice told Julia of her young married life, her husband, Roscoe Hardee, and her children.

It is doubtful that Bernice shared the darkness of her early years. Though Ollie Graves had taken Bernice into her home, raised her in the Pentecostal tradition, and taught her right from wrong, she had not given Bernice the thing she needed the most: maternal love. Ollie was "particular to an extreme," Bernice remembered, not just strict, but physically brutal. At ten, faced with the taunting of classmates ("Your ma ain't your ma!"), she finally learned of her adoption, her mother, Julia Anderson, and her lost half brother, Bruce. Though school was in Cerro Gordo, where Julia had waited tables so many years ago, and there were Anderson relatives everywhere, whenever they saw any of Bernice's "real kin," Ollie ordered her "to put my head down . . . and walk to the other side of the street." As she got older, Bernice grew bold enough to at least acknowledge the Andersons cursorily, but she was still too cowed by Ollie to stop and talk.

Now, a grown woman, Bernice was less afraid to make her feelings known. The day after her night alone with Julia, she walked next door, where Ollie and Atlas lived, and asked for permission to invite her birth mother for Sunday dinner. It was as much of a "telling" as an "asking" and Ollie agreed, as long as family and neighbors were invited, too. Bernice killed and cooked a chicken, baked a cake, and when Julia entered, "she looked like a rose that had just blossomed. I couldn't talk to nobody but her." A little neighbor girl tried to get Bernice to play, but Bernice ignored her altogether: "I just wanted my mother, and I knew she was going to have to go."

Bernice was not the only one who felt the reunion was too short. Before she left, Julia invited Bernice to move to Mississippi, to bring her husband Roscoe and their children and settle there. The proposition tugged at Bernice's heart, but Ollie and Atlas were getting old; as unkind as they had been, "they had taken care of me," and she had to do the same for them.

Julia understood, of course. Nonetheless, it was as if she were losing Bernice all over again. Nearly two decades after the adoption, she felt its pain fresh: Julia had failed Bernice. She had not been able to be her mother. But because she knew Bernice forgave her, because God forgave her, perhaps finally Julia was able to forgive herself.

When they said good-bye, Julia asked Bernice to walk away from the Graveses' home first, so she could watch her. She sat down on a rocking chair on the porch and "put her hands to her face." Bernice walked home, and whenever she turned, Julia was still sitting, motionless, watching her.

AFTER JULIA'S DEATH, it was her children Hollis and Jewel who finally had the chance to reunite with her other lost child. But these encounters offered none of the catharsis and reconciliation of Julia's visit with Bernice.

In the early 1940s, Hollis was a young man, working in the Poplarville icehouse. On one particularly busy day, a stranger came in and asked for Horace Rawls. Hollis told the stranger that Horace was his older brother, and he didn't work there, then darted off to tend to a customer wanting ice. When Hollis looked over again, the man still lingered. Hollis made his way back over, and at last, the man introduced himself: his name was Bobby Dunbar. Distracted, Hollis barely absorbed what the man had said before he was called back to work again. When it finally began to dawn on him, Hollis returned, his heart now thumping just as hard as Bobby's must have been.

"We talked," Hollis remembered, "but it was just talk. He told me he was from Opelousas," but little else. In lieu of conversation, the men studied each other carefully. It occurred to Hollis to ask Bobby up into the back office where they could speak in private, but customers weren't allowed there, and he was anxious about getting in trouble. And the real customers, those wanting ice, were piling up. The next time Hollis headed over to wait on one, Bobby Dunbar left.

Only once he was gone did Hollis begin to absorb the full weight of Bobby's appearance. That was his half brother, and he had come, Hollis believed, to find out about his past. To get to the truth. Over the years, as Hollis revisited the incident and tortured himself with regret that he hadn't handled things differently and made more time to talk, dozens of questions popped up that he should have asked Bobby. What *he* thought had happened; what *he* remembered. "I'll always believe that he knew," Hollis insisted over a half century later. "I'll always believe that he knew something about the situation that he wasn't telling."

At least a decade later, Hollis's sister Jewel and her husband, Tony, were running a service station just outside of Poplarville—Tony was a mechanic and Jewel was in charge of the café and cash register—and one day, some ladies appeared with a flat tire. When it came out that they were from Opelousas, Jewel told them that she had a brother there, Bobby Dunbar, and asked them, when they got home, to "check and find out if he's still there . . . still living or what." Around this time, Julia's Mississippi kin had heard a rumor that Bobby had died. The ladies agreed to look him up, left, and Jewel forgot all about it. Until a month later when a strange man came into the café, said he was looking for a salvage yard, but then sat for a full hour drinking a cup of coffee. He talked, and asked Jewel all kinds of questions, paying no attention to Tony, who was working just outside, or any other customers. Only Jewel. Only after he left did Jewel put the visit together with the ladies from Opelousas. This had been Bobby, she felt absolutely certain, and looking back in relation to her brother Hollis's own encounter, she said, "I believe he had come to talk to us again."

If Bobby had come to Poplarville, why could they not go to Opelousas? It wasn't that Julia's family did not think of it, or that they could not afford the half-day's drive. But from all they had heard from their mother, who herself had experienced the discomfort and terror of being an unwanted outsider in that community, they knew that their appearance in Opelousas would be seen as an act of aggression. A challenge not just to the Dunbars, who they had heard were a very powerful family, but also to the community itself. This family had committed a kidnapping, and the town had given them legal sanction. They had savaged their mother and done their best to have an innocent man hung. What else were they capable of?

And so Bobby remained a mystery, a ghost, a source of wonder and speculation, increasingly abstract with every passing generation of the Anderson-Rawls family. "I don't think we thought of him as anything but this little boy," recalls Jewel's daughter Linda, looking back on her own childhood understanding of her lost uncle Bobby. "[W]e always had that little picture."

As MUCH AS Julia and her descendants wondered over that little picture, as much as Walters yearned to hear what kind of man Bobby Dunbar had become, the fullest answers to all of their questions could only be found by knowing the life that Bobby had lived *between* that little picture and becoming a man, the life they had been left out of. And the story of Bobby's upbringing is also the story of those who raised him. After the Walters trial, Percy and Lessie Dunbar had publicly wished for a "return to normal," but that outcome was impossible. It was not just a young boy's identity and fate that had been forever altered; it was their own.

Chapter 26

Envelope in the Dunbar family scrapbook

ON APRIL 23, 1915, just months after the case against Walters had finally been dropped, New Orleans police chief Reynolds released to the press a recent letter that Percy Dunbar had written, praising Reynolds and his team for their work in successfully resolving a far lesser known, and much shorter-lived, kidnapping case: the snatching and ransom of Joseph Martinez. "Mrs. Dunbar and myself have watched every paper," Percy told Reynolds, and remained ever confident that the boy would be found. After all, their own prayers for Bobby's return had been answered, two years earlier almost to the day. "Thanking you for the interest you have taken on behalf of these poor people," Percy concluded, careful to add, "and for past favors, I am, yours very truly, C. P. Dunbar."

For Percy and Lessie, another kidnapping in the news did more than force them back into their own past nightmare. It did more than break their hearts for parents who were suffering as they had. It gave them the chance to revise their experience of losing and recovering Bobby, to simplify and purify that experience. *They were just like these other parents,* they insisted to themselves and to the world.

Cynical observers would be quick to note that April 23, 1915, was also the date of the much-advertised theatrical premiere of William Walters in Pass Christian, Mississippi. In Walters's version of the story, the Dunbars were anything but ordinary, sympathetic parents. And if one were looking for an ulterior motive for the writing or release of the Dunbars' letter—beyond simply to neutralize Walters in the court of public opinion—one only needed to wait a few weeks.

In late May, at a state farmers' convention in Baton Rouge, Percy formally announced his candidacy for registrar of the state land office. Conveniently, Walters was silenced behind bars in New Orleans again, so Percy could deliver his news without threat of distraction. "Will you take 'Bobby' around the state with you?" a reporter asked. It was a reasonable question, particularly given the boy's summerlong statewide homecoming rally in 1913. But Percy bristled. "Not on your life," he snapped back. "I want the job, but I don't want it bad enough to try to get it through any such notoriety."

Incumbent Fred Grace was a popular and formidable opponent, and Percy faced two other challengers, too. Comparatively, he was not much of a public speaker, and his pockets were not as deep, but he boasted an enviable campaign team: District Attorney Garland as chairman, John Lewis and Mayor Loeb as committee members, and alderman E. K. Eastham (who, at the trial, had been forced to recall the peculiarity of Bobby Dunbar's footprint at Swayze Lake) as campaign secretary.

By early fall, though, it was obvious what name on Percy's ticket was the biggest draw. In its endorsement of Mr. Dunbar, the *Jackson Independent* in Jonesboro gossiped: "And in response to a suggestion from Sheriff McBride, [Mr. Dunbar] says he may bring little Bobbie (who is now going to school) with him to Jonesboro when he comes later to meet our people." There is no record of Bobby actually accompanying his father to Jonesboro, or to any other campaign stop, but whether he actively exploited his son's fame or not, Percy's campaign most certainly depended on it. Throughout the race, headlines advertised son over father: "Father of Kidnapped 'Bobbie' Would Be Land Office Registrar," "Bobbie Dunbar's Dad Is in New Orleans over Politics." And while editorial endorsements nodded to Percy's years of experience in land matters, and praised him for his affability, generosity, and even his perseverance in the face of physical handicap, it was his heroic role in the search for his son and the "reserve" he displayed during Walters's trial, that garnered the most acclaim.

For Percy personally, the kidnapping case had other resonances with his campaign. With Walters onstage denouncing *him* as a coldhearted child snatcher, he again felt the flare of public doubt, and his months-long, statewide handshaking tour was infused with the same fervor to correct the record as his investigation had been two years prior. "Percy Dunbar has been located at last!" quipped the St. Landry paper after one extended stint on the campaign trail. And even once he had returned, Percy found respite out in the woods, hunting. Anywhere, it seems, but with his family.

In early 1916, as the race reached its climax, the all-powerful Democratic Ring closed ranks behind incumbent Grace, and Percy balked to the press that he had even lost the advantage of his name: "[M]y name will appear on the ticket as Clarence Percy Dunbar instead of C. P. Dunbar, as I am better known." Grace carried the election easily, with Dunbar a distant second, though at least he prevailed in St. Landry.

A few days later, Bobby Dunbar finally reemerged in the flesh. On West Landry Street in Opelousas, the seven-year-old darted from the sidewalk into traffic and was run down by an approaching Ford. The driver cut his engine, stopped the car, and rushed out to find Bobby, prone on the street, battered and bruised, but very much alive. Once again, the "famous kidnap boy" made the New Orleans tabloids. From the *Opelousas Enterprise* came this smiling prognosis: "It is stated that he will be in his usual form again within a few days." The accident was a minor interruption in an otherwise sunny childhood. A polite thought, typical of a friendly small-town paper. But it was not true.

As BOBBY GREW up, John M. Parker—the one man, more than any other, who had determined his identity and fate—was a larger-than-life figure, a household hero. When Parker swept into Opelousas on April 8, 1916, as Louisiana's Progressive candidate for governor, the Dunbars were first among the eight hundred citizens to cram into the courtroom to hear him. Old Judge E. D. Estillette's voice trembled as he delivered his introduction, recalling the event in 1913 for which Opelousas knew Parker the best: "The governor of Mississippi needed a citizen of Louisiana of such ability and character as would guarantee exact justice." Applause shook the courtroom, and all eyes turned to seven-year-old Bobby. Throughout the speech, he "clapped his little hands whenever others cheered," and afterward, as the throngs were pushed back for Parker to exit, Bobby stepped forward with a ribbon-adorned bouquet in his outstretched arms.

In the Dunbar family scrapbook is a full-page Parker campaign ad from 1916, boasting a distinguished photographic portrait of the candidate. Scrawled in handwriting at the top is this: "The man that helped us when in distress."

Four years later, during Parker's second try at the governorship, it was Percy Dunbar, out of all of his elite Opelousas supporters, who was elected chairman of his St. Landry campaign. But on the eve of the Democratic primary, tragedy befell the chairman, just a few miles from its first striking place back in August 1912. At Second Lake, where he was now officially a shareholding member, Percy and several other men were out hunting, with the club's longtime black caretaker, Sebe Frilot, serving as guide. When the baying hounds chased a deer their way, the hunters readied to fire from their elevated wooden stands, and Sebe, wearing his standard khaki jacket, crouched and scurried aside. Percy saw the soft brown shape bouncing in front of the hounds, and fired twice, filling Sebe's head and back with buckshot. He soon died.

When Percy returned home, his jacket was stained with Sebe's blood, and his shame filled the Dunbar household. At fourteen, Bobby was old enough to understand what had occurred. Word of the death spread from the black communities of the Lakes to the homes of the wealthiest whites of Opelousas, where Sebe was well known and admired. On Tuesday, as his body was carried to town for burial, politics marched on. White men came out in force to vote, and toast their new governor. St. Landry carried the largest majority for John M. Parker of any parish in the state.

PERCY'S NEXT ACT of violence was not accidental.

In the spring and summer of 1920, he was estimating, and advertising in the trade journal *National Lumberman*, the sale of cypress and longleaf pine tracts in Florida, anywhere from 50,000 to 150,000 acres for $10 to $20 an acre. As Lessie later recalled, this was business of such a magnitude that Percy felt it necessary to move to Orlando, apparently near where the property was located. He had been gone for four full months when the incident occurred, in the lobby of the Empire, "Orlando's Most Popular Medium Priced Hotel." It was the night of August 23, 1920, the eight-year anniversary of Bobby's disappearance.

Later, Percy would admit that he'd drunk some moonshine, but would insist it had not contributed to his actions. Other elements of his account are equally implausible. He had his knife out, he would explain, because he was trimming a bit of leather from his shoe. Surrounded by a group of men, he was disparaging restaurant cuisine in Orlando, particularly the "rotten food" he'd recently been served at the Palace Café. A nineteen-year-old waiter from the Palace named Perry Joiner happened to be in the lobby at the same time and took offense. Words were exchanged, and according to eyewitnesses, Percy made the first move, lunging with his knife suddenly. At least one of the gashes in Joiner's body was in the back. Joiner turned and counterattacked with blows to Percy's eyes and face. He seized Percy and the two toppled to the floor, Joiner punching and Percy slashing. By the end of it, young Joiner had six knife wounds, some "several inches long," and was rushed to the hospital. Percy was arrested and taken to jail.

He remained behind bars for at least a few days, and possibly as long as two weeks, as Perry Joiner recovered, losing fifteen pounds by the time of his release from the hospital. On September 6, Percy appeared before the Orlando mayor on charges of aggravated assault, but pled guilty to a lesser charge of disturbing the peace by fighting. He was fined $125 and ordered to pay Joiner's medical bill.

A few days into his jail time, Percy was approached by a reporter for the *Tampa Morning Tribune*, who gleaned that he was in fact the father of the famous Bobby Dunbar. In the interview, Percy did everything he could to win sympathy, asserting that he had spent $20,000 in the search for his son, boasting of his sterling political reputation in Louisiana and prominent business references in Florida, asserting that this brush with violence was "the first trouble I got into," an anomaly, and that he was a victim as well: "I might have hit him first, but he sure did work on me." He also expressed his sincere desire that news of the violence would not reach his wife and children back home.

The New Orleans dailies might have overlooked the story, but in mid-September, it made the news in at least two smaller Louisiana papers, neither too far from Opelousas. Lessie undoubtedly found out. And it wasn't her only discovery, either. Percy had all his mail sent to his office, but at one point, she caught sight of a letter from Orlando, in what she knew to be a woman's handwriting. She also spotted in Percy's possession a photo of an unfamiliar woman, whom he insisted was his cousin.

Alongside her marital mistrust and embarrassment over the assault boiled an older unhappiness with life in Opelousas. A sizable portion of the town either doubted or disbelieved that the child she was raising was her son. By extension, they saw Lessie herself as either pitifully delusional, a hardened and brittle liar, or vacillating somewhere between the two. Any person would find life within that spectrum intolerable.

But when she asked Percy to consider a move to New Orleans, he resisted: he was the parish notary now, and his Opelousas business, "at my age," was impossible to just move. What's more, he admitted later, "I owed large sums of money and to secure the same had obtained endorsements of friends which I was forced to protect." In other words, if he appeared to be running away from debt, Percy would destroy not just his own good name, but that of his friends. Lessie told him she could go to work herself to help, but still Percy refused. She suggested that they could keep up residences in both places, but that was even more financially imprudent. Eventually she took a firm stand for herself. "She became insistent and determined and finally left for New Orleans," Percy later recalled, adding—an afterthought to them both—"leaving our two children with my parents in order that they might complete their scholastic year."

Though Lessie had family in New Orleans, on both her side and Percy's, she took up a more neutral residence in a boardinghouse run by the Sisters of Mount Carmel. Special to Lessie since her girlhood at their school in Washington, Louisiana, the order provided sanctuary from a fraying marriage, and—in Lessie's flight from a community that doubted her—a home free of judgment.

Word of Lessie's arrival in New Orleans quickly reached the new city editor of the *States*, Mrs. Christian Schertz, who in May 1913 had persistently invited Bobby Dunbar to be the guest of honor at the Sunshine Society's spring carnival. A working woman herself and a suffragist, Mrs. Schertz leapt at the opportunity to report not just on the arrival of the famous mother from Opelousas but on her fledgling business venture. Her February 1922 feature was titled "Bobbie Dunbar's Mother True Blue; Comes to New Orleans to Develop Her Splendid Talent":

> For years Lessie Dunbar has realized that she was possessed of a gift for design, its form taking a sartorial twist. She has developed from a child with deft fingers for doll clothes into a woman with fairy fingers and a genius for drawing lovely garments. She has come to New Orleans to engage in this work. It would be a long time before the gifted young woman could finance a shop of her

own, so she expects to work with others or to [do] private work in order to be self-sustaining while "playing for place."

The true purpose for Lessie's new business, as Mrs. Schertz reported it, was to earn enough to afford a proper education for Bobby and Alonzo, in New Orleans. Lessie's move from home, then, was a selfless act, "her mother sacrifice."

Percy's version of these events was more complicated: while Lessie "paid in cash a portion of the expenses of [the] children," he himself was footing most of the bill, not just for the boys but also for Lessie herself. And over time, her New Orleans "experiment" became less and less possible for him to sustain.

On the dicey issue of the Dunbars' financial woes, Mrs. Schertz's report gave the sunniest spin: Percy had spent everything he had during his heroic search for his son nine years ago, and the Dunbars had refused a "small fortune" to put the boy in pictures. And as she had done in 1913, Mrs. Schertz gossiped about the boy's health. Though she coaxed it into a prettified quote from Lessie, the raw, underlying facts were chilling:

> We both feel that we have been blessed for [keeping Bobby out of the limelight], for Bobby has undergone four operations and only the quiet country life we live could have pulled him through. He has never fully recovered from the cruelties to which he was subjected, his shyness of everyone, and nerves preventing perfect concentration in his school work. But, at last he is coming out of the fog he has been in and been gently treated in every way.

For almost the entire past decade, from childhood into adolescence, Bobby Dunbar had been suffering, physically and mentally, from the effects of his kidnapping.

In the absence of medical records, it is impossible to know what these four "operations" were. Adenoid removal was the procedure most mentioned back in 1913. After Bobby was hit by a car in 1916, an operation may have been required, though Mrs. Schertz's and/or Lessie's implication was that all of the procedures stemmed from maladies acquired during Bobby's travels with Walters. Hookworm, which he may well have had back in 1912–13, requires nothing like an "operation," but it does necessitate treatment, sometimes repeatedly. If untreated or incompletely treated, hookworm can result in anemia, whose symptoms, according to Dr. Bass, the hookworm pioneer of Marion County, Mississippi, can include: "melancholia, hypochondriasis . . . [i]nsomnia, and night terrors," and trouble keeping awake during the day.

Of course, nervousness, "shyness of everyone," and lack of concentration in school probably had less to do with what might have happened, and might still be happening, to the boy's body, and more to do with what had happened, and was still happening to his mind. For those *States* readers who believed that Bobby was truly Bruce Anderson—and there were many—these words of Lessie's must have had a far different implication than what she had intended: "He has never fully recovered from the cruelties to which he was subjected." What sorts of cruelties, subjected to him by whom or what, and when? It had been a cruelty to rip Bruce away from his caretaker, to force on him a new name and fill his head with memories and terrors that he never had. It had been a cruelty to parade him across the state, to allow the whole world to stare at and photograph him, and to repeatedly undress and probe him in public. It had been a cruelty to teach him, directly or indirectly, to rebuff his true mother and hate his guardian. To these readers, Lessie's words in 1922 must have resurrected a wellspring of outrage, the very opposite of the inspiration that Mrs. Schertz had hoped to convey. If the child had suffered through all of that, how could he help but now be "shy of everyone"? How could he help anxiety and constant distraction? *The boy didn't know who he was.*

Yet, regardless of what Lessie had done in the past, her desire to see the boy thrive *was* a great part of her desperate, impractical motivation to move. She knew that, as Bobby grew up, the same doubt that Opelousas had leveled at her would be leveled at him, and that he would only grow more and more conscious of it. Outside of Opelousas he had a better chance to escape that doubt, if not unscathed, then at least not destroyed. In New Orleans, they would still know his name, but they were more likely to know him simply as the "kidnapped boy found." Lessie's impulse to erase the past was self-serving, to be sure, but it was the only way she saw to give her son a future.

The earliest official records of the boys' school attendance in New Orleans come from the following year, when both were enrolled at Holy Cross College, a private preparatory school run by its namesake Catholic brotherhood, situated on the site of an old orphanage on the banks of the Mississippi in the Lower Ninth Ward. The school boasted a stained-glass chapel for daily Mass, a modern gymnasium for athletics, and a formal dining room. With paths along the levees, acres of playing fields, and a herd of Holsteins, it was a pastoral campus, yet just a quick streetcar ride away for the New Orleans parents who came by for visiting hours, on Sunday or Thursday afternoons.

In the 1923–24 school year, Bobby and Alonzo were both enrolled in the Preparatory Department, "designed for those students that are not sufficiently advanced to take up high-school studies." At fifteen, Bobby was in grade 7A. Meanwhile, their fifteen-year-old cousin George Kelt (who'd been used at the Walters trial as a "decoy double" for Bobby) was already a sophomore in high school, singled out as one of the brightest in his class. As freshmen and sophomores took up algebra, Latin, civil government, and public speaking, Bobby—alongside his younger brother—studied arithmetic, reading, penmanship, and geography. His delayed "advancement" was not altogether unusual: judging by their group photo in the Holy Cross yearbook, the "Preps" appear to have ranged in age from early teens to midteens. But by the end of 1924, only Alonzo Dunbar was a graduate of the Preps course; Bobby was not. And only Alonzo would return the following year.

During Bobby's brief stint at Holy Cross, Lessie and Percy were not the only ones working for his tuition. In September 1923 Bobby was granted an employment permit, with Lessie's signed approval. It specified "No Night Work," so whatever the job, he likely was working it after school and on weekends.

In the spring, Bobby did have time for an extracurricular activity. The boy who had thrown the first pitch during his hometown's summer winning streak eleven years ago was a member of Holy Cross Junior Baseball Team. In the group photo, Bobby stands at the far right, one of the two shortest players, his eyes squinty and bagged, and his mouth upturned into the slightest of half smiles.

After Holy Cross, the next chapter of Bobby and Alonzo's education unfolded along the shorefront of Gulfport, Mississippi, where stood the stark barracks of the Gulf Coast Military Academy. "Send us the boy, and we will return you the man" was the academy's slogan, advertised in magazines nationwide, boasting "excellent moral tone and surroundings," followed by reassurance to parents that "the nearest town is five miles away." No official records of the Dunbars' stint at the institution survive, but one student from a decade later, biologist E. O. Wilson, chronicled his own academy experience, which affords insight into Bobby's and Alonzo's. Wilson, too, was a child of a dissolving marriage: "While my parents untangled their lives," he wrote, "they looked for a place that could offer a guarantee of security . . ." The academy experience was nearly as strict and brutal as the military itself, he recalled, a "lockstep" bugle-punctuated daily routine, from six in the morning to nine thirty at night. And though the white sand and gentle Gulf were always in full view, just yards away, there was little time for leisure.

The only surviving record of the Dunbar boys' time here is a photo, this one a parent-child school portrait. Alonzo and Bobby stand on either side of Lessie, their trousers tucked into knee-high boots, gray wool uniform jackets fastened up to the collar, smiles on both faces. Lessie stands between them, in a long lace-collared coat, a simple veiled hat, and a rolled-up and ribbon-tied document, perhaps a prop, clutched in her gloved hand. Her pose, flanked by her two beaming boys, would suggest pride, but her expression itself is a cipher. If she was preparing or attempting to smile, her mouth shows no trace of it. If anything, Lessie looks self-conscious, distracted, and sad.

In private, her marriage was crumbling beyond repair. "During [Lessie's] residence in New Orleans and when I could spare the time to go and see her," Percy later recalled, "she would become quarrelsome and abusive and accused me of immoral conduct and breaches of my marriage vows." Specifically, it was Percy's life in Florida that ate at Lessie, not just the 1920 trip to Orlando but also several more extended visits since. According to Lessie's later recollection, after repeated confrontations, he finally admitted to an affair.

All the while, parenting was an afterthought, at best. Unbeknownst to Percy, Lessie allowed Alonzo to sign up for service aboard two international commercial steamships, at the tender age of fifteen. From April to June 1925, the *West Hobomac* took him to Naples, Italy, and other Mediterranean ports, then back to New Orleans, where he boarded the *Duquesne* for a two-month voyage to and from the United Kingdom. On both trips, Alonzo worked in the engine room, as a wiper, the department's only "beginner" position, cleaning, polishing, and helping out with repair. He earned somewhere around $75 a month, and the service certificate for his second voyage noted that he was of very good character and ability. That certificate also lists his age as eighteen. When Percy found out, he was outraged, as much at the trip and age deception as at his wife's reckless complicity.

Meanwhile, Lessie further inflamed her husband by seeking to turn their older son against him. In a letter to Bobby, back in Opelousas for summer vacation, "she repeated the charges of immorality on my part," recalled Percy, who read the letter himself, "stating therein that she proposed to go to Florida to support her charges of infidelity, and greatly to my mortification and shame." While the letter itself has not survived, its likely envelope was affixed in the Dunbar family scrapbook. On the envelope's exterior, where anyone bringing in the mail could have read it (unless it was secreted inside another envelope), Lessie wrote, "Read this *my* boy and be good, for all I have suffered for *you*, I would gladly suffer it again."

The "my" was underlined twice. It was probably Lessie's theatrical way of asserting to Percy her primacy in a looming custody battle. Whether or not the other connotation of an emphasized "my" occurred to Lessie or not (Bobby was hers as opposed to Julia Anderson's), the question of identity was very much on the young man's mind in his teenage years. And he would soon give voice to it himself.

Bobby wasn't the only one with whom Lessie shared too much. In a 1925 letter to Percy, she wrote that she had run into John Lewis in a New Orleans department store "and brought up our domestic trials," making it clear that divorce was the only option. Her letter closed with this: "Be good to my Boy and see that he takes good care of his body." Irate at Lessie's public exposure of him, and fearful of greater exposure still, Percy took action, calling upon Lewis in September 1925 to file papers for separation. The petition detailed Lessie's move to New Orleans, her recent letter to Bobby, and her threat to go to Florida, all of which "constitutes cruelty toward him and renders their living together insupportable and unbearable." As to her charges of infidelity, Percy's petition offered a flat denial. In terms of custody, the petition proposed that the boys were old enough to decide for themselves which parent they wanted to live with.

To Lessie, the charge of "cruelty" was outrageously unjust, and Percy's denial was a boldfaced lie. Though she received a summons to appear before the Opelousas court, she did not honor it. In her absence, Judge Pavy rendered a judgment of separation, noting that "the undisputed testimony evidences a character of cruelty which justifies" the court's action. Without Lessie present, Judge Pavy had little choice but to take Percy's word that her allegations were both false and malicious.

For Lessie, this could not be the last word. In mid-1926, despite Percy's alleged threats "to kill me" if she did so, she finally went to Florida. What she discovered there was far more devastating than anything she had imagined. Through police detectives in Tampa and Orlando, she cobbled together what appeared to have been a lengthy affair with one woman,

Atrice McCoullough. She and Percy had been found and charged with "occupying a room for immoral purposes" at least two times and likely more.

The most recent incident occurred in March 1926 in Tampa (likely sparked by Lessie's own investigation). According to a police detective's report, when he arrived at McCoullough's boardinghouse room just before midnight with two warrants, the woman, dressed in a "loose house dress and red room slippers," commenced a vicious verbal assault. Mr. Dunbar, whose coat was off and collar was unfastened, claimed that "he was single and was going to marry this woman." The detective reminded Percy of his wife in Louisiana, to which Percy barked that "it was none of my damn business." After their arrests, both were released on $50 bonds.

But the worst blow to Lessie was not an assault or an act of adultery, but a marriage record that finally tied the whole sordid affair together. In Lessie's handwriting, on the packet of divorce papers that she saved for her entire life, the union is recorded: "Atrice A. McCoullough, Nov. 3, 1923, married [Perry] Joiner in Orlando."

With this, it all made sense. Lessie could only conclude that Percy had been romantically involved with Atrice McCoullough since 1920. Even then, it had been far more than a dalliance. It had been her that Percy and Perry Joiner fought over, not Orlando's "rotten food." Even when Perry won her in marriage three years later, Percy and Atrice continued their affair. In 1926, when Percy told the detective that he intended to marry Atrice, he probably was telling the truth. After all, he had filed his own divorce papers in Opelousas and was legally separated. And if Lessie's investigation were to be believed, he had given Atrice his wife's diamond rings.

For several months, Lessie remained in Florida, gathering arrest records and sworn affidavits. She tried to file for divorce in Orlando, but her lawyer backed out, so she found another lawyer and filed in Tampa. In September 1926 and again in January 1927, she testified before a stunned Hillsborough circuit court judge who grilled her on her rationale for seeking divorce in Florida instead of Louisiana and expressed skepticism over the veracity of her claims. While her testimony does smack of a spurned wife's jealous ravings, the judge could not disbelieve the sworn words of two police officers. On January 21, he granted Lessie a divorce based on Percy's infidelity. Though Lessie had petitioned for custody of the boys and alimony as well, the Florida court issued no judgment in those matters.

Less than two weeks later in Opelousas, Judge Pavy granted Percy a divorce based on the couple's inability to reconcile during their separation. Further, Pavy awarded full custody of both boys to their father.

By now Bobby and Alonzo were living in Opelousas and attending public high school. From 1925 to 1927, Bobby supplemented the family income by serving in the Louisiana National Guard, an extended stint that earned him longevity pay. His 1927 discharge lists him as unqualified in marksmanship, in good physical condition, and of excellent character. Even before his discharge was official, he and Percy went to court to file for his emancipation, which "relieved [him] of the disabilities that attach to minors, with full power to do and perform all acts as fully as if he had attained the age of twenty-one years." At nineteen, Bobby was now free to work as an adult. When or if he graduated from high school is unknown.

Returning to Opelousas in his late teenage years, Bobby was something of an outsider at first, but his childhood celebrity status—which had not worn off—afforded him social entrée. Aline Perrault, who had chased after Bobby at his 1913 homecoming, recalls attending parties and gatherings at her aunt's home as a teenager where Bobby was often the center of attention. Invariably, the subject of the kidnapping came up, and by now Bobby probably had a practiced way of telling his parents' version of the story. But on more than one occasion, the deeper and thornier layer of the story came to the surface: the debate over his true identity. And on this question, Bobby had no stock answer at the ready. In fact, he was so troubled by the matter that he confessed to both Aline and her aunt, more than once, that, deep down, he did not know who he was.

As Bobby grappled with the question of his identity, and struggled to understand his tumultuous childhood and his parents' ugly divorce, he was largely on his own. Even if he could have turned to Lessie for answers, she was not there.

After the divorce, she fled again, this time farther from Opelousas than ever before. It is unknown why she landed in Oceana, Virginia, and how she survived there. But in her reinvention, at least one element of her old self was still alive: the need to be needed. Lessie became a loyal caretaker to an old man who owned an iris farm. "[S]he has been so attentive to me, and has nursed me for the last six years without cost to me," the man wrote in his 1932 will, bequeathing to her his entire estate. For Lessie, who had just been humiliated by a brief, ill-fated second marriage (her husband, it turned out, was still wed), care for the farmer was a welcome pursuit, with little emotional complication.

Meanwhile, Percy Dunbar's health had been declining for years, and in 1931, after a protracted illness, he died.

For all practical purposes, Bobby was an orphan at twenty-five.

NOT LONG INTO his return to Opelousas, he met a girl from Eunice, Louisiana, at a dance. Her name was Marjorie Byars and she had never heard of Bobby Dunbar, the famous kidnapped child of yesteryear. In fact, she turned down his first request for a dance. Only when his name came up at home did Marjorie learn his history from her mother, who had—like mothers across the state—cried over his loss and return.

But while the trauma of Bobby's childhood endeared him to Marjorie's family, and served as a bond between Bobby and Marjorie herself, who had lost her father when she was a little girl, it was not the defining characteristic of their budding romance. In fact, quite the opposite: with Marjorie and in her home at Eunice, Bobby was free of his past, welcomed without doubt or question, and able to discover and create himself, as part of a family, honestly and openly for the first time in his life. For Bobby, Marjorie Byars's mother and stepfather, a larger-than-life Cajun named Onezime Babineaux, were parents he had never had. They were stable, decent, and loving.

Very early in the relationship, Bobby asked Marjorie to marry him. He knew they belonged together, and in her heart, she did, too. But, as the family story goes, she was more practical, insisting that before they got married and started a family, they needed at least something of a savings.

There may have been more to Marjorie's hesitation than finances. She had come to peace with the pain of her childhood, but the same could not be said of Bobby. If he told Aline Perrault that he didn't know who he was, he was sure to have shared that sentiment with Marjorie. And during the year before and the year after Percy Dunbar's death, events would conspire to force Bobby's doubts to the surface again.

First there was the 1930 letter to Alex Robertson from William Walters, a man Bobby had grown up to remember and fear as a deranged and abusive kidnapper. What kidnapper would write a letter, gently wondering what kind of man his victim had turned out to be? Surely, if Bobby had any relationship with Percy at all in 1930, he would have broached that subject and probed that question.

Knowing that he faced death, Percy quite possibly could no longer give Bobby a ready answer. Before he died, he told Alonzo—the *younger* son—to take care of his brother. Not the other way around. For all his past hubris and unhinged vitriol, in his final years, Percy could see that Bobby was still lost.

One year after Percy's death, almost to the day, the Lindbergh baby was kidnapped. When reporters came around for interviews with Louisiana's own famous kidnapping victim, regardless what answers Percy had given Bobby before he died, Bobby was now faced with retelling the story *as he himself remembered it,* in his own words.

On the core question of his identity, Bobby seemed comfortable and certain enough to crack jokes: "A lot of people still believe I was eaten by an alligator. I can assure you I was not." In telling of his abduction, his memory largely mirrored the case built by the Dunbars and prosecutors in 1913: his hair had been dyed red, he had been dressed like a girl, taken around to beg for food. He was beaten horribly by Walters, particularly when he tried to tell people who he was, and he still had scars on his body.

But time, a hazy memory, and confusion over conflicting retellings had all taken their toll (and perhaps again reporters got elements of the interview wrong). Bobby recalled that former governor John M. Parker had actually been part of the search for him, back in the fall of 1912. In one interview, he suggested that the unwed mother of the "other boy" was the kidnapper's sister. And in one interview, he referred to Walters as "Walton."

Sometimes Bobby's memory had a fable-like quality: a story he had been told rather than lived. "Another incident outstanding in his then childish mind was the Christmas morning spent with Walters. No toys, Bobby remembered, and, as Walters told him, "nothing for you but ashes and switches."

But it is in Bobby's description of his abduction at Swayze Lake that something far more profound than a foggy childhood memory emerges: "When I realized what had happened, I was frightened, of course, and suppose I cried, but can't remember it very distinctly."

In describing the fate of the "other boy," Bobby was similarly speculative about his emotional state: "[Walters] and a man we had picked up, who was riding with us, buried him in the woods. I must have been frightened at this but I don't remember my emotions clearly. Maybe I was too young to be affected."

He could piece together what had happened to him, and he may have even been able to see glimpses of it in his mind. *But he could not feel it.*

By contrast, Bobby remembered the 1912 floods, and "an experience when practically all the foodstuff in Walters's buggy was dumped in a creek . . . when the buggy in which he and Walters were riding sank. This, he says, was one of the few funny incidents he experienced in the eight months."

Giddy laughter aboard a tipping, sinking wagon was a *feeling* that Bobby still remembered distinctly. Unlike crying or being frightened, this laughter was a lived memory. In the midst of what should have been an ordeal of terror, Bobby remembered the pure childish glee in witnessing calamity, and adult powerlessness in the face of it.

The tension between true memory and inherited legend came to a head in Bobby's commentary *after* he described the fate of the "other boy." "And I don't believe it ever come out that the child had been killed," he was quoted. "I must have been too young to tell anything about it coherently, and no one else except Walton knew about it." Of course, the other boy's death had been no secret at all in 1913–14. Neither he nor Cowart had been allowed to swear to it on the stand, but the public knew all about it.

And yet, almost twenty years later, Bobby felt it *had not* been known, its significance still had not been understood, or it hadn't been fully believed. Indeed, as Judge Pavy's daughter Ida recalls, Opelousans grew up hearing about the Bobby Dunbar case, and adults debated it publicly for decades, not simply as a crime of yesteryear, but "like one of those unsolved mysteries." In telling it now, Bobby hoped, the thing would at last be settled. For the public, but also for himself.

As haunted as he was by unknowing, that was not the most startling element of his reflections back. According to one report, "Speaking of his kidnapping Bobby calls it 'a terrible experience, *but one I would not take anything for.*'" In another report, he is quoted on the subject of Walters: "He just stole me for a companion—he didn't want money." And finally: *"I would love to see him and talk to him."* This is a sentiment that Bobby may never have uttered in public with Percy still alive, the one person most invested in a portrait of Walters as a ruthless villain. How could he yearn to reconnect with a man who beat him without mercy? How could he feel such unguarded nostalgia and affection?

The Associated Press ran one of these 1932 "looking back" interviews, and it was published in newspapers across the south. William Cantwell Walters, wherever he was, could hardly have missed it. Though no record of further correspondence or a reunion between the two exists, Bobby's statement—*"I would love to see him and talk to him"*—was certainly a response to Walters's 1930 letter. It was more than an offering of peace; it was an invitation. Having just lost Percy, Bobby was reaching out to the only other man who had come close to being his father.

AT THE TIME of his return to the headlines, Bobby was working in a steam laundry in Opelousas, saving up so that Marjorie might finally marry him. He was an orphan in love. The morass of his early childhood had just been resurrected, but more than that, Bobby was still reeling from the chaos and abandonment he had lived through afterward. "Those boys weren't raised up," Alonzo's wife, Anna Lee, would later recall, "they were jerked up." And with the two people most responsible for that "jerking-up" gone from his adult life altogether, Bobby was consumed with, and trapped in, a volatile adolescent anger. Marriage, family, a stable adulthood, all of that was still a remote dream.

Fittingly, both of the calamities that next befell him occurred in this limbo of time and place, the road from Opelousas (his past) to Eunice (his future). Both times, Bobby was on his way to pick Marjorie up for a date.

In one accident, the family story goes, his car veered off the road and ended up on its side. Bobby flew into a panicked rage and heaved himself into the automobile. At last, he managed to right it, and return it—battered but operative—back onto the road.

Another night, the Opelousas-to-Eunice highway was closed for construction. Determined to make his date with Marjorie, Bobby concocted a lunatic scheme with Alonzo for him to get there: they drove their uncle Archie's car up onto the railroad tracks and took the tires off, so that its rims rested on the rails. Bobby took off in the car and rode along smoothly, but before he got to Eunice, the lights of an approaching train appeared. Unable to jump the car off the rails, Bobby did his best to signal the train—to no avail. It was not going to stop, and it was going to kill him. At the last minute, Bobby leapt out of the car and away from the inevitable collision. "You can imagine what happened to the car," his friend Earl Briggs recalls with a wry smile only possible with decades of retrospect. Archie's car was demolished.

The wedding was postponed until Bobby could make a dent in repaying his uncle for the car. Even then, unbeknownst to Marjorie, Bobby had to borrow $50 from Archie to convince her of his fiscal solvency.

In 1935, after nine long years of courtship, they finally were wed.

Even this milestone of Bobby's new life, however, was shadowed by the events of his childhood. "Wedding Recalls 1912 Kidnapping" was the headline of the *Times-Picayune* story, which, like most of the wedding coverage, resurrected details of Bobby's abduction and recovery, with scant attention to bride or ceremony.

Three months later, a stranger from that past, his attention sparked by reportage of the wedding, reached out to the newlywed husband in a letter: Heyman Gabriel, the jeweler/dairy farmer from Mobile, who, in late 1912, had spotted one of the earliest crippled tramps to be arrested, Edgar Hooks. But by 1935, Gabriel's memory of his role in the case had become much grander: "I am the man who was instrumental in your recovery from the one-legged tinker who had kidnapped you," he insisted erroneously. Though he "distinctly remember[s] your late father coming to Mobile to pay me a reward which I, of course, declined," it wasn't money he was now after. Gabriel was writing his memoirs at the request of his son, and wanted Bobby to furnish information on the case.

Bobby did not write back. One month later, Gabriel wrote again, this time petulant and aggrieved:

> Not having heard from you, I am just wondering whether my letter reached you, or whether you objected to showing me the courtesy of a reply.
>
> Of course, you realize that I have other ways of getting the information that I desire, such as newspaper files, etc. But if you really object to answering my letter, please so advise me so I will not expect this information from you and not be delayed in my purpose, and I assure you that I will have no ill feeling against you as a result of your refusal to furnish me this data.

Even if the first letter were just a source of bemusement, the aggression of the follow-up must have unnerved not just Bobby but Marjorie as well. To a great many strangers out there, the man Marjorie had just married was a celebrity, who by the accident of an event in his childhood, had forever relinquished his claim to privacy. The public would always feel entitled to Bobby Dunbar and his story.

By now Bobby himself knew that he couldn't fight this celebrity, and was savvy enough to make it work *for* him. He christened his new career venture, an all-night operation in downtown Opelousas, the Bobby Dunbar Service Station, and business boomed.

"All he had to do was put his pants on the bed, and I'd get pregnant," Marjorie would later joke. Within three years, they had two sons, Bobby

Jr. and Johnny. Marjorie lost a pair of twins, then had daughter Mary, and fifteen years after Bobby Jr. had been born came little Gerald.

When World War II broke out, Bobby did his part, shuttering the service station and moving his young family to New Orleans to work as a welder in the Avondale Shipyard. It was welding, he later recalled, that ruined his eyes. Returning to Opelousas, he went to work as a salesman for his brother Alonzo, who owned a booming welding supply business servicing all of southern Louisiana. But as with all his professional successes, Alonzo easily grew restless, sold the company and moved on, leaving Bobby, who didn't get along with his new boss, to scramble for a better job. He turned to his friend Earl Briggs, who had worked for Bobby at the service station and now ran a fledgling electrical supply company. Bobby offered to be Earl's salesman, using his own car and working solely on commission. Earl could hardly refuse, and in his first year working, Bobby brought in a flood of new business and the company saw record-breaking profits. Soon enough, Bobby had a salary, a company car, and the beginning of a lifelong career. His childhood fame may have opened the doors of the homes and businesses he knocked on, but it was Bobby's way with customers—his fond smile, gentle manner, and easy rapport—that was key to his success. He was a salesman that people *wanted* to see.

Early in their marriage, Bobby and Marjorie "shopped around" for a church to join. Marjorie pressed for the Catholic church, but Bobby— perhaps owing to his difficult upbringing in that tradition—was less than enthusiastic. But like everything in their married life, they found and created a religious life for themselves, apart from their pasts. Over the years, as Bobby grew more personally devoted, his commitment to the church strengthened. Church was not just a place for worship but also for dances, barbecues, and socializing. It was the focus of his and Marjorie's community. After his induction into the church's fraternal organization, the Knights of Columbus, Bobby fast became a passionate and highly respected member, active in charity efforts and work with local Boy Scouts, eventually reaching the order's highest rank.

But it was neither church nor work by which Bobby defined his life most deeply. Every morning before he left home, he dabbed a bit of Marjorie's perfume on his handkerchief, so that she would be with him while he traveled. And though his route took him far from Opelousas each day, he was always back by suppertime. "Where's my baby?!" he called out when he opened the door. If he happened to find Marjorie gone, their children recalled, Bobby would grow anxious, pace the floors and panic. Without her there, he was not quite home. He was not settled or safe.

Bobby took to fatherhood naturally and with passion, dedicating his heart to the project of raising and teaching his children. He gave them the childhood he himself had barely had, protected it ferociously, and lived in it with them.

Bobby taught the children to swim, hunt, fish, and drive. He built a platform in the oak tree in the front yard, strung up a cable and pulley to create a zip line all the way to the Catawba in back. He welded together four-inch iron pipes to create a swing set. One day he brought home cypress logs and supervised the construction of a fourteen-foot pirogue. Before every family outing, they would fill the boat with water from the hose to swell the wood and seal the cracks, then mount two outboard motors. On the bayous, the Dunbars spent long afternoons fishing and exploring, the whole family crowded into the boat, one or two children dragging along behind on a homemade surfboard.

In the late 1940s, Bobby Jr. and Johnny—like other preadolescent boys across the nation—caught the model airplane fever. When their local club, the Flying Cajuns, fell apart, Bobby Sr. could not see these boys' spirit of flight crushed, and so he stepped in to resurrect it. Assuming the title of club "advisor" was not at all against his will, either: Bobby was an avid model plane builder and flyer himself. Every Wednesday night in the summers and Fridays during the school year, the boys and their fathers met in the Dunbars' garage to build new planes, rebuild wrecked ones, paint, perfect, and test their models in the field at nearby City Park.

These were not tiny plastic kit models, meant for posing on a shelf or dangling from a bedroom ceiling. These were homemade and hand-crafted, with wingspans as big as a buzzard's. Powered by gasoline, teth-ered by long piano wire to handheld control gear operated by the boys, these machines swooped, circled, looped, and corkscrewed. For blocks around, for days on end, the summer air was filled with their distinctive buzz. The Cajuns even built an airplane for Alonzo's young daughter, Elizabeth, who recalls fondly that she wrecked it.

In meets with clubs from other towns, the boys competed in "combat," with two planes vying to rip through streamers attached to their oppo-nent's craft. They won prizes for best stunts and worst crack-ups. Both Johnny and Bobby were team stars, and in the summer of 1951, Bobby was allowed to take the train to Dallas to compete in a national competi-tion. Bobby Sr. took the Cajuns to another national meet in Philadelphia.

When Johnny took up football in high school (Bobby, too, though he spent most of his time on the bench), their father found a new way of staying involved in their pastimes. He was in charge of the team's mascot, a live wildcat. At every game, Bobby hauled the caged cat on his trailer to the field and parked it in the end zone, and watched the game from there.

So close in age and with so many overlapping interests, Bobby and Johnny, quite naturally, shared a fraternal competitive streak. For the most part, it was friendly. But once, when their father found them in a physical scuffle, he intervened with unforgettable emotion. "You can fight with the whole world," he told them, "but don't fight with your brother."

Bobby Jr. was musically inclined, and during his teenage years, late into the night, could be found at the piano in the living room. The neighbors may have complained, but for Bobby Sr., in bed with Marjorie, the music wafting through the house was like a lullaby. It had been so since his own childhood.

As the only girl, Mary enjoyed a special place in her father's life and heart. Piling onto their parents' bed around the radio, or later sitting in front of the television, it was she that got first dibs on Bobby Sr.'s lap. As he rewired lamps, installed sockets, or strung a rosary of blue Christmas lights on the front porch, Mary followed her father around and picked up his knack for all things electrical, a talent she'd carry for the rest of her life. On cold winter nights, after Bobby had checked under her bed for vampires or monsters, he placed a quart mason jar, filled with hot water, at her feet to keep her warm. He knew what cold sleep felt like.

One of Mary's favorite spots was at her father's side as he tended the barbecue pit in the backyard. The barbecue was, and is, a sacred tradition in the Dunbar family, inherited by Bobby and Marjorie from the Byars family, a regular feature of their courtship. As Mary remembers, Bobby would start the fire early Sunday morning, then go to Mass. By the time he returned, bearing donuts for the kids, the coals were perfect and the meat was ready to go on.

On school vacations and over the summer, Bobby made an event of taking his children, individually, out on his sales route, for a day here and there, or a few days in succession. It afforded Marjorie somewhat of a break, and for the kids, young Gerald especially, it was an adventure.

As Bobby idled the Ford Fairlane at the gate of St. Mary's Ironworks, Gerald recalls his heart racing with excitement. There were stacks of massive pipes, trucks, and cranes everywhere. This was another world. When they parked and headed to the office, Bobby fitted a hard hat snugly onto

Gerald's head. "How you doing, Bobby?" the manager greeted with a smile. Then, nodding down at Gerald standing by his side: "I see you got a helper today."

At around noon, Bobby and his helper would break out a packed lunch or, if they were near Eunice, they would stop and eat with Marjorie's relatives. Best of all was gumbo and a hot plate lunch from the Yellow Bowl in Franklin. Passing through sugarcane fields or spotting a clump of cut cane that had fallen from a truck, Bobby would stop to "harvest" dessert, cutting the stalk into quarters, sucking on them with the kids until all the juices were gone, then spitting out the fiber.

When Bobby was not out on the job, he could often be found in the back shed, at work on a new project. Usually, it was easy to tell what he was working on, but one late fall day, Gerald spotted something he'd never seen before on his father's workbench: a giant round metal contraption, some kind of wheel with spokes. The mystery object stayed out there for some time, and Gerald wondered over it silently, what it was and what kind of tinkering his dad was doing on it. The next time he saw it, it was in downtown, the centerpiece of a Christmas display in the window of Sandoz Hardware Store. It was a Ferris wheel, each of its chairs carrying a small Christmas gift suggestion around and around and around. Not only was it now electrified to rotate constantly but also the frame and each chair had been wired with twinkling Christmas lights. The spinning lights dazzled passersby and sparked many a holiday smile. But the pleasure was far deeper for Gerald, who could privately appreciate its transformation from a lifeless hulk of metal, who knew that it was his father who had brought it to life.

ONCE HE HAD created his own family, Bobby was not crippled by the events of his childhood and questions over his identity. But nor was he free from them. Unbeknownst to his children, and possibly even his wife, he had visited the Poplarville, Mississippi, family of Julia Anderson Rawls at least once. Pearl River County was well beyond the borders of his sales route, but still within a day's drive.

As late as 1963, Bobby was drawn to revisit the site of another key event in his contested childhood history. The Dunbars had driven to Cincinnati for Johnny's wedding, a milestone that certainly stirred deep emotion in Bobby. At fifty-four, his health was in decline as well—his heart was bad—and he was keenly aware of his mortality. On their way back home, traveling through a blizzard, Bobby spotted a sign for Columbia,

Mississippi, and asked Marjorie if they should stop. In the front seat, Marjorie looked over at her husband; she knew what Columbia meant in his childhood. And she knew by his question, and his tone, what he wanted her to say. If you feel like you should, yes, she replied, then let's stop. In the backseat, thirteen-year-old Gerald and eighteen-year-old Mary listened with curiosity.

Bobby pulled off and stepped into a store, where he was pointed to another location, as Mary remembers it, a pharmacy. Here, with the family waiting out in the car, Bobby went inside to talk. He stayed inside for thirty minutes, Gerald recalled, and when he finally returned, not much was said. He did not seem upset, but just quiet, which was not altogether unusual for their father. Who had he spoken to, the children wanted to know?

Those were people who had helped find him, the parents explained. Or possibly, Gerald remembers his father putting it this way: "Those were the people they came to pick me up from."

Bobby may have just wanted to reconnect with a seminal moment in his childhood, plain and simple. And during that conversation in the pharmacy, the deeper question of who he truly was may not have even been on his mind, much less out of his mouth.

But even if Bobby had made peace with that question himself, it was still being raised all around him. And his children had yet to fully face it.

Epilogue

Bobby and Marjorie Dunbar, 1965 (Courtesy of Elizabeth Dunbar)

YOU'RE NOT DUNBARS, you're Andersons."

Particularly when the case was resurrected in the news, the Dunbar children recall being harassed by anonymous phone calls that challenged their father's, and by extension their own, identity. Mary remembers hearing those very words at least two times from an adult female on the other line. Old enough to understand what the caller meant, she alerted her parents, who seemed resigned. Let it go, they told her, there is nothing we can do. While the children grew up believing the callers to be "those people from Mississippi," they could have come from anyone, from anywhere, who recalled their father's story.

As a teenager, Gerald once found himself in a group telling the kidnapping story. When he concluded that his father had been proven to be Bobby Dunbar, as he'd grown up hearing the story told, an elderly gentleman balked. It was never "proven," the man insisted to Gerald; rather the boy simply had been awarded to the Dunbars. There was a difference. Gerald was stunned and unsettled by the correction.

In his late teens, Bobby Jr. had an even more direct experience of doubt about his father's past. The 1953 kidnapping and murder of six-year-old Bobby Greenlease in Missouri again brought public attention to the Dunbar case, including a lengthy retelling of the story, entitled "A Case for a Solomon," written by renowned true-crime reporter Ruth Reynolds and syndicated across the nation. A pair of journalists visited the house to gather research and interview Bobby Sr., and as he spoke, his eldest son listened in. It was the first time that Bobby Jr. had heard all the details of the case, and he was filled with unease. Suddenly the story that he had grown up with had become so much more complicated, no longer a straight-forward case of kidnapping, but a question of contested identity. And in Bobby Jr.'s mind, the answer to that question was far from resolved.

That summer, he was being initiated into the Knights of Columbus. Intended as a rigorous emotional and spiritual challenge, the initiation involved probing the young men with questions tailored to their known vulnerabilities. "Your daddy was that little boy who was kidnapped, right?" they grilled Bobby Jr. "And they didn't find him for a year? How do you know you're who you think you are?"

FOR BOBBY SR. himself, the most troubling reminders of his childhood came with the return to Louisiana of Lessie Dunbar. In the late 1940s, after decades of distance from their mother, Bobby and Alonzo took two separate trips up to Oceana, Virginia. Bobby Jr. and Elizabeth, who traveled with their fathers, remember the same details: an endless field of irises, a farmhouse so run down that Alonzo literally stepped through the broken screen door, and Grandma Lessie, whom they'd never met, smoking a corncob pipe. She was living, it appeared, in ruin and isolation.

The sons eventually persuaded Lessie to return to Opelousas, with the idea that she could help care for Elizabeth, who had recently lost her mother. Instead Elizabeth was sent off to boarding school, and Lessie moved in for about a month with Bobby, Marjorie, and their children.

During that time, the relationship between mother and son, already strained and distant, worsened considerably. It wasn't just that Lessie told Bobby Jr. that Santa Claus didn't exist before he was ready to hear it, or that she was not particularly "grandmotherly," as Elizabeth put it kindly. It wasn't just that she was overbearing and demanding of her hosts, or that she doted over Bobby in a manner that Bobby Jr. observed to be both infantilizing and false. Marjorie Dunbar, who got along with everyone in the world, did not like Lessie Dunbar at all. Beyond that, she did not trust her. Bobby Jr. recalls that it was an ultimatum from his mother that led to Lessie's eviction: "her or me."

But for Bobby, now, the choice was not a difficult one.

The life that he and Marjorie were forging together was not just *unlike* his childhood, under Lessie's care; it was a *reaction against that.* And no matter what Bobby knew or did not know about his blood, Marjorie had given him enough strength of self by now to see and feel just how divorced from reality Lessie had become. Underneath her notorious vanity, behind the affected eccentricity of the corncob pipe, Lessie was lost. Bobby loved her and ached for her, but she was a stranger. There was no place for her—no place for her way of being—in his new family.

She did not last much longer with Alonzo and his new wife, Anna Lee. Alonzo offered her one of his rental homes for a time, then she remarried and moved to Bunkie. In retrospect, Elizabeth recalled the relationship between Lessie and Alonzo as closer, more affectionate, and easier than the one between Lessie and Bobby. As early as the second generation into Bobby's new family, his mother was such a remote presence that they thought her name was "Leslie."

When Alonzo died suddenly in 1959, Bobby Jr. remembers Lessie grieving visibly and loudly over his casket. Sometime after that, she and family members were going through old photos. They came upon a portrait of Bobby Dunbar as an infant, his eyes wide and round, in a white gown holding a toy—the same photo that had been enlarged and perched atop his high chair at the 1913 homecoming. When Lessie turned over the photo, she spotted "Alonzo Dunbar" written on its back. She bristled, snatched a pen, scratched out "Alonzo" and wrote in "Robert." "Don't you think I know my own son?" she snapped. Though the ink color is different, the handwriting of both the original name and its revision appears similar, which would mean that Lessie was, in fact, correcting herself. Whoever made the mistake, it was an understandable one: Alonzo's eyes had retained their round shape for his whole life.

In 1965 Bobby suffered two heart attacks. On the eve of Mary's wedding, no one knew if he would be strong enough to walk her down the aisle. But he made it, crying the whole way. Bobby adored Mary's new husband, Leon, but he had lost his daughter. When the newlyweds pulled out of the driveway for their honeymoon, Bobby said to Bob Jr., "I'll never see her again." He died six weeks later, on March 8, 1966.

Hundreds of Opelousans flooded the Catholic church to pay their respects. But there was one noticeable absence. After attending Mary's wedding and with Bobby's health plainly precarious, Lessie took the train across the country to California to visit her old friend and relative, Ola Fox, now remarried. It was Ola who had been at Lessie's side in April 1913 when she received late-night word from Percy in Columbia that the child there might be their son. Ola had been with Lessie for the entire two-year ordeal that followed. And when Lessie got word that Bobby died, Ola was there again.

Rather than fly back home, Lessie returned on the train. She did not alert anyone that she had arrived in time for the funeral, so many family members assumed she was still in transit. A neighbor, however, saw Lessie alone in her yard on that day. For this son, she was grieving in private.

Lessie lived for another decade after Bobby's death. Elizabeth took faithful care of her throughout, selling her car after one too many fender benders, trying to get her on welfare to supplement her husband's meager pension. Other than Elizabeth, whom she adored, Lessie had only one regular companion in her final years in Opelousas: a family friend named Mrs. Richard, who stopped in to visit, do laundry, clean, and take Lessie for drives. Elizabeth was paying Mrs. Richard from Lessie's savings, but out of respect for the friendship and Lessie's feelings, they kept that arrangement a secret.

A few years before her death, Lessie was hospitalized for leg vein surgery, and during one of Elizabeth's visits, she found her grandmother supine, her hand raised and her fingers tweaking the air. Against her wishes, Lessie had been given morphine, to which she was allergic, and was hallucinating that string was dangling down at her from the ceiling. "She would just pick string," Elizabeth recalls, "for hours and hours and hours."

Lessie donated her body, specifically her horseshoe kidney, to the Tulane School of Medicine. After her death, Elizabeth found the records of her divorce from Percy hidden in a butter churn, complete with detective reports and court transcripts detailing his adultery in Florida. On the outside of the sheaf, Lessie had scrawled, "For Elizabeth Dunbar, to read after my death so she may know why I stayed in my shell of grief." Lessie had not lost her flair for drama ("Read this <u>my</u> boy"), nor had she given up her grudge against Percy. Nor, this close to her own death, had she faced the true source of her unending grief: the boy who had gone unmourned since 1912.

★ ★ ★

BY 2004, THE newly unearthed historical record and the challenges that it posed to the biological identity of Bobby Dunbar and his descendants were—for some in the family—too glaring to ignore. After long deliberation and with grave apprehension, Robert Dunbar Jr., son of Bobby Dunbar, and David Dunbar, son of Alonzo Dunbar, agreed to a paternity test. Their DNA, the test revealed, did not match.

Julia Anderson's children and grandchildren had long known this truth. But to hear it, delivered as scientific fact, and in person by none other than Bobby Dunbar Jr., who had traveled, still in shock, all the way to Mississippi from North Carolina, this was a singular and unforgettable experience. "We loved to hear it from somebody that knew. That knew the facts," Julia's son Hollis recalls. "He knew himself that he was our kinfolk."

On May 1, 2004, Julia's birthday, Bobby Jr. made the announcement at the Walters Homecoming, a family reunion held in Lumber River State Park, North Carolina—only a few miles from where his father, Bruce Anderson, had spent the first four years of his life. Descendants of the Walters clan, for whom the case had long been shrouded in mystery and family shame, erupted in cheers. Both Jean Cooper and Barbara Moore, Rad Walters's granddaughters, were present, beaming at the news that their odd old great-uncle Cant was finally exonerated.

For the Dunbar family, the revelation was far more fraught. Beyond the embarrassment of unwanted and persistent notoriety, beyond moral discomfort with the actions of Percy and Lessie Dunbar a century past, even beyond their own very real existential questions about who they were or what family they belonged to, Bobby's descendants have been most worried that a modern investigation of his birth and childhood will taint or eclipse the man that they knew and loved. They worry that the life Bobby Dunbar lived—the life they lived with him—will be branded an impersonation or a lie. They want Bobby Dunbar remembered not for the tabloid tragedy foisted upon him in childhood, but for the life he made in spite of it. They want him known not for his blood, but for his character and his soul.

The greatest piece of wisdom they will ever find comes from Bobby Dunbar himself.

Raw with doubt after the 1954 interview and the Knights of Columbus grilling, Bobby Dunbar Jr. stood in the hallway and asked his father point-blank, "Who are you? Who you do *think* you are?"

His father looked him "square in the eye" and answered with words that Bobby Jr. would never forget: "I know who I am, and I know who you are, and nothing else matters. It's how we live our life."

Bobby considered his father's words. Though he couldn't understand exactly why at the time, they satisfied him. Fifty years later, he would observe that his father had given him "a pretty good piece of information." *What matters is how we choose to live our life.* "My daddy could have had all the excuses in the world," Bob Jr. knows, "to be a drunk and a child abuser, or anything, a rascal. . . . He had a terrible, traumatic young life. But he chose my mother. And he chose to be a family man. And he chose to be a parent to the children. And that was his world."

Bobby Sr.'s answer to his son had grown out of decades of struggle and searching. He knew the answer to his son's question so readily because he had been asking it of himself since he was a boy. He knew the answer to the question because he had discovered it, in his own life.

OUT ON HIS sales rounds and after lunch, Gerald recalls, his dad would make a beeline to the most shaded and accessible live oak along the roadside, then pull over. Gerald, who has "always been a big car sleeper," was usually conked out in the backseat by the time his father found his spot. And so Bobby kept the window rolled down so that Gerald could sleep with a breeze, and so he could hear him if he woke and called out. Then he stretched out under the tree nearby and closed his eyes. Ten minutes was all Bobby needed. But if Gerald happened to wake up before he did, he felt no need to call out, no need to panic. He knew his father was just a few feet away. It felt as safe as sleeping in his lap.

Acknowledgments

Margaret Dunbar Cutright

Throughout this journey, I have been blessed with friends who kept me company and gave me inspiration. Darla Turner was at my side during my first Opelousas research trip. Tanya Ruthven Sisk taught me how to embrace the experience of *not* knowing. Melinda Marshall has believed passionately in this story, and the need to tell it, and has been a mentor and collaborator, encouraging me to honor *all* of its voices. Sharon Bond played an essential role in the seeking and discovering of the truth behind my family legend, introducing me to genealogical research and, crucially, to the descendants of Julia Anderson Rawls.

Susan Kirk has been my constant confidante, helping me to think through the moral and ethical issues of writing this book. Kim Mackey gave feedback on an early draft. Thanks to Dr. Donald Pavy and Professor James Starrs for a 101 lesson in DNA. And to Dr. Denise Barnes, who has shared wisdom that keeps my feet firmly planted on the ground. My cherished friend Virginia Norris Jones helped me to understand loss and grief at a far-too-early age. Tim, *how I wish you were here.*

I am forever grateful to my grandparents Bobby and Marjorie Dunbar, who instilled in their family by example the way of unconditional love. *I'll be loving you, always.* And to my brothers and sisters for their love and support: Marie and John Cummings, Leah Dunbar, Ron and Deb Dunbar, Swin Dunbar, especially my brother Robbie, whose premature passing sparked my journey.

My father, Robert C. Dunbar Jr., who put me on the path of this journey, guided me through its most difficult chapters and provided immeasurably wise feedback. My mother, Imelda, has been a model in the art of persistence and my inspiration.

My children, Angela and Daniel, and grandson, Tyler, have heard me tell this story for their whole lives. Long after it stopped being a childhood fable, they helped me to keep it alive and remained convinced—even when I wasn't—that I would find a way to tell it.

Wayne Cutright, my husband, has never wavered in his encouragement. He never said, "No, you can't," but instead, "Whatever you need, I'm here waiting." Without his love and respect this book would not exist.

Tal McThenia

During my months in New Orleans, Aaron Alterman and Caroline Heymann were a source of constant support (and food!). Adrian Nicole Leblanc taught me to honor my instincts about when this book was ready. Susan Kaufman has been a careful reader and an unflagging champion. Ian Chorao and Sylvia Sichel have been making my writing better for decades. Terence Dougherty, Shane Dubow, Pierre Duleyrie, Saskia Grooms, Alan Huffman, Peter Koblish, Sunny Neater, Alison Shonkwiler, Julie Silverman, Stefanie Spina, A. K. Summers, and Rob Young have provided love, sanity, fresh air, and family.

As for biological(ish) family, I am blessed to have been coddled and prodded through this process by Jon Adams, Donna Barnett, Barry Berk, Derek Berk, Scott Berk, Stacie Berk, Kathy Cannon, Rob Eggers, Sandyha Huchingson, Andy McThenia, Paige McThenia, and Terri White.

Colin Dickerman has been my best friend and shepherd. He told me I could write this book, and draft after draft, gave sharp, challenging notes without ever losing patience.

Uncas McThenia has been my father for forty-four years and the legal advisor on this book for four. He combed court records, waded through the manuscript, offered clarifications and corrections, and helped us to see all of these lawyers as human.

Brett Berk reveled in the nightly ritual of "Today in Bobby Dunbar" for years, moved with me to New Orleans, and has had to live with just my shell as the rest of me disappeared into this manuscript. He has saved me and loved me for twenty-two years.

Anne Whitley McThenia was my co-witness to the miraculous and lifelong knowing that exists between a mother and her son. I was not at all ready to lose her.

Margaret Dunbar Cutright and Tal McThenia

Our collaboration started during the production of the radio documentary "The Ghost of Bobby Dunbar" for *This American Life*. Julie Snyder gave rigorous feedback, and Ira Glass gave freely of his storytelling wisdom. Alex Blumberg, a brilliant producer, championed the story in both radio and book form.

In Opelousas, we've had an abundance of hosts and supporters: Caroline Dejean, Juergen and Etha Amling, Freddy Lafleur, Sylvia David Morel, Richard Hollier, St. Landry clerk of court Charles Jagneaux, Kelsey Soileau, and many others. We are especially grateful to descendants of the story's local legal figures: Ida Pavy Boudreaux and her husband, Albert Boudreaux; Ed Dubuisson; Lee Halphen; Laura Lewis; and Huey Lambert. David and Sherry Dunbar fed and entertained us, and David was a generous storyteller and Atchafalaya tour guide. Chris Dunbar shared amazing photographs. Ronald Buschel gave us a rare window into how this story has been whispered down through generations. J. A. Allen gave us beautiful Opelousas sketches and memories.

Earl Briggs shared with us memories of his lifelong friendship with Bobby. Aline Perrault offered Margaret vivid, firsthand accounts of Bobby as a boy and a young man. Estelle Perrault has been this book's greatest local champion, organizing public presentations and unlocking doors we didn't even know existed. She shared local history and moral support.

Kevin Fontenot uncovered a little-known recording, "The Mystery of the Dunbar Child," and has given us wise counsel on Louisiana history. Kendall Horton was our gracious host and guide in Natchez. Louis Morgan offered us textured Marion County history. We are so thankful to James C. Rawls for memories of his grandfather, Hollis C. Rawls, and to George Daly, Ben and Bill Lampton, and Buddy Moody, descendants of other figures in the book, to Krae Morgan, Greg Price, Sr. Therese Gregoire and Sr. Germaine Lauzen of the Mt. Carmel Archives, and Gerard Lagarde of Holy Cross School. Since Margaret's first research trip to Columbia, Allison Rawls Bullock has been an invaluable resource.

In North and South Carolina, Paula Smith, R. Maxcy Foxworth Jr., and Jo Church Dickerson eagerly aided our search for Bruce Anderson's birthplace and provided reams of genealogy.

Among the many dedicated librarians and archivists who helped us, special thanks to Keith Fontenot at the St. Landry Courthouse Archives, Gale Thomas at Tulane University, Gabe Harrell at Louisiana State

University, Chris Watts and Ann Atkinson Simmons of the Marion County Museum and Archives.

We have been fortunate to know descendants from all three families involved in this century-old story. From the Walters family, Bob Burton, Janie Perrin, Michael Walters, Ellen Luciano, and Margie Standard have provided genealogical research and boundless enthusiasm. Cora Lutie Walters Bass shared rich family stories. Becky and George Fain gave generous hospitality, and Becky provided us with the only known photo of the Walters homestead. Barbara Moore's memories of her uncle Cant gave us insight into his warmth and oddity. And listening to Jean Cooper was almost like listening to William Walters himself.

Julia Anderson's family has opened their hearts to us. We are so grateful to Charlotte Foster, Jimmy and Tracey Hardy, Suzette Hardee Spencer, Shelly Hardy Willoughby, Denise Norris, Nelda Hennis, Peggy Marble, Will and Zodie Norris, Ricky Rawls, Ronny Rawls, Vergie Rawls, and Betty Redden. Tammy and Gerald Westmoreland provided genealogy expertise, support, and friendship.

Linda Tarver, Julia's granddaughter, has been our beloved friend, a moral compass and giddy accomplice. Julia's daughter Jewel Rawls Tarver opened her memory and heart, and allowed us to relive her childhood under her mother's loving care. Julia's son Hollis Rawls has been a reverent protector of his mother's honor, and offered essential insight into her enduring grief and her spiritual transformation. For Margaret, meeting Julia's oldest daughter, Bernice Hardee Graves, was a miracle.

For twelve years, Elizabeth Dunbar has been our enthusiastic supporter, sharing photos, court records, and rich memories of her grandmother Lessie. We have treasured every moment with Alonzo's wife, Anna Lee Dunbar.

Between them, Bobby Dunbar's children have memories of their father that are worthy of their own book, and it is through them that this story has found its redemption. Gerald and Helaine Dunbar opened their hearts and home to us. Mary Cole has shared not just her memories as Bobby and Marjorie's only daughter; she and her husband, Leon, offered a lifetime of affectionate wisdom. John Dunbar and his wife, Sally, have helped us to grasp the tremendous responsibility that comes with writing this book. Robert C. Dunbar Jr. has shared vivid and unforgettable stories, and his process of coming to understand his father has inspired and humbled us.

We are deeply grateful to our agent, Zoë Pagnamenta, who fell in love with this story, found its proper home, and supported us without fail. At Simon & Schuster/Free Press, Sydney Tanigawa has been a rigorous reader, and Daniella Wexler has given us friendly support.

Our editor Leah Miller breathed fresh life and energy into this project at just the right time, and her passion and vision have thrilled and inspired us. Before her, our editor Hilary Redmon asked all the right questions and pushed us to ever-deeper human truths. She nourished and protected this story, and our experience with her has been a remarkable collaboration.

Notes

Abbreviations of Frequently Cited Sources

Individuals

D&R   Dale and Rawls

Collections

DFS	Dunbar Family Scrapbook
EHP	Ethel Hutson Papers (Tulane University Special Collections)
ELBP	Earl L. Brewer Papers (Mississippi Department of Archives and History)
GHDC	Gerald and Helaine Dunbar Collection
HFP	Hutson Family Papers (Tulane University Special Collections)
JMPP	John M. Parker Papers (University of North Carolina at Chapel Hill Libraries)
JWC	John Wilds Collection (Historic New Orleans Collection)
WWDF	William Walters Defense File

Newspapers

ATT	*Town Talk,* Alexandria, LA
AWTT	*Weekly Town Talk*
BDH	*Daily Herald,* Biloxi, MS
BRSTA	*State Times Advocate,* Baton Rouge, LA
JDL	*Daily Ledger,* Jackson, MS
JDN	*Daily News,* Jackson, MS
MCP	*Marion County Progress,* Columbia, MS
MA	*Advertiser,* Montgomery, AL
MR	*Register,* Mobile, AL
NODP	*Daily Picayune,* New Orleans
NODS	*New Orleans Daily States,* New Orleans

NOTD	*Times-Democrat,* New Orleans
NOTP	*Times-Picayune,* New Orleans
NOI	*New Orleans Item,* New Orleans
OC	*Opelousas Courier,* Opelousas, LA
OE	*Opelousas Enterprise,* Opelousas, LA
PFP	*Free Press,* Poplarville, MS
SLC	*St. Landry Clarion,* Opelousas, LA

Foreword

xv   *"Can you talk":* Marjorie Dunbar, oral history interview by Mark Dunbar, May 1993, GHDC.

xvi *"Fifty Years from Now":* W. K. Patrick, illustration, NOTD, June 10, 1913; handwritten note, DFS.

xvii *"Julia had a son":* From "Notes for Julia Anderson," on genealogical page, Genealogy of Tammy Howard Westmoreland.

xviii *"I knew that":* Linda Tarver, interview by author, January 2008.

Chapter 1

1 *She harbored no illusion:* See Lessie's testimony, NOTP, April 17, 1914; other Swayze Lake witnesses in NOTP, April 16, 1914.

1 *his baby ring:* NOTD, June 6, 1913.

1 *swollen and bloodshot:* NOI, April 23, 1913.

2 *"Craw-fish Are Vamoosing":* SLC, July 27, 1912.

2 *there was also the chore:* NOTP, April 16, 1914.

2 *five-foot-wide bank:* NODS, April 16, 1914.

2 *needed the deed transfer notarized:* NOTP, April 16, 1914; Thornton-Rideau land sale, #71762, Mortgage Book 47a, 546, St. Landry Parish Clerk of Court.

2 *He couldn't:* NOI, April 16, 1914.

2 *the rubber band strap:* NOTP, April 16, 1914.

3 *he instructed the boy:* NOI, August 24, 1912.

3 *rotund Oge challenged rotund Wallace Dunbar:* NOTP, April 17, 1914.

3 *cleaned, fried, and then drained:* Ida and Albert Boudreaux, interview by authors, February 2009.

3 *He often took:* NOI, April 16, 1914; NOTP, April 17, 1914.

3 *she warned:* NOTP, April 14, 1914.

3 *the lake plunged:* NOTP, April 16, 1914.

3 *Searching the water:* Strange to D&R, May 5, 1913, WWDF, book 1, 77a–80b; NOTP, April 16, 1914; NOTD, April 16, 17, 1914, and June 7, 1913.

4 *Later, no single person:* NOTP, April 16, 17, 1914; NODS, April 16, 1914.

4 *"Bobby's last words":* NODS, April 16, 1914.

4 *"Get out of the way":* NODS, April 23, 1913.

5 *"willing to lay down":* NOTP, April 17, 1914.

5 *"suddenly disappeared":* NOTP, NODS, April 16, 1914.

6 *A crossbred dog:* NODS, NOTP, April 16, 1914; NOTP, April 17, 1914.

7 *"To have an idea":* William Darby, *A Geographical Description of the State of Louisiana* (Philadelphia: John Melish, 1861), 136.

7 *For the next century:* Martin Reuss, *Designing the Bayous: The Control of Water in the Atchafalaya Basin, 1800–1995* (College Station: Texas A&M University Press, 1994), 17–101.

7 *Waud's drawing:* A. R. Waud, "Cypress Swamp on the Opelousas Railroad," *Harper's Weekly,* December 8, 1866.

7 *Percy Dunbar had hunted:* NODS, April 16, 1914.

8 *Second Lake was private:* Editors, *Opelousas Daily World, St. Landry History from the 1690's,* July 29, 1998, 236.

8 *"the energy and good taste"*: SLC, August 3, 1912.

8 *And for one season*: NOTD, May 10, 1911. For history of water hyacinth, see also NODP, December 10, 1898, and McFadden Duffy, "Flowering Death on Our Waters," *Louisiana Conservationist* 21 (July–August 1969): 24–30.

8 *"a real 'parky' appearance"*: SLC, July 27, 1913.

9 *a thick cable:* NOTP, April 16, 1914.

9 *At last, the explosions:* NOTP, NODS, April 16, 1914.

9 *John Oge was one:* NOTP, April 17, 1914.

9 *Just a few miles:* OC, October 10, 1908.

9 *A poisonous snake:* SLC, August 31, 1912; NOI, August 27, 1912.

9 *three-year-old Harry Frye:* NODP, May 15, 1908; *Grand Forks Herald,* May 18, 1908; *Wilkes-Barre Times-Leader,* May 15, 1908.

9 *"the search was abandoned"*: SLC, May 23, 1908.

10 *But the Dunbars had moved:* NODP, May 25, 1913.

10 *Morales:* T. Lindsay Baker, *Ghost Towns of Texas* (Norman: University of Oklahoma Press, 1986), 99–100.

10 *horseshoe kidney:* Elizabeth Dunbar, interview by authors, February 26, 2010.

11 *In the academy's tuition books:* Sisters of Mt. Carmel Archives, New Orleans, LA, Washington Collection, No. of Boarders—1902–1903, 240–41.

11 *At first:* Paul L. Lastrapes, ed., *Looking Back at Washington, LA: The Memoirs of David Jasper MicNicoll* (Saline, MI: McNaughton & Gunn, 1996), 115.

11 *As a boy: Winfield Times,* reprinted in OE, November 23, 1915; other descriptions of accident and cork leg: NOTD, May 21, 1913; NOI, June 6, 1913, November 23, 1915; *Tampa Morning Tribune,* August 28, 1920.

12 *"noblest Creole sons"*: SLC, September 22, 1906.

12 *In late 1906:* SLC, December 8, 1906.

13 *"a popular and accomplished"*: SLC, June 22, 1907.

13 *"genial and indefatigable"*: OC, June 22, 1907.

13 *Nearly every afternoon:* NOTD, May 2, 1913.

13 *Bobby had also taken:* NODP, April 25, 1913.

14 *He was "simply outrageous": Lexington Advertiser* (Lexington, MS), approximate date May 22, 1913 (found in DFS and WWDF, book 1, 7–9); see also testimony of Mrs. Mornhingveg, NODS, April 23, 1914.

14 *"prostrate with grief"*: NOTD, August 26, 1912.

Chapter 2

15 *Searchers flooded in:* SLC, August 31, 1912.

15 *The hunt had widened:* NOTP, April 17, 1914.

15 *Perhaps Bobby:* ATT, August 26, 1912.

16 *"stragglers"*: NODP, August 28, 1912.

16 *"They even cut"*: NODS, April 23, 1913.

16 *Before they cut:* For description of alligator hunting methods, see Malcolm L. Comeaux, *Atchafalaya Swamp Life Settlement and Folk Occupations* (Baton Rouge: Louisiana State University School of Geoscience, 1972), 91–92.

16 *For years now:* NOI, November 13, 1910; Louis M. Megargee, ed., "A Talk About Alligator Skins," *Seen and Heard* 4, no. 4 (August 17, 1904): 4419–28.

16 *the hat still there:* NOI, August 27, 1912.

17 *"Now dear ones"*: Aunt Pam to Lessie and Percy, August 28, 1912, DFS.

17 *"vast army"*: SLC, August 31, 1912.

18 *$1,000.00 Reward!:* Reward poster, DFS.

18 *a parish-wide massacre:* Carolyne E. Delatte, "The St. Landry Riot: A Forgotten Incident of Reconstruction Violence," *Louisiana History: The Journal of the Louisiana Historical Association* 17, no. 1 (Winter 1976): 41–49.

19 *"to use an expression"*: NOI, April 22, 1906.

19 *Time and time again:* SLC, January 24, February 14, 1914.

19 *"There are seldom pistol shots"*: SLC, February 22, 1913.

20 *"the woman at the oars":* NOTD, August 31, 1912.

20 *"Italian Woman":* SLC, September 7, 1912.

20 *Most notoriously:* William Ivy Hair, *The Kingfish and His Realm: The Life and Times of Huey P. Long* (Baton Rouge: Louisiana State University Press, 1991), 10–14.

20 *the horrific case of Walter Lamana:* New York Times, June 24, August 15, 1907.

21 *"I only wish":* Boagnis to Dunbars, August 31, 1912, DFS.

21 *A new possibility:* NODP, September 13, 1912; NOTD, September 2, 1912.

21 *"Suspicion Turns":* NOTD, September 2, 1912.

22 *At Swayze Lake:* NODS, April 24, 1913.

22 *By now state militia:* NODS, April 23, 1913.

22 *"Parents Offer $10,000":* Omaha World-Herald, August 31, 1912; see also *Denver Post,* August 30, 1912.

22 *his Biloxi cousins wrote:* Rosa Balthrope to Lessie, September 6, 1912, DFS.

22 *"I went into":* NOI, April 22, 1913.

22 *In a September 8 letter:* Percy to Lessie and Alonzo, September 8, 1912, DFS.

23 *"My dear Mrs Dunbar":* Smith to Dunbar, September 8, 1912, DFS.

23 *"Chief Police Poplarville":* Archie Dunbar to C. P. Dunbar, September 11, 1912, DFS.

24 *"little bare feet":* MR, September 25, 1912.

24 *heading to his sister's house:* MR, September 20, 1912.

24 *"Yours of":* Ibid.

24 *"[H]e is forcing":* MR, September 25, 1912; additional reporting of this search is found in NODP, September 21, 1912.

24 *So-called tramp laws:* Elbert Hubbard, "The Rights of Tramps," *Arena* 9 (April 1894): 593–600.

25 *"[H]e did not tally":* BDH, September 23, 1912; see also NODP, September 23 and 24, 1912.

25 *ancient "fakir":* ATT, September 27, 1912.

25 *A string of more plausible leads:* NOTD, April 23, 1913; NOI, May 2, 1913.

26 *"I'll give":* NODP, October 5, 1912.

26 *"I know where":* NOI, November 17, 1912; see also NOTD, April 23, 1913.

26 *"perhaps the only detective":* New York Times, December 4, 1911.

27 *In Tennessee:* NOI, May 2, 1913; NOTP, November 12, 1912.

27 *"I believe that":* NOI, November 17, 1912.

27 *In a chilling coincidence:* Vance McLaughlin, *The Postcard Killer: The True Story of J. Frank Hickey* (New York: Thunder's Mouth Press, 2006), 19–32.

28 *The* Item's *report:* NOI, November 20, 1912.

29 *"[M]y 18-month-old":* NODP, April 25, 1913.

Chapter 3

31 *"deep in the canebrake":* MR, December 13, 1912.

32 *"a bed of freshly gathered":* NODP, December 12, 1912.

32 *Lessie took the call:* Ibid.

32 *By nightfall:* Ibid.

33 *"had to do away with":* NODP, December 15, 1912.

33 *"Kidnappers Killed":* Kansas City Star (Kansas City, MO), December 14, 1912.

33 *"I am convinced":* NOI, December 14, 1912.

33 *"I love my wife":* NODS, December 14, 1912.

33 *When the suspects reached:* NOTD, December 26, 1912.

34 *"This alleged confession":* ATT, December 17, 1912.

35 *On December 18:* Magnolia Gazette, December 21, 1912; ATT, December 20, 1912.

35 *From the Alabama canebrake:* MR, December 29, 1912.

35 *"suspicious man here named Walters":* Copy of telegram, Smith to Loeb, December 30, 1912; Loeb to Carriere, December 30, 1912, WWDF, book 1, 46a–46b; affidavits of D. F. Smith, H. G. Anderson, April 6, 1914, WWDF, book 1, 47a–47b.

35 *"What, are you":* NODP, December 18, 1912.

35 *"Pretty as a girl":* SLC, March 1, 1913.

36 *"I will admit"*: BDH, January 14, 1913.
36 *On January 15:* BDH, January 16, 1913.
37 *"drank coffee"*: SLC, March 1, 1913.

Chapter 4

41 *"Walters told four different ways"*: Mrs. Rankin's letter to the editor, NOI, May 23, 1913.
42 *his young son had died:* NOI, April 23, 1913.
42 *"He remembers"*: Shreveport Journal, March 12, 1932.
43 *"seven or eight others"*: NOI, April 22, 1913.
45 *"audbeel"*: NODP, April 22, 1913.
45 *"The scar is somewhat"*: NOTD, April 22, 1913.
45 *Percy also described:* Ibid.
45 *"Mr. Dunbar said"*: NODS, April 18, 1914.
46 *"He was a"*: NOTD, April 22, 1913.
46 *"He wears"*: NOTD, April 23, 1913.
46 *"I tried to talk"*: NOTD, April 22, 1913.
47 *"sort of a 'smart aleck' "*: NOTD, April 23, 1913.
47 *"It was not until"*: NOTD, April 22, 1913.
47 *"was given to me"*: NOI, April 21, 1913.
48 *"[A]t this time and place"*: Affidavit of Jack F. Storm, June 14, 1913, WWDF, book 2, 37a.
49 *"several reliable men"*: NODP, April 22, 1913.
49 *If he wasn't just:* Rawls and Dale biographical information: Cliff Rawls, interview by author, July 8, 2002.
50 *"Old man"*: NOI, April 12, 1914.
50 *Walters had $50:* Robesonian, July 29, 1914.
51 *"My name is"*: NOTD, NOI, April 22, 1913.
52 *Deputy Day was:* NOI, April 23, 1913.
53 *"I think that"*: NOTD, April 22, 1913.
53 *"It's too good"*: Ibid.
53 *another passenger:* Ibid.
54 *the lynching of whites:* William Fitzhugh Brundage, *Lynching in the New South: Georgia and Virginia, 1880–1930* (Champaign: University of Illinois Press, 1993), 86–102.
55 *"morbid"*: NOI, April 22, 1913.
55 *as unstoppable:* Ibid.
55 *With his one arm:* NODP, April 22, 1912.
55 *prayed silently:* NOTD, April 22, 1913.
55 *"I do not know"*: NODP, April 22, 1912.
56 *"plain to everyone"*: NOI, April 12, 1914.
56 *comatose or drugged:* NOI, April 22, 1912; NOTD, April 22, 1912.
57 *candy and lemonade:* NOTD, April 22, 1912.
57 *a full half hour:* NOI, April 22, 1912.
57 *"It needed but a cry"*: Ibid.
57 *"Keep quiet"*: NOTP, April 17, 1914.

Chapter 5

61 *Wallace wanted:* NOTP, April 16, 1914.
61 *mansion:* Details of Lampton home from: Chimneys, pamphlet for Arthritis Benefit Coffee, the R. Roy Newsom Home, October 26, 1979.
62 *Percy lifted:* NODS, April 23, 1913.
62 *Lessie spoke of their life:* NODS, April 22, 1913.
62 *He asked:* NOTD, April 23, 1913.
63 *darker than Lessie remembered:* NODS, April 23, 1913.
64 *"Now I'll take"*: NOTD, April 24, 1913.
64 *"within an hour"*: NOTD, April 23, 1913.
65 *They had roped in Day:* NOTP, April 16, 17, 1914.

66 *"First they cheered; next they cried"*: NOTD, April 23, 1913.
67 *"Between you, me, and God"*: NOI, April 23, 1913.
68 *"I immediately"*: NOI, April 12, 1914.
69 *As his daughter Claudia:* Claudia Brewer Strite, *Biography of Earl Leroy Brewer*, ELBP, 2–3.
69 *"A great crowd"*: NOTD, April 23, 1913.
70 *"To hell with that"*: NOI, April 12, 1914.
70 *reward imbroglio:* Deputy Jeff Wallace never received the reward; nor did anyone. In 1915 he sued the *Item* for libel for its report that he had delayed the Dunbars' entry to his home before their nighttime visit, conveniently omitting his elaborate subsequent efforts to claim the reward. A decade later, a hardened eighty-year-old moonshiner, Wallace beat his wife, Saphronia, to death with a twig broom while two of their children looked on, and after a speedy trial, was executed in Columbia.

Chapter 6

72 *George Benz was the only journalist:* All quotations and observations are found in his report, NOI, April 23, 1913.
74 *"long-necked mass"*: NODS, April 23, 1913.
75 *At the end:* A history of this portion of the New Orleans paper wars is found in *John Wilds, Afternoon Story: The History of the New Orleans States Item* (Baton Rouge: Louisiana State University Press, 1976), 81–182.
75 *solely one of words:* JWC, Box 4. In the summer of 1912, the *States* and the *Item* attacked each other over competing circulation claims, each betting publicly that the other was lying, and the *Item* proposed bringing future governor John M. Parker in as a referee.
76 *"Overcome with joy"*: NODP, April 24, 1913.
76 *"Alone on the lawn"*: NODP, April 23, 1913.
77 *"Walters came"*: NODS, April 23, 1913.
77 *"Grandma"*: BRSTA, April 24, 1913.
78 *"swelling"*: NOI, April 23, 1913.
79 *He paused:* NODS, April 24, 1913.
79 *"That's Robbie Dunbar!"*: NOTD, April 24, 1913.
79 *According to:* NOI, NOTD, April 24, 1913.
79 *"gouged his eyes"*: NODP, April 25, 1913.
79 *"I see that you got Bruce"*: Walters to Mr. and Mrs. C. P. Dunbar, April 23, 1913, WWDF, book 1, 50a–51b.
80 *"Come to Daddy"*: NODS, April 24, 1913.
80 *"battle royal"*: NOI, April 24, 1913.
81 *"Silent Salesmen": The Clothier and Furnisher*, November 1896, 54–55.
81 *" 'Robbie' Knows"*: NODS, April 2, 1913.
81 *Percy Dunbar had telephoned:* SLC, April 22, 1913.
82 *"You see, gentlemen"*: JDN, April 24, 1913.
83 *"go see Mr. and Mrs. Dunbar"*: NOTD, April 25, 1913.
83 *"Owing to all the circumstances"*: NODS, April 24, 1913.
83 *"Little Robbie Dunbar"*: NOTD, April 25, 1913.
84 *"Mamma has a cut eye"*: NOI, April 23, 1913.
84 *"Both his mother and I"*: NOTD, April 25, 1913.
85 *"he told me"*: NOTD, April 24 and 25, 1913.
85 *" 'I had a' "*: NODS, April 25, 1913.
85 *"To His Excellency"*: NOTD, April 25, 1913.
87 *"the malformation"*: Ibid.
87 *"Those two little"*: NODP, April 25, 1913.
87 *heredity:* NODP, April 25, 1913.
87 *"not a doubt"*: NOTD, April 24, 1913.
87 *"I have had"*: NODP, April 25, 1913.
88 *"I intend"*: Ibid.
88 *"I sincerely hope"*: Brewer to Dunbars, reprinted in NOTD, NODP, NODS, April 25, 1913.
88 *"The head"*: NODS, April 25, 1913.

Chapter 7

90 *"with no"*: NODS, April 24, 1913.
91 *As the train inched:* Details of the train ride, NODP, NOTD, April 26, 1913; NODS, April 25, 26, 1913; NOI, April 25, 1913.
91 *"Well, he's going to make"*: NODS, April 25, 1913.
92 *A giddy smile:* NODS, April 16, 1914.
92 *He gave no sign:* NODP, NOTD, April 26, 1913.
92 *"If they declare"*: NOI, April 25, 1913.
92 *"Of course he's mine"*: NODP, April 26, 1913.
93 *"On the streetcars"*: NODS, April 25, 1913.
93 *"I know of no precedents"*: NOI, April 24, 1913.
93 *pseudoscience typical:* Frank Luther Mott, *American Journalism, A History: 1690–1960* (New York: MacMillan, 1962), 524.
94 *the Tichborne case:* NOTD, April 24, 1913; Robyn Annear, *The Man Who Lost Himself: The Unbelievable Story of the Tichborne Claimant* (Melbourne, Australia: Text Publishing, 2002).
94 *John Norris of the New Orleans Police Department:* NODS, April 25, 1913.
94 *Down on Canal Street:* NODS, April 25, 1913.
95 *It was the children:* NOI, NODS, April 25, 1913.
95 *It was rumored:* NODS, April 26, 1913.
95 *"That's him!"*: NODP, April 26, 1913.
95 *Only the* Item: NOI, April 26, 1913.
96 *"That's the kid!"*: *Atlanta Journal*, April 26, 1913.
96 *In the* Item's *photo of the room:* NOI, April 26, 1913.
96 *"[T]he chair had been so changed"*: NODS, April 26, 1913.
97 *Then the playmates arrived:* NODS, NOTD, April 26, 1913.
97 *"Recognizes Playmates"*: NOTD, April 26, 1913.
98 *from Rapides Parish:* ATT, April 25, 1913.
98 *sightings:* NOI, April 25, 1913; NODP, April 26, 1913.
98 *"The ladies at Hub wrote me"*: NOTD, April 27, 1913.
98 *"he had his own 'gang' "*: NOI, April 26, 1913.
99 *Affidavit of Julia Anderson:* NOTD, NOI, April 26, 1913.
100 *Withholding character judgment:* NOI, NOTD, April 26, 1913.
100 *two examinations:* NOI, April 26, 1913.
100 *"If Julia Anderson"*: NODP, April 26, 1913.
102 *"I would like to see"*: NODS, April 27, 1913.
102 *"Everywhere he went"*: Aline Perrault, interview by author.
102 *little red paper flags:* NODS, NOI, April 27, 1913.
103 *"Not one-half"*: JDN, April 30, 1912.

Chapter 8

105 *scandalized stares:* NODP, April 30, 1913. See also Taylor, 173–74.
105 *Narrowly beating out:* Robesonian, April 28, 1913; NODP, April 27, 1913; NOI, May 1, 1913.
106 *"Mr. Thomson declined"*: *Atlanta Journal*, April 29, 1913.
106 *Her sole recent foray:* E. Hutson to C. W. Hutson, March 24, 1913, HFP, box 43, folder 9; NOI, March 23, 1913.
107 *Last year:* NODP, July 7 and January 7, 1912.
107 *Since her arrival:* See Hutson to Dowling, October 7, 1913, EHP, box 4, folder 5; Moise to Hutson, November 10, 1912, EHP, box 4, folder 3; Hutson to Moise, July 26, 1913, EHP, box 4, folder 4; Hutson to Thomas, September 19, 1913, EHP, box 4, folder 4.
107 *"light, feminine touch"*: E. Hutson to C. W. Hutson, March 24, 1913, HFP, box 43, folder 9.
107 *The daughter of:* Biographical information on Ethel Hutson and family provided by Mary Sue Roniger and Martha Sullivan.
107 *with an assistant:* Ethel Hutson to Mary Hutson Nelson, August 7, 1913, HFP, box 44.

107   *"was then removed"*: NOI, May 1, 1913.

107   *"modern apartments"*: NOI, May 3, 1913.

107   *"immediate members"*: NOI, May 1, 1913.

108   *ongoing publishing collaborations:* A grade-school English primer, a collection of the works of New Orleans writer Lafcadio Hearn.

108   *there was art:* Examples of and background on Ethel's and Charles's art found in collections of Mary Sue Roniger, the Ogden Museum of Southern Art, New Orleans, and in William A. Fagaly, "The Gifted Amateur: The Art and Life of Charles Woodward Hutson," *Folk Art* 22, no. 3 (Fall 1997): 50–57.

108   *"long, quiet talk"*: NOI, April 30, 1913.

108   *townspeople would flock:* Ann Courtney and Ward Little, eds., *Columbus County, North Carolina: Records and Recollections* (Whiteville, NC: Columbus County Commissioners and Columbus County Public Library, 1980), 162.

109   *if a family expected:* See Roy G. Taylor, *Sharecroppers: The Way We Really Were* (Wilson, NC: J-Mark, 1984), 8–14.

109   *A "free school"*: Courtney and Little, 168.

109   *"no wedding gowns"*: Taylor, 170.

109   *the heavyset Rev. Moses Pridgen:* Genealogical notes of Jeanie Blanton Tremble, March 16, 2003; Raymond Pridgen, ed., "A Man of Great Faith: Story of Wilson Daniel Pridgen."

110   *"He was crazy"*: NOI, April 30, 1913.

110   *swelling ranks:* David L. Carlton, *Mill and Town in South Carolina, 1880–1920* (Baton Rouge: Louisiana State University Press, 1982), 10; for South Carolina mill town history, see also Carlton, 13–81.

110   *(even eleven-year-old George):* For discussion of evasion of minimum age laws, see Carlton, 212–14.

110   *a spacious new hotel:* photograph, Courtney and Little, 187.

110   *Phin Williams:* Courtney and Little, 187.

111   *You wait on a man:* Illinois, General Assembly, Senate Vice Committee, Report of the Senate Vice Committee (Chicago: Allied Printing, 1916), 819, as quoted in Ruth Rosen, *The Lost Sisterhood: Prostitution in America, 1900–18* (Baltimore: Johns Hopkins University Press, 1983), 151–52.

111   *"I was a woman"*: NOTP, April 14, 1914.

111   *"Bastardy"*: Thomas J. Jerome, *The North Carolina Criminal Code and Digest* (Raleigh, NC: Edwards & Broughton, 1908), 77–86.

112   *"I don't know what"*: NOTP, April 14, 1914.

112   *"Just the usual"*: NOI, April 30, 1913.

112   *"I'm going to see"*: NODS, April 29, 1913.

113   *By midweek:* NOTD, May 1, 1913.

113   *"Nobody knew anything"*: NODS, May 1, 1913.

113   *"I wish it was over"*: NOI, May 1, 1913.

113   *May 1, 1913:* In the retelling of the events of May 1 and May 2, 1913, footnotes cite quotes and observations that the text itself does not clearly note, either by reporter or newspaper. Reporters identified are James Edmonds for the *Item*, F. S. Tisdale for the *Daily States*, and reporters for the *Times-Democrat* and the *Daily Picayune* were present as well.

113   *As dawn broke:* NOI, May 2, 1913.

114   *Unfortunately, both men:* State of Louisiana v. Walters, Note of Evidence on trial of motion and supplemental and amended motion of defendant for a new trial, May 18, 1914 (hereafter abbreviated as NOE), testimony of R. L. Garland, "11," 131.

114   *Mrs. Lewis drew the blinds:* NOTD, May 2, 1913.

114   *"Her eyes were red"*: NOI, May 2, 1913.

115   *Dr. Saizan would later testify:* Testimony of Dr. Saizan, NOE, "G," 99.

116   *Cornered, Mr. Lewis sputtered:* NODS, May 1, 1913.

116   *By noon:* NOI, May 1, 1913.

117   *Julia's hands were shaking:* NOTD, May 2, 1913.

118   *A sharp hand clap:* The hand clap and exclamation "She has failed to recognize the

child" are detailed in: NOE, testimony of Leon Dupre, "F," 93–94; testimony of Dr. Saizan, "G," 96–97; testimony of Kelley Andrus, "9," 126; testimony of E. P. Veazie, "10," 127–30.

118   *Dr. Haas glowered:* NOE, testimony of E. P. Veazie, "10," 128.

118   *"Perhaps a dozen":* NOTD, May 2, 1913.

118   *"she looked like":* NOE, testimony of Dr. Saizan, "G," 97.

118   *"I locked the door":* Ibid.

119   *leaving only Tisdale:* NOI, May 2, 1913.

119   *Percy Dunbar objected:* NOTD, May 2, 1913.

119   *The door was locked:* NOE, testimony of Dr. Saizan, "G," 97–98.

119   *"statements and actions":* NOE, testimony of Leon Dupre, "F," 93–94.

120   *"I can't":* NOTD, May 2, 1913.

122   *"dumb with fright":* Ibid.

124   *"This is the hardest thing":* Times-Democrat, May 2, 1913.

124   *"I am Mrs. Dunbar":* NODS, May 2, 1913.

125   *He suggested:* NOE, testimony of E. P. Veazie, "10," 128; NOTD, May 2, 1913.

125   *"Your child has":* NOTD, May 2, 1913.

125   *He felt his task:* NODS, April 24, 1914.

125   *By late afternoon:* NOE, testimony of R. L. Garland, "11," 131.

125   *She was heard:* NOTD, May 2, 1913.

Chapter 9

126   *In the most optimistic moments:* NOI, May 3, 1913.

129   *"Gentlemen":* NODS, May 2, 1913; NODP, NOI, May 3, 1913.

129   *"[H]is actions and":* BRSTA, May 2, 1913.

129   *"What about the scar":* Ibid.

129   *"How about the mole":* NODS, May 2, 1913.

129   *Taking a cue:* NODP, May 5, 1913.

130   *impatience:* NOI, May 1, 1913.

131   *"I wasn't afraid":* NODP, May 4, 1913.

131   *But in just two months:* Threats against Julia, see Anderson to Dale, July 5, 1913, WWDF, book 2, 65a–66b; NODS, April 23, 1914; Hollis Rawls and Jewel Tarver, interview by author, January 2008.

131   *"my heart says":* NOI, May 2, 1913.

133   *"was self-hypnotized":* Ibid.

135   *Marshall Ballard:* Wilds, 221.

135   *Julia would later:* Anderson to Dales and Rawls, quoted in NODS, June 2, 1913.

136   *According to Benz:* NOI, May 3, 1913; *Linotype Machine Principles: The Official Manual* (Brooklyn, NY: Merganthaler Linotype Company, 1940), chapters 1 (linotype operation) and 34 (slug melting); Jay Thornwaldson, "When Hot Type Went Cold at the *Palo Alto Times*," in the *Hellbox*, internal newsletter for *Palo Alto Times*, 1977 (hot slug prank).

Chapter 10

139   *When Dale suggested:* Statements and telegrams are found in NOTD, May 4, 1913.

139   *One memoirist recalled:* T. H. Harris, *The Memoirs of T. H. Harris, State Superintendent of Public Education in Louisiana, 1908–1940* (Baton Rouge: Louisiana State University, 1963), 83–84.

139   *"Was it Bobby Dunbar":* Sunday Enterprise, undated, Lee Halphen Collection.

140   *In late April:* NOTD, April 30, 1913.

141   *"He said he":* NOI, May 5, 1913.

141   *"Monday morning":* SLC, May 10, 1913.

142   *courthouse square fountain:* NODP, April 26, 1913; NOTD, May 2, 1913.

142   *"Mamma, I know":* SLC, May 10, 1913.

142   *The first sentence:* McMullen's interview: NODS, May 4, 1913.

144   *"[W]hen Walters would":* Goleman's letter: NOTD, April 26, 1913.

144 *When the lawyers:* McMullen's community interviews: NODS, May 5, 1913.
147 *"with him very familiar":* NOTD, April 28, 1913. After much finger-pointing, Marion County's district attorney later admitted to authoring the petition, and another local Dunbar sympathizer admitted to distributing it. But there was another possible force behind this sudden "grassroots" frustration toward Governor Brewer: Lieutenant Governor Theodore Bilbo, who had been in the Columbia courtroom for the identification, though he emphatically denied he was in town on business related to the Dunbar matter (NOTD, May 12, 1913).
149 *"Things may shape up":* NODP, May 17, 1913.
150 *"our man in New Orleans":* Hollis Rawls to T. A. Rawls, May 20, 1913, WWDF, book 1, 113.
150 *The driver rushed:* T. A. Rawls to Hollis Rawls, May 19, 1913, WWDF, book 1, 110b.
150 *"wiseacres":* NOI, May 19, 1913.
151 *"[R]esponding to a fear":* Garland to D&R, May 22, 1913, WWDF, book 1, 114a–b.
152 *"Someone had evidently":* NOTD, May 21, 1913.

Chapter 11

153 *the two accounts:* Key details of the swap theory are found in NOI, May 18, 1913; NOTD, May 17, 1913.
155 *"Dunbars Seek 'Bruce' ":* NODS, May 21, 1913.
155 *"If Bruce Anderson":* Hattiesburg News, May 20, 1913.
155 *In Poplarville, they heard:* NOI, May 21, 1913.
156 *"to prove an alibi":* Ibid.
156 *"fund for the prosecution":* NOTD, May 26, 1913.
156 *"manifestly reticent":* Hattiesburg News, May 22, 1913.
156 *"a mysterious automobile mission":* NOI, May 21, 1913.
156 *"Are you positive":* NOI, May 17, 1913.
157 *"The fact":* NODP, May 25, 1913.
157 *Over 2,800 words in length:* D&R's statement was carried in full or synopsized in the New Orleans dailies, as well as in the Mississippi newspapers; we cite it here: "Movements of Walters," WWDF, book 1, 39a–41b.
159 *"hill of beans":* NODP, May 25, 1913.
160 *"Now, as I am a Negro":* Joseph Galloway to Tom Ford, April 24, 1913, WWDF, book 1, 69a–b.
160 *"I do not intend":* NOTD, May 18, 1913.
160 *"[T]he report has been":* Brewer to Garland, May 24, 1913, WWDF, book 1, 122a–b.
161 *"fizzle":* NODP, May 28, 1913.
161 *two or more:* NOTD, May 25, 1913; NODS, May 26, 27, 1913; see also NODP, May 25, 1913; NOI, May 28, 1913.
161 *"for the purpose":* NOTD, May 25, 1913; see also NOTD, May 28, 1913.
162 *whose portrait of Percy:* No surprise, then, that in a Dunbar family scrapbook of news clippings, an angry hand has scrawled atop two pages of reporting from Robert Ewing's afternoon daily, "States Rot."
162 *a national hookworm pioneer:* See Rudolph Matas, "Dr. Charles C. Bass: An Appreciation," New Orleans Medical and Surgical Journal 92 (April 1940): 545–50.
162 *By one estimate:* Marion County Historical Association, History of Marion County, Mississippi (Marceline, MO: Walsworth Publishing Company, 1976), 68.
163 *His study focused:* George Dock and Charles C. Bass, Hookworm Disease: Etiology, Pathology, Diagnosis, Prognosis, Prophylaxis, and Treatment (St. Louis: C. V. Mosby Company, 1910), 86–93.
163 *"It is often possible":* Ibid., 90.
163 *In his observations:* Ibid., 137–41.
163 *In listing home remedies:* Ibid., 207–9.
163 *Sufferers became anemic:* Ibid., 115–54.
164 *Yet the malady:* Ibid., 213–14.
164 *"A child with":* Ibid., 230.

165 *"This Dunbar case"*: *Lexington Advertiser* (Lexington, MS), approximate date May 22, 1913 (found in DFS and WWDF, book 1, 7–9).

167 *On day eleven:* NODP, June 4, 1913.

167 *"Dunbar Trying to Exploit"*: NODS, June 2, 1914.

167 *Not unlike Jane Quick:* George Behe, "Winnifred (Quick) Van Tongerloo," *Titanic Commutator* 17, no. 2 (1993).

168 *drastically lower counteroffer:* The *States* even claimed to have plucked from its archive a quote from Percy at the time: "I had been to an exhausting expense hunting for the boy, and if he had made me an offer that there was something in, I might have taken up the subject." (Reprinted in ATT, June 5, 1913.)

168 *Columbia attorneys were privately angling:* D&R to Julia Anderson, June 2, 1913, WWDF, book 2, 6a; D&R to J. Frank, June 2, 1913, book 2, 6b; see also Julia Anderson to Dale, June 7, 1913, book 2, 25a–b; Padgett and Watson to D&R, October 8, 1913, book 2, 143a–b.

170 *More than one recent:* Hattiesburg News, May 22, 1913.

171 *In a fitting postscript:* NODS, NOI, June 5, 1913.

Chapter 12

173 *two jarring telegrams:* Lewis to Parker, Brewer to Parker, June 6, 1913, JMPP, box 4, folder 44.

174 *"Will with pleasure comply"*: Parker to Brewer, June 5, 1913, JMPP, Brewer, box 4, folder 44.

174 *"God has been"*: NODP, June 6, 1913.

174 *"[A]lways when we"*: Interview with Lessie, NODP, June 6, 1913.

175 *"peach kiss"*: NOI, June 6, 1913.

175 *This was the first time:* All observations are from NOI, NODP, June 6, 1913.

176 *"You may rest"*: NOTD, June 7, 1913.

176 *Julia Anderson wrote:* Anderson to Dale, June 6, 1913, WWDF, book 2, 25a–b.

177 *On Saturday morning:* NOI, June 7, 1913.

177 *The day before:* NOTD, NODP, June 7, 1913.

177 *"not as a witness"*: NOI, June 7, 1913.

178 *"arisen from a sickbed"*: NOI, June 7, 1913.

178 *"This is going"*: NODP, June 7, 1913.

178 *"the Dunbar Investigation"*: Unless otherwise noted, all direct quotes from these proceedings are found in Oliveira's transcript, "The Dunbar Investigation," June 7, 1913, WWDF, book 2, 9a, 1–30.

179 *"Dear Sir"*: JMPP, box 4, folder 44.

180 *"anxious faces"*: NODS, June 8, 1913.

185 *"[I]t took two"*: Ibid.

185 *"There it is"*: Ibid.

185 *"A score of heads"*: NODP, June 8, 1913.

185 *"I don't see any web"*: NODS, June 8, 1913.

185 *"It wasn't"*: NOI, June 7, 1913.

186 *"Did you notice that?"*: Ibid.

186 *"showed no signs"*: NOI, June 8, 1913.

186 *"Hello, Bruce"*: Ibid.

186 *"acting as though"*: NOTD, June 8, 1913.

186 *purse:* NODP, June 8, 1913.

187 *At the time:* NOI, May 18, 1913.

188 *"It seems to me"*: NODS, May 5, 1913.

189 *"was not produced"*: NOI, June 8, 1913.

189 *"just 'leaked out' "*: Ibid.

189 *"intermission"*: NODS, June 8, 1913.

189 *Mr. and Mrs. Goleman:* Though Mrs. Goleman knew of no physical peculiarity, Mr. Goleman reiterated his blunt assessment of the boy's behavior: "I know he is a rude and mischievous child, always going around."

190   *"plain backwoods"*: NODP, June 8, 1913.
190   *"one of the largest"*: NODP, November 16, 1903.
191   *Mr. Parker stood*: NODS, June 8, 1913.
191   *"straight and stiff"*: Ibid.
192   *"hung his head"*: NOI, June 8, 1913.
192   *"large blue bellboy"*: NODS, June 8, 1913.

Chapter 13

193   *"Mamma, it was Bruce"*: NODP, June 8, 1913.
194   *"Bruce what?"*: Ibid.
195   *"I want my dinner"*: NODS, June 8, 1913.
195   *Lessie fanned*: NODP, June 8, 1913.
195   *"Let me hug"*: NOI, June 7, 1913.
195   *"Mr. Parker has just"*: NODP, June 8, 1913.
195   *"I thought so"*: NOI, June 7, 1913.
195   *In 1848*: Foster and "Uncle Ned": Stephen Collins Foster Collection, Center for American Music, University of Pittsburgh.
196   *"too slick"*: NODP, June 8, 1913.
196   *"I want to shake"*: Ibid.
196   *"[A]nchored by"*: Ibid.
196   *"bowing and smiling"*: NOI, June 8, 1913.
196   *"I tried to get"*: NOI, June 9, 1913.
197   *two doors down*: David G. Sansing and Carroll Waller, *A History of the Mississippi Governor's Mansion* (Jackson: University Press of Mississippi, 1977), 113.
197   *"exhibited a lively interest"*: NOI, June 7, 1913.
197   *read its copy*: NODS, June 8, 1913.
197   *five full Day Letter forms*: Parker to Brewer, June 7, 1913, JMPP, box 4, folder 44.
198   *"I will not make"*: NODS, June 8, 1913.
198   *"I knew it"*: NOI, June 8, 1913.
198   *"I am a good Methodist"*: NODP, June 8, 1913.
198   *"practically dictated"*: NOI, June 7, 1913.
198   *prior (albeit lopsided) political and personal relationship*: In 1911 Lewis was president of the local chapter of Parker's Good Government League, and the men were close enough for Parker to have granted Lewis a personal loan without interest. See Lewis to Parker, April 20, 1911, and Parker to Lewis, April 24, 1911, JMPP, box 3, folder 40; and Parker to Lewis, August 12, 1912, JMPP, SV1184/1 (lettercopy book).
199   *"Mr. Parker was frank enough"*: NOTD, NOI, NODP, June 9, 1913.
199   *"When I was asked . . . On the other hand"*: NOI, April 11, 1914.
199   *he had just received*: J. M. Walters to W. C. Walters, June 6, 1912, WWDF, book 2, 4a–5a.
200   *"whether it would be"*: NOI, April 10, 1914.
200   *Surgical experts*: Walter Hamilton Acland Jacobson, *The Operations of Surgery*, vol. 1, 6th ed. (New York: Macmillan, 1915), 79–82; Herbert William Allingham, *Operative Surgery* (New York: William Wood & Company, 1904), 66–67; De Forest Willard, *The Surgery of Childhood* (Philadelphia: J. P. Lippincott Company, 1910), 576–77.
200   *"They all told me"*: NOI, April 10, 1914.
200   *two young men*: The drowning of Will Miller is recounted in BDH, June 9, 1913, and NODP, June 9, 10, 1913. Parker's explanation of grocery clerk Henry Andresen's statements is found in Parker telegram to Brewer, June 8, 1913, JMPP, box 4, folder 44.
201   *a journalist for the* Pic: NODP, June 10, 1913.
201   *two more letters*: Parker to Brewer, June 17, 1913, and Parker to Brewer, June 19, 1913, JMPP, box 4, folder 44.
201   *"the two boys"*: Parker's account in NOI, April 10, 1914.
201   *"a small boy"*: MR, September 25, 1912.
201   *politely pandering reply*: Brewer to Parker, June 21, 1913, JMPP, box 4, folder 44. Similarly, Brewer's earlier thank-you letter to Parker for his verdict was subtly dismissive: see Brewer to Parker, June 9, 1913, JMPP, box 4, folder 44.

201   *"John M. Parker"*: *Shreveport Journal*, March 12, 1932.
202   *"[A]t all times"*: Affidavit of Jobie Sweeney, June 13, 1913, WWDF, book 3, 104a.
203   *"I have been"*: Brewer's original statement, and the most comprehensive account of this meeting, is found in *Marion County Progress* (Columbia, MS), June 21, 1913.

Chapter 14

206   *"Q. How many brothers"*: Transcript of In the Matter of W. C. Walters' Application for Writ of Habeas Corpus, Fifteenth Judicial District Court, July 2, 1913, 43.
206   *"about a year"*: Bledsoe's prepared statement to press, NOTP, NODS, NOI, April 14, 1914.
206   *"It was an army"*: Lawrence S. Early, *Looking for Longleaf: The Rise and Fall of an American Forest* (Chapel Hill: University of North Carolina Press, 2004), 141.
208   *"I dare say"*: NOTP, NODS, NOI, April 14, 1914.
208   *"quit him"*: NOI, April 30, 1913.
208   *Her accusations in court*: "[D]amn bitch" and other details found in *Mary A. Walters v. William C. Walters*, Libel for Divorce, Montgomery County Superior Court, January 26, 1901.
208   *he'd locked them*: NODP, April 27, 1913.
208   *By late summer*: NODS, NOTD, May 5, 1913.
208   *On September 9*: Ibid.
208   *A doctor cut open*: See J. H. Mitchell, "Injuries to the Patella with Their Medical Treatment," *New York State Journal of Medicine* 10, no. 2 (February 1910): 75–77; J. J. Cassidy, "Metallic Sutures in Fracture of Patella with an Improved Method of Introducing the Sutures," *Dominion Medical Monthly* 4, no. 6 (June 1895): 153–56.
209   *"I could hardly walk"*: Walters's testimony, Habeas, 40.
209   *"had been run away with and fixed up"*: Ibid., 42.
209   *"I stayed in"*: Ibid., 40–41.
209   *David Bledsoe was*: W. R. Surles, "Memorial to David L. Bledsoe, One of Robeson's Illustrious Sons," *Robesonian*, June 23, 1932.
209   *"He has been trying"*: NOTP, April 14, 1914.
210   *"a little old rake"*: Walters's testimony, Habeas, 41.
210   *To supplement his income*: Letter from R. L. Caldwell, NOI, May 4, 1913.
210   *famously pungent*: Jack M. Willis, "Sulphur Springs Was Famous Resort," *Piney Woods Journal*, June 2001.
210   *Walters was still hobbling*: This detail and other testimony regarding Walters's travels during this time: letters from Sheriff W. J. McBride and A. H. May to *Shreveport Times*, reprinted in *Jackson Independent* (Jonesboro, LA), May 8, 1913.
210   *"He came to my home"*: Letter from R. L. Caldwell, NOI, May 4, 1913.
210   *"[A]bout the last of 1910"*: Walters's testimony, Habeas, 39.
211   *although the actual string count*: Ibid.
211   *"at my old home"*: Ibid.
213   *"Keep Walters"*: NODP, July 4, 1913.
213   *"all the way"*: NOI, July 4, 1913.
213   *"worked in our town"*: McManus's testimony, Habeas, 62.
213   *In the past month*: See extensive series of letters between Brown and D&R, May 15–July 24, 1913, WWDF, book 2.
214   *"Julia Anderson did not"*: NOI, July 3, 1913.

Chapter 15

215   *run out of names*: Jean Cooper and Barbara Moore, interview by author, January 2008.
215   *"They've got"*: NOI, April 30, 1913.
216   *assault with a deadly weapon*: Criminal Court Docket, Superior Court, 1902–1912, Robeson County, NC: July 1910 term, 97; September 1910 term, 229, November 1910 term, 268, 290, at NCSA.

216 *Iredell Williamson came up:* Affidavit of Iredell Williamson, April 30, 1913, WWDF, book 1, 70b.

216 *fornication and adultery:* Criminal Court Docket, Superior Court, 1902–1912, Robeson County, NC, July 1911 term, 368, at NCSA.

217 *The criteria for admissible charges:* Jerome, 279–84.

217 *she "loved":* Interview with Walters, NOTP, April 29, 1914.

217 *"rounder":* Jean Cooper, interview by author, January 2008.

217 *"I didn't think":* NOI, April 30, 1913.

217 *"a reputable farmer's daughter":* NOTP, April 29, 1914.

217 *Julia and Bunt were charged:* Criminal Court Docket, Superior Court, 1902–1912, Robeson County, NC, September 1911 term, 409, November 1911 term, 438.

217 *Bunt skipped:* NOTD, April 26, 1913.

218 *"Dear Sir":* Julia to Dale, July 5, 1913, WWDF, book 2, 65a–66b.

219 *"flirting a small":* Point Coupee Banner, July 5, 1913; SLC, July 5, 1913.

219 *In the same edition:* ATT, July 15, 1913.

220 *official parade:* AWTT, July 18, 1913; NODP, July 19, 1913; NOI, July 19, 1913.

220 *"did it just as":* NODP, July 20, 1913.

220 *"Mama, let's come here":* AWTT, July 18, 1913.

221 *"I never saw":* ATT, April 25, 1913.

221 *At the corner of:* ATT, May 3, July 17, 1913; AWTT, July 18, 1913.

221 *"W. C. Walters and his brother":* ATT, July 17, 1913.

221 *George the evicted hotel alligator:* ATT, July 22, 1913.

222 *Negotiating the sale:* See D&R's correspondence with Frank Walters, J. B. Walters, J. M. Walters, and R. R. Barnes, May 1913–July 1913, WWDF.

222 *"Dunbar Funds":* ATT, July 7, 1913; BRSTA, July 19, 1913.

222 *In Opelousas:* SLC, August 2, 1913.

222 *When a desperate:* NODS, July 18, 1913.

222 *"Little Dunbar":* NODP, July 19, 1913.

222 *"Bruce Anderson Is Buried":* NOI, July 30, 1913.

222 *a New Orleans criminal attorney and his brother:* Joseph R. and Frank T. Echezabal, *The Tinker and the Boy* (New Orleans, July 8, 1913).

222 *Aline Richter:* NODS, July 26, 1913; NODP, July 28, 1913.

222 *from "Willie Barton":* Echezabal and Echezabal, 1–41.

222 *"starts in the air":* NODS, July 28, 1913.

223 *"We may be criminals":* B. and H. to Lessie, printed in NOI, August 5, 1913.

223 *B. and H.'s rationale:* Outlined in B. and H. to Percy, printed in NOI, August 3, 1913.

224 *"They can't bluff":* NOI, August 5, 1913.

224 *their goriest threat yet:* NOI, August 8, 1913.

225 *the Item's editorial:* NOI, August 9, 1913.

225 *he painstakingly transcribed:* All of Walters's transcription and commentary to follow comes from Walters to D&R, August 21, 1913 (WWDF, book 1, 12a–16), and Walters's letter to D&R, August 19, 1913 (WWDF, book 2, 84a–b).

227 *"I have findley":* Julia to Dale, August 22, 1913, WWDF, book 2, 77a–b.

227 *Rawls's response:* Rawls to Julia, August 26, 1913, WWDF, book 2, 80a–b.

228 *Julia wrote back:* Julia to D&R, August 29, 1913, WWDF, book 2, 91–92.

228 *"Since Bobbie's return":* Lake Charles American Press, quoted in SLC, September 6, 1913.

228 *"the center of all":* BRSTA, September 1, 1913.

229 *"I think we shall":* ATT, September 2, 1913.

229 *the station matron:* James Peabody, *Railway Organization and Management* (Chicago: LaSalle Extension University, 1920), 103–4.

229 *"peculiar actions":* NOI, September 12, 1913.

230 *"stay with her people":* D&R to J. M. Walters, September 13, 1913, WWDF, book 2, 95a–b.

230 *Julia remained:* Inevitably, the media got wind. The story was local at first. Then it hit New Orleans, was promptly sensationalized and syndicated, and over the next

few weeks, broadcast across the entire nation. The tabloid version of Julia's Savannah stranding, along with a portrait photo of her from May, made front pages as far away as Grand Forks, North Dakota.

Chapter 16

231 *"hands [were] scarce"*: Robesonian, November 30, 1911.
232 *"Cantwell Walters sure had"*: NOTD, May 3, 1913.
232 *"He tried to"*: NOI, April 30, 1913.
232 *That was not all he tried:* Entire crop-theft attempt story is told in NOI, April 30, 1913.
233 *"as good an opinion as I should have"*: NOI, April 29, 1914.
233 *Slowly but surely:* NOTD, May 3, 1913.
233 *"Ugly Papa"*: Affidavit of Iredell Williamson, April 30, 1913, WWDF, book 170b.
233 *"Julia proved"*: NOI, April 29, 1914.
233 *a financial scheme:* NOI, April 30, 1913.
234 *"That during"*: Affidavit of Julia Anderson, May 30, 1913, WWDF, book 1, 128a.
235 *Dock Williamson:* NOTD, April 26, 1913.
235 *"She . . . told"*: NOI, April 30, 1913.
235 *She was barefoot:* PFP, May 7, 1914.
236 *"He went down"*: NOI, April 30, 1913.
236 *July 16, 1912:* Robeson County, NC, sealed adoption record.
236 *fluid, provisional:* "I am helping to raise her now, although she is not under my direct care," she is quoted two years later: NOTP, April 14, 1914.
237 *"It has occurred"*: D&R to Padgett and Watson, August 26, 1913, WWDF, book 2, 79a–b.
237 *"[I]f I have not"*: J. M. Walters to D&R, September 9, 1913, WWDF, book 2, 93b–94c.
238 *"would have already"*: D&R to J. M. Walters, September 13, 1913, WWDF, book 2, 95a–b.
238 *("She is a lady")*: Padgett to D&R, September 15, 1913, WWDF, book 2, 96a–b.
238 *"have our immediate attention"*: D&R to Padgett and Watson, September 17, 1913, WWDF, book 2, 136a.
239 *Padgett responded:* Padgett to D&R, October 8, 1913, WWDF, book 2, 143a–b.
240 *"[I]f the Supreme Court"*: NOI, October 8, 1913.
240 *"agitators"*: BDH, January 1, 1914.
240 *Bilbo, though still under indictment:* As the case against Bilbo proceeded through the courts in 1914, anonymous kidnapping threats were made to Governor Brewer. They never made the news, but Brewer and his wife, Minnie, were sufficiently alarmed to assign a black convict working in the mansion to the job of bodyguard for their young daughter Claudia (Strite, 14).
241 *"prima facie"*: Ex Parte Walters, No. 17,120 (Supreme Court of Mississippi, January 12, 1914).
241 *"they cannot eat me"*: ATT, January 13, 1914. Walters was not just being colorful. He was referring to the Atakapa, a native American people who once inhabited southern Louisiana, including the region of St. Landry Parish, and were thought to have fed on their enemies. In Choctaw, Atakapa means "eater of human flesh."

Chapter 17

243 *"W. C. Walters Left Us"*: Columbian (Columbia, MS), February 5, 1914.
243 *"I'm going to show you"*: ATT, February 3, 1914.
243 *"accustomed to"*: NODP, February 2, 1914.
243 *a written statement:* NOTD, February 1, 1914.
244 *"I want to be tried"*: NOTD, February 2, 1914.
244 *"with the modest air"*: ATT, February 2, 1914.
244 *"Sheriff Swords"*: NODP, February 2, 1914.
244 *a withering report:* SLC, January 24, 1914.
245 *"Many of the young"*: SLC, February 28, 1914.

245 *provocative letter:* Ibid.

246 *"rose in strains":* NOI, April 11, 1914.

246 *"The little tots":* NODS, April 13, 1914.

246 *"I Have worried":* Walters to D&R, March 10, 1914, WWDF, book 3, 24a–b.

247 *"If Walters must":* NODP, January 14, 1914.

247 *Louisiana law:* Warren M. Billings, "Origins of Criminal Law in Louisiana," *Louisiana History: The Journal of the Louisiana Historical Association* 32, no. 1 (Winter 1991): 63–76; James W. Garner, "Proposed Criminal Code for Louisiana," *Journal of the American Institute of Criminal Law and Criminology* 1, no.10: 480–83.

248 *From Baxley:* Padgett to D&R, February 2, 1914, WWDF, book 3, 4a–b.

248 *"as you know":* D&R to Padgett, February 5, 1914, WWDF, book 3, 5a–b.

249 *two dollars a day:* Minutes of St. Landry Police Jury, February 2, 1914, at LSUSC.

250 *legal limit:* H. G. Lastrapes, *Code of Practice of Louisiana* (New Orleans: F. F. Hansell & Bro., 1914), 344.

250 *"in a quiet way":* D&R to Dubuisson, February 9, 1914, WWDF, book 3, 18a–b.

250 *Less than a month:* Kleinpeter to D&R, March 17, 1914, WWDF, book 3, 30a–b.

250 *Eleven days later:* Kleinpeter to D&R, March 28, 1914, WWDF, book 3, 31a–b.

251 *"a mowing machine":* SLC, April 4, 1914.

252 *"With clumsy":* NODS, April 12, 1914.

252 *Just before the trial:* Seiferth interview with Dunbars, including quotes: NOTP, April 14, 1914.

Chapter 18

255 *"Do you know":* NOTP, April 14, 1914.

255 *"eye-sore":* SLC, January 31, 1914; for additional *Clarion* complaints about the courthouse, see also SLC, January 24, April 11, 1914.

256 *"an overripe plum":* Wilds, 209; see also NOI, April 1, 1914.

257 *"The* Times-Picayune*":* NOTP, April 11, 12, 1914.

257 *eschewed "inaccuracy":* NOTP, March 5, 1929.

257 *"Oh, I'm going to have":* This and other details of Hall's biography: Lane Carter, "Retired Reporter Takes a Trip Down Memory Lane," *Birmingham News Magazine,* January 10, 1960, 12–13.

257 *before being wooed away:* Ethel Hutson to Charles Hutson, March 24, 1913, HFP, box 43, folder 9.

258 *His first big:* NOI, December 28–30, 1912.

258 *In 1919:* Cy Q. Faunce, *The Airliner and Its Inventor, Alfred W. Lawson* (Columbus, OH: Rockastel Publishing Co., 1921), 165.

258 *prescient stipulation:* See Blair's December 22, 1920, report; Clara disputed the will story, and, though she was acquitted, no will materialized (NODS, August 1, 1920).

259 *"Identity of Boy":* NOI, April 9, 1914.

259 *"first motion picture record":* BRSTA, April 15, 1914.

260 *"just one step":* NOTP, April 14, 1914.

260 *"Mrs. C. P. Dunbar":* NOI, April 12, 1914.

261 *On Monday afternoon:* NOTP, NODS, April 14, 1914.

261 *"[W]e came on":* NOTP, April 15, 1914.

261 *"[H]ot words":* NOTP, April 14, 1914.

261 *"Go'wn, Dunbar":* NODS, April 14, 1914.

261 *"Item Adds Forgery":* NODS, April 15, 1914.

261 *screed:* NOI, April 14, 1914.

261 *taunt:* NOI, April 15, 1914.

261 *mature admonishment:* NOI, April 20, 1914.

262 *James Thomson regretted:* Wilds, 210; for circulation reports, see also JWC, Box 4.

262 *As Walters limped:* The fullest account of Walters's encounter with Mrs. Sloan and Mrs. Nix is found in NOTP, April 14, 1914.

263 *He collapsed in:* The account of Bunt's visit is found in NOTP, April 15, 1914.

Chapter 19

264 *the little boy:* NOI, April 15, 1914; NODS, NOTP, April 16, 1914.

264 *Tucked in the room's:* NOTP, April 15, 1914.

264 *"scarce ten feet":* Ibid.

265 *Finding a jury: Louisiana v. Mrs. Zee Runge McRee,* testimony of M. L. Swords, October 25, 1911; NOTP, April 15, 1914.

265 *shot and killed four black men:* NODP, March 14, September 25, 1904, and October 5, 1906; NOTP, April 28, 1914.

265 *an estimated eighty:* NOTP, April 16, 1914.

266 *the journalists:* For the *Item,* Sam Blair, Mignon Hall, and Lee Hawes; for the *Daily States,* A. J. McMullen and Rudolph Ramelli; for the *Times-Picayune,* Stanley Ray and Herman Seiferth. In the retelling of the trial, footnotes cite quotes and observations that the text itself does not clearly note, either by reporter or newspaper.

266 *"On the stand":* NOTP, April 16, 1914.

266 *"I knew the child":* Ibid.

266 *"I wouldn't have":* Ibid.

266 *"Lessie, you go":* Ibid.

267 *Ever since:* Lucy S. McGough, *Child Witnesses: Fragile Voices in the American Legal System* (New Haven, CT: Yale University Press, 1994), 18–21.

267 *"Recognizing on":* 1 Wigmore 1904, § 509, 640, as quoted in McGough, 10.

268 *"He looked him":* NOTP, April 16, 1914.

268 *"Then he turned":* Ibid.

269 *Yes, Percy answered:* NOTP, NOI, NODS, April 16, 1914.

269 *"How long":* NOTP, NOI, April 16, 1914.

269 *"Didn't you say his eyes":* NOTP, NOI, NODS, April 16, 1914.

270 *"My wife jumped":* NOTP, NOI, April 16, 1914.

270 *"Indistinctly":* Ibid.

270 *As Lessie ushered:* Ibid.

270 *On April 25, 1913:* NOTP, April 25, 1913.

271 *"Before issuing":* NODS, December 13, 1912.

271 *he had told her:* NODS, April 16, 1914.

271 *On cue:* Telegram, Loeb to Carriere, December 30, 1912, and telegram, Smith to Loeb, December 30, 1912, WWDF, book 1, 46a–46b.

271 *"were unable to":* Affidavits of D. F. Smith, H. G. Anderson, April 6, 1914, WWDF, book 1, 47a–47b.

272 *"Some of":* NOTP, NOI, April 16, 1914.

272 *"many people thought":* NOTP, April 16, 1914.

273 *A wedge:* NOTP, April 17, 1914.

274 *"I have heard":* Ibid.

275 *"the marshes":* Ibid.

275 *Her tea-gown:* NOI, April 16, 1914; image in NOTP, April 17, 1914.

275 *"proudly erect upon":* NOTP, April 17, 1914.

275 *"Robert's, I know them":* Ibid.

276 *Through her tears:* NOTP, NODS, April 17, 1914.

276 *"I would not have taken":* NOTP, April 17, 1914.

276 *"engaged in the gentlest":* NOTP, NODS, April 17, 1914.

277 *After Virginia Military:* Dubuisson's biography: James Clark Fifield, *The American Bar: Contemporary Lawyers of the United States and Canada, 1918,* 260; Democratic Party (LA) State Central Committee, ed., *The Convention of '98,* 19.

277 *politely brutal cross-examination:* NOTP, April 30, 1912; NOI, April 30, 1912.

277 *"she was willing":* NOTP, April 17, 1914.

277 *Was there anyone:* Ibid.

277 *Dubuisson then lifted:* NODS, NOTP, April 17, 1914.

277 *"Left foot had been":* SLC, August 31, 1912.

278 *"at the tragedy's inception":* NOTP, April 17, 1914.

278 *taking stenography for Governor:* NOTP, July 1, 1936.

278 *As she stood:* NOTP, April 17, 1914.
279 *"Miss Maud Taylor":* NODS, April 17, 1913.
279 *She cocked it:* NODS, NOTP, April 17, 1914.
280 *He had known:* Loeb's testimony: NOTP, NODS, April 17, 1914.
280 *He had been accompanied:* NOTP, April 17, 1914.

Chapter 20

282 *Originally, Mallett had sworn:* NOI, May 2, June 6, 1913.
282 *In Poplarville:* All citations for witnesses' earlier habeas testimony can be found in Habeas transcript.
282 *Now, on the stand:* NOTP, April 17, 1914.
282 *"[h]e wanted":* NODS, April 17, 1914.
282 *Her husband, William:* NODP, March 7, 1911; NOI, May 22, 1911.
282 *his wife's motivations:* Three years later, William McManus was recommended for pardon by the Board of Parole, but denied. Six months later, their son Robert exploded again. Confronting his wife, Matilda (whom Robert had wildly insisted that Walters romanced during his earlier stay in Louisiana), in the act of fleeing their home and marriage, Robert fired three shots through her body, then brought the pistol to his own mouth for the fourth. Clemency for William was refused again in 1919. Finally, in 1923, his freedom came from Governor John M. Parker.
283 *A year ago:* NODP, April 27, 1913.
283 *"the guilty party":* NODS, April 17, 1914.
283 *the following observations:* NOTP, April 18, 1914; NOI, NODS, April 17, 1914.
284 *A bit more subtly:* NOI, April 17, 1914.
284 *"Q. He didn't tell":* King's testimony, Habeas, 75.
285 *"It was the same expression":* NOTP, April 18, 1914.
285 *"He did not":* NODS, April 17, 1914.
287 *"as long as Dunbar":* NOTP, April 17, 1914.
289 *"could not stand it":* NODS, April 18, 1914.
289 *"His ire seemed":* NOTP, April 18, 1914.
290 *An ancient farmer:* NOTP, NOI, April 18, 1914.
290 *Overnight, placards:* NODS, April 18, 1914.
290 *The child's face:* Shute's examination is detailed by all three New Orleans newspapers, NOTP, April 19, 1914; NOI, April 18, 19, 1914; NODS, April 18, 1914.
292 *"As Professor Roltair":* Quote, photos, and explanation of "half-spider" acts are found in W. B. Robertson, "A Gallery of Mystifying Pictures," *Cassel's Magazine Limited Illustrated* 8 (January–November 1900): 50–51.

Chapter 21

295 *"a postcard bearing":* NOI, May 21, 1914.
296 *"scattered about town":* NODS, April 18, 1914.
297 *"I would tell it":* NODS, April 19, 1914.
297 *the courtroom filled:* NOI, April 19, 1914.
298 *"Can you give":* Ibid.
298 *Of Nurse:* Walters's rebuttal of Loveless, Stogner, and McManus quoted and summarized in NOI, NOTP, NODS, April 19, 1914.
298 *"crazy":* Veazie's questioning, NOI, NODS, April 19, 1914.
298 *"Ask God that":* Walters's rebuttal, NOI, April 19, 1914.
299 *"Did you beat":* Ibid.
299 *"That child found":* Ibid.
299 *Over panicked objections:* NOTP, April 19, 1914.
300 *"Can you tell us":* Ibid.
301 *"Could a man":* NOTP, April 21, 1914.
301 *When Emile Thigpen:* NOTP, April 22, 1914.
301 *"Walters tried":* Ibid.

301 *"No, that don't"*: Ibid.
302 *peritonitis:* NOTP, April 27, 1914.
302 *the abscess:* NOTP April 21, 1914.
302 *"was a very severe one"*: NODS, April 23, 1924.
302 *"temporary relief"* . . . *"compulsory"*: NOTP, April 26, 1914.
303 *It was Murray:* NODS, April 28, 1913.
303 *"Remarkable man"*: NOTP, April 21, 1914; NODS, April 20, 1914.
303 *"Don't you think"*: NODS, April 20, 1914.
303 *All it took:* Questioning of Murray and Stephens, NODS, NOI, April 20, 1914; NOTP, April 21, 1914.
304 *"What are the greatest"*: D. L. Bledsoe, *Bledsoe's Catechism on Music: Two Hundred and Eighty Concised, Pointed Questions and Answers* (Clyde, GA: J. B. Vaughan, 1893).
304 *"[R]eputed to be wealthy"*: NOTP, April 20, 1914.
304 *Bledsoe's eyes:* NOTP, April 21, 1914.
305 *They asked him:* Ibid.
305 *"Robert Dunbar"*: Ibid.

Chapter 22

306 *They took the first step:* NOTP, April 23, 1914.
306 *St. Joseph's lilies:* NOTP, April 18, 1914; NODS, April 23, 1914.
307 *"What is your name?"*: NODS, April 23, 1914.
308 *"That's my boy"*: NOI, April 23, 1914.
308 *"Come here, darling"*: NOTP, April 23, 1914.
308 *The boy scampered:* Entire exchange reported in NOTP, April 23, 1914.
310 *"Did you hear"*: NODS, April 23, 1914.
310 *"If the child was"*: Ibid.
310 *The jury brought:* NOTP, NOI, April 23, 1914.
310 *"She readily denied"*: NOI, April 23, 1914.
311 *"Although not yet"*: NOI, April 16, 1914.
313 *In October:* NOI, April 30, 1913.
313 *"Bruce is as fat"*: NODS, April 25, 1913.
314 *"[W]hile they were"*: NOTD, April 26, 1913.
314 *"he was about to get"*: NOI, April 30, 1913.
314 *the county coroner:* Robesonian, March 6, April 10, 1913.
315 *"them Arnett folks"*: NOTD, May 3, 1913.
315 *white phosphorous matches:* See New York Times, January 28, 1912; ATT, July 9, 1913.
315 *"Deare Sur"*: Julia to Walters, March 1, 1913, unmarked evidence, *State of Louisiana v. Walters.*
316 *"I've done seen"*: NOTP, April 23, 1914.

Chapter 23

322 *"I ask you"*: NODS, April 23, 1914.
323 *at the crack of dawn:* Entire Cowart account is found in NOI, April 22, 1914.
323 *Koenig had a confession:* NOTP, April 20, 1914.
329 *"sneaking"*: NOTP, April 24, 1914.
329 *"the rankest kind of hearsay"*: NODS, April 24, 1914.
329 *"very camp"*: NOI, April 24, 1914.
329 *"at a time"*: Paraphrased in NOTP, April 25, 1914.
330 *"startling testimony"*: Dupre to *Item*, NOI, April 25, 1914.
330 *"[A]s I have been"*: Childs to *Item*, NOI, May 4, 1914.
332 *young George Baylis:* NOI, April 12, 1914.
334 *"Some members"*: Dubuisson's closing argument is found in NOTP, April 26, 1914.
334 *Mrs. Dunbar's body:* Ibid.
335 *Veazie wrangled:* NOI, April 27, 1914.
335 *Lewis flung:* Lewis's closing argument is found in NOI, April 25, 1914.

335 *Piny Woods Statesman:* NOTP, April 23, 1914.
336 *"I had a man":* NODS, April 23, 1914.
336 *Deputy Day approached:* NOTP, April 17, 1914.
336 *"Dear Father and Mother":* Walters to parents and Julia, unmarked evidence, *State of Louisiana v. Walters.*
336 *"A Child lost about His Age":* Defense contended that Walters wrote "A child lost about His age." Prosecutors insisted the "A" was a "1" (one). "1 (one) child lost about His age" would imply that he was in possession of multiple children.
337 *"a key by which":* NOTP, April 28, 1914.
337 *raw, bloody scrapes:* Ibid.

Chapter 24

338 *"Sheriff Swords points":* NODS, April 27, 1914.
339 *fear of mistrial:* NOTP, April 28, 1914.
339 *Mignon Hall's hand:* NOE, testimony of Lawrence Andrepont, "D," 77.
339 *On Union Street:* Dunbar celebration reported in NOTP, April 28, 1914.
340 *"In the beginning":* NOTP, April 24, 1914.
340 *"smiled weakly":* NOTP, April 27, 1914.
340 *When news:* NOTP, April 28, 1914.
341 *"You cannot say":* NOI, April 25, 1914.
341 *"not entirely unexpected":* NOI, April 28, 1914.
342 *"erroneous in law": State of Louisiana v. Walters,* Supreme Court of Louisiana, Transcript of Appeal, bill of exception #3.
342 *"Owing to my":* NOE, testimony of Dubuisson, "18," 140.
342 *It was Assistant District Attorney Veazie:* NOE, testimony of E. P. Veazie, "10,"127.
343 *"after voicing a strong":* NOI, May 3, 1914.
343 *She made her way up:* PFP, May 7, 1914.
343 *she had forgotten to proffer:* NOTP, April 24, 1914.
344 *"It is therefore ordered":* Supreme Court decision, *Southern Reporter* 66, 364–77.
345 *Up in Poplarville:* Accounts of this event, NODS, July 1, 1914; NOTP, July 2, 1914.
346 *"Even if convicted":* NOI, June 17, 1914.
347 *Three days later:* NOTP, June 21, 1914.

Chapter 25

349 *"[i]t is doubtful if":* NOTP, January 20, 1915.
350 *Two weeks later:* PFP, May 13, 1915.
350 *On his arrest record:* New Orleans Police Department Arrest Books, TP35 Roll #871, May 9–June 26, 1915, New Orleans Public Library.
352 *Cant reached out: Shreveport Journal,* March 3, 1932.
352 *home was a farm:* For this portion of the book, quotations and information are culled from authors' interviews with Julia's children Bernice Graves Hardee, Hollis Rawls, Jewel Rawls Tarver, and Julia's granddaughter Linda Tarver, 2000–11.
353 *she found herself enveloped:* For details on conversion experiences, the history of Pentecostalism in Mississippi and the Murray Hill Church of God, see Louis F. Morgan, *Streams of Living Water: 100 Years of the Church of God in Mississippi, 1909–2009* (self-published, 2009).

Chapter 26

358 *"Mrs. Dunbar and myself":* Percy Dunbar to Reynolds, NODS, April 23, 1915.
359 *"Will you take 'Bobby' ":* NOTP, May 29, 1915.
359 *"And in response":* Reprinted in OE, September 4, 1914.
359 *headlines advertised:* NOTP, May 29, 1915; undated source paper (Grace scrapbook, Lucille Grace Collection, LSU); see also ATT, September 7, 1915.
360 *"Percy Dunbar has":* OE, November 27, 1915.

360   *"[M]y name"*: NODS, January 22, 1916.

360   *"It is stated"*: OE, February 12, 1916.

360   *all eyes turned:* NOI, NODS, April 9, 1916.

361   *ribbon-adorned bouquet:* NOTP, April 9, 1916.

361   *Parker campaign ad:* DFS.

361   *Four years later:* In 1916, Parker won St. Landry, but the establishment Democrat garnered a sweeping majority. Barely registering defeat, Parker accepted the Bull Moose
nominee for U.S. vice president that same year. But when his running mate and friend,
Theodore Roosevelt, abandoned the Progressives at the last minute to endorse a
Republican, Parker's sense of betrayal was so deep that he crisscrossed the nation and
threw all of his political weight into the successful reelection of President Wilson,
whom he had formerly opposed. Louisiana and the Democratic Party welcomed him
back as a national hero.

361   *elected chairman:* NOI, November 7, 1919.

361   *a shareholding member: St. Landry History from the 1690's,* 236.

361   *Word of the death:* All details from shooting, funeral, and community reaction, SLC,
January 24, 1920.

361   *St. Landry carried:* A week later, Percy emerged from a fog of remorse and disgrace to
send Parker a noticeably tardy note of congratulations from the entire Dunbar family.
"I expect this is, not excepting your own, the happiest family in the whole state over
this election," Percy gushed, though at that moment, it must have been a lie. "Pledging
both generations signing this to support you," the letter ended with all four Dunbar
signatures. If Parker knew of the shooting, his generically gracious reply did not let
on. A year later, as governor, he appointed Percy to be the St. Landry notary public
(Dunbar Family to John M. Parker, January 27, 1920; John M. Parker to Dunbar Family,
January 30, 1920, JMPP, Box 20; NOTP, February 9, 1921).

361   *August 23, 1920:* Accounts of the incident are found in *Tampa Morning Tribune,* August
24 and September 9, 1920; *Abbeville Press* (Abbeville, LA), September 11, 1920; *Rice Belt
Journal* (Welsh, LA), September 11, 1920; see also *Lela C. Dunbar v. Clarence P. Dunbar,
Action for Divorce.* Circuit Court of Hillsborough County, Florida. Testimony, September 10 and January 29, 1926; Final Decree, January 21, 1927.

363   *"For years Lessie Dunbar"*: NODS, February 1, 1922.

364   *"We both feel"*: Ibid.

365   *"melancholia, hypochondriasis"*: Dock and Bass, 152.

366   *"designed for those"*: *Catalogue of Holy Cross College,* 1923–24, 45. See also *The Chalmette,*
1923–24, 1924–25.

366   *grade 7A:* Work permit, GHDC.

366   *"No Night Work"*: Ibid.

366   *"Send us the boy"*: See *Cosmopolitan* 61(August 1916): 20.

366   *"While my parents"*: Edward O. Wilson, *Naturalist* (Washington, DC: Island Press,
2006), 17; see also pages 16–20 for description of Gulf Coast Military Academy life.

367   *"During [Lessie's]"*: See *Clarence Percy Dunbar, husband, v. Lela C. Whitley, wife,* No. 23582.
16th District Court St. Landry Parish. Filed September 18, 1925. Final decree, February
3, 1927.

367   *From April to June 1925:* Department of Commerce Certificate of Seaman's Service;
GHDC.

368   *"Read this"*: Lessie to Bobby, DFS.

368   *"and brought up"*: Lessie to Percy, 1925, evidence in *Dunbar v. Whitley.*

370   *From 1925 to 1927:* Louisiana National Guard certificate of discharge, Robert Dunbar,
October 15, 1927, GHDC.

370   *"relieved [him]"*: Robert C. Dunbar Emancipation, No. 24279. 16th District Court St.
Landry Parish. September 1927.

370   *Aline Perrault:* Aline Perrault, interview by author, 2002; Estelle Perrault, interview by
author, January 2011.

370   *"[S]he has been"*: Will of R. E. Gornto, February 11, 1932. Filed, Circuit Court of Princess Anne County, VA, January 15, 1945.

371   *Not long into:* The story of Bobby's early relationship with Marjorie comes from

numerous interviews by authors with Robert Dunbar Jr., Gerald Dunbar, and Mary Dunbar Cole, 2000–10.

372   *When reporters came around:* Two reports in *Shreveport Journal,* March 12, 1932.

373   *"like one of those":* Ida and Albert Boudreaux, interview by authors, February 2009.

373   *The Associated Press: Dothan Eagle* (Dothan, AL), March 16, 1932.

374   *"Those boys weren't":* David Dunbar, interview by authors, 2007; Anna Lee Dunbar, interview by authors, February 2009.

374   *"You can imagine":* Earl Briggs, interview by author, January 2008; additional information on Bobby's accidents from Robert Dunbar Jr., Gerald Dunbar, and Mary Dunbar Cole, interviews by authors, 2007–11.

375   *But by 1935:* Heyman Gabriel to Robert Dunbar, August 8, 1935, DFS.

375   *One month later:* Heyman Gabriel to Robert Dunbar, September 13, 1935, DFS.

375   *"All he had":* Gerald Dunbar, interview by authors, February 2009.

375   For the final portion of this chapter and the Epilogue, all quotations and information are culled from authors' interviews with Bobby's children: Robert Dunbar Jr., Mary Dunbar Cole, and Gerald Dunbar, as well as his niece Elizabeth Dunbar and his life-long friend Earl Briggs, 2008–11.

Epilogue

385   *Their DNA:* The test compared the Y-chromosome, which is passed on from a father to his sons. While this established that Bobby was not the son of Percy and Lessie Dunbar, it did not prove, scientifically, that he was Bruce Anderson. To do this, it would be necessary to examine mitochondrial DNA, which is passed down from a mother to her children, but only passed on to the next generation by her female offspring. Such a test, then, would involve exhumation of Bobby Dunbar's body, an avenue that no member of either the Dunbar or the Anderson-Rawls family wishes, or feels the need, to pursue.

Bibliography

Legal Records

Clarence Percy Dunbar, husband, v. Lela C. Whitley, wife, No. 23582 (16th District Court St. Landry Parish; filed September 18, 1925; final decree, February 3, 1927).

Criminal Court Docket, Superior Court—1902–1912; Deeds and Conveyances. Robeson County, North Carolina. (North Carolina State Archives, Raleigh, NC).

Deeds and Conveyances (Archives, St. Landry Parish Clerk of Court, Opelousas, Louisiana).

The Dunbar Identification, held at the Hotel Monteleone, New Orleans, LA (John M. Parker, presiding, June 7, 1913).

Ex Parte Walters, No. 17,120 (Supreme Court of Mississippi, January 12, 1914).

Jail, Circuit Court, Grand Jury Dockets, 1911–24 (Marion County, MS, Courthouse, Marion County Museum and Archives).

Lela C. Dunbar v. Clarence P. Dunbar, Action for Divorce (Circuit Court of Hillsborough County, FL; testimony, September 10, 1926, and January 29, 1926; final decree, January 21, 1927).

Mary A. Walters v. William C. Walters, Libel for Divorce (Montgomery County Superior Court, GA, January 26, 1901).

In the Matter of W. C. Walters's Application for Writ of Habeas Corpus (15th Judicial District Court, MS, July 2, 1913).

Mississippi Governor's Order of Extradition: William C. Walters, June 18, 1913 (Mississippi Department of Archives and History).

New Orleans Police Department Arrest Books, TP35 Roll #871, May 9–June 26, 1915 (New Orleans Municipal Archives, New Orleans Public Library).

Robert C. Dunbar Emancipation, No. 24279 (16th District Court St. Landry Parish, September 1927).

St. Landry Police Jury Minutes, 1912–14 (Louisiana State University, Special Collections, Hill Memorial Library).

State of Florida v. C. P. Dunbar, No. 5222 (Aggravated Assault, Orange County Criminal Court, filed September 7, 1920).

State of Louisiana v. William C. Walters, No. 20687 (Louisiana Supreme Court). Transcript of appeal from 16th Judicial District Court, in and for the Parish of St. Landry. Brief on behalf of defendant and appellant. Full court decision, filed November 21, 1914 (University of New Orleans Supreme Court Archives).

State of Louisiana v. William C. Walters, No. 7962. Note of evidence on trial of motion and supplemental and amended motion of defendant for a new trial, May 18, 1914.

State of Louisiana v. William Walters, No. 7962 (District Court Criminal Docket). Witness summonses, court minutes, unmarked evidence, and verdict.

William C. Walters Defense File (Columbia, MS).

Will of R. E. Gornto, February 11, 1932 (filed in the Circuit Court of Princess Anne County, VA, January 15, 1945).

Archival Collections

Bobby Dunbar Collection (Opelousas Museum and Interpretive Center).
Dunbar Family Scrapbook.
Earl L. Brewer Papers (Mississippi Department of Archives and History).
Ethel Hutson Papers (Special Collections, Howard–Tilton Library, Tulane University).
Gerald and Helaine Dunbar Collection (Lafayette, LA).
Holy Cross College Archives and Records (New Orleans, LA).
Hutson Family Papers (Special Collections, Howard–Tilton Library, Tulane University).
John M. Parker Papers (University of North Carolina, Chapel Hill, NC).
John Wilds Research Notes (Williams Center, Historic New Orleans Collection).
Lucille Grace Collection (Louisiana State University, Baton Rouge, LA).
Vieux Carré Survey (Williams Center, Historic New Orleans Collection).
Washington Collection (Archives of the Sisters of Mt. Carmel, New Orleans, LA).

Principal Newspapers

Advertiser, Montgomery, AL
Columbian, Columbia, MS
Daily Herald, Biloxi, MS
Daily Ledger, Jackson, MS
Daily Picayune, New Orleans, LA
Daily Register, Mobile, AL
Daily Signal, Crowley, LA
Daily States, New Orleans, LA
Free Press, Poplarville, MS
Item, New Orleans, LA
Marion County Progress, Columbia, MS
News, Hattiesburg, MS
Opelousas Courier, Opelousas, LA
Opelousas Enterprise, Opelousas, LA
Robesonian, Lumberton, NC
St. Landry Clarion, Opelousas, LA
State Times Advocate, Baton Rouge, LA
Times-Democrat, New Orleans, LA
Times-Picayune, New Orleans, LA
Town Talk, Alexandria, LA
Weekly Town Talk

Principal Authors' Interviews

Bass, Lutie Cora Walters
Boudreaux, Albert
Boudreaux, Ida Pavy
Briggs, Earl
Buschel, Ronald
Cole, Mary Dunbar
Cooper, Jean
Dunbar, Anna Lee
Dunbar, David
Dunbar, Elizabeth
Dunbar, Gerald
Dunbar, Robert Jr.
Fontenot, Kevin
Halphen, Lee Garland
Hardee, Bernice Graves
Moore, Barbara
Morgan, Louis
Perrault, Aline
Perrault, Estelle
Rawls, Cliff
Rawls, Hollis
Sylvestrie, Mary
Tarver, Jewel Rawls
Tarver, Linda
Walters, Michael

Select Books, Articles, and other Manuscripts

Abramson, Phyllis Leslie. *Sob Sister Journalism*. New York: Greenwood Press, 1990.
Allen, J. A. *Sketchbook and Tourist Guide of Historic Opelousas and Surrounding Areas*. Opelousas, LA: Andrepont Printing, 1975.
Andrepont, Carola Ann. *Opelousas: The Place You'll Want to Be, Presented by the City of Opelousas; The Story of a Community, Its People, and Their Culture*. Opelousas, LA: Andrepont Printing, 1992.
Annear, Robin. *The Man Who Lost Himself: The Unbelievable Story of the Tichborne Claimant*. Melbourne, Australia: Text Publishing, 2002.

Arceneaux, William. *No Spark of Malice: The Murder of Martin Begnaud*. Baton Rouge: Louisiana University Press, 1999.

Ashe, W. W. *The Forests, Forest Lands, and Forest Products of Eastern North Carolina*. Raleigh: Joseph Daniels, State Printer and Binder, 1894.

Banks, Elizabeth L. "American Yellow Journalism." *Twentieth Century* 44 (August 1898).

Billings, Warren M. "Origins of Criminal Law in Louisiana." *Louisiana History: The Journal of the Louisiana Historical Association* 32, no. 1 (Winter 1991).

Blackford, Katherine M. H. "An Afternoon with Bertillon." *Outlook* 100, no. 8 (February 1912).

Bledsoe, D. L. *Bledsoe's Catechism on Music: Two Hundred and Eighty Concised, Pointed Questions and Answers*. Clyde, GA: J. B. Vaughan, 1893.

Blum, Howard. *American Lightning: Terror, Mystery, the Birth of Hollywood, and the Crime of the Century*. New York: Crown, 2008.

Borchard, Edwin M. *Convicting the Innocent: Errors of Criminal Justice*. New Haven: Yale University Press, 1932.

Boss, Pauline. *Ambiguous Loss: Learning to Live with Unresolved Grief*. Cambridge, MA: Harvard University Press, 1999.

———. "Ambiguous Loss: Working with Families of the Missing." *Family Process* 41 (2002).

Brown, Richard "Rabbit." "The Mystery of the Dunbar Child." Victor Recording, (March 11, 1927).

Brundage, William Fitzhugh. *Lynching in the New South: Georgia and Virginia, 1880–1930*. Urbana: University of Illinois Press, 1993.

Caesar, Gene. *Incredible Detective: The Biography of William J. Burns*. Englewood Cliffs, NJ: Prentice-Hall, 1968.

Cain, Albert C., and Barbara S. Cain. "On Replacing a Child." *Journal of the American Academy of Child Psychiatry* 3 (1964).

Campanella, Richard. *Time and Place in New Orleans: Past Geographies in the Present Day*. Gretna, LA: Pelican Publishing, 2002.

Campbell, W. Joseph. *Yellow Journalism: Puncturing the Myths, Defining the Legacies*. Westport, CT: Praeger, 2001.

Carlton, David L. *Mill and Town in South Carolina, 1880–1920*. Baton Rouge: Louisiana State University Press, 1982.

Carstens, C. C. "The Rural Community and Prostitution." *Social Hygiene* 1 (1914–1915).

Ceci, Stephen J., and Maggie Bruck. *Jeopardy in the Courtroom: A Scientific Analysis of Children's Testimony*. Washington, DC: American Psychological Association, 1995.

Chapin, Henry Dwight, and Godfrey Roger Pisek. *Diseases of Infants and Children*. New York: William Wood, 1911.

Chase, Sidney M. "Asahel and Lavinia at the Fair." *Outlook* 100, no. 8 (February 1912).

Chauvin, Mrs. O. J., and Harry Weston. "I Have Found My Child at Last," from *The Finding of the Dunbar Child*. Abbeville, LA: Mrs. O. J. Chauvin, 1913.

Clarke, Samuel Fessenden. "The Habits and Embryology of the American Alligator." *Journal of Morphology* (Wistar Institute of Anatomy and Biology, 1891).

Comeaux, Malcolm L. *Atchafalaya Swamp Life Settlement and Folk Occupations*. Baton Rouge: Louisiana State University School of Geoscience, 1972.

Corrales, Barbara Smith. "Deviant Women and the Politics of Privilege: Two Louisiana Murder Cases, 1911–1913." *Louisiana History: The Journal of the Louisiana Historical Association* 48, no. 3 (Summer 2007).

Cresswell, Stephen. *Rednecks, Redeemers, and Race* (Heritage of Mississippi Series, no. 3). Jackson: University Press of Mississippi for the Mississippi Historical Society, Jackson, 2006.

Cresswell, Tim. *The Tramp in America*. London: Reaktion Books, 2001.

Cunningham, George E. "The Italian, a Hindrance to White Solidarity in Louisiana, 1890–1898." *Journal of Negro History* 50, no. 1 (January 1965).

Darby, William. *A Geographical Description of the State of Louisiana*. Philadelphia: John Melish, 1861.

Davis, Natalie Zemon. *The Return of Martin Guerre.* Cambridge, MA: Harvard University Press, 1983.

DeLatte, Carolyn E. "The St. Landry Riot: A Forgotten Incident of Reconstruction Violence." *Louisiana History: The Journal of the Louisiana Historical Association* 17, no. 1 (Winter 1976).

DePastino, Todd. *Citizen Hobo: How a Century of Homelessness Shaped America.* Chicago: University of Chicago Press, 2003.

DeYoung, Robert, and Barbara Buzzi. "Ultimate Coping Strategies: The Differences Among Parents of Murdered or Abducted, Long-Term Missing Children." *Omega: Journal of Death and Dying* (2003).

Dock, George, and Charles C. Bass. *Hookworm Disease: Etiology, Pathology, Diagnosis, Prognosis, Prophylaxis and Treatment.* St. Louis: C. V. Mosby, 1910.

Earley, Lawrence S. *Looking for Longleaf: The Rise and Fall of an American Forest.* Chapel Hill: University of North Carolina Press, 2004.

Echezabal, J. R., and F. T Echezabal. *The Tinker and the Boy: Melodrama in 4 Acts.* New Orleans, 1913.

Edelson, Micah, et al. "Following the Crowd: Brain Substrates of Long-Term Memory Conformity." *Science* 333, no. 108 (July 2011).

Editors, *Opelousas Daily World, St. Landry History from the 1690s* (July 1998).

Erickson, Franklin C. "The Cotton Belt of North Carolina." *Economic Geography* 20, no. 1 (January 1944).

Fass, Paula S. *Kidnapped: Child Abduction in America.* New York: Oxford University Press, 1997.

Fontenot, Kevin. "Times Ain't Like They Used to Be." *Jazz Archivist: A Newsletter of the William Ransom Hogan Jazz Archive* 13 (1998–99).

Fontenot, Marshall P. *Grand Prairie—Looking Back.* Opelousas: Andrepont Printing Company, 1988.

Fortier, Alcee. *Louisiana: Comprising Sketches of Parishes, Towns, Events, Institutions and Persons, Arranged in Cyclopedic Form,* vols. 1–3. LA: Century Historical Association, 1914.

Garner, James W. "Proposed Criminal Code for Louisiana." *Journal of the American Institute of Criminal Law and Criminology* 1, no. 3 (September 1910).

Glasgow, Vaughn L. *A Social History of the American Alligator: The Earth Trembles With His Thunder.* New York: St. Martin's Press, 1991.

Gomez, Gay M. "Describing Louisiana: The Contribution of William Darby." *Louisiana History: The Journal of the Louisiana Historical Association* 34, no. 1 (Winter 1993).

Green, Elna C. *Southern Strategies: Southern Women and the Woman Suffrage Question.* Chapel Hill: University of North Carolina Press, 1997.

Hair, William Ivy. *The Kingfish and His Realm: The Life and Times of Huey P. Long.* Baton Rouge: Louisiana State University Press, 1991.

Harris, T. H. *The Memoirs of T. H. Harris, State Superintendent of Public Education in Louisiana, 1908–1940.* Baton Rouge: Bureau of Educational Materials and Research, Louisiana State University College of Education, 1963.

Hobbs, G. A. *Bilbo, Brewer and Bribery in Mississippi Politics.* Memphis: Dixon-Paul Printing Co., 1918.

Holmes, William F. "Whitecapping: Agrarian Violence in Mississippi, 1902–1906." *Journal of Southern History* 35, no. 2 (May 1969).

Hubbard, Elbert. "The Rights of Tramps." *Arena* 9 (April 1894).

Jackson, George Pullen. *White Spirituals in the Southern Uplands: The Story of the Fasola Folk, Their Songs, Singings, and "Buckwheat Notes."* Chapel Hill: University of North Carolina Press, 1933.

Jackson, Joy J. *New Orleans in the Gilded Age,* second edition. Lafayette: Louisiana Historical Association, 1997.

Kane, Harnett T. *The Bayous of Louisiana.* New York: William Morrow & Company, 1943.

Landon, Charles E. "The Tobacco Growing Industry of North Carolina." *Economic Geography* 10, no. 3 (July 1934).

Lastrapes, Paul L., ed. *Looking Back at Washington: The Memoirs of David Jasper McNicoll.* Baton Rouge, LA: Paul L. Lastrapes, 1996.

Lawrence, Robert C. *The State of Robeson.* New York: J. J. Little and Ives, 1939.

Lee, Robert E., and Jason B. Whiting. "Foster Children's Expressions of Ambiguous Loss." *American Journal of Family Therapy* 35 (2007).

Little, Ann Courtney Ward, ed. *Columbus County, North Carolina—Records and Recollections.* Whiteville, NC: Columbus County Commissioners and Columbus County Public Library, 1980.

Lockwood, C. C. *Atchafalaya: America's Largest Basin River Swamp.* Baton Rouge, LA: Claitor's, 1982.

Loftus, Elizabeth. "Creating False Memories." *Scientific American* 277 (1997).

Lutes, Jean Marie. *Front Page Girls: Women Journalists in American Culture and Fiction, 1880–1930.* Ithaca, NY: Cornell University Press, 2006.

Marion County Historical Association. *History of Marion County, Mississippi.* Walsworth Publishing Company, 1976.

Marshall, F. Ray. *Labor in the South.* Cambridge, MA: Harvard University Press, 1967.

Mattoon, Wilbur R. *The Southern Cypress.* Washington, DC: United States Department of Agriculture, 1915.

McClowery, S. G., E. B. Davies, K. A. May, E. J. Kulenkamp, and I. M. Martinson. "The Empty Space Phenomenon: The Process of Grief in the Bereaved Family." *Death Studies* 11 (1987).

McGough, Lucy C. *Child Witnesses: Fragile Voices in the American Legal System.* New Haven, CT: Yale University Press, 1994.

McLaughlin, Vance. *The Postcard Killer: The True Story of J. Frank Hickey.* New York: Thunder's Mouth Press, 2006.

Melius, Louis. *The American Postal Service: History of the Postal Service from the Earliest Times.* Washington, DC: National Capital Press, 1917.

Mintz, Steven. *Huck's Raft: A History of American Childhood.* Cambridge, MA: Belknap Press of Harvard University Press, 2004.

Mitchell, C. Ainsworth. *Science and the Criminal.* Boston: Little, Brown, 1911.

Monkkonen, Eric H., ed. *Walking to Work: Tramps in America, 1790–1935.* Lincoln: University of Nebraska Press, 1984.

Morgan, Louis F. *Streams of Living Water: 100 Years of the Church of God in Mississippi, 1909–2009,* vol. 1 (2009).

Mott, Frank Luther. *American Journalism: A History of Newspapers in the United States Through 250 Years, 1690–1940.* New York: Macmillian, 1950.

Oney, Steve. *And the Dead Shall Rise: The Murder of Mary Phagan and the Lynching of Leo Frank.* New York: Pantheon, 2003.

Our Heritage: Robeson County, North Carolina, 1748–2002. Robeson County Heritage Book Committee and County Heritage, Inc.: Waynesville, NC, 2003.

Outland, Robert B. *Tapping the Pines: The Naval Stores Industry in the American South.* Baton Rouge: Louisiana State University Press, 2004.

Owsley, Frank Lawrence. *Plain Folk in the Old South.* Baton Rouge: Louisiana State University Press, 1949.

Pfeifer, Michael James. *Rough Justice: Lynching and American Society, 1974–1947.* Chicago: University of Illinois Press, 2004.

Post, Lauren C. "Some Notes on the Attakapas Indians of Southwest Louisiana." *Louisiana History: The Journal of the Louisiana Historical Association* 3, no. 3 (Summer 1962).

Pride, Nancy. "Incidents Preceding the Louisiana Child Labor Law of 1912." *Louisiana History: The Journal of the Louisiana Historical Association* 19, no. 4 (Autumn 1978).

Reuss, Martin. *Designing the Bayous: The Control of Water in the Atchafalaya Basin, 1800–1995.* College Station: Texas A&M University Press, 2004.

Roosevelt, Theodore. *A Book-lover's Holidays in the Open*. New York: Charles Scribner's Sons, 1916.

Rosen, Ruth. *The Lost Sisterhood: Prostitution in America, 1900–1918*. Baltimore: Johns Hopkins University Press, 1983.

Rosof, Barbara D. *The Worst Loss: How Families Heal from the Death of a Child*. New York: Henry Holt, 1994.

Rowland, Dunbar, ed. *Mississippi, Comprising Sketches of Counties, Towns, Events, Institutions, and Persons, Arranged in Cyclopedic Form*, vol. 2. Atlanta: Southern Historical Publishing Association, 1907.

Rubin, David C. *Remembering Our Past: Studies in Autobiographical Memory*. New York: Cambridge University Press, 1999.

Sansing, David G., and Carroll Waller. *A History of the Mississippi Governor's Mansion*. Jackson: University Press of Mississippi, 1977.

Schacter, Daniel. *Searching for Memory: The Brain, the Mind, and the Past*. New York: Basic Books, 1996.

Schott, Matthew J. *Louisiana Politics and the Paradoxes of Reaction and Reform, 1877–1928*. Lafayette: Center for Louisiana Studies, University of Louisiana at Lafayette, 2000.

———. "The New Orleans Machine and Progressivism." *Louisiana History: The Journal of the Louisiana Historical Society* 24, no. 2 (Spring 1983).

Smallwood, W. W. "Notes on a Two-Headed Calf." *Anatomical Record* 22 (August–December 1921).

Smith, Barbara A., and Richard G. Graham. *Ford's Creek: A Place Called Home*. 2007.

Smith, J. Denson. "How Louisiana Prepared and Adopted a Criminal Code." *Journal of Criminal Law and Criminology* 41, no. 2 (July–August 1950).

Smythe, Ted Curtis. *The Gilded Age Press, 1865–1900*. Westport, CT: Praeger, 2003.

Spence, Donald P. *Narrative Truth and Historical Truth: Meaning and Interpretation in Psychoanalysis*. New York: W. W. Norton, 1982.

Stelly, Antoine B. *The Murder of Marion L. Swords, Sheriff of St. Landry Parish, 1900–1916*. Unpublished, 1988.

Stewart, Gilbert Holland. *Legal Medicine*. Indianapolis: Bobbs-Merrill Company, 1910.

Strite, Claudia Brewer. *Biography of Earl Leroy Brewer*. Unpublished, 1972.

Tanner, Amy Eliza. *The Child: His Thinking, Feeling and Doing*. New York: Rand McNally, 1904.

Taylor, Roy G. *Sharecroppers: The Way We Really Were*. Wilson, NC: J-Mark, 1984.

Thigpen, S. G. *Next Door to Heaven*. Kingsport, TN: Kingsport Press, 1965.

———. *Pearl River: Highway to Glory Land*. Kingsport, TN: Kingsport Press, 1965.

Vanstory, Burnette. *Georgia's Land of the Golden Isles*. Athens: University of Georgia Press, 1981.

Walters, William B., Laura Jane Cabaniss Walters, Warren Alfred Lewis, and Michael Earl Walters. *The Descendants of William Walters Sr. of Robeson County, North Carolina, 1794–1994*. Winston-Salem, NC: W. B. Walters, 1994.

Wilds, John. *Afternoon Story: A Century of the New Orleans States-Item*. Baton Rouge: Louisiana State University Press, 1976.

Williams, Robert W. Jr. "Martin Behrman and New Orleans Civic Development, 1904–1920." *Louisiana History: The Journal of the Louisiana Historical Association* 2, no. 4 (Autumn 1961).

Wilson, Edward O. *Naturalist*. Washington, DC: Island Press, 1994.

Workers of the Writers' Program of the Works Progress Administration in the State of Louisiana, comp. *Louisiana: A Guide to the State*. New York: Hastings House, 1941.

Index

Page numbers in *italics* refer to illustrations.

About the Authors

TAL MCTHENIA reported and wrote "The Ghost of Bobby Dunbar," a one-hour radio documentary for the acclaimed public radio series *This American Life* that aired in March 2008 and is the focus of this book. Tal works in documentary film and television production and is a freelance writer. He has received residencies at the ShenanArts' Playwrights' Workshop and the MacDowell Colony. He lives in New York.

MARGARET DUNBAR CUTRIGHT is the granddaughter of Bobby Dunbar, the victim of the kidnapping that is the subject of this book. She has researched this case for more than a decade, gathering and analyzing legal documents, family correspondence, and newspapers, and has had extensive and ongoing contact with descendants of all three of the families involved in the story. She lives in North Carolina.

364.1 MCT
McThenia, Tal.
A case for Solomon :
  Bobby Dunbar and the kidnap

PER